CHRISTIANITY

and

BARTHIANISM

CORNELIUS VAN TIL

Distributed by

BAKER BOOK HOUSE

Grand Rapids, Michigan

Library of Congress Catalog Card Number: LC 62-15431

Printed in the United States of America

In Memory of Jessie den Dulk

The Author

Born in the Netherlands in 1895, Dr. Van Til is a graduate of Calvin College (A.B.), of Princeton Theological Seminary (Th.M.), and Princeton University (Ph.D.). After a year in the pastorate he spent one year (1928-29) as Instructor of Apologetics at Princeton Theological Seminary. After the reorganization of that institution he was asked to remain by the new Board of Control but chose rather to accept the position of Professor of Apologetics in the newly formed Westminster Theological Seminary. He continues to hold this position to the present time.

Dr. Van Til is the author of *The Defense of the Faith, The Case for Calvinism, Christianity and Idealism, Common Grace, The Theology of James Daane* and *Christianity and Modern Theology* as well as numerous theological brochures and syllabi.

He is joint-editor of *Philosophia Reformata*, a quarterly devoted to Calvinistic philosophy, and a contributor to *The Westminster Theological Journal*.

Preface

Some years ago the prediction was made that Karl Barth's theology would soon disappear from the scene. It was said to be nothing more than an expression of post-war pessimism. But, as Barth's recent visit to America has emphasized, he is now regarded as the great prophet of the twentieth century.

In particular it is Barth's Christology that has, it is said, spoken the liberating word for our day. In it, we are told, God's sovereignty above man and his gracious presence with man, are kept in proper balance.

Moreover, it is through his view of the Christ that Barth has become the great ecumenical theologian of our day. By his return to and by his development of a true Reformation theology, he has, it is said, paved the way for a union of all true Protestants. Surely all Protestants gladly accept the Christ as the electing God and the elected man. In this Christ heaven and earth are being reconciled. Thus, Barth's theology is rapidly becoming the rallying point for modern ecumenism. Roman Catholic and New Protestant theologians alike rejoice as Barth replaces the Christ of Luther and of Calvin with a Christ patterned after modern activist thought.

Those who, with the Reformers, believe that through the death and resurrection of Christ in history sinners are saved from the wrath of God to come, have the responsibility of upholding Biblical Christianity against this new and concerted attack.

The present writer is of the opinion that, for all its verbal similarity to historic Protestantism, Barth's theology is, in effect, a denial of it. There is, he believes, in Barth's view no "transition from wrath to grace" in history. This was the writer's opinion in 1946 when he published *The New Modernism*. A careful consideration of Barth's more recent writings has only established him more firmly in this conviction.

Appreciation is hereby expressed to the following publishers for

the use of quotations from their books. Additional acknowledgment
is made in the various footnotes:

Wm. B. Eerdmans Publishing Company for G. C. Berkouwer's
The Triumph of Grace in the Theology of Karl Barth, and several
other books in Berkouwer's Dogmatical Series; Harper & Brothers
for Karl Barth's *Protestant Thought: From Rousseau to Ritschl;*
John Knox Press for Karl Barth, *A Shorter Commentary on Romans,*
and Karl Barth, *The Humanity of God;* The Macmillan Company
for Richard Kroner, *The Primacy of Faith;* Princeton University
Press for Søren Kierkegaard, *Concluding Unscientific Postscript;*
Søren Kierkegaard, *On Authority and Revelation;* Søren Kierkegaard,
The Concept of Dread; Søren Kierkegaard, *The Sickness unto Death;*
and the University of Chicago Press for Richard Kroner, *Culture
and Faith,* Richard Kroner, *Kant's Weltanschauung;* Johannes-
Verlag for Hans Küng's *Rechtfertigung;* Oxford University Press
for Søren Kierkegaard's *Training in Christianity,* and The World
Publishing Company for Karl Barth's *The Faith of the Church.*

Special thanks are due to Mr. Hendrik Krabbendam for checking
much of the translation of Dutch and German material, to Miss
Dorothy Newkirk for the typing of the manuscript, to Mr. Richard
Von Dohlen for making the index, to Mr. Rousas J. Rushdoony for
reading the manuscript and helpful suggestions, and to Mr. Leslie
W. Sloat for editing the proofs.

Cornelius Van Til

June 1962

Contents

Orientation

1. Writings of Barth

Quite properly men speak of Karl Barth as the most influential theologian of our time. We must therefore seek to understand him.

Brief personal conferences with Barth will not materially help us for this purpose. Such conferences may impress us with Barth's deep sincerity and his gracious Christian character. They may even give us glimpses of his theology. For a full and careful statement of this theology, however, we must turn to his writings.

The writings of Barth may, for our purposes, be put into two classes. On the one hand there are the more popular, and on the other hand there are the more scholarly works. Among the more popular works are the summaries of his theology written as expositions of Calvin's catechism, the Heidelberg catechism and the Apostles' Creed. The "simple Christian" can read these for himself. Is not this enough? Is Barth's general position not plainly expressed in these works?

The answer is that Barth's position is much more fully and more carefully articulated in his scholarly than in his popular works. Barth would have every reason to complain if we sought to analyze his views in terms of his popular writings alone, especially if we found it necessary to differ with him. Due respect for Barth requires us to listen at length and with patience as he speaks in his major theological writings. Even the more popular writings must finally be seen in the light of the *Church Dogmatics* and its companion works.

The *Church Dogmatics* is a truly monumental work. In reading it one's admiration for Barth knows no bounds. One must look back to the *Christian Dogmatics* of 1927 and even to the commentary on Romans, as well as to other earlier works, in order to trace the development of Barth's thinking. But in the *Church Dogmatics* we have the ripe fruition of a long lifetime of arduous reflection and research.

Barth's influence springs primarily from this great work. The theology of this work is being stated, restated, and modified in ever more popular form by many of Barth's followers and partial followers. Even if he has not read a word of Barth or scarcely knows his name, the "simple believer" in effect listens to his theology from many a pulpit of the land.

It is at this point that the question of "traditional phraseology" has its significance. The "simple believer" is all too often given new wine in old bottles. It is our solemn duty to point out this fact to him. The matter is of basic importance and of the utmost urgency.

2. *Barth and Schleiermacher*

Ever since the appearance of his *Romans* (1918), Barth has been concerned to set off his theology from that of Friedrich Schleiermacher. Schleiermacher is often called the "father of modern theology," and the emphasis of modern theology is commonly recognized as being immanentistic. Emil Brunner states that Schleiermacher's theology is controlled by the principles of an identity philosophy.[1]

Barth himself speaks constantly of Schleiermacher and his followers as "consciousness-theologians." Such theologians, he says, begin with the fact of man's self-consciousness as something given. From their own self-consciousness as a starting-point, these theologians proceed to inquire about the possibility of knowing anything of God.[2] Over against this consciousness-theology Barth wants to set a theology of the Word. Instead of beginning with a discussion of possibilities in general, we must begin, he asserts, with the reality of God.

But how can man speak of God? It is impossible! Yet by God's election or predestination the impossible takes place. A true the-

---

1. *Die Mystik und das Wort*, Zweite Auflage, Tübingen, 1928.
2. *Die Lehre vom Worte Gottes*, Vol. I of *Die Christliche Dogmatik im Entwurf*, München, 1927, hereafter referred to as *Dogmatics* in distinction from the *Church Dogmatics* (1932——).

ology will therefore set the doctrine of election at the center of its efforts. By means of this doctrine we are to cut ourselves loose from all correlation and even from all relation with the consciousness of man.[3]

But, says Barth, the doctrine of election must at once be related to Christ. Jesus Christ is "the beginning of all the ways and works of God." He is both the "electing God" and the "elected man." Election is therefore always election by Christ and in Christ.

The whole of Christian theology must, accordingly, be Christologically interpreted, and this, moreover, in terms of Barth's concept of Christology. Schleiermacher's theology was basically anthropological rather than Christological. He did indeed assert the absoluteness of Christianity. In this he was no doubt sincere.[4] But "at the back of even his most forceful protestations . . . stands the fact he established in the *Addresses* that the basic outlook of every religion is in itself eternal, since it forms a supplementary part of the infinite whole of religion in general in which all things must be eternal."[5] Thus the Christ of Schleiermacher "has only an incomparably greater quantity of that which we see in ourselves as our Christianity . . ." [6]

The conclusion of Barth's estimate of the theology of Schleiermacher is that for all his desire to elevate Jesus Christ to a place of unique importance he did not really succeed in doing so. The Christ of Schleiermacher is, after all, no more than a projection of the general religious consciousness of man.

Having no truly Christological theology Schleiermacher also fails to have a true theology of the Word. The "historical element in religion, the objective motif, the Lord Jesus, is a problem child" for Schleiermacher.[7] He did not clearly presuppose the "divinity of the Logos" as did the Reformers.[8] According to Schleiermacher "Christ is the Revealer and Redeemer" only "in so far as he effects the higher life."[9] Thus the objective moment of religion dissolves into the subjective. According to Schleiermacher, it is not to Christ alone that we must look for our knowledge of God.

3. *Fate and Idea in Theology* in *Zwischen den Zeiten*, 1929, pp. 309 ff.

4. Article on Schleiermacher in *Protestant Thought: From Rousseau to Ritschl*, New York, 1959. This is a translation of eleven chapters of *Die Protestantische Theologie im 19. Jahrhundert*. Zürich, 1952, pp. 351-352.

5. *Ibid.*, p. 352.   8. *Ibid.*, p. 343.
6. *Idem.*   9. *Ibid.*, p. 347.
7. *Ibid.*, p. 342.

Nor does Schleiermacher's doctrine of the Holy Spirit save the situation. "In a proper theology of the Holy Spirit there could be no question of dissolving the Word."[10] But Schleiermacher explains the working of the Holy Spirit too in the familiar form of the religious consciousness.[11]

However much then we must hold that "in some depth of his mind Schleiermacher intended otherwise,"[12] it remains true that for all his effort to elevate the Scriptures and the Christ he had neither the Christ of the Word nor the Word of the Christ.

It is therefore, Barth argues, our prerogative and duty to turn away, however reluctantly, from Schleiermacher and go back to the Reformers. "With Luther the divinity of the *Logos* demands in the most direct way possible the divinity of the Spirit."[13] The Reformers interpreted man in terms of Christ and his Word as they were led by the Holy Spirit. Let us return to them and then go beyond them in their spirit.

Did Barth really turn away from consciousness-theology? Did he really return to the principles of Reformation theology? Before answering these questions, let us consider further Barth's own analyses of theological trends and factors.

3. Barth and Feuerbach

In his survey of nineteenth-century theology, Barth writes a chapter on Ludwig Feuerbach, the philosopher. This chapter follows immediately upon the one dealing with Schleiermacher. Elsewhere too Barth concerns himself with Feuerbach.[14] Again and again he appears on the surface in the *Church Dogmatics*.

And why trouble with Feuerbach? Because he has rightly reduced consciousness-theology to skepticism. In two famous books, *The Essence of Christianity* (1841) and *The Essence of Religion* (1851), Feuerbach told the consciousness-theologians that their theology was only under-cover anthropology. In worshiping God, he stated, they were merely worshiping a projection of themselves. Why not frankly admit that it is the apotheosis of man that all of us are after?

Was Feuerbach completely in the wrong? Not so far as Schleiermacher and many others are concerned. Feuerbach too "is singing

10. *Ibid.*, p. 352.   12. *Idem.*
11. *Ibid.*, p. 353.   13. *Ibid.*, p. 343.
14. Article on *Ludwig Feuerbach* in *Die Theologie und die Kirche*, München, 1928.

his *Magnificat*."[15] And his song is not too different from that of consciousness-theology.

Patching up consciousness-theology will not help us to escape the cool smile of Feuerbach. To escape him we must be able to laugh in his face. Feuerbach did not understand the significance of death and of evil.[16] He had no true sense of sin. It is this fact that makes him confuse the nature of God with that of man. Only a truly Christological approach in theology enables us to laugh at Feuerbach. Skepticism can only be answered if we begin our theology with Christ. Again, only a theology of the Word enables us to laugh at Feuerbach; the problem of sin and death can only be solved in terms of the *Yes* of God spoken to men in Christ.

Does Barth really have a theology that can answer skepticism? Does he really have a biblical view of sin? Does he really give answers to men as sinners in terms of the Christ of the Word? We shall seek answers to questions like these.

4. Barth and Strauss

Only brief mention must be made here of Barth's discussion of the theology of D. F. Strauss. Strauss' *Leben Jesu, kritisch bearbeitet* (1835-36) brought to the forefront of attention the question of God's revelation in history.[17] Strauss "was not the anti-Christ by any means."[18] But he did offer to his time "the sight of a theologian who has become an unbeliever, for all to behold and without denying it."[19] Our historical information about Jesus, he argues, is "incomplete and uncertain." Expounding Strauss Barth says: "It is out of the question that faith and salvation can depend on things only the smallest part of which are not in doubt. And, in any case, it is a matter of principle that there should be no such dependence. 'Just as certainly as the destiny of man is a universal one and accessible to all, so the conditions upon which it is to be achieved . . . must be accorded to every man'; the perception of the goal must 'not only be an accidental one, a historical perception coming from without, but a necessary perception of reason, which each man can find in himself'."[20]

Here then in Strauss, argues Barth, is a skepticism equal to that of

15. *Protestant Thought*, etc., p. 356.
16. *Die Theologie und die Kirche*, p. 237.
17. *Protestant Thought*, etc., p. 363.

18. *Ibid.*, p. 370.
19. *Ibid.*, p. 368.
20. *Ibid.*, p. 373.

Feuerbach. Theologians had sought in the historical Jesus some measure of objectivity. But "something absolute as a part of world and of human history as such is a sword of lath. Strauss' book made this very plain and well understood, and those who read it were shaken to the core, for it was precisely upon the card of history that they had staked no less than half their means, the other half being on that of religious consciousness. The situation was such that in running away from Feuerbach they ran straight into the arms of Strauss. And if they managed somehow to escape Strauss they were still not free of Feuerbach. That was the deeply disturbing feature of the state of theological discussion a hundred years ago: the deeply disturbing background to the history of theology in all the ensuing decades."[21]

With critics such as Strauss and Feuerbach in the background, Barth constructs his theology. In recent times Rudolf Bultmann has been prominent in his thought. Is Christianity as a direct revelation merely an illusion? When dealing with God's coming into history and the miracles the gospels speak of in connection with that coming, are we to think of myth alone?

Barth's own answer to these men, as to many others, is again in terms of the Christ. In Christ God is wholly revealed. In his resurrection is the objective factual basis for the believer's faith. Thus Barth answers Feuerbach and Bultmann. We have objective truth in Christ. But God is wholly hidden as well as wholly revealed in Christ. Our objectivity need not be and cannot be found directly in history. Objectivity is primarily to be found in primal history, that is, in *Geschichte*.

The idea of *Geschichte*, Barth argues, does full justice to the fact that in Christ God is both fully revealed and fully hidden to man. In the idea of *Geschichte* we can see that God is *indirectly* identical with man. It is only in the idea of *indirect* identification of God and man that the priority of God over man can be maintained.

5. Barth and Romanism

Romanism does not realize this point. With its notion of the analogy of being it has developed a natural theology. By means of this natural theology Romanism thinks it possible for man to have

21. *Ibid.*, p. 383.

direct knowledge of God. Romanism does not realize that while revelation is historical, history is never, as such, revelational. Accordingly, Romanism cannot do justice to the fact that God's grace is prior to all the decisions of men. How then could Romanism do justice to the truly scriptural idea of God's revelation to man in Christ? The idea of analogy of being as espoused by Romanist theology makes it impossible for us to join hands with it. We should have no answer for Feuerbach if we adhered to Romanism.

6. *Barth and Reformation-theology*

Barth is therefore wholeheartedly committed to a "Reformation-theology." And of Reformation theologians it is Calvin rather than Luther whom he follows.

But Barth finds it necessary to go *beyond* Calvin too. He thinks that the Reformation principle requires him to do so. If we are really to hold to justification by faith alone, as the Reformers held, then we must think in terms of Christ as *Geschichte*. Did the Reformers, and in particular, did Calvin adequately realize this fact? Did the Reformers not, in spite of themselves, sometimes do what Romanism had done, namely, identify revelation with history? Does it really help us to reject the natural theology of Rome if we do not reject all direct revelation in history? Do we really understand the Scriptures as they want to be understood if we directly identify them with revelation? And do we really have the Christ if we directly identify him with Jesus of Nazareth?

Barth makes it perfectly plain that Calvin did not have an adequate idea of the *indirect* character of every contact between God and man. In other words, Barth seeks to go beyond Calvin as he went beyond Romanism in terms of *Geschichte*. In terms of *Geschichte* alone can there be the genuine priority of revelation and of grace that Calvin was seeking but could not find.

The true priority of grace implies both its sovereignty and its universality. God in Christ is always the *subject*, the initiator of grace. He creates that which is wholly new for man and wholly undeserved by man. At the same time God is always the subject of *grace*. It is his glory to humiliate himself for the exaltation of man. Therefore grace is always the primary relation of every man to God. However wretched the reality of his sin, and however dreadful the wrath of God upon man's sin, it is settled *in advance* by the very nature of God, that man, every man, will ultimately participate in the being of God. Calvin did not have such a view of the grace of God. We must therefore go beyond Calvin. He had no eye for Christ as *Geschichte*.

7. Barth and Protestant Orthodoxy

Calvin's failure to see Christ in terms of *Geschichte* was largely in spite of himself. Such is no longer the case with later orthodox theologians. They made a virtue out of the idea of direct revelation in Scripture and in Christ. Of course, even they meant well. But their basic allegiance is to direct revelation. And the idea of direct revelation is *profane*. It fetters the freedom or sovereignty of grace. God is then no longer wholly hidden in his revelation. It fetters also the universality of grace. God is then no longer wholly revealed as grace in Christ. He then may be something other than grace to some men and even to all men.

If then we are to laugh in Feuerbach's face we can do so only in terms of Christ as *Geschichte*, as the indirect identification of God with man. Such being the case, we shall need to develop and restate the Reformation principle.

We need to *start* with Christ and interpret both God and man in terms of him. All meaning comes from Christ. All possibility and impossibility must be in the light of the fact of his existence as truly God and truly man. Only thus do we have grace that is truly sovereign and as such truly universal. Only thus do we have God who really speaks from above and who is yet surely present with every man as his redeemer. Only in terms of Christ as the *indirect* identification with man does his resurrection from the dead spell true objectivity. Without the Christ as *Geschichte*, we should have, as does Bultmann, a mere parthenogenesis of the faith.

8. Geschichte and Historie

Of particular importance in Barth's dealing with all such men and movements as have been mentioned is the question of the relation between *Geschichte* and *Historie*. By *Historie* Barth means history as the past, history as studied by the average historian, whether Christian or non-Christian. How is Barth's view of *Geschichte* related to ordinary history? There is clearly an overlapping of the two, but there is never identification.

It is our purpose in this book to analyze Barth's basic position as it centers around his idea of Christ as *Geschichte*.

In the first section it is our aim to understand Barth's principle by dealing with his view of Christ and of grace in relation to Romanism, Calvin, and orthodoxy, and to set forth his own view of the relation of *Geschichte* to *Historie*.

This will lead on from the idea of understanding Barth to the beginning of an evaluation of his theology. We therefore ask in the second section what some Reformed theologians and philosophers have said about Barth's theology. Must we follow Barth in going beyond Calvin and orthodox theology in terms of his idea of *Geschichte*? We shall need both a Christian theology and a Christian philosophy to determine this.

In the third section we deal with the basic principle of dialecticism. A comparison is made between ancient dialecticism with its influence on Romanist theology and modern dialecticism with its influence on Barth's theology.

In the fourth and final section our understanding and evaluation of Barth's theology lead us to a discussion of his relation to some modern thinkers. In particular, we there seek to answer the question whether, with his idea of Christ as *Geschichte* he has succeeded in getting beyond the immanentistic view of theology which he tries so hard to escape. Is Barth's theology perhaps, after all, a new and refined form of consciousness-theology? How can it be anything else since he will not start from the Christ as this Christ is found in the Scripture as the direct revelation of God? Is not Barth's Christ, after all, a Christ fashioned according to the principles of modern reconstruction? And if it is, can it then be properly spoken of as a Protestant theology?

Section One

Barth's Main Doctrines

Chapter I

Barth's View of Jesus Christ

It is well known that Barth seeks to approach every problem of theology Christologically. When we talk about God and man and their relation to one another, we must do so by speaking of Jesus Christ, who is both truly God and truly man. Unless we speak of God and man by speaking of both through the God-man, Jesus Christ, we are speaking of pure abstractions.

1. Christ as Geschichte

For Barth, when we speak of Jesus Christ we must at once speak of his work as the mediator between God and man. If we spoke first of his person and then of his work, we should again be speaking of abstractions. Christ's person is identical with his work as redeemer. So also if we spoke first of his divine nature and then of his human nature, we should again be speaking of abstractions. As we cannot speak of God in himself apart from Christ, so we cannot speak of the divine nature of Christ apart from the human nature of Christ. So also, as we cannot speak of man apart from Christ, we cannot speak of the human nature of Christ apart from its relation to the divine nature of Christ.

How then can we speak truly, that is concretely, rather than abstractly about Christ? We can do so only by speaking of him as *Act*. Abstract thinking is thinking of static entities, such as God in himself and man in himself. To think truly, that is concretely, about God is to think of him as living and therefore as acting for man in

13

Christ. So also to think truly, that is concretely, about Christ is to think of him as the Act, or work of saving man unto God.

The English word "history" does not adequately convey what Barth means by *Geschichte*. Barth himself distinguishes between *Geschichte* and *Historie*. The latter indicates the facts of the world as the neutral historian sees them. Thus the resurrection appearances of Christ deal with facts that could be seen and felt by the physical eye and hand. But the resurrection must not, says Barth, be directly identified with any such fact. To do so would be to forget that while revelation is historical nothing historical is, as such, revelational. To do so would be to deny that God in Christ is the subject of the resurrection. To do so would be to forget that God is wholly hidden even when wholly revealed and wholly revealed when revealed at all.

The real resurrection must therefore be seen as *Geschichte*. That is to say it is an actual event. As such it lies at the foundation of our faith. The resurrection as *Historie* is only a subordinate aspect of the resurrection as *Geschichte*. The real relation between God and man takes place in terms of Christ as *Geschichte*. In it alone do we do justice to the idea that God is really, that is, fully man in Christ. God *is* Jesus Christ. In it alone do we do justice to the idea that man is fully man only by participation in Christ.

The distinction Barth makes between *Geschichte* and *Historie* must therefore be kept in mind. But frequently Barth uses the term *Geschichte* as inclusive of *Historie*. It is only at peculiarly critical junctures, such as the creation of the world and the resurrection of Christ, that he makes the distinction between them.

2. Geschichte as a Reformation Principle

By speaking of Christ in terms of *Geschichte* Barth seeks to accomplish two objectives. In terms of *Geschichte* Barth expresses, as he thinks, the principle of Reformation theology. But he realizes that in his view of Jesus Christ as *Geschichte* he is not only expressing but also going beyond the theology of the *Reformers*. He makes, as he thinks, a necessary correction of, as well as a supplementation to, the theology of the Reformers by his idea of *Geschichte*. The correction pertains especially to the tendency of the Reformers to identify *Geschichte* with *Historie*. They did not realize adequately that while the revelation of God in Christ and in Scripture is historical, it cannot be said that history as such is revelational. Accord-

ingly, they did not properly recognize the *hiddenness* of God in his
revelation. They sought to bring down the *freedom* of God into the
given facts of history. Thus God was bound by his own revelation
and no longer truly sovereign. Over against this Barth asserts that
God is *wholly hidden* in his revelation to man in Christ. In the idea
of *Geschichte* we recognize that in God's revelation in Christ and in
Scripture as the witness to Christ, the wholly free and sovereign
God is speaking.

A second weakness in the theology of the Reformers, says Barth,
corresponds to the first. They failed to see that God was *wholly* revealed in Christ as they failed to see that as *wholly* revealed he is at
the same time *wholly* hidden.

The Reformers, and especially Calvin, sought for God beyond
Christ, as though he were not wholly revealed in Christ. For them
there was some abstract, mysterious being back of Christ who arbitrarily chose some to salvation while passing others by. This created
a fear and uncertainty unworthy of God and his love in Christ.

Seeing Christ as *Geschichte* enables us to sense the fact that God's
final word to mankind is *Yes*. Grace is grace for all men or it is not
grace at all.[1]

Thus the idea of *Geschichte* helps Barth, on the one hand, to
reach a theology with the proper view of God's transcendence and,
on the other hand, to reach a theology with the proper view of God's
immanence. God's revelation in Christ is and remains *God's* revelation. It is always God's secret (*Geheimnis*). At the same time this
revelation reveals God *wholly*. Man need never fear that he is or
can be anything but the object of God's grace. In Christ the grace of
God is truly grace; it is wholly *undeserved* and wholly *new*. Thus
only by sovereign election in Christ can man be saved. At the same
time this truly free and sovereign grace *certainly* reaches down to
man and to *all* men. Both of these aspects are expressed in the idea
of Jesus Christ as *Geschichte*.

3. *Geschichte as an Answer to Critics*

In addition to using the idea of *Geschichte* in order to return to
and go beyond Reformation theology Barth solves his problem and
meets his critics with it.

His problem is, as already noted, how to have a theology that can

---

1. *Kirchliche Dogmatik*, IV:2, p. 589. (We shall refer to this work by num-
bers only.)

laugh in Feuerbach's face. Feuerbach said that theology was really nothing more than a projection on the part of the autonomous consciousness of the theologians.

This charge is largely to the point, argues Barth, as against the theology of Schleiermacher and his followers. It is true also of traditional orthodoxy which, often enough, has led to an immanentistic theology such as Schleiermacher held. It is true also of the natural theology of Rome. It is true even of Brunner's theology.

The mistake in all of these approaches is basically the same, that of starting one's theological thinking from the bottom up, from the consciousness of man as intelligible to itself in its environment. A true theology must start from the top down. It must offer the light of the revelation of God in Christ as that in terms of which alone man knows himself. If the consciousness of man itself must be interpreted in terms of revelation, then the problem of faith and reason, or theology and philosophy, has been solved and we can laugh in Feuerbach's face. If the facts of history *(Historie)* must themselves be interpreted in terms of *Geschichte,* then the uncertainties of *Historie* need no longer trouble us and Strauss has been answered. If the resurrection of Christ is primarily *Geschichte,* then the problem of fact and myth is solved and we need not follow the demythologizing procedure in order to have men believe in Christianity. If faith were to be founded upon the resurrection as a fact of *Historie* as such, then Bultmann would be right. Such facts are, all of them, lost in a sea of relativity. But if the resurrection is primarily *Geschichte* and only peripherally *Historie* then we can boldly assert that our faith is based on a fact, a *fact* as an *Event,* namely, the meeting of Christ, after his resurrection, with the apostles.

4. Jesus Christ, the Mediator

Corroboration and amplification of this general statement on Barth's view of Christ must now be given.

In doing so we begin with the nature of reconciliation or atonement. For Jesus Christ is reconciliation.[2] Christ exists as mediator between God and man,[3] i.e., he exists as the fact of the mediation between God and man.

Jesus Christ is reconciliation because he is truly God and truly

2. IV:1, p. 35.—Jesus Christus ist die Versöhnung.
3. *Ibid.,* p. 135.

man. He is a human person.[4] "His being as man is His work."[5] And
his work is the work of saving all men. The man Jesus "is the coming
kingdom of God . . ."[6]

But Jesus is the kingdom of God because he is "in the Word of
God."[7] As such he is identical with the divine Subject.[8] And in this
identification of himself as both God and man he is the salvation of
every man.[9]

The gracious God and the reconciled man are one in Jesus Christ
as *Geschichte*.[10] The existence of Jesus Christ as truly God and truly
man constitutes the finished act of man's reconciliation with God.[11]
"His being as such is His *Geschichte*, and His *Geschichte* is identical
with His being."[12] Because Jesus Christ is wholly God and wholly
man in *Geschichte*, God accomplishes the turning about of all men
to himself.[13] Jesus Christ is both the reconciling God and the reconciled man.[14] As such he was born, died and rose again for all men.[15]
In Christ all men are objectively justified, sanctified and called.[16]

There is absolute identity between God and man in Jesus Christ
as *Geschichte*. But this identity is not a direct identity. Barth wants
no identity philosophy. His identity is a living one, the identity of
Geschichte. Only by means of such a living, or indirect, identity,
can we escape the hopeless mysteries and abstractions of a God in
himself and a man in himself. With the idea of God wholly revealed
in the man Jesus and with the idea of mankind fully brought to light
in the same man Jesus, the slate is clear for the doctrine that God's
attitude to men, to all men, is ultimately that of grace.

5. Jesus Christ, the Lord as Servant

But since the identity between God and man in Jesus Christ is
the living identity of *Geschichte*, Barth can, he thinks, also furnish
the proper stress on the priority of God in relation to man. There is

4. III:2, p. 69.—Er ist menschliche Person.
5. *Idem.*
6. *Ibid.*, p. 80.   7. *Ibid.*, p. 80.
                                       8. *Ibid.*, p. 81.
9. *Ibid.*, p. 81. Wie die Geschichte der göttlichen Rettung für alle und jeden
Menschen ganz und gar und ausschliesslich Er ist, so ist Er ganz und gar und
ausschliesslich die Geschichte der göttlichen Rettung für alle und jeden Menschen. . . . Er ist selbst diese Geschichte.
10. IV:1, p. 138.   14. *Ibid.*, p. 149.
11. *Ibid.*, p. 139.   15. *Ibid.*, p. 163.
12. *Ibid.*, p. 140.   16. *Idem.*
13. *Ibid.*, p. 143.

a genuine difference, he says, between God and man. God is always sovereign and free in all that he does for man. God's grace toward man is inherently universal grace because of the identity between God and man inherent in *Geschichte*. Similarly, this same grace is inherently sovereign and free because of the difference inherent in *Geschichte*. Thus the act of God, as free act, always precedes and initiates the response of man. Before we discuss Jesus Christ, the Servant as Lord, we must, says Barth, discuss Jesus Christ the Lord as Servant.

In doing so Barth starts with asserting anew that reconciliation is *Geschichte*.[17] But it is a very special type of *Geschichte*.[18] It is the most original *Geschichte* of every man.[19] "Reconciliation is, noetically expressed: the *Geschichte* of Jesus Christ; ontically expressed: the *Geschichte* of Jesus Christ Himself."[20]

God comes down to man in Jesus Christ. In the man Jesus God is not only the "electing creator, but also the elected creature, not only the giver of grace *(der Gnädige)* but also the receiver of grace *(der Begnadete)*, not only the commander but also the one called and obliged to obey."[21]

Jesus Christ is the elected man because as the substitute for man he is negated by God. God has promised to be true and faithful to him. Yet he stands under the condemnation and judgment of God.[22]

---

17. *Ibid.,* p. 171.
18. *Idem.* Höchst besondere Geschichte.
19. *Idem.*

20. *Ibid.,* p. 172.
21. *Ibid.,* p. 186.

22. *Ibid ,* p. 189; Engl. tr. p. 173. "Because he negates God, the man elected by God, the object of the divine grace, is himself necessarily, and logically, and with all that it involves, the man negated by God. It is also true that God has sworn to be, and actually is, faithful, that God's grace does not fail but persists towards Him. But within these limits it is unconditionally the case that as a sinner He is rejected by God, that He not only stands under the wrath and accusation of God, but because this wrath is well-founded and this accusation is true, He stands under His sentence and judgment. The grace of God is concealed under His sentence and judgment, His Yes under His No. The man elected by God is the man who with his contradiction is broken and destroyed by the greater contradiction of God. He cannot stand before Him, and therefore he cannot stand at all. He chooses a freedom which is no freedom. He is therefore a prisoner of the world-process, of chance, of all-powerful natural and historical forces, above all of Himself. He tries to be His own master, and to control His relations with God and the world and His fellow-men. And as He does so, the onslaught of nothingness prevails against Him, controlling Him in death in an irresistible and senseless way and to His own loss. This is the *circulus vitiosus* of

But how is it possible that the Son of God could thus become identical with man? How can the Son of God come under the judgment of God? Is not the Son of God, as well as the Father, the unchangeable one?

The basic answer to this is that we must learn of the nature of God from the Christ as *Geschichte (das Christusgeschehen)*. This point is of the utmost importance for Barth. Failure to learn of the nature of God through *das Christusgeschehen* leads right back to all the evils of consciousness-theology.[23] In particular we should then become the victims of a false view of the hiddenness of God (*Geheimnis*). We should be the victims of all the arbitrariness, the fears and uncertainties of an absolute and unchangeable decree of an absolute and unchangeable God.

We may therefore work back from the atonement to the incarnation. But we need not and cannot really work back. For the incarnation is reconciliation. The identity between them lies again in the idea of *Geschichte*. When the Word becomes flesh he becomes therewith subject to the wrath of God.[24] God himself becomes the subject of human reconciliation by his identification with Jesus of Nazareth.[25]

Through reconciliation God wants to make men participate in the "internal *Geschichte* of his divinity."[26] But this participation of the world in the being of God requires that God first participate in

the human plight presupposed and revealed in and with the grace of God. And there is no man who, whether he experiences it or not, is not in this plight. But the man elected by God not only suffers and experiences it. He knows it. He knows that He must perish. He considers that He must die. The connexion between His guilt and the righteous judgment of God is constantly before Him."

23. *Ibid* , p. 193; Engl. tr. p. 177. "The meaning of His deity—the only true deity in the New Testament sense—cannot be gathered from any notion of supreme, absolute, non-worldly being. It can be learned only from what took place in Christ. Otherwise its mystery would be an arbitrary mystery of our own imagining, a false mystery. It would not be the mystery given by the Word and revelation of God in its biblical attestation, the mystery which is alone relevant in Church dogmatics. Who the one true God is, and what He is, i.e., what is His being as God, and therefore His deity, His "divine nature," which is also the divine nature of Jesus Christ if He is very God—all this we have to discover from the fact that as such He is very man and a partaker of human nature, from His becoming man, from His incarnation and from what He has done and suffered in the flesh. For—to put it more pointedly, the mirror in which it can be known (and is known) that He is God, and of the divine nature, is His becoming flesh and His existence in the flesh."

24. *Ibid.*, p. 202.   26. *Ibid.*, p. 236.
25. *Ibid.*, p. 217.

the being of the world, namely, that "his own being, his own *Geschichte*, work itself out as world-history *(Weltgeschichte)* and therefore under the entire burden and in the entire danger of world-history."[27]

If we are used to thinking in static categories, we might demur at this point. Would God still be God if he submitted himself to *Weltgeschichte?*

Thinking Christologically, we reply that it is the nature of the Son of God to express the freedom of God. God in his freedom can become wholly unlike himself and yet remain the same.[28]

Thus God becomes visible to us in the man Jesus.[29] But in this very revelation he remains wholly hidden.[30] God is present in history but revelation is never a predicate of history.[31] Thus God can and does reveal himself in Jesus Christ. And therewith God has reconciled the world to himself.[32]

God is free to become a creature and free to take his divinity back into himself. God is free to lift the creature in the strictest and most perfect sense into unity with his own divine being.[33] In relation to the world God is *totus intra et totus extra*. He is this in Christ.[34] What happens in God must be continued in the world. Eventuation in God is inherently also eventuation with respect to and in us.[35]

In his incarnation, therefore, Jesus Christ expresses the *Geschichte* of God and man in unity. "He who says man says creaturehood and

27. *Ibid.*, p. 236.
28. I:1, p. 337; Engl. tr. p. 367. "But, be that as it may, the Lordship which becomes visible in the Biblical revelation consists in God's freedom to distinguish Himself from Himself, to become other than Himself, and yet to remain as He was: in fact more, to be the one God equal to Himself and to exist as the one sole God by the very fact that He thus, so inconceivably deeply, distinguishes Himself from Himself, that He is not only God the Father but also—in this direction this is the comprehensive meaning of the entire Biblical witness—God the Son. That He reveals Himself as the Son is what is primarily meant by saying that He reveals Himself as the Lord. Actually this Sonship is God's lordship in His revelation."

29. *Ibid.*, p. 40.   31. *Ibid.*, p. 64.
30. *Ibid.*, p. 42.   32. *Ibid.*, p. 172.

33. II:1, p. 354; Engl. tr. p. 314-315. "God is free to conceal His divinity from the creature, even to become a creature Himself, and free to assume again His Godhead. He is free to maintain as God His distance from the creature and equally free to enter into partnership with it, indeed, to lift the creature itself, in the most vigorous sense, into unity with His own divine being, with Himself."

34. *Ibid.*, p. 354.
35. *Ibid.*, p. 176 (see next chapter).

sin, limitation and distress. One must also say both of these of the man Christ Jesus."[36] But all this is included in the nature of God. God is inherently coexistent as well as existent.[37]

Looking at things Christologically, that is, from the fact of the incarnation as *Geschichte* we see that in Christ eternity becomes time without ceasing to be eternity. God's eternity is itself beginning, succession and end. In the incarnation God submits himself to the conditions of time.[38]

If we think of the attributes of God statically and abstractly, then we are horrified at this truth. Thinking concretely, that is, Christologically, we see that the living God himself is eternity.[39] "God is who he is in the act of his revelation."[40] And in the incarnation time is that form of creation, by which it becomes fit to be the place where God displays his deeds.[41] If creation were eternal, then God would be limited by its and by his own eternity.[42] It is only in time and in space that God can be and express his own eternal being. In the incarnation, therefore, the glory of God flows into time.[43] Incarnation is a free, sovereign act of God. In Christ God elects himself so that we can only believe in the non-rejection of all men.[44] Here is our true beginning as men.[45]

6. *Jesus Christ, the Servant as Lord*

Barth says he has actualized the doctrine of the incarnation. The entire relation between God and man exists in their common *Geschichte* which is Jesus Christ. Jesus Christ is the finished act of the reconciliation of man with God.[46] Thus the primary relation of men,

---

36. IV:1, p. 143. 37. II:1, p. 521; *cf.* p. 578.

38. *Ibid.*, p. 694; Engl. tr. p. 616. "The fact that the Word became flesh undoubtedly means that, without ceasing to be eternity, in its very power as eternity, eternity became time. Yes, it became time. What happens in Jesus Christ is not simply that God gives us time, our created time, as the form of our own existence and world, as is the case in creation and in the whole ruling of the world by God as its Lord. In Jesus Christ it comes about that God takes time to Himself, that He Himself, the eternal One, becomes temporal, that he is present for us in the form of our own existence and our own world, not simply embracing our time and ruling it, but submitting Himself to it, and permitting created time to become and be the form of His eternity."

39. *Ibid.*, p. 720. 43. II:2, p. 130.

40. *Ibid.*, p. 288. 44. *Ibid.*, p. 184.

41. *Ibid.*, p. 523. 45. *Ibid.*, p. 704.

42. *Ibid.*, p. 523.

46. IV:1, pp. 138-139; Engl. tr. p. 127. "But His being as God and man and God-man consists in the completed act of the reconciliation of man with God."

of all men, to God is their oneness with Jesus Christ. Christ is the act of God in coming down into time and space for the purpose of saving men, and men are the act of participation in the being of God through Christ.

Thus the divine and the human natures flow into one another. They do this in terms of *Geschichte*. And the two states of Christ in his work of saving men, the state of humiliation and the state of exaltation, also flow into one another.[47] They too do this in terms of *Geschichte*. The relation between God and man is always *indirect*, through Christ as *Geschichte*.

As therefore Christ is the electing God, so he is also the elected man. As in speaking of God we must begin with Christ, so, in speaking of man, we must also begin with Christ. We must begin with Christ and his finished work for all men. We must start from the idea of completed salvation-history.[48] We must say that this *Heilsgeschichte* happened. He stepped into our place as our substitute.[49] He is the judge who was judged for us.[50]

Really to begin with Christ as the elected man is, therefore, to see him as the only reprobate or rejected man. "God's entire freedom and His entire love become identical with this decree, with the election of Jesus Christ."[51] But this election is a double election (*praedestinatio gemina*).[52] The negative side of election is reprobation. God speaks *no* as well as *yes*.

But if we are truly to know what reprobation is, it must be clear to us that it strikes only God himself in Jesus Christ.[53] The *no* of God is not spoken to other men.[54]

There is therefore no equal ultimacy between the negative and the positive aspects of election. God's *no* to man is his penultimate but his *yes* is always his *ultimate* word to man.

God gives himself *into danger*, but it is always *God* who gives himself into this danger. He is therefore certain of victory over sin and death. That which was danger for God was sure to be salvation for man.[55] All has become new.[56] There is one man, and only one man of whom it may be said that he bears the image of the

47. *Ibid.*, pp. 145-147.
48. *Ibid.*, p. 250, objektiv für uns geschehene Heilsgeschichte.
49. *Idem.*
50. *Ibid.*, p. 251.
51. II:2, p. 176.
52. *Idem.*
53. *Ibid.*, p. 180.
54. *Ibid.*, p. 181.
55. *Ibid.*, p. 177.
56. *Ibid.*, p. 289.

glory of God.[57] This man is Jesus Christ, and he is such in his oneness with the Church. This man, with this wife, his church, is the
one for whom Adam was created.[58] This man *is* the kingdom of
God.[59]

Other men are therefore fellow men with Jesus. To be man is,
for other men, to be together with God.[60] Christ is the reprobate
man while and because he is the elect man.[61] There are, accordingly, no reprobate men other than he.[62] No sin can exclude us from
our election in Christ.[63]

What then is the groundform of humanity? "Our criterion for
answering this question is the humanity of the man Jesus."[64] To say
this is not to fall back on the idea of analogy of being. It is rather to
speak of an analogy of relation.[65] God's subjecting of himself in
Christ to the limitations of humanity and man's participation in the
being of God take place in Christ as *Geschichte*. In it one has the
true identity of God and man with one another. In it one also has
the genuine difference between God and man and priority of God
over man.

It is thus, says Barth, that we have actualized the doctrine of

57. III:1, p. 228.   59. III:2, p. 80.
58. *Idem.*
60. *Ibid.*, p. 161. Der eine Mensch Jesus aber steht allen Anderen eben so,
gerade real, gerade absolut gegenüber, weil er, dieser Einzelne, in seiner Eige-
nart, in seiner Beziehung zu Gott einzig ist: so einzig wie Gott selber im Verhältnis zu allen Kreaturen einzig ist. Es ist in der Tat die Einzigkeit und damit
die Transzendenz Gottes, die in ihm, die in diesem Menschen und also in der
Mitte aller anderen Menschen ihre kreatürliche Entsprechung, Wiederholung
und Darstellung findet. Es ist in der Tat der in der vollen Majestät Gottes allen
Menschen Ungleiche, der als dieser eine Mensch ihnen allen gleich ist. Und so
heisst Menschsein, indem es mit Jesus zusammen ist: Zusammensein mit dieser
Entsprechung, Wiederholung und Darstellung der Einzigkeit und Transzendenz
Gottes, Zusammensein mit diesem Ungleichen. So heisst Menschsein: Sein in
diesem, dem realen, dem absoluten Gegenüber. Menschsein heisst infolgedessen
grundlegend und umfassend: mit Gott zusammen sein. Was der Mensch in
diesem Gegenüber ist, das ist ja offenbar die grundlegende und umfassende
Bestimmung seines eigenen Seins.
61. II:2, p. 389.   62. II:2, p. 389.
63. III:2, p. 162. Gottlosigkeit ist infolgedessen keine Möglichkeit, sondern
die ontologische Unmöglichkeit des Menschseins. Der Mensch ist nicht ohne,
sondern mit Gott. Wir sagen damit selbstverständlich nicht, dass es kein gott-
loses Menschsein gibt. Es geschieht, es gibt ja zweifellos die Sünde. Aber eben
die Sünde ist keine Möglichkeit, sondern die ontologische Unmöglichkeit des
Menschseins. Wir sind mit Jesus, wir sind also mit Gott zusammen. Das bedeutet,
dass unser Sein die Sünde nicht ein-, sondern ausschliesst. Sein in der Sünde,
Sein in der Gottlosigkeit ist ein Sein wider unser Menschsein.
64. *Ibid.*, p. 269.   65. *Ibid.*, p. 262.

the incarnation.[66] Thinking in concepts of pure movement, we have transmuted all the terms pertaining to the incarnation into the idea of *Geschichte*.[67]

But this *Geschichte* is presence.[68] That is to say, this *Geschichte* happens at every time.[69] In *Geschichte* as presence humiliation can at the same time be exaltation.[70] How can we say of a *Geschichte* that happened then (*damals*), that it is happening now and that that which happened then and is happening now will happen again?[71]

The answer is again that we must think of all things else in terms of the Christ-Event. In this Christ-Event God's eternity is present in and even subject to time, that is, Christ's humiliation. In this Christ-Event man's time is taken up into God's eternity. In the existence of Jesus Christ we deal with the common realization of divine and human being.[72] The divine "works itself out in the human" and the human "serves and gives witness to the divine."[73]

It is because we know that time is taken into eternity by means of *Geschichte* that we have the true, objective basis for our faith, for

66. IV:2, p. 116.   67. *Ibid.*, p. 118.

68. *Ibid.*, p. 119. diese Geschichte ist Gegenwart.

69. *Ibid.*, p. 119; Engl. tr. p. 107. "But when we speak of this history, we mean the history which took place once and for all in the birth and life and death of Jesus Christ and was revealed for a first time in His resurrection. To that extent it unquestionably belongs to a definite time. It has happened. But in so far as it has happened as this history, the act of God, it has not ceased to be history and therefore to happen. As this history it is not enclosed or confined in that given time. "My words shall not pass away" (Mk. 13:31). They have not passed away, they have not become merely historical fact. "Lo, I am with you alway" (Mt. 28:20). Who? Jesus Christ. But that means the history in which He, the Son of God, becomes and is the Son of Man, going into the far country as the Son of God to come home again as the Son of Man. "Jesus Christ lives" means that this history takes place to-day in the same way as did that yesterday —indeed, as the same history. Jesus Christ speaks and acts and rules—it all means that this history is present. Whether confessed and acknowledged or not, it is the great decisive event of to-day. It is the most up-to-date history of the moment. Is it only that? Does it only take place to-day, in the present? Does it take place only as a reflection of our own present history? No, it has a backward reference. It took place then, at its own time, before we were, when our present was still future. And it has also a forward reference. It is still future and will still happen—"even unto the end of the world." In other words, when we say that Jesus Christ is in every age, we say that His history takes place in every age. He is in this *operatio*, this event. This is the new form which we have given to Christology in our present understanding and development of it."

70. *Ibid.*, p. 120.   71. *Idem.*

72. *Ibid.*, p. 126; Engl. tr. p. 113. "Our first point, in relation to the main concept, is that it is a matter of the existence of Jesus Christ in the common *actualisation* of divine and human essence."

73. *Ibid.*, p. 128.

then we have the central point of *Geschichte*.[74] This is Christ revealing himself as the risen and ascended one.[75]

To be sure, the resurrection is physical and historical, but this is true only in the sense that, though it is primarily *Geschichte*, it is *also* an innerworldly something.[76] In this sense Christianity is not exclusively eschatological. It is not as though eternity touches time merely as a tangent touches a circle. God is really present in history. Pontius Pilate must have a place in the creed. Barth says that in his commentary on Romans he did not adequately bring out this point.

In fact, Barth now holds that only on the basis of the idea of *Geschichte* can one avoid Docetism. Even so, Barth's view of *Geschichte* as presence *(Gegenwart)* excludes as thoroughly as could be the identification of the resurrection of Christ with a fact of history. To be truly the Christ-Event, and, as such, the climax of the revelation of that event, the resurrection must primarily be *Geschichte* and only secondarily *Historie*.

If the resurrection were directly identified with anything in *Historie*, then, as earlier indicated, it could be no truly objective basis for the believer's faith. Only when seen as *Geschichte* and therefore only secondarily as *Historie*, does the resurrection indicate the presence of God in act.

In Christ the risen one, the kingly one, all men have been sanctified.[77] In Christ as risen his substitutionary reconciliation for all men is apparent.[78] The New Testament tells of salvation-history and

74. *Ibid.*, p. 146. zentralen Geschichte aller Geschichte.

75. *Ibid.*, p. 148; Engl. tr. p. 132. "But 'Jesus Christ in this character' means Jesus Christ as He reveals Himself in His resurrection and ascension. The significance of this event is to be found here. It is not to be found in a continuation of His being in a changed form which is its fulfilment. The being of Jesus Christ was and is perfect and complete in itself in His history as the true Son of God and Son of Man. It does not need to be transcended or augmented by new qualities or further developments. The humiliation of God and the exaltation of man as they took place in Him are the completed fulfilment of the covenant, the completed reconciliation of the world with God."

76. *Ibid.*, p. 160.   77. *Ibid.*, p. 173.

78. *Ibid.*, pp. 298-299; Engl. tr. pp. 269-270. "For what was it that really took place in the event which we then recognized and described as the homecoming of the Son of Man, as His elevation and exaltation to fellowship with God, to the side of God, to participation in His lordship over all things, as the *communicatio idiomatum et gratiarum et operationum?* Was it just the isolated history of this one man? This is certainly the case, for what took place and has

therefore of salvation-time. This is the time of the life of Jesus Christ.[79] It is the time of Revelation. It is God's time and therefore real time.[80] This time is *also* that which we call historical time.[81] But it is primarily the divine presence which overarches and touches historical time equally in the past, the present and the future. "The Word of God is. It is never 'not yet' or 'no more.' No becoming and therefore no passing away underlies it and in consequence no change. And this applies also to the Word that became flesh and entered time."[82] Christ's true time takes the place *(tritt an die Stelle)* of our problematic, unauthentic time.[83] Christ's time *triumphs over our time.*[84]

In his resurrection, therefore, Christ triumphs over his own subjection to our time, his own reprobation for us. As such Christ is the substitute for the sin of men, of all men. It is Christ who envelops men from all sides. For what time is there of which he is not the Lord?[85] In the resurrection all men participate in the glory of God.[86]

---

to be noted as this communication between divine and human being and activity in this One was and is only, as the reconciliation of man with God by God's own incarnation, His own history and not that of any other man. But for all its singularity, as His history it was not and is not a private history, but a representative and therefore a public. His history in the place of all other men and in accomplishment of their atonement; the history of their Head, in which they all participate. Therefore, in the most concrete sense of the term, the history of this One is world history. When God was in Christ He reconciled the world to Himself (2 Cor. 5:19), and therefore us, each one of us. In this One humanity itself, our human essence, was and is elevated and exalted. It is in perfect likeness with us, as our genuine Brother, that He was and is so unique, so unlike us as the true and royal man. To that in which a man is like all others, and therefore a man, there now belongs brotherhood with this one man, the One who is so utterly unlike him and all other men. To human essence in all its nature and corruption there now belongs the fact that in the one Jesus Christ, who as the true Son of God was and is also the true Son of Man, it has now become and is participant in this elevation and exaltation. There is no human life which is not also (and primarily and finally) determined and characterised by the fact that it can take place only in this brotherhood. And therefore there is no self-knowledge which does not also include, which does not necessarily have primarily and finally as its object, the fact that man as such is the brother of this one man. Its true theme and origin can only be a declaration of the Christmas message."

79. III:2, p. 529. Es verkündigt die Heilsgeschichte und eben darum und damit die Heilszeit. Die Lebenszeit Jesu ist diese Heilszeit.

80. I:2, p. 54.
81. *Ibid.*, p. 55. Deus praesens.
82. *Ibid.*, p. 58.
83. *Ibid.*, p. 61.

84. *Ibid.*, p. 62.
85. III:2, p. 694.
86. *Ibid.*, p. 760.

7. Jesus Christ, the True Witness

The salvation of all men has taken place in the resurrection of Christ.[87] Not only has it taken place there, but the fact that it has taken place there we know only in the Christ-Event. Jesus Christ is our only prophet. He is himself our ground of knowledge of him. He is the Revealer of God to men and he is the light of life. How can he be the light of life to men? Because he is present to them in the manner of God.[88] He is present, therefore, as pure act (*actus purus*),[89] present as God realizing himself, so that his act of life is identical with that of God, and his *Geschichte* identical with that of God.[90] Inasmuch as Christ lives, he speaks for himself. He makes himself known to other men.[91] His life is *Geschichte*. As such it is *Heilsgeschichte*, and it is also revelation-history (*Offenbarungsgeschichte*).[92] This *Offenbarungsgeschichte* is inherently clear.[93] Grace as such gives light.[94]

The Church, as the body of Christ, confesses her Lord as her life and her light.[95] The light of the Christ-Event is *the* final light for men.[96] In terms of it alone all true answers are given and all proper questions asked.[97]

How else could Christ be known by men than by his authoritative speech to them? "Geschichte is the life of all men realized in Jesus Christ; Geschichte is the covenant fulfilled in Him."[98] This *Geschichte* is light as well as life and is inherently overarching in character.[99]

This *Geschichte* as overarching revelation cannot be evaded by men, for their confrontation with it is unavoidable,[100] since man with his response is enveloped and taken into the Christ-Event.[101]

87. IV:3; 1, p. 343.
88. *Ibid.*, p. 41.
89. *Ibid.*, p. 42.
90. *Idem.*
91. *Ibid.*, p. 49.
92. *Ibid.*, p. 50.
93. *Ibid.*, p. 87.

94. *Ibid.*, p. 90.
95. *Ibid.*, p. 130.
96. *Ibid.*, p. 182.
97. *Ibid.*, p. 184.
98. *Ibid.*, p. 206-207.
99. *Ibid.*, p. 209.
100. *Idem.*

101. *Ibid.*, p. 213-214. Wir hörten: Offenbarung und Erkenntnis Jesu Christi ist die Geschichte, in der er den Menschen mit sich selbst konfrontiert, in der also der Mensch und seine Geschichte in die Geschichte Jesu Christi einbezogen, in sie hineingenommen wird: eben mit ihm und seiner Geschichte nun aber auch der Widerstand, den er ihm entgegensetzt, und konkret: der Widerspruch, in welchem er sich seiner Offenbarung und Erkenntnis verweigern, die Obstruktion, in der er sie schon in ihrem Anheben und damit auch

Thus the prophecy of Jesus Christ envelops the entire history of the world and of every man.[102]

Summing up the question of man's knowledge of Christ, Barth says: "The reconciliation of the world with God in its totality is Geschichte."[103] This is true especially when we deal with the question of prophecy or truth. As such it breaks through all limitations and it envelops all that happens so as to reform it to participation with its own eventuation.[104] Christ as *Geschichte* is the reconciliation of the whole world and of all men. Precisely as such does it wish to be understood and thus will it be accepted by all men.[105]

The recognition of Christ as *Geschichte* on the part of men becomes *Geschichte* in turn. Springing from the reconciliation in *Jesus-Geschichte*, it too is *Heilsgeschichte*. In it the *Heilsgeschichte* accomplished in Jesus Christ reproduces and extends itself.[106] This process of extension continues till the "Geschichte of Jesus Christ envelops the Geschichte of the world and of all men."[107] And this continuation of *Heilsgeschichte* in the form of Christian knowledge is itself Jesus Christ.[108] Believers participate in the being and work of Jesus Christ, and, finally, all men stand in the light of the resurrection of Jesus Christ.[109] No one can finally deny his election in

---

in ihrem Fortgang und Vollzug verhindern und unterdrücken will. Einbezogen in die Geschichte Jesu Christi wird mit dem Menschen und seiner Geschichte also auch das Nichtige, das Böse, das in der noch nicht erlösten Welt noch und noch gegenwärtig und wirksam ist.

102. *Ibid.*, p. 225.   104. *Ibid.*, p. 241.
103. *Ibid.*, p. 240.

105. *Idem.* Sie ist ja die Versöhnung der ganzen Welt, aller Menschen. Aber eben als das muss und will sie nun auch von der ganzen Welt, von allen Menschen begriffen und ergriffen werden. Dass das geschehe, dafür sorgt sie selber in dieser ihrer dritten Gestalt, in der ihre Wirklichkeit auch Wahrheit, Gottes Tat in Jesus Christus auch Gottes Wort, in der das Leben auch das Licht ist.

106. *Idem.* neuen Geschichte: einer weiteren Geschichte
107. *Ibid.*, p. 244.

108. *Ibid.*, p. 247-248. Dieses Heilgeschehen ist Jesus Christus und Jesus Christus ist dieses *Heilgeschichte*. Und wenn nun Jesus Christus, der selbst dieses Heilsgeschehen ist, sich selbst und also dieses Heilsgeschehen offenbart, wenn er sich und also dieses Heilsgeschehen zum Gegenstand, Grund und Inhalt menschlicher, der christlichen Erkenntnis mach, dann heisst das: Er gibt dem seiner Offenbarung teilhaftigen und in ihrer Macht ihn erkennenden Menschen eben damit gnädigen Anteil an dem Sein und Tun, das zunächst nur eben sein eigenes ist und also an dem Heilsgeschehen, das zunächst nur Gottes in ihm geschehene Heilstat, nur eben in seiner Person für die ganze Welt, für alle Menschen Ereignis ist.

109. *Ibid.*, p. 519.

Jesus Christ.[110] For the truth is "identical with the living Jesus Christ."[111] In Jesus Christ every man's election to participation in God's being is settled before the foundation of the world. This is the meaning of Ephesians 1:4.[112]

8. Geschichte—Review

Christ therefore is truly God and truly man, and Christ's person is his work. The work is the reconciliation of all men to God.

Thus Christ as *Geschichte* is the act of revelation whereby God is wholly revealed and wholly hidden to man. Man's faith in this act becomes participation in God's revelation. But Christ as revelation is the actual identification of his whole being of God with the man Jesus. Man's faith in Jesus thus becomes participation in his being and therewith in the being of God. Finally, God as identical with his revelation in the incarnation is the act of the reconciliation of all men. Christ as *Geschichte is* the reconciliation of all men. The faith of man is therefore the inevitable response to the victory of God in Christ as *Geschichte*. Through Christ as *Geschichte* all men receive the grace of God. An analysis of Barth's view of grace must be our next concern.

---

110. *Ibid.,* p. 534.   111. *Ibid.,* p. 547.
112. IV:3;2, p. 556. Zuerst in Gott selbst steht der Mensch schon im Lichte des Lebens. Der Mensch: jeder Mensch, alle Menschen! So gewiss des Menschen Erwählung seine Erwählung in Jesus Christus, dem Sohne Gottes, ist, den der Vater und der sicht selbst nicht nur für diesen und jenen, sondern für alle Menschen erwählt und der nicht nur diesen und jenen, sondern alle Menschen für sich erwählt hat.

Chapter II

Barth's View of Grace in Christ

In discussing the doctrine of grace, Barth argues again and again, we must do so Christologically.

Speaking Christologically of grace is, in effect, speaking of Christ. It is not to speak of the *principle* of grace; it is rather to speak of "the living person of Jesus Christ himself."[1] Christology must *"per definitionem"* be that which grounds all our theological thinking. It must therefore also, and in particular, control us in our view of the relation of sin to grace.[2] We cannot first establish views concerning God, man, sin, and grace and afterward shore them up with Christological considerations.[3]

Thinking Christologically of grace is to keep the two aspects of grace in proper balance. On the one hand grace is inherently *free* grace. It is *sovereign* grace. It *produces* works in man which are new, takes sin seriously, and is incomprehensible. When man is saved by grace, there is a genuine turning-about in his life. On the other hand, grace is inherently universal grace. The primordial and unchangeable relation of God to man is that of grace in Christ, and the primordial and unchangeable relation of man to God is that of the receiver of grace in Christ. Sin is an "ontological impossibility" for man. "The real man is the sinner who participates in God's grace."[4]

1. IV:3;1, p. 198.
2. *Ibid.*, pp. 198 ff. In this section Barth rejects G. C. Berkouwer's charge that his theology is speculative in that for him grace makes it a foregone conclusion that sin will be defeated. Barth says that this charge is without foundation because he deals with the Person of Christ, not with the principle of grace.
3. *Ibid.*, p. 200.   4. III:2, p. 36.

If we think of grace as a principle instead of simply as the person of Christ, then we might think of Barth's theology as being speculative. Noting Barth's stress on the *free* character of grace, we might even think of his position as being nominalistic. Is it not nominalism to say that God does not need his nature, that he is so free as to be able to participate in the being of man and then to take man's being into participation with his own divine being?

Thinking of grace as a principle might, however, also make us think of Barth's position as realistic. Is it not realism to say that all men will be and even have been saved in Christ from all eternity? Is he not then virtually a Platonist?

Barth's answer to both charges is that speaking Christologically of grace is not to speak speculatively in any direction. One may freely use the language of any school of philosophy.[4a] But one must, as a theologian, be free from the control of all philosophy.

Thinking Christologically of grace enables us, says Barth, to speak along the lines of Reformation theology. Thinking Christologically of grace enables us to escape the Romanist approach to grace and the free will of man. Romanism thinks along the lines of the analogy of being, and in doing so, is largely controlled by philosophical speculation. It is this philosophical speculation that accounts for its use of natural theology. In Romanist theology Christ comes into the picture too late; he comes in *afterwards*, and a Christ coming in *afterwards* is, in effect, Christ not coming in at all.

Against this the Reformers, thinking Christologically, gave God the true priority over man, and grace the true priority over man's participation in it.

But the Reformers did not consistently work out the relation of grace to sin along Christological lines. They were unable to fathom the full implication of their own idea of the sovereignty of grace. They did not realize that the full freedom and glory of God's grace to man in Christ is expressed in the very idea of his being the one who suffers the wrath of God for man.

Again, the Reformers, and notably Calvin, had no full appreciation for the biblical universalism involved in the true idea of grace. We must therefore go beyond the Reformers in stressing both the full sovereignty and the full universality of the nature of grace.

Instead of thus going beyond the Reformers, later orthodox the-

---

4a. *Grundfragen, beantwortet von Prof. Dr. Karl Barth,* Nykerk, 1935, p. 24.

ologians all too often fell back on natural theology and on the idea of direct revelation in history. Thus they tended once more to make the consciousness of man think of itself as autonomous. And thus they became, all too often, the forerunners of the consciousness-theology of Schleiermacher and his followers.

This in turn prepared the way for a theology which was, in effect, as Feuerbach maintained, nothing more than an undercover anthropology.

If then we are to work out the true Reformation principle of theology, and therewith escape the synergistic views of Romanism, we must think of grace Christologically. And if we are to escape the narrowness of an evil orthodoxy and the subjectivism of the consciousness theologians, we must think of grace Christologically. And finally if we are really to enjoy the full certainty of the gift of the grace of God in Christ for all men, and in doing so laugh in Feuerbach's face, then we must think of grace Christologically.

1. Reconciliation as Geschichte

Speaking of grace Christologically is to speak of grace as *Geschichte*. For Christ is *Geschichte*.

In Christ as *Geschichte* Christ is identical with his work, and his work is that of the salvation of all men. Barth stresses this "biblical universalism," as he calls it, over and over. As *biblical* universalism it differs from philosophical universalism. Biblical universalism is, says Barth, not based upon man's inherent goodness. It in no way resembles the philosophical optimism of Leibniz and others. Biblical universalism wants to take sin seriously.

Man in himself and as such is utterly undeserving. He is under the wrath of God. He is blind.[5] His time is "problematic and unauthentic."[6] He is sinful and fallen. As such he is boastful of his own power.[7] He will not admit that he is lost and must live by the mercy of God.[8] As a religious being he speaks but will not listen to the revelation of God. Moreover, his speaking and thinking is grasping and as such is contradictory of the revelation of God.[9] He is a fabricator of idols,[10] and is such because he thinks that he can

5. I:2, p. 33.
6. *Ibid.*, p. 61.
7. *Ibid.*, p. 67.

8. *Ibid.*, p. 172.
9. *Ibid.*, p. 330.
10. *Ibid.*, p. 355.

possess the truth, failing to see that "no religion is true."[11] He seeks
for a god beyond and apart from Christ, failing to realize that God
can be known by God only.[12] He seeks for an analogy of God's
knowledge in his own knowledge, not realizing that not he but only
God is an authentic person.[13] When he thinks of God, he thinks of
abstractions. He thinks of freedom rather than of God as free.[14]

In all this man as he is in himself is and thinks as an unbeliever,
as a sinner, thinking and acting against the grace of God in Christ.
He sins "against his created being."[15] He chooses that which, according to his election in Christ, is impossible for him to choose. He
chooses the "satanic possibility."[16] "And because the divine election
of grace, because Jesus Christ, is the beginning of all the ways and
works of God, man chooses that which is in itself nothing when he
returns to this satanic possibility, when he chooses isolation in relation to God. His choice itself and as such is, therefore, null. He
chooses as and what he cannot choose. He chooses as if he were
able to choose otherwise than in correspondence to his election."[17]

Man in himself sins against grace. He does not realize that his own
true being as man is his being elected in Christ. Says Berkouwer:
"Probably no one will wish to venture a prophecy as to the direction
in which Barth will further develop his thought. It is quite possible,
however, to state in a nutshell his central thesis. This is that the
triumph of election means, centrally and determinatively, the a
priori divine decision of the election of *all* in the election of Christ.

"This a priorism as the content of the proclamation of the
Church involves as a direct consequence for Barth the ontological
impossibility of sin. For is not this unbelief opposition to that which
overcomes the bitterest opposition, namely, God's gracious election?"[18]

The sin of man is therefore the act of rebellion against Christ as
the electing God and the elected man. Christ as the electing God and
elected man is the *Geschichte* of God saving all men. To understand
the sin of man we must, accordingly, note that it is against God and
his grace as expressed in the incarnation.

11. *Ibid.*, p. 356.
12. II:1, pp. 47, 200.
13. *Ibid.*, p. 305.
17. *Ibid.*, p. 347. Engl. tr. p. 316.
18. *The Triumph of Grace in the Theology of Karl Barth*, p. 290.

14. *Ibid.*, p. 360.
15. III:2, p. 29.
16. II:2, p. 347.

2. *Jesus Christ as the Electing God*

The nature of sin can be understood only in terms of the cross of Christ where it was defeated by Christ as the victor over chaos. And Christ is victor over chaos because he is true God and true man. He is the electing God and the elected man.

For the purpose of understanding Barth's Christological view of sin and grace we can best begin with Christ as the electing God.

But we must not, says Barth, attempt to go beyond this point. We must not speak about God as he is in himself apart from and prior to Christ. Accordingly, we must not speak of a decree of such a God as the source of man's election. For the *"decretum absolutum"* we must substitute the *"decretum concretum."*

If we establish our doctrine of election upon the counsel of God in himself prior to Christ, then we involve ourselves in meaningless mystery, since our very idea of God, as the triune God, must be stated in terms of the revelation that we have in Jesus Christ.[19]

We may and even must, says Barth, speak of an immanent trinity. So we may and must also distinguish between God's essence and his works. But this distinction is to be made only in the interest of stressing that God's works are works of grace.[20] God is therefore to be thought of as identical with his revelation in Christ. To speak of the triune God properly is to speak of his free Lordship over himself and over his creatures. "The doctrine of the trinity is nothing more than the development of the confession that Jesus is the Christ or Lord."[21]

If we thus interpret the trinity Christologically we realize that God is our Creator because he is first our Father and he is our Father because he is first the Father of the Son. The Son is God as reconciler. Through the Son, and only through the Son, the Father speaks.[22] Thus the hiddenness of revelation, of revelation as reconciliation, comes to expression in our midst through Jesus Christ as Lord.[23] Christ as the Word wholly reveals and wholly hides the triune God. "The same revelation thus compels us to separate God and His word and to combine them in one."[24] Only thus can we have the idea that in Jesus Christ God is both *wholly* revealed and *wholly*

19. I:1, p. 313.
20. *Ibid.*, p. 391.
21. *Ibid.*, p. 353.

22. *Ibid.*, p. 430.
23. *Idem.*
24. *Ibid.*, p. 457.

hidden. And only while understanding that God is wholly revealed in Christ and yet wholly hidden when thus revealed can we also understand that the grace of God is at the same time universal and sovereign.

"As this word, which God Himself thinks or speaks eternally by Himself, the content of which, therefore, can be naught other than God Himself—Jesus Christ, as the second mode of God's existence, is God Himself. But here too we shall not need to be blind to the fact that this language also in our mouths and in our concepts is inappropriate language. We know not what we say when we call Jesus Christ the eternal Word of God. We indeed know no such Word as, being distinct from the speaker, should yet contain and reproduce the entire essence of the speaker, no *Logos* with an adequate complement of *Nus*, and no *Nus* that could be expressed exhaustively in one *Logos*, no thought or language which should leave behind it the contrast between knowing and being, overcoming it by a synthesis. In short, we know no true word. And therefore neither do we know the true Word above the true word, the Word of God! Once more we must say what we said about the Father-Son relationship: that the true Word is, for us who think and speak in the doubly veiled sphere of creatureliness and sinfulness, strictly and exclusively the eternal Word hidden in God, Jesus Christ Himself. It is not the case that our creaturely thought and language, in relation to the creaturely reason that produces such a creaturely *logos*, should in itself have a command of allegory to justify us in a claim to think and speak the truth, when we call Jesus Christ the Word of God. But it requires revelation and faith, it requires the continuous gracious event of the incarnation of the eternal Word and the outpouring of the Holy Spirit, ever and again to arouse and lift up what we know as the Word to such a command of allegory, that it may become the truth when we call Jesus Christ the Word of God."[25]

On this basis, Barth argues, we realize that God is inherently gracious to all men. For we do not deal with a principle of love or a principle of grace. We deal with Jesus Christ. "By being the Father in Himself from eternity, God brings Himself forth from eternity as the Son. By being the Son from eternity, He comes forth from eternity from Himself as Father. In this eternal bringing forth of Himself and coming forth from Himself, He posits Himself a third time

25. *Ibid.*, pp. 458-459. Engl. tr. p. 499.

as the Holy Spirit, i.e., as the love which unifies Him in Himself."[26] This must now be shown under the following headings.

(a) THE EXISTENCE OF GOD

"Love is God, the highest law and the ultimate reality, because God is Love and not *vice versa*."[27] It is, we are told, by holding fast to this that we first consider the idea of the existence of God.

It is because God, the triune God, is love, that he "negates in Himself, from all eternity, in His utter simplicity, existence in loneliness, self-sufficiency, self-dependence."[28] And since God's being is his revelation in Christ, and this revelation is reconciliation, therefore man exists in his being reconciled to God in Christ. "The Love which meets us in reconciliation and, looking backwards from that, in creation, is therefore and thereby Love, the highest law and the ultimate reality, because God is Love antecedently in Himself; not merely a supreme principle of the connection of separation and communion, but Love which wills and affirms, seeks and finds in separation the other thing, the Other Person in communion also, in order to will and to affirm, to seek and to find communion with it (Him) in separation also. Because God is Love antecedently in Himself, therefore love exists and holds good as the reality of God in the work of revelation and in the work of creation. But He is Love antecedently in Himself, by positing Himself as the Father of the Son. That is the interpretation and proof of the *qui procedit ex Patre*."[29]

Basic, then, to an understanding of the very existence of God is the fact that he is Act. He is *Geschichte*. "God is, who He is, in His works." To be sure, "He is also, who He is, not *only* in His works." But what he is in himself is not different from what he is in his works. In his works he is himself revealed for what he is.[30]

The older theology, including protestant orthodoxy, failed to see this basic point. It was not truly Christological in its approach. It sought for formal-logical foundations for its doctrine of the trinity back of the revelation of God in Christ.[31] Over against this we must

---

26. *Ibid.*, p. 507. Engl. tr. pp. 552-553.
27. *Ibid.*, p. 507. Engl. tr. p. 553. So ist er der Vater des Sohnes, das er mit dem Sohne den Geist, die Liebe, hervorbringt und so in sich selber der Geist, die Liebe, ist.
28. *Idem.*
29. I:1, *Idem.* Engl. tr. p. 553.
30. II:1, p. 291.
31. *Ibid.*, p. 292.

insist that "God is, who He is, in the act of his revelation."[32] Thus
do we deal with the living God, not with some abstract essence.[33]
Only thus do we deal with God as a person.[34] And thus we can
speak of God's being as "self-moved being."[35]

Here we have the foundation for grace that is truly sovereign
grace, because it is grace of the sovereign God. "God's revelation
draws its authority and evidence from the fact that it is founded on
itself apart from all human foundations. God's commandment, God's
grace, and God's promise have a unique force because they are without reference to human strength or weakness. God's work is triumphant because it is not bound to our work, but precedes and follows
it in its own way, which may also be the way of our work."[36] "Every
statement of what God is, and explanation how God is, must always
state and explain what and how He is in His act and decision. There
is no moment in the ways of God which is over and above this act
and decision."[37]

As the only self-moved being, God is the only real or authentic
Person. "The real person is not man but God. It is not God who is
a person by extension but we. God exists in His act. God is His
own decision. God lives from and by Himself."[38]

(b) THE INCARNATION

But now we must proceed to consider the manifestation of this
God of self-decision as this manifestation appears in the names of
the Father, the Son, and the Spirit.[39] Without proceeding thus, we
should only have tautology. But the God of act in himself is, at the
same time the God of act beyond himself. God seeks and establishes
communion with man. God does not need this communion. He establishes it freely. "It implies so to speak an overflow of His essence
that He turns to us. We must certainly regard this overflow as itself
matching His essence, belonging to His essence. But it is an overflow which is not demanded or presupposed by any necessity, con-
straint, or obligation, least of all from outside, from our side, or by

32. *Idem.*

33. *Ibid.*, p. 293.

34. *Ibid.*, p. 300.

35. *Ibid.*, p. 303.

36. *Ibid.*, p. 303; Engl. tr. p. 271.

37. *Ibid.*, p. 305; Engl. tr. p. 272. Es gibt kein Moment im Wesen Gottes
oberhalb dieser Tat und Entscheidung.

38. *Idem.*; Engl. tr. *Idem.*

39. *Ibid.*, p. 306.

any law by which God Himself is bound and obliged."[40] "This seeking and creating finds its crown and final confirmation in the future destiny of mankind as redeemed in Jesus Christ, in His destiny for eternal salvation and life. What God does in all this, He is: and He is no other than He who does all this."[41] "He does not will to be Himself in any other way than He is in this relationship."[42] The goodness of God is so great that it overflows as goodness toward us as men.

On the basis of what has just been said about God as act, whose decision is his being, and whose being as decision freely overflows into the communion with man, we have the two aspects of grace again brought back to their final source in God.

God's grace is sovereign or free. God's grace is inherently inclusive of all men. These two aspects of grace are based upon the fact that God is his work of salvation of all men in Christ.

The sovereignty or freedom of grace rests upon the fact that God's own being exists and is by virtue of his own decision. "He cannot 'need' His own being because He affirms it in being who He is."[43] Here is the sovereign God indeed. This sovereign freedom by which God chooses his own being is the basis of his sovereign or free choice of men to communion with him. If God is free or sovereign in the choice of his own being, then he is certainly, and if possible, more definitely free in his choice of men and their salvation. If God chooses his own being freely, he certainly chooses the overflow of his being or essence freely.

On the other hand, the being of God does not need the affirmation of God's choice. "It is not, of course, that His being needs this affirmation."[44] Not God himself, but only his creature *needs* the affirmation of God. "When we say that God is free to exist, we do not say that God lifts Himself, as it were, out of non-existence into existence, that He makes Himself free to exist. What we say is that the mode of existence is proper to Him which is exempt from any limitation by the possibility of its non-existence. He is the One who is in Himself the Existent. By existing in this way He is not subject to any necessity, as though He must first exist in order to be who He is. But by His existence He simply reaffirms Himself."[45]

40. *Ibid.*, p. 307; Engl. tr. p. 273.   43. *Ibid.*, p. 344; Engl. tr. p. 306.
41. *Ibid.*, p. 307. Engl. tr. p. 274.   44. *Ibid.*, p. 344; Engl. tr. p. 306.
42. *Ibid.*, p. 308; Engl. tr. p. 274.
45. *Idem.* Nicht weil er dieser Bestätigung bedürfte, sondern weil er es damit *faktisch* bestätigt.

Here then is the basis for grace that is inherently universal. The God who *freely* chooses himself, chooses *himself* as "the Existent." As "the Existent" he is not threatened by non-existence. Only his creatures are threatened by non-existence. Their existence must therefore, surely, be existence by the sovereign grace of God. For God's existence is his revelation of grace. So man's existence must be existence by participation in the being of God that does not need the affirmation of God. God is free but he is free as the God whose nature it is to seek communion with men.

(c) The Attributes of God

Immediately involved in the reality of a God who is free in his love is the idea that in discussing God's attributes we must always subordinate those that would condemn man to those that would save him.

God is holy. When we speak of God's holiness we speak of his judgment upon the sin of man. But God is gracious even as the God of wrath. "God is He who in His son Jesus Christ loves all His children, in His children all men, and in men His whole creation. God's being is His loving. He is all that He is as the One who loves."[46]

God is righteous. His condemnation rests upon guilty men. But this condemnation or wrath is itself a form of the grace of God. Wrath is real but real only as a mode of grace.[47]

(d) Christ as Man's Substitute

This does not mean that the guilt of man goes unpunished. It means rather that God will certainly take upon himself the punishment of sin. That is to say he will visit this punishment upon Jesus Christ, who is truly God and man. Thus the idea of Jesus Christ as man's substitute is immediately implied in the idea of grace as free and universal.

3. *Jesus Christ as the Elected Man*

The doctrine of the grace of God must also be studied by considering the fact that Jesus Christ is the elected man as well as the electing God. Failing to think of Christ as the electing God has made

46. *Ibid.*, p. 394; Engl. tr. p. 351.   47. IV:1, pp. 545-546.

men fail to see both the freedom and the universality of grace. They
then looked into the dreadful face of a God, beyond Christ, who
arbitrarily might elect or might not elect them. Such arbitrariness
is not true freedom. Such arbitrariness caused men to live in dread.
And such arbitrariness excluded the universality as well as the freedom of grace.

Similarly failing to think of Christ as the elected man leads to the
idea of grace as neither free nor universal.

Let us then think with Barth of Christ as the elected man.

This, as noted above, means first that Christ, and he alone, is *the*
rejected man.

As noted above, God's wrath must be appeased. Sin is real. Sin
must be punished. But the wrath of God is a mode of his grace.

Hence the punishment for the sin of man must be placed upon
Jesus Christ as the God-man. Upon him the wrath of God expends
itself completely. Thus other men must first of all be regarded as
those whose sins are forgiven in Christ as their substitute.

More than that, since Jesus Christ as the electing God is identical
with Jesus Christ as the elected man, it follows that his work as the
substitute for men is inherent in the Christ as the Eternal Son. Election is the eternal election of the Church by and in Jesus Christ.[48]

Jesus Christ has accepted the grace of God in our place.[49] The
readiness of God for man in Christ envelops the readiness of man
for God in Christ.[50] "In the Holy Spirit as the Spirit of the Father
and of the Son there is, in the height of God, no 'Against us' but only
the 'For us' which has been spoken and is true once for all. Just because this is how it is and not otherwise in this height, in the height
of God, it cannot be otherwise in our depth. What depth can be so
deep that it is withdrawn from what is true and valid in the height
of God; that something else can be true and valid in it; that everything in it that seeks to be true in and for itself is not unmasked from
this height as a lie? So then between us and God, however it may
be with ourselves and our enmity against grace, there can be no
strife. So then our enmity is outstripped and overcome. So then the
world is reconciled to God (2 Cor. 5:19). And this is just as certain
as that Father, Son and Holy Spirit are the one eternal and almighty

48. II:2, p. 215.
49. II:1, p. 170. an unserer Stelle Gottes Gnade angenommen und damit
Gott den Gehorsam dargebracht hat.
50. *Ibid.*, p. 167.

God, and that between the Son and the Father in the height there is no strife, but peace and unity in the Holy Spirit from eternity to eternity. Thus everything that is to be said about our participation in the person and work of Jesus Christ, here in the depth as such, can properly consist only in this: It lies in the nature of what happens there in God, in eternal continuation of the reconciliation and revelation accomplished in time, that in full reality it happens here also to and in us—even in face and in spite of what we are to and in ourselves as long as 'there' and 'here' still mean two different things. This participation of ours in the person and work of Jesus Christ does not have to be added as a second thing. As the one thing which has to be done it is already wholly and utterly accomplished in Him."[51]

We see then that the freedom and the universality of grace are involved in Christ as the elected man. For as such he is, from eternity, the one who has borne the wrath of God for all men. Thus we have the objective completion of the work of redemption for all men once for all, because from eternity it was accomplished in Christ.

Sin becomes therefore an impossible possibility for other men. Man is to be defined as that being who is the object of God's grace.[52] The real man is the one who participates with Christ as the victor over Chaos. Men are men only as fellow-elect with Jesus Christ.[53] God protects them in advance (*zum vornherein*) from the power of Chaos (*das Nichtige*).[54] Man's being is being in the *Geschichte* as grounded by Jesus.[55] To be man is to have experienced redemption, to be preserved by God's mercy.[56] "The Word, the call of God to all and every man, is the existence of the man Jesus." God's grace is the meaning of the man Jesus, and God's grace is that which in him is directed to all men. That which constitutes the existence of men is the fact there is among them one man, the man Jesus, to whom God says that he is gracious to him.[57]

Barth calls his position on election one of purified supralapsarianism. He calls it this in order to bring out the fact that grace is both sovereign and universal. Purified supralapsarianism hinges on the idea that Christ is both the electing God and the elected man. Hav-

51. *Ibid.*, p. 176; Engl. tr. p. 157.
52. III:2, p. 34-35.
53. *Ibid.*, p. 175.
54. *Idem.*

55. *Ibid*, p. 193.
56. *Ibid.*, p. 194.
57. *Ibid.*, p. 196.

ing a proper view of grace, we know of no men and of no class of men who are permanently rejected of God. The form of the reprobate is a fleeing and disappearing one.[58] When we think of the destiny of the reprobate, everything depends on the point that we must not ascribe to him more than an unauthentic and dependent fellow-existence.[59] We must think of him as having a shadow-form that is receding, fleeing and disappearing.[60]

It was Jesus Christ, alone true man, who alone was rejected of God.[61] Therefore the rejection of all other men is inherently rejected by God.

"Barth's preference for the supralapsarian view," says Berkouwer, *"is nothing else than the reverse side of the ontological impossibility of sin."*[62] It is also true that his preference for the supralapsarian position springs from his idea of the freedom or sovereignty of grace. The sovereignty and the universality of grace are always involved in one another for Barth.

58. II:2, p. 507.
59. *Ibid.*, p. 502.
60. *Idem.*

61. *Ibid.*, p. 506.
62. *The Triumph of Grace*, etc., p. 256.

Chapter III

Beyond Romanism

It will help us in understanding Barth's view of God's grace in Christ to know how he sets it off from Roman Catholicism. At the time when Barth began the publication of the *Church Dogmatics* (1932), he said: "My whole work is concerned with the desperate question of achieving an evangelical theology which can stand worthily over against Roman Catholicism which I hold to be *the* great heresy."[1] And in the introduction to the first volume of that work, he thinks of the Romanist idea of *analogia entis* as a discovery of the Antichrist.

How then are we to meet this spirit of the Antichrist? Certainly not by setting over against the philosophy of Romanism another, a more Christian philosophy. We must have done with all philosophy. Philosophy starts from the bottom up. It thinks of the consciousness of man as a self-sufficient, self-intelligible something. Over against every kind of philosophy, including our own, we must start from the top down. We must start with Christ. In him, and in him alone, is the identity of being and of knowing. Our whole approach must be Christological.

Of course, Roman Catholic theology is also Christological. Does it not subscribe to the Chalcedon creed? Does it not, in subscribing to this creed, maintain the proper orthodox doctrines with respect to the relation of the divine and human natures of Christ? Is there then anything lacking in Rome's Christology?

1. *Theologische Blätter*, 1932, p. 221-222, quoted by Berkouwer *op. cit.;* p. 171, note.

Yes, there is! A true Christology must be one that speaks of Christ as Act, as *Geschichte*. "God is, who He is, in His works."[2] We may indeed concern ourselves with the being of God. But we must not think of being as prior to act.

So also, and this is for Barth basically important, we must actualize the incarnation. The Chalcedon statement on the relation of the two natures of Christ must be so interpreted as to allow for the idea of Christ being identical with *Geschichte*. As noted in the first chapter, this means that in Christ God is free to submit himself to the limitations of the creature, and man can be taken up into participation with the very being of God.

Actualizing the incarnation means also to realize that his work in the steps of exaltation does not follow in history on his work in the steps of humiliation. Christ as *Geschichte* involves his contemporaneity with us. God in the fullness of his being is both wholly revealed and wholly hidden in his act of decision in Jesus Christ. God exists only in the act of his decision which is Jesus Christ. "There is not a moment in God's being outside of this act and decision."[3]

It is in terms of this Christ as the act and decision of God that Barth opposes Romanism. It is in terms of this Christ alone that the character of grace appears in its sovereign universality. It is in terms of this Christ that man is interpreted from above.

For here, precisely, says Barth, the basic error of Rome is to be found. Romanism interprets man largely in terms of himself. Romanism claims to know to some extent what God is apart from Christ. That is to say, it has a natural theology. Romanism also claims to know to some extent what man is apart from Christ. It starts from man as a given intelligible something. The grace of God is not therefore given its rightful place of priority in the interpretations of man. Hence its claim that man is able to cooperate with the grace of God. Hence, in short, its synergism. Hence its claim that man knows the nature of sin before he knows grace. Hence also its claim to *possess* the truth about God and man and even about Christ. Hence, in short, its pride. Hence also its claim that the Church alone knows the truth. Hence its claim that there is no salvation outside the church as it understands the church. Hence, in short, its exclusiveness.

2. II:1, p. 291.
3. *Ibid.*, p. 305. Es gibt also kein Zurückgreifen hinter diese Tat und Entscheidung, hinter die Lebendigkeit Gottes, es gibt nur das Ergreifen seiner Lebendigkeit daraufhin das wir in seiner Offenbarung von ihr ergriffen sind.

All of these objections of Barth against Romanism may, however, be said to have their center in the idea of *analogia entis*. He speaks of it as "the cardinal doctrine" of Romanism.[4] The Mariolatry of Rome is but an expression of it. In the *analogia entis* idea we have a misrepresentation of the whole God-man relation.

It is not that Barth wishes to reject every form of the analogy idea.[5] He does not wish to do this any more than he wishes to forbid us to speak of the being of God. But as he wishes us to speak of God as he is revealed in Christ, so he wishes us to speak of man primarily as the one who has faith in Christ. He wishes therefore to replace the analogy of being with the analogy of faith. He also calls this analogy of faith the analogy of relation. Man is to be interpreted from above through the relation that he sustains to Christ. Man can come to a true knowledge of God only if he has this knowledge in Christ.[6] Man is "taken up by the grace of God and determined to participation in the veracity of the revelation of God."[7] It is only when man is conquered by the grace of God that he truly knows God. It is only in Christ as his substitute that man can know God. But in Christ it is certain in advance that all men know God.

It is thus from the point of view of Christ as *Geschichte* that Barth analyzes all Romanist theology and in particular the analogy of being idea.

1. *The Analogy of Faith*

The idea of analogy of being means primarily that man may start with an objective state of affairs.[8] Over against this Barth urges that even faith as an experience of man cannot as such be said to be real experience. "Let us hold on to the fact that faith is experience, a concretely fixable temporal act of this man's or that, the act, in short, of acknowledgment. But it does not go without saying that experience is real experience, experience of the Word of God. Of no experience as such, however perfect a form it may have, could this be said. Therefore, it is not as experience that faith is faith, i.e., real experience, although it is certainly experience."[9] It will be noted that Barth includes the idea of the acknowledgment of the truth in his description of experience. "Or, the act of acknowledgment is not as such acknowledgment of the Word of God. Nor is it so in virtue of

4. *Ibid.*, p. 275.
5. *Ibid.*, p. 256.
6. *Ibid.*, p. 230.

7. *Ibid.*, p. 239; Engl. tr. p. 213.
8. *Cf.* Berkouwer *op. cit.*, p. 181.
9. I:1, pp. 241-242; Engl. tr. p. 263.

any degree of perfection with which it may be achieved. But it is the Word, it is Christ, to whom faith is related, because He gives Himself as object to it, who makes faith into faith, into real experience."[10]

Faith is, therefore, not a possibility inherent in man. "Faith takes its absolute or unconditioned rise in the Word of God, independently of inborn or inherited characteristics and possibilities in man . . ."[11]

In apparent allusion to Emil Brunner, Barth says of faith: "We cannot fix it by, so to speak, turning our back upon the Word of God, in order to consider ourselves and to discover in ourselves an openness, a positive or at least a negative point of contact, for the Word of God."[12]

It is only when in Christ we actually hear the Word that the possibility of hearing it is fixed. Our faith in Christ "arises and consists purely in the object of real knowledge."[13] Our faith as experience is at most a hint of the object to which it is attached. Where God is present in his revelation, he is always hidden in it. The moment we should wish to regard faith as in any way belonging to us, we should lose it.[14]

At this point we draw near to the precise distinction Barth makes between the analogy of being and the analogy of faith.

All our stress on the fact that the possibility of our faith in Christ must be based on the fact of the actuality of its object, namely, Christ, must not make us deny that in faith we become conformable to God. Speaking of man and his faith, Barth says: "By really apprehending the Word of God in faith he is actually made fit to apprehend it. Were this to be denied we could no longer characterise and regard faith as the act and experience of man, or man as the subject of faith. But if we ascribe to man a qualification—not belonging to him, but one lent him in faith, and not one to be contemplated but only one to be used in faith, still a qualification—for apprehending the Word of God, then, we could not resile from speaking of a conformity with God proper to him in faith. Apprehension of the Word of God could not take place, were there not in and along with this event something in common between God who speaks and man who hears, an analogy, a similarity, for all the dissimilarity involved in

10. *Idem.*
11. *Ibid.*, p. 249; Engl. tr. p. 271.
12. *Idem.*
13. *Ibid.*, p. 250.
14. *Idem.*

the difference between God and man, a 'point of contact'—now we may use this concept too—between God and man."[15]

How then, asks Barth, are we to distinguish our "conformity with God" from the Romanist idea of analogy of being? "'Conformity with God' was the name we gave to the possibility of apprehending the Word of God. That is also expressed by the concept of the *imago Dei*. We must be quite clear that that puts us into hairbreadth proximity to the Catholic doctrine of the *analogia entis*. But even in and because of this proximity our doctrine will have to be quite a different one from that."[16]

In our analogy of faith we, therefore, stress the idea that it is man's *decision* that is similar to the decision of God. Only thus can we avoid the idea of the deification of man. The decision of man always depends on a prior decision of God. "In faith man is in conformity with God, i.e., capable of apprehending the Word of God, capable in his own decision of so corresponding with God's decision made about him in the Word, that the Word of God is now the Word heard by him, he himself is now the man addressed by this Word. This capacity is not to be sought among the remainder of the possibilities belonging to him, the statement about the indwelling of Christ which takes place in faith may not be converted into an anthropological statement."[17]

Here we have the heart of the matter. Man's faith is real. It is his own genuine experience. But it is a real and genuine experience not as such but as the bearer of the revelation of Christ. And this revelation or presence of Christ in man is wholly hidden in man's faith. "And once again and over and over again, what has to be said here cannot be intended as the analysis of a present reality, for as such it is withdrawn from our grasp and our knowledge, but strictly only as a reminder of the promise and as a hope of fulfilment to come. But in that case and in that way, this involution, nay, oneness of the divine *Logos* and the human in faith cannot and may not be either hushed up or denied. This involution or oneness is the knowability of the Word of God, the possibility of Church proclamation, regarded from the preacher's as well as from the hearer's standpoint,

15. I:1 Engl. tr. p. 273; *Cf.* I:1, p. 251. Die Versöhnung des Menschen mit Gott in Christus schliesst auch das in sich oder fängt schon damit an dass der verlorene Anknupfungspunkt neu gesetzt wird.
16. I: 1, p. 252; Engl. tr. p. 274. *Cf.* also p. 251.
17. *Ibid.*, p. 253; Engl. tr. p. 275.

and thereby the possibility of dogmatics also. By the Church furnishing the ministry of proclamation, by our pursuit of dogmatics, we confess our belief in this possibility. We have every reason to be pretty clear at this point, in spite of the threatening proximity of the *analogia entis,* mysticism and the philosophy of identity, and all other existing 'dangers' so-called."[18]

Thus "we have to think of man in the event of real faith as, so to speak, opened up from above. From above, not from beneath!"[19] "The opening up from above, achieved in the event of real faith, remains as hidden for us as this event itself and as God Himself."[20]

In this idea of the hiddenness of faith we recognize the great stress on the complete otherness of God found in Barth's *Romans.* Barth rejects the *analogia entis* idea because it has no proper place for the priority of God in relation to man. It has no proper place for the sovereign freedom of God in his grace toward man.

Berkouwer puts the matter very strikingly in his book, *Karl Barth.*[21] In this book there is a chapter dealing with Barth's basic motif. Are we not, Berkouwer asks, in danger of imposing a scheme of our own on Barth's work? Are we not in danger of oversimplifying Barth's comprehensive and complicated views?

Berkouwer answers that there is no real danger here. Barth keeps hammering without interruption on one theme. "That theme, in which all the lines of Barth's theology are brought into focus, is that of the freedom, sovereignty and actuality of God in his revelation."[21a] This point will appear to be of basic importance when we seek, in the next chapter, for an answer to the question of Barth's relation to the Reformers. For the moment, however, it must be indicated that Barth is as anxious to stress the real and universal presence of God's revelation to man as he is to indicate its sovereignty.

This is true, even in *Romans.* When we have stressed the meaninglessness of history with all our power, we begin to understand that "the positive relation between God and man, which is the absolute

18. *Ibid.,* p. 255; Engl. tr. p. 277. Barth quotes the following sentence from Thurneysen with apparent approval: Der Satz der Offenbarung: Gott redet ist identisch mit dem Satze: der Mensch hört!

19. *Ibid.,* p. 255; Engl. tr. p. 278.

20. *Ibid.,* p. 256; Engl. tr. p. 278.

21. This book was published in Kampen, 1936, and includes a discussion of the *Church Dogmatics,* volume one, part one.

21a. *Op. cit.;* p. 75.

paradox, veritably exists" and this becomes to us "the theme of the gospel . . . proclaimed in fear and trembling, but under pressure of a necessity from which there is no escape. It proclaims eternity as an event."[22]

It is this overpowering, this universalistic aspect of God's grace, that is emphasized by Barth in his *Church Dogmatics*. But Barth himself says that this is only a matter of emphasis and not a change of basic motif. He says that *from the beginning* it was his purpose to point out that grace is not only inherently free but also inherently universal.

The idea of universality is inherent in the idea of sovereignty. The idea of sovereignty expresses itself especially in the denial of direct revelation. If the revelation of God in history were to be identified with any fact of history, then this revelation would, ipso facto, be the possession of some men and not of all. But since the revelation of God is wholly hidden in history even when wholly revealed there, then God is not limited in the expression of his grace. The indirectness of the communication of God's grace involves, for Barth, the universality, because of the originality of the *Yes* of God toward all men.

The true Christological interpretation of grace, as Barth says he saw more clearly after 1932 than before, requires both absolute sovereignty or freedom and absolute universality. But both elements were present even in *Romans,* as he himself says. Berkouwer recognizes this fact but in his second book he greatly emphasizes the universalistic or "triumphal" character of Barth's theology. He now thinks of this triumphal character in itself as the main theme of Barth's view of the gospel. But the very idea of the universal Yes of God presupposes the idea of its sovereignty and freedom or hiddenness. If God had bound himself to a direct revelation in history, given to some men only, then he could speak no word of *Yes* to all men everywhere.

This question of the relation of the sovereignty or freedom of grace to its universality interests us just now only so far as it bears on Barth's treatment of Romanism. It is quite impossible to understand Barth's rejection of the *analogia entis* idea if we think of Barth's own view as being either that of sovereign or of universal grace. In his discussion of faith Barth stresses both aspects. Sover-

22. *Romans,* Engl. tr. p. 94.

eign grace is not sovereign unless it is also universal grace. Universal grace is not universal unless it is also sovereign grace. And this is the case because we deal with the Christ as *Geschichte*. Man knows by being known of God. "Man acts by believing, but the fact that he believes by acting is God's act. Man is the subject of faith. It is not God but man who believes. But the very fact of a man thus being subject in faith is bracketed as the predicate of the subject, God, bracketed exactly as the Creator embraces His creature, the merciful God sinful man, i.e. so that there is no departure from man's being a subject, and this very thing, the Ego of man as such, is still only derivable from the Thou of the Subject, God."[23] Here we have the analogy of faith.[24]

Barth's view of man's knowledge and of man's will are, naturally, similar to his view of man's faith. He sets forth all three of them in opposition to the *analogia entis* idea.

In the Roman Catholic church the Molinists, like G. Pohle, have been the champions of *scientia media*. Thomists, like F. Diekamp, were their vigorous opponents. A middle position is occupied by a man like B. Bartmann.[25] But the basic error, common to all three of these points of view is that of the *analogia entis*. Accordingly, the true notion of man's relation to God can never come to expression in the Romanist church. Relatively speaking, the position of the Thomists is far better than that of Molinism. But with its adherence to the idea of *analogia entis*, even Thomism has a God-man scheme of thought that is inherently speculative in character. "For the school of Thomas has done far more than its opponents to consolidate the basis it has in common with the Jesuits, the great error of the *analogia entis* as the basic pattern of Catholic thinking and teaching. The most secure basis for this pattern is the work of Thomas Aquinas himself, so that every step a Thomist takes, even if it seems to take him far from the Jesuit counter-thesis, really serves implicitly to justify this counter-theory in advance."[26]

If then the Thomists were to be effective in their rejection of *scientia media*, they would have to become Protestant. For though many a Protestant theologian held to views lower than those of the Thomists, it is of the genius of Protestantism to correct its own errors. A true Protestant opposition to Molinism is possible only when "theology dares to be theology and not ontology, and the

23. I:1, p. 258; Engl. tr. p. 281.   25. II:1, p. 641.
24. *Ibid.*, p. 257; Engl. tr. p. 279.   26. *Ibid.*, p. 658; Engl. tr. p. 584.

question of a freedom of the creature which creates conditions for God can no longer arise. But this can happen only when theology is orientated on God's revelation and therefore Christology."[27] But the theology of Thomism is still only an ontology. Only on the Protestant view do we have a theology that is not an ontology.

Thus the meaning of man's faith, of his freedom, of his will and of his knowledge must all be interpreted from above. Man's faith, will and knowledge are what they are because their object is Christ.

Only thus can the sovereignty of grace in relation to man be maintained. "Only if it begins with the knowledge of Jesus Christ can theology so think and speak that the divine and the creaturely spheres are automatically distinguished and related in a way that makes wholly impossible the replacement of the order A-B by the order B-A. It must be wholly and from the very first, and not merely occasionally or subsequently, a theology of revelation and grace, a Christological theology, if it is to speak at this point conclusively and effectively. If it is not this, or not this absolutely, then the protest against the inversion will come too late and can never be effective."[28] "Thus our own opposition to the doctrine of the *scientia media* must have as its starting-point the simple recognition that the relation between God and the creature is grace, a free act of the divine mercy. This is true generally, and it is therefore true of the relation between His omnipotent knowledge and the free creaturely actions."[29]

2. *The Unity of Grace*

In dealing with the question of the *analogia entis*, Barth lays great stress on the priority of God in Christ as over against man. Man has no knowledge or will in terms of which he can in any form cooperate with God. The Romanist views on cooperation, on the sacraments, and on Mariolatry are all condemned because they all indicate the ability of man to make choices independent of the grace of God.

The other side of the picture must, however, not be forgotten. If man can make no decisions apart from Christ, it does not mean that he does not make them in Christ. In fact man does know, he does

27. *Ibid.*, p. 657; Engl. tr. p. 583.
28. *Ibid.*, p. 658; Engl. tr. pp. 583-584.
29. *Ibid.*, p. 660; Engl. tr. p. 585.

believe because he does so in Christ. Man does have a real choice, but it is a choice in Christ.

As noted in the previous chapter, sin is an impossible possibility for man because man as man is elected in Christ for participation in God's aseity.

This "biblical universalism" must also be maintained against Romanism. Only thus can we reject false Romanist distinctions in the area of grace. There are many of them. So, for instance, Romanism speaks of *gratia praeveniens* and *gratia concomitans*. But how can grace be anything but prevenient grace?[30] Again, Romanism distinguishes between *gratia sufficiens* and *gratia efficax*. The latter is added to the former and "lends it the necessary force." "We ask: Is grace as such ever *sufficiens* without being *efficax*? Is it ever effective objectively without being effective subjectively?"[31] We need not mention the other distinctions Romanism makes in the idea of grace. The most remarkable among them is the one between *gratia Christi* and *gratia Dei* or *gratia supernaturalis* and *gratia naturalis*. Romanism claims that the *gratia Dei* is a *gratia sanitatis* "granted to man in paradise when he was at any rate not positively unworthy of it." Even after the fall, something of this *gratia sanitatis* remains in the form of *gratia naturalis*.

Is then, exclaims Barth, the grace of Christ "only a kind of generic name for all the other graces? Are they merely called the grace of Christ, or are they all really His one grace? And if they are called this because they really are, is it enough to say that they are because the merits of Christ constitute the possibility and condition of their distribution?"[32]

Away with all such abstractions! Grace in Christ cannot even properly be said to be prevenient grace "because it is itself the only true grace and all that grace."[33]

Thus the basic fault of the Roman Catholic doctrine of grace is that it is not Christologically conceived. For this reason Romanism cannot do justice to grace as inherently given from above and as inherently universal. "The heart and guiding principle of the Romanist doctrine of grace is the negation of the unity of grace as always God's grace to man, as His sovereign act which is everywhere new and strange and free."[34]

---

30. IV:1, p. 90; Engl. tr. p. 85.
31. *Ibid.*, p. 91; Engl. tr. p. 86.
32. *Ibid.*, p. 91; Engl. tr. p. 86.

33. *Idem.*
34. *Ibid.*, p. 89; Engl. tr. p. 84.

Barth's criticism of Romanism is, therefore, at every point, in accord with his basic principle that God in Christ is not bound to his revelation in history. Christ is the electing God. There is no God, and no decree of God beyond Christ. Christ is also the elected man. There is no man except he be a man in Christ. Man cannot choose against him in any final way. Man's existence is taken "into unity with" Christ's "God-existence."[35] "Jesus Christ is the propelling power given to all men unto eternal life."[36] All God's works have their origin in the grace that is in Christ.[37] Since Christ is the electing God and the elected man, the movement of grace toward man is "an eternal movement, and therefore one that encloses man in his finitude and temporality."[38]

All men are elected in Christ. And since creation is the external ground of the covenant, all men are created in Christ and are saved in Christ. Only thus can we, according to Barth, do justice to Ephesians 1:4.

---

35. I:2, p. 57; Engl. tr. p. 51.
36. II:2, p. 630.
37. Ibid., p. 98.
38. Ibid., p. 99; Engl. tr. p. 92.

Chapter IV

Beyond the Reformers

There is no doubt that Barth aims to set forth a Reformation theology. He rejects Romanism, he says, in terms of the Reformation principle. He seeks to build upon the theology of Luther and of Calvin. This is generally recognized. "Everyone acknowledges that Barth has been the leader of the so-called revival *of the spirit* of Reformation theology in the present day, and that this means for him primarily reformed theology."[1]

A second point is equally important. It is the fact that Barth not only seeks to work in accordance with but also to go beyond the theology of the Reformers. Vahanian expresses this point when he says: "What perhaps is surprising is that never has Calvin himself so compelled us to tread other paths than his own as when he is heard through Barth's interpretation. It will be seen that, for the sake of an equal and common fidelity to the living reality of God, Barth can be marvelously free from Calvin. He can reject him without any feeling of disobedience."[2]

It must be our concern now to discover why and in what way Barth wants to go beyond the Reformers. Is it because he merely disagrees with them on one doctrine or another? It might seem so. When writing on Calvin's catechism on the Apostles' Creed, does not Barth largely agree with Calvin? Does he not, with Luther and Calvin, speak of God's revelation in Christ as the only norm in

1. Gabriel Vahanian in his Introduction to *The Faith of the Church* in which Barth deals with Calvin's Catechism, Engl. tr. p. 7.
2. *Ibid.*, p. 8.

theology?[3] Barth says that for Calvin, "Jesus Christ holds a central position. There is not an 'essence' of God's love that one could know as such, and then a 'manifestation' of such a love whose eminent representative is Jesus Christ. No distinction is made between the principle and the person, between the message and the messenger. *Jesus Christ is what he brings forth.* He is the mercy of God, he is the love of God, he is the open heart of God."[4]

In thus starting with the revelation of God in Christ Calvin gives the proper place to faith as being what it is because of its object, Jesus Christ. "Calvin does not begin by saying to us: This is what you should be! He begins by saying: We are enabled to put our whole life in God's hands through Jesus Christ."[5]

Calvin thinks Christologically and therefore thinks of grace as sovereign or free. Thinking Christologically Calvin even thinks of grace as objectively accomplished in Christ and therefore universal. The Apostles' Creed makes no mention of hell but only of eternal life.[6] This is the case, says Calvin, "since nothing is held by faith except what contributes to the consolation of the souls of the pious."[7]

In the *Church Dogmatics* too the Reformers are said to have set the true view of grace over against the false views of Rome.[8]

The question of immediate importance is whether the Reformers fully understood the doubly indirect nature of revelation.[9] Did they understand that the whole transaction between God and man is expressed in the one act of Jesus Christ as the indirect identification of God with man?

The followers of Calvin surely did not. They believed in a closed canon of Scripture. They believed therefore in direct revelation. In short they believed in *Offenbartheit* and therefore in *Inspiriertheit.* And therewith they committed themselves to a position no better than that of Rome.

The question is whether, according to Barth, these followers of Calvin could find any foundation for their false thinking in Calvin. The high orthodoxy of the seventeenth century did not see that the Bible "is not 'a,' not even the highest 'Truth.' "[10] They did not realize that the Bible "is not an instrument of direct impartation."[11] Their

3. *Ibid.*, p. 33.
4. *Ibid.*, p. 38.
5. *Ibid.*, p. 39.
6. *Ibid.*, p. 171.
7. *Idem.*

8. I:1, p. 71.
9. I:1, p. 174.
10. I:1, p. 141.
11. I:2, p. 562.

doctrine of the perspicuity of Scripture is poles apart from the true idea of Scripture. "We know what we say when we call the Bible the Word of God only when we recognize its human imperfection in face of its divine perfection, and its divine perfection in spite of its human imperfection."[12]

What about Calvin on this basic matter? Did he realize that the Bible is not a book of divine *Offenbartheit?* Did he realize that "the vulnerability of the Bible, i.e., its capacity for error, also extends to its religious or theological content"?[13] Did Calvin really hold that God is both wholly revealed and wholly hidden in Christ and in Scripture?

Barth's answer is that Luther and Calvin restored the true idea of mystery to the idea of revelation. This idea had been largely lost prior to the Reformation. "What took place in the sixteenth century proved itself a Reformation of the Church by the fact that with the restoration of the authority and lordship of the Bible in the Church there now arose a new reading and understanding and expounding of Scripture in accordance with this authority and lordship."[14]

The Reformers took over the idea of the verbal inspiration of Scripture. For them God is the author of the Bible. On occasion they made use of the idea of dictation through the biblical writers.[15] But they realized that the inspiration of Scripture by the Holy Spirit is not "any kind of miracle." "It rests on the relationship of the biblical witnesses to the very definite content of their witness."[16] The content of Scripture is Christ. And Christ cannot be understood because he is God, says Luther.[17] By recognizing the incomprehensibility of God "the doctrine of the inspiration of the Bible is restored as the doctrine of a divine mystery which we cannot grasp and which is therefore true and redemptive."[18] Accordingly "for them [the Reformers] the literally inspired Bible was not at all a revealed book of oracles, but a witness to revelation, to be interpreted from the standpoint of and with a view to its theme, and in conformity with that theme."[19]

Calvin (*Institutes*, I, 7, 1) uses terms with respect to inspiration that might make us doubt whether he has really preserved the mystery of revelation. He uses concepts that seem to point in the

12. *Ibid.*, p. 564; Engl. tr. p. 508.
13. *Ibid.*, p. 565; Engl. tr. p. 509.
14. *Ibid.*, p. 577; Engl. tr. p. 519.
15. *Ibid.*, p. 577; Engl. tr. p. 520.

16. *Ibid.*, p. 578; Engl. tr. p. 520.
17. *Ibid.*, p. 578; Engl. tr. p. 521.
18. *Idem.*
19. *Idem.*

direction of direct revelation. But "in spite of the use of these concepts neither a mantico-mechanical nor a docetic conception of biblical inspiration is in the actual sphere of Calvin's thinking."[20]

It is therefore the new content and the context in which the Reformers set the doctrine of Scripture that is all important. This content and context is the Christ-Event. "If we take Luther and Calvin together, we can say that the way to that universal and moving view of inspiration which answers to the majesty of God, and as we find it in Scripture itself, was again opened up by the Reformation. The Reformers' doctrine of inspiration is an honouring of God, and of the free grace of God. The statement that the Bible is the Word of God is on this view no limitation, but an unfolding of the perception of the sovereignty in which the Word of God condescended to become flesh for us in Jesus Christ, and a human word in the witness of the prophets and apostles as witnesses to His incarnation. On their lips and understanding this is the true statement concerning the Bible which is always indispensable to the Church."[21]

The Reformers knew how to speak properly of the backward and forward relations in which the Scripture must be placed.[22] They did not believe in Scripture as the "paper Pope" the way a later orthodoxy did. And because they saw that Scripture witnesses to the Christ-Event, they were able truly to challenge Romanism. For only if the true mystery of the Revelation of God in Christ and in the Bible is maintained can the idea of direct revelation of Romanist theology be challenged. If the Bible is truly to stand above the church, we must conceive of it as witnessing to the Act of God's revelation in Christ.

It is time now to turn to Barth's analysis of the content of Scripture in relation to the Reformers. As noted, Barth says that the Reformers maintained the proper view of the mystery of Scripture. They did this because they said the proper things about its content, the Christ. And this they did backwards and forwards.

However, when we look at Barth's analysis of what Calvin said about Christ, something quite different appears. To speak properly of the Scriptures is to speak of Christ as the electing God and the elected man. Calvin did neither. He believed in an electing God back of the electing Christ. He had an absolute God with an abso-

20. *Ibid.*, p. 578; Engl. tr. p. 520.   22. *Ibid.*, p. 579; Engl. tr. p. 521.
21. *Ibid.*, p. 579; Engl. tr. p. 522.

lute decree. Accordingly, Calvin also believed in a permanent separation between some men who were elected and others who were not.[23] He did not realize that the primary relation of every man is his election in Christ.

Thus in reality, according to Barth, neither backwards nor forwards did Calvin supply the proper context for the *mystery* of revelation as witnessed to in Scripture.

We turn first to the question of Christ as the electing God.

1. The Backward Context

In introducing his chapter on election, Barth says: "I would have preferred to follow Calvin's doctrine of predestination much more closely, instead of departing from it so radically."[24] And this is important, since in dealing with election we deal with the sum of the gospel.[25] Here we bring to climactic expression the fact that God is *free* to be gracious to all men. There is nothing in his nature, not even his righteousness, that keeps his electing grace from including all men.

The foundation of election must therefore not be sought in a "God in general" back of Christ.[26] We must have no abstract absoluteness and no naked sovereignty. The first and last question with respect to man's relation to God must be answered in terms of Christ alone. How else can we attain a sure knowledge of God and of ourselves?[27]

Now Reformation theologians did indeed make an effort to set us free from the useless speculations of Thomas Aquinas, with their idea of Christ as the *speculum electionis*.[28] "By this Christological reference Reformation theology did assert and defend the honour and dignity of the divine self-revelation as such against all the attempts of man to be his own instructor in the things concerning God and himself."[29]

But Reformation theology did not adhere to this line. "The Christological reference was warmly and impressively made, but it is left standing in the air."[30] So Bullinger does not ascribe the function of the electing God to Christ. For him, Christ is only "the organ

23. IV:2, p. 588.
24. II:2, p. vii.
25. *Ibid.*, p. 9.
26. *Ibid.*, p. 52.

27. *Ibid.*, p. 68.
28. *Ibid.*, p. 69.
29. *Ibid.*, p. 69; Engl. tr. p. 65.
30. *Ibid.*, pp. 69-70; Engl. tr. p. 65.

which serves the electing will of God, as a means toward the attainment of the end foreordained for the elect."[31] "Now, according to John's Gospel, the electing of the Father and that of the Son are one and the same. And according to Ephesians 1:4 we are not only called and redeemed in Christ, but are already elected to calling and salvation in Him. Bullinger not only says nothing of all this, but in the formula mentioned he expressly denies it, although he never returns later to this background truth."[32] Luther too talked of an election apart from Christ.[33] The entire work on *De servo arbitrio* is devoted to a discussion of the majestic will of a God beyond Christ.[34] In spite of all his warnings to the contrary, Luther therefore deals only with a relative truth about God. "In defiance of all such warnings and prohibitions, will not the question of the hidden God emerge one day as the question of the true God?"[35] "Is there not something necessarily spasmodic and artificial about the reference to Jesus Christ when in fact it is accompanied by the assertion of a quite different *voluntas maiestatis?* And we must ask the same question of Calvin."[36]

To be sure, Calvin refers those men who are elect to consider their election in relation to Christ. "But what does Calvin mean when he says that on His side God begins *a se ipso* (in contradistinction to *a Christo*) when He elects us, i.e., when the Father gives us the Son, when He predestinates us members of the body of this Head and partakers of His inheritance? And what is this *gratuitum beneplacitum* which plainly here precedes and is superior to the being and work of Christ? The question of the election is really the question of this *gratuitum beneplacitum* as such. And the reference to Christ as the One who executed the *beneplacitum* is only an answer to the question of the *beneplacitum* if the *beneplacitum* as such is understood to be Christ's, if Christ is already thought of not merely as the executive instrument of the divine dealings with man ordained in the election but as the Subject of the election itself. But Calvin was not prepared to think of Him in this way."[37] "The fact that according to Eph. 1:4 the *electio Patris* which preceded the *donatio* is to be thought of as taking place *in Christo* is something which Calvin will not acknowledge. He says the direct opposite:

31. *Ibid.*, p. 70; Engl. tr. p. 65.
32. *Ibid.*, p. 70; Engl. tr. p. 65.
33. *Idem.*
34. *Ibid.*, p. 71; Engl. tr. p. 66.
35. *Idem.*
36. *Idem.*
37. *Ibid.*, p. 71; Engl. tr. pp. 66-67.

Qui ad Christum accedunt, iam filii Dei erant in eius corde . . . et quia praeordinati erant ad vitam, Christo dati sunt (De praed. C. R. 8, 292). It was inevitable, then, that in spite of the christological reference the main emphasis in Calvinistic doctrine should come to rest in effect upon this reference to the secret *electio Patris.* But how, then, could the first reference have any force? Assent might be given to it, but it was inevitable that a secret dissatisfaction should lead to its supersession by the real truth to be found *in Deo incipiente a se ipso,* in the *beneplacitum gratuitum* which was before Christ and behind Him and above Him. It was inevitable, then, that little store should be set by the revelation when there was no need to adhere strictly to it. It was inevitable that even within the revelation the main concern should be, not with a relative truth, but quite unreservedly and unhesitatingly with this real and inward truth concerning God."[38]

All in all then, Reformation theologians failed to give a proper interpretation of Christ as the electing God. In the early church there were some theologians, notably Athanasius, who made Jesus Christ "the eternal basis of the whole divine election."[39] It was to be expected that later Romanist theology would lose this proper Christological insight. But the Reformers too ignored it altogether. "They did state that Jesus Christ is for us the *lumen* or *speculum electionis.* But they thought it sufficient to base this belief upon the reference to Jesus Christ as the first of the elect according to His human nature. They restricted themselves to this basis with the same exclusiveness as Thomas. They missed the fact that this basis is quite insufficient to explain the ἐν αὐτῷ of Eph. 1:4."[40]

The failure of the Reformers, and especially of Calvin, to think of Christ as the electing God substitutes a false for a true idea of mystery. The believer may no longer look into the face of Jesus Christ for the assurance of salvation. With statements and assurances of the lovingkindness of a God beyond Christ the believer cannot be satisfied. "How can we have assurance in respect of our own election except by the Word of God? And how can even the Word of God give us assurance on this point if this Word, if Jesus Christ, is not really the electing God, not the election itself, not our election, but only an elected means whereby the electing God—

38. *Ibid.,* p. 71; Engl. tr. p. 67.   40. *Idem.*
39. *Ibid.,* p. 118; Engl. tr. p. 110.

electing elsewhere and in some other way—executes that which He has decreed concerning those whom He has—elsewhere and in some other way—elected? The fact that Calvin in particular not only did not answer but did not even perceive this question is the decisive objection which we have to bring against his whole doctrine of predestination. The electing God of Calvin is a *Deus nudus absconditus*. It is not the *Deus revelatus* who is as such the *Deus absconditus*, the eternal God. All the dubious features of Calvin's doctrine result from the basic failing that in the last analysis he separates God and Jesus Christ, thinking that what was in the beginning with God must be sought elsewhere than in Jesus Christ. Thus with all his forceful and impressive acknowledgment of the divine election of grace, ultimately he still passes by the grace of God as it has appeared in Jesus Christ."[41]

It appears then that both Calvin and Barth speak of mystery in relation to man's election by God. But on the *nature* of that mystery they differ.[42] According to Barth, Calvin leads men to look past Christ into the incomprehensible darkness of a God who arbitrarily elects some and not others. Therewith he takes away the comfort of election. Therewith he destroys the biblical idea of grace.

Is it then this sort of Christ which Calvin preaches as the content of the Scriptures? Is it a Christ who is merely the instrument of carrying out the arbitrary behests of a God who stands behind him? Surely, says Barth, even the Bible *could not* tell us about such a Christ. The only Christ of which the Word could tell us, argues Barth, is the one who is the electing God. Therefore the only proper way in which Calvin could have safeguarded the properly active concept of Scripture as the witness to the Christ, would be by a Christ in which, according to Barth, Calvin does not believe.

If then we are to take seriously Barth's vigorous rejection of Calvin's view of the Christ and his relation to God as the source of man's election, then we cannot take seriously his earlier statement on Christ and his relation to the Scripture. According to Barth, Calvin has the wrong view of *mystery*. Calvin's non-Christological view of mystery is the source of all static and arbitrary decisions on the part of God. Such a non-Christological view of the electing God fits in perfectly with the idea of Scripture as *Offenbartheit*. It does not fit with Barth's own activist view of revelation.

41. *Ibid.*, p. 119; Engl. tr. p. 111. 42. *Ibid.*, p. 158.

From Barth's point of view, then, Calvin did *not* furnish the proper context backwards for the idea of the hiddenness of the revelation of God in Christ. In fact what Calvin offers at this point is, according to Barth, completely destructive of the idea of sovereign, universal grace.

2. *The Forward Context*

What then of the context of Scripture looking forward? Calvin has the wrong view of mystery in failing to think of Christ as the electing God. Does he, in spite of this, have the right view of mystery in holding Christ to be the elected man?

To answer this question, we may turn first to Barth's work on anthropology. In it he gives what he thinks of as the proper context forward to the idea of Scripture as a witness to revelation. Barth tells us frankly that in offering his doctrine of man he has departed still further from the "dogmatic tradition" than he did in his discussion of predestination.[43]

Election is, says Barth, inherently universal. God's ordinary word to mankind is Yes. Calvin failed to see this.[44] He believed in two classes of men. According to him, the wrath of God abides forever on one of these two classes. Only some men are elected in Christ. Only some are saved by Christ.

Over against this Barth asserts that the final rejection of all men has been taken to himself by God in Christ. Jesus Christ is the only rejected one. Since Christ has borne the rejection of God for all men, those who oppose Christ cannot finally escape their own election in Christ.[45]

The doctrine of creation and of man is worked out in accordance with this basic principle. Creation is said to be the external ground of the covenant, while the covenant is said to be the internal ground of creation. The original relation of every man is therefore that of his election in Christ.

Christ as the only real man is before Adam.[46] Therefore man's acceptance with God is an accomplished fact before his creation.

43. III:2, p. vii.   45. IV:2, p. 589.
44. IV:2, p. 588.

46. Karl Barth—*A Shorter Catechism on Romans*, London, Richmond, 1959, p. 62. Adam "precedes Christ merely as a shadow and an example. He is only apparently the first."

His redemption has taken place in God before he exists: "That the Creator Himself willed to endure, and has endured, and still endures the contradiction in creaturely life is the first point to be noted in the foundation revealed in His self-revelation. For the real goodness of the real God is that the contradiction of creation has not remained alien to Himself. Primarily and supremely He has made it His own, and only then caused it to be reflected in the life of the creature. His rejoicing and sorrow preceded ours. For before light could gladden us and darkness torment us, He was aware of both, separating and thus co-ordinating them. Before life greeted us and death menaced us, He was the Lord of life and death, and bound them both in a bundle. And He did not do all this in such a way that He confronted it in mere superiority, so that it was alien and external to Him, but in such a way that in the full majesty of His Godhead He participated in these antitheses and their connexion, in eternal mercy causing them to be internal to Himself, and to find their origin in His own being. This is how we must put it if on the basis of His self-revelation we affirm that His covenant with man is the meaning and the goal and therefore the primary basis of creation. If this is so, He has taken the creature to Himself even before it was, namely, in His own Son, who willed to live and die as a man for all men, as a creature for all creatures. He thus took it to Himself even in its very contradictions. He made His own both its menace and its hope. He did not spare Himself. He first placed Himself under the stern law of the twofold aspect of being. What are all the severity and relentlessness of its contradiction as known and experienced by us in comparison with the relentlessness and severity which He caused to be visited on Himself, on His own heart, even before He acted as Creator?"[47]

Thus creation is in Christ because election is in Christ. A proper view of election in Christ involves this idea of creation in Christ.[48] For that reason the Genesis account of creation must not be taken as *historische Geschichte*.[49] "The history of creation is 'non-historical' or, to be more precise, pre-historical history."[50] Creation has nothing in it that can be manipulated by human percepts and concepts.[51] If it did Adam would be prior to Christ. Only the idea of every man's

47. III:1, p. 436; Engl. tr. p. 380.   48. *Ibid.*, p. 57.
49. *Ibid.*, p. 84; Engl. tr. p. 78.—For this reason it is not history in the historical sense, and there can be no history of it.
50. *Ibid.*, p. 87; Engl. tr. p. 80.   51. *Ibid.*, p. 90; Engl. tr. p. 82.

election and therefore creation in Christ can escape false mystery.[52]

To what extent does Calvin give proper recognition to the fact that all men are elected and created in Christ? Did he really found his anthropology on Christology? Did he realize that it is not Christ who must participate in human nature but rather it is human nature that must participate in Christ?[53]

The answer is as follows. In the beginning of his *Institutes*, Calvin does relate man at the outset to God. But it is not clear from what point of view he says this.[54] Who is this man who can only subsist in God? And who is this God whose knowledge is so indispensable for the knowledge of man? Having no clarity on these points, we must take Calvin's statements and place them squarely on the foundation of our knowledge of Jesus Christ.[55]

Standing on our own Christological basis we can, says Barth, say something more precise than Calvin did.

Barth makes his "more precise" statement in the following six points.

3. Beyond Calvin

(1) In a true anthropology priority must be given to Jesus Christ. This is the case because we have found that in his identity with himself we have also God's identity with himself.[56] It is through identity of the man Jesus with God that all men are also related to God. It is because of this identity that their primary relation is to God.

(2) More precisely, it must be added that through this identity with the man Jesus, it is God's nature to be active for and in all men.[57] God is identical with his revelation in Jesus Christ. His presence with men is an *act*. This act has meaning or purpose. And this meaning is salvation (Rettung).[58] In his identity with Jesus Christ, God's presence in and among men is the act of their salvation. Men are inherently participants in Jesus Christ as the *Geschichte* of salvation for all men. Thus grace is inherently universal.

(3) But grace is also inherently free. For God's identification with Jesus Christ is itself an act of freedom. It is his very nature to be

52. *Ibid.*, p. 436.
53. III:2, p. 69.
54. *Ibid.*, p. 84.
55. *Idem.*

56. *Ibid.*, p. 79, 85.
57. *Idem.*
58. *Ibid.*, p. 79.

coexistent as well as existent. His very glory is expressed in this his utter humiliation. Therefore God's being as *Geschichte* is Christ's being as *Geschichte*. And this *Geschichte* must "*a priori* be considered as divine-human *Geschichte*."[59] Man is what he is in the participation of the *Geschichte* as the sovereign or free grace in Jesus Christ.

(4) Man therefore has his being in his freedom for God through Christ. Man exists inasmuch as and in so far as God is present in him as the Saviour of all men. Man can never escape the lordship of Christ over him.[60]

(5) Thus man exists in his indirect identity with the divine subject.[61] On the one hand the *Geschichte* of the salvation of all men is wholly and exclusively identical with Jesus Christ. On the other hand Jesus Christ is wholly and exclusively identical with the salvation of every man.[62] With all the difference between Christ and other men, their essence must be that of their participation in him.[63]

(6) Finally, man's participation in the *Geschichte* of Christ must be an active participation. Man is the being who is for God.[64] We may call this reciprocity. But it is such as expressive of God's work in him. Man is man because God's work takes place in him, because God's kingdom comes in him, and God's word is heard through him.[65] This is true first of all in Christ. But it is also true of every man, since every man is man through active participation in the work of Christ. Man as man serves God in Christ.[66]

One thing would seem to be obvious from the six points now discussed, namely, that Barth thinks Calvin's view of man to be equally as defective as his view of God. Calvin did not provide for the proper hiddenness of God's revelation in Christ through Scripture forward any more than backward.

From his point of view, Calvin *has after all not* supplied a proper Christological context for the idea of Scripture as the witness to Christ either backward or forward. Failing to think of Christ as the electing God, Calvin also fails to think of Christ as the elected man.

How then can Calvin be expected to see that sin is an ontological impossibility?[67] How could he see that sin and unbelief are defeated

59. *Ibid.*, p. 80.
60. *Ibid.*, pp. 79, 85.
61. *Ibid.*, pp. 81, 85.
62. *Ibid.*, p. 81.
63. *Ibid.*, p. 85.

64. *Ibid.*, p. 82.
65. *Idem.*
66. *Ibid.*, p. 86.
67. *Ibid.*, pp. 162, 174.

in advance *(zum vornherein)*?[68] Having an arbitrarily electing God
back of Christ, how could Calvin see the essence of *all* men is their
election in Christ?[69] How could he see that God's final word to man
as man is that he is gracious to him?[70] If Calvin holds to a false idea
of mystery in his view of God, what else can one expect him to have
than a false view of mystery in his view of man?

In view of Barth's analysis of Calvin's view of God and of man,
one cannot help but ask how Barth can think of the Reformers, and
particularly of Calvin, as being able, in any adequate sense, to challenge the defects of Romanist theology. Barth challenges Romanism
in terms of his Christ as *Geschichte*. But when Barth analyzes Calvin's doctrines of God and of man, he finds the same defects there
that he finds in Romanism. Calvin has the twofold defect of thinking
of a God in himself apart from Christ and of a man in himself apart
from Christ. The proper Christological foundation is lacking in
Calvin's thinking on the relation of God and man no less than it is in
Romanism. Without the proper Christological approach, that is,
without the idea of Christ as the divine-human *Geschichte*, it is not
possible to understand either the sovereign or the universal nature
of Christ. Therefore the simple pronouncement must be made that
Calvin has no proper view of grace. And not understanding the true
nature of Christ as *Geschichte*, Calvin could not really maintain the
idea of the indirectness of revelation which marks the true Reformation principle.[71]

---

68. *Ibid.*, p. 175.
69. *Ibid.*, p. 193—Sein Sein aber ist ein Sein in der von Jesus begründeten
Geschichte.
70. *Ibid.*, p. 196.
71. II:2, p. 119; Engl. tr. p. 111.

Chapter V

Against Orthodoxy

Barth claims to have built his theology upon that of the Reformers. He also claims to have gone beyond them. But, as for orthodoxy, Barth is simply against it.

This is not to say that, according to Barth, orthodox theologians did not mean to hold to the doctrine of grace. Neither does it mean that they were not sometimes formally right in the words they used to describe grace. It does not even mean that the doctrine of free, universal grace did not sometimes shine through their words. But it does mean that their central teaching is destructive of the idea of Christ as the electing God and the elected man, that is, of Christ as divine-human *Geschichte*.

By orthodoxy Barth indicates mainly the theology of sixteenth and seventeenth century theologians. There is, he says, a Lutheran and a Reformed orthodoxy.

The followers of Calvin soon forgot to think in terms of the living Christ. They thought of saving revelation as something that had taken place in the past. For them revelation had taken place directly in history. They had no eye for the double indirectness of revelation. They believed in *Offenbartheit*. With respect to the Bible this was *Inspiriertheit*. They said that "there is revelation" and that "there is faith." They believed in the "profane 'there is'."[1]

But the personal relation of God to man in Christ can be expressed only in terms of pure act. Not only the theologians of the left but also the theologians of the right have failed to see this fact.[2] "On

1. I:1, p. 40—das profane 'es gibt'.
2. *Ibid.*, p. 41.

the left we say: the essence of the Church is *actus purus,* divine action beginning with itself, the source and means of its own insight, therefore action unpredictable on an anthropological basis. On the right we say: the essence of the Church is *actus purus,* free action, not a continuously present relation; grace is an event of personal approach, not a transferred tangible state of the soul. Left and right our first question can only be, how it could be otherwise, if the essence of the Church is identical with Jesus Christ."[3]

Revelation always takes place in the present. Scripture does not wish to be taken as identical with revelation. Not only heterodoxy but also "hyperorthodoxy" were mistaken in thinking it to be such.[4]

Unfortunately orthodoxy could appeal to Calvin on this point. He too did not really understand the fact of the "double indirectness" of Scripture.[5] He too had no proper appreciation for the fact that God's revelation comes into a world in which it must be wholly hidden. There simply can be no revelation of God in which he is not wholly hidden. "Put more briefly, only because there is a veiling of God can there be an unveiling, and only by there being a veiling and unveiling of God can there be a self-impartation of God."[6]

It is only in terms of this correlativity of unveiling and veiling (*Enthüllung* and *Verhüllung*) that we can meet the challenge of Romanism, for this correlativity expresses the idea of the analogy of faith. And only by the analogy of faith can we effectively oppose the Romanist notion of the analogy of being.[7]

Thinking of revelation as identical with Scripture, orthodoxy also thought that faith in this revelation requires men to hold as true all that the Bible contains. Orthodoxy believed in the miracles of Scripture as directly revelational of God. It did not realize that the miracles of Scripture are only *signs* of the revelation of which they gave witness.[8]

In particular, orthodoxy had a mistaken concept of religion. For orthodoxy, religion consisted in holding as true all the various teachings of Scripture. There was here, as elsewhere, too much of Romanism.

True, even Aquinas did not really think of religion as a general concept to which the Christian religion must be subject.[9] As for Cal-

---

3. *Ibid.,* p. 41; Engl. tr. p. 44.   7. *Ibid.,* p. 257.
4. *Ibid.,* p. 115.   8. I:2, p. 71.
5. *Ibid.,* p. 174.   9. *Ibid.,* p. 310; Engl. tr. p. 284.
6. *Ibid.,* p. 383; Engl. tr. p. 417.

vin, even though in humanistic fashion he spoke of the object of theology as *christiana religio*, he took his theology from Scripture.[10] "Therefore the concept of *religio* as a general and neutral form has no fundamental significance in Calvin's conception and exposition of Christianity. For him *religio* is an entity x, which receives content and form only as it is equated with Christianity, i.e., because as it is taken up into revelation and fashioned by it."[11] Many of the "older orthodox" theologians followed Calvin in this respect. Among them we may count "A. Polanus, *Synt. Theol.*, 1609, p. 3694f."[12] "At the same time, we can find in J. Wolleb (*Christ. Theol. comp.*, 1626, II 4, 1) the very thing which Polanus obviously tried to avoid. It is concealed and rendered innocuous by the context, but it is there all the same: a general and neutral definition of the concept 'religion' (*Religio . . . generali significatione omnem Dei cultum, specialiter cultum Dei immediatum, specialissime vero aut internum solum aut externum et internum simul denotat*), to which the concept *vera religio* (*ib.* 4, 3) can be subordinated as a species."[13]

In "a Dutch pupil of Polanus, Anton Walaeus" and in "the *Synopsis purioris Theol.*, Leiden 1624" we find an apologetic to support the truth of Scripture by an appeal to the general concept of religion as known from conscience or nature.[14] This was, in itself, not too serious. "For Walaeus and the Leiden men it does not actually amount to much. But we can already foresee what it will amount to some day."[15]

We can see these results in A. Heidan who "like many of his theological contemporaries, particularly in Holland" had for his aim "to unite Calvin and Descartes."[16] Of course, even Heidan, and no one more strongly than he, insisted that "faith and theology must be based on revelation." "But then Heidan remembers the atheists of his time, and his Cartesian heart begins to flutter." So he speaks of a natural religion innate in every man. "But Calvin stirs again." So he insists that even "Adam had knowledge of God only by revelation." "As soon as he forgets the atheists, Heidan again speaks only as a theologian of revelation."[17]

But the problem could not be left in such an uncertain state. Soon "M. F. Wendelin (*Chr. Theol.*, lib. duo, 1634, I, 1) tried to make the

10. *Idem.*
11. *Ibid.*, p. 310; Engl. tr. p. 285.
12. *Idem.*
13. *Idem.*

14. *Ibid.*, p. 311; Engl. tr. p. 285.
15. *Ibid.*, p. 311; Engl. tr. p. 286.
16. *Idem.*
17. *Idem.*

vera religio the *obiectum theologiae* . . . putting it at the head of his theological system as a form-concept." Even Wendelin, however, did not fill out the concept of true religion from nature and conscience. The concept "is filled out by him in a wholly objective and Christian way."[18] Thus the "secret catastrophe" does not fully come to light. "The same can still be said of F. Burmann."[19] Even so in Burmann the downward trend appears more strongly than it does in his predecessors. Calvin and Descartes are gradually being synthesized.

"There were similar developments on the Lutheran side. This is true even of the Lutheran High Orthodoxy in the second half of the 17th century . . ."[20] Barth mentions A. Calov, J. F. König and A. Quenstedt. In all of their works we find that the chapter on Scripture is preceded by one on the Christian religion which is described as the *obiectum theologiae generale.*

Of course, even here the idea of the Christian religion is traced back to Adam in paradise prior to the Fall. And therewith we are back to Scripture. "It is just that there is a change of emphasis. The question of the *religio christiana* has acquired an autonomous interest."[21] There is a "strange vacillation between spiritual and carnal argumentation. Yet even here no one can point to a single passage in which there is any notable deviation from the line adopted by Calvin."[22] "As a Lutheran parallel to Burmann we might mention D. Hollaz . . ."[23] "Hollaz is one of the last and strictest representatives of the theory of verbal inspiration. Therefore theoretically he was a scriptural theologian. Yet the Bible was not so important to him that he had to mention it consistently at the point where mention of it has such a basic importance. Such was the power of that concern which was then about to make itself autonomous and all-powerful under the caption *religio.*"[24] Of course, there can be no question that even Hollaz "finds the true religion in that which is built upon the foundation of Jesus Christ . . ."[25]

But the catastrophe was bound to come to expression. "In this as in other matters the catastrophe occurred, and Neo-Protestantism was truly and openly born, in the movement of so-called rational orthodoxy at the beginning of the 18th century. We can watch it happen in two theologians, on the Reformed side in Salomon van Til

18. *Ibid.,* p. 312; Engl. tr. p. 286.
19. *Ibid.,* p. 312; Engl. tr. p. 287.
20. *Ibid.,* p. 313; Engl. tr. p. 287.
21. *Idem.*
22. *Idem.*
23. *Idem.*
24. *Ibid.,* p. 313; Engl. tr. p. 288.
25. *Idem.*

(1643-1713, *Theologiae utriusque compendium cum naturalis tum revelatae*, 1704), and on the Lutheran side in J. Franz Buddeus (1667-1729, *Institutiones Theologiae dogmaticae*, 1724).[26] In these men Dogmatics begins openly "with the presupposition of the concept and the description of a general and natural and neutral 're-ligion,' which as *religio in se spectata* is the presupposition of all religions."[27] "As a convinced Cartesian" van Til gives an independent, non-biblical definition of natural religion. "Van Til, in part I of his compendium, develops this natural theology in a broad doctrine of the nature and attributes of God, creation and providence, the moral law of nature, the immortality of the soul, and even sin."[28] Buddeus proceeds in similar fashion. Of course, Buddeus and van Til still seek to place the revelation of Scripture above that in nature. With all exponents of natural revelation Buddeus and at last even van Til make the reservation that for the knowledge of eternal salvation one must go to the Bible.[29] Even so in "van Til natural theology culminates in a doctrine *De praeparatione evangelica*, in which: (1) from the presuppositions and data of natural religion there is logically postulated the necessity of a reconciliation between God and man; (2) again on the principles of natural religion the conditions of such a reconciliation are adduced; and (3) and lastly, the heathen, Jewish, Mohammedan and Christian religions are mutually compared, and the latter is shown to answer to the adduced conditions and is therefore recognisable as the revealed religion. *Theologia naturalis . . . ad ista rationis dictamina religiones qualescunque explorat, ut inde elicias, religionem christianam (licet mysteria agnoscat naturalis scientiae limites excellentia) tamen plus quam reliquas cum lumine naturae consentire (Praef. ad lectorem).* That is the programme which van Til and Buddeus set themselves and carried out to the best of their ability (the first time that such a programme was ever put forward in Protestantism without being condemned as unconfessional)."[30]

What these men achieved can never be overestimated either in its basic significance or in the seriousness of its historical consequences. "With these theologians there emerged clearly and logically what was perhaps the secret *telos* and *pathos* of the whole preceding development. Human religion, the relationship with God which we

26. *Idem.*   29. *Ibid.*, p. 314; Engl. tr. p. 289.
27. *Ibid.*, p. 314; Engl. tr. p. 288.   30. *Idem.*
28. *Idem.*

can and actually do have apart from revelation, is not an unknown but a very well-known quantity both in form and content, and as such it is something which has to be reckoned with, as having a central importance for all theological thinking. It constitutes, in fact, the presupposition, the criterion, the necessary framework for an understanding of revelation. It shows us the question which is answered by revealed religion as well as all other positive religions, and it is as the most satisfactory answer that the Christian religion has the advantage over others and is rightly described as revealed religion. The Christian element—and with this the theological reorientation which had threatened since the Renaissance is completed —has now actually become a predicate of the neutral and universal human element. Revelation has now become a historical confirmation of what man can know about himself and therefore about God even apart from revelation."[31]

The "sad story of recent Protestant theology" here takes its start. Buddeus and van Til, as well as the many who took similar positions, "were all men of an admitted seriousness and piety. And in points of detail they were outspokenly conservative. They knew how to safeguard in their theology the full rights of revelation, at any rate in appearance."[32] But their "untenable compromise preceded the work of the so-called Neologians of the second half of the 18th century."[33] For these Neologians reason was the supreme authority. After this came Kant, Schleiermacher, Hegel, D. F. Strauss, and others till we reach L. Feuerbach for whom "there is room only for natural religion as the illusory expression of the natural longings and wishes of the human heart."[34] A. Ritschl said that the Christian Religion is true because in it the supreme value of human life "is most perfectly realised," and E. Troeltsch sought to ascertain the proper place for Christianity by "'entering hypothetically' into the phenomena of general religious history . . ."[35] "And then at last and finally there came that tumultuous invasion of the Church and theology by natural religion whose astonished witnesses we have been in our day. Of all this, of course, the doughty van Til and the equally doughty Buddeus never even dreamed. Yet they and their generation must still be regarded as the real fathers of Neo-Protestant theology, for which the way was not unprepared by the very differ-

31. *Ibid.*, p. 315; Engl. tr. p. 289.
32. *Ibid.*, p. 315; Engl. tr. p. 290.
33. *Ibid.*, p. 316; Engl. tr. p. 290.
34. *Idem.*
35. *Idem.*

ent Reformation tradition. All these more or less radical and destructive movements in the history of theology in the last two centuries are simply variations on one simple theme, and that theme was clearly introduced by van Til and Buddeus; *that religion has not to be understood in the light of revelation, but revelation in the light of religion.* To this common denominator the aims and the programmes of all the more important tendencies of modern theology can be reduced. Neo-Protestantism means 'religionism.' Even the conservative theology of these centuries, the supra-naturalistic of the 18th and the confessional, biblicistic and 'positive' of the 19th and 20th, has, on the whole, co-operated, making such concessions to the prevailing outlook that in spite of the immanent resistance which it has put up it cannot be regarded as a renewal of the Reformation tradition."[36]

According to Barth, then, orthodoxy led directly into the modern reversal of revelation and religion. The incline from van Til and Buddeus toward the German Christians, has nothing more solid than rough edges of inconsistency by which one might hope to stop short of final catastrophe. And the final catastrophe of a purely subjective theology sprang from the orthodox doctrine of *Offenbartheit.*

One point must be specially observed in this connection. Those who believe in direct revelation but do not believe in natural theology might overlook it. The point is that the real enemy Barth is after in his criticism is not natural theology. Yes, natural theology, as based on the idea of *analogia entis* is, for Barth, a manifestation of the spirit of the Antichrist. But when dealing with Protestant orthodoxy, Barth's main objective is to slay *"das profane 'es gibt'."* And this idea came to climactic expression in Buddeus and van Til. If Barth were out to destroy nothing but natural theology, then most recent followers of Calvin would agree. Barth is right, they might say; Protestant orthodoxy all too soon incorporated into its thought the essentially Romanist notion of natural theology.[37] And Reformed theologians all too often sought to combine Calvin and Descartes. Shall we not rejoice in the fact that Barth has pointed out this fact?

To drop the matter here would, however, result in confusion. In the last analysis, the issue is not natural theology but direct revelation. And even here the point must be sharpened. The issue is not revelation in nature over against revelation in Scripture. Barth

36. *Ibid.,* p. 316; Engl. tr. pp. 290-291.
37. G. C. Berkouwer—*Algemene Openbaring.*

praises some theologians for going back from an appeal to conscience and nature to the Bible. Even Buddeus and van Til are commended for doing this. But the final question goes still further back. Of what help is it if men go back from revelation in nature to revelation in the Bible so long as they have no eye for the hiddenness of God's revelation in it? Revelation has not been reinstated to its priority over religion on Barth's view unless and until the basic rule is observed that there is no revelation at all unless it is wholly hidden. There is, for him, as noted, no *Enthüllung* without *Verhüllung*.

Barth approves of orthodoxy then in so far as it wants a scriptural theology. He too would say that the Bible *is* the Word of God. He too would proceed in simple exegetical fashion to discover what the Bible says. We must believe what the Bible says because it is the Bible that says it *(weil es so in der Bibel steht)*. But Barth is opposed to the "diffuse peripheral biblicism" of orthodoxy.

This diffuse peripheral biblicism derives, he says, from the static categories with which orthodoxy works. Orthodoxy thinks that in the Bible it *possesses* the revelation of God. It does not realize that Scripture does not itself want to be identified with revelation. The Bible points to the living Christ in whom the act of saving all men is accomplished.

No true exegesis of Scripture can be carried on except in terms of Christ as the act of the saving revelation of God. In failing to see this fact, orthodoxy is, argues Barth, really scholastic and speculative. Its idea of the Bible as the direct revelation of God is therefore, for Barth, really only another form of natural theology. All theology that does not start with the Christ as truly God and truly man is really natural theology. To think according to Scripture *(schriftgemässes Denken)* is to think in terms of the identity of God with man and of man with God in Jesus Christ as act, i.e., *Geschichte*.[38] On the one hand we must say that God is identical with Jesus Christ. On the other hand we must say that the being of the Church is identical with Jesus Christ. This identification of God with man is *in act*.[38a] The true priority of God over man is maintained in Christ as *Geschichte* alone. In fact both the genuine contact between God and man and the genuine priority of God over man can be maintained only in terms of the God-man as act, as *Geschichte*. It is here where orthodoxy failed. In holding to *das profane 'es gibt,'* orthodoxy did not allow the living Christ to speak to it.[39]

1. *Orthodoxy on the Doctrine of God*

In the previous chapter it was indicated that according to Barth, Calvin had no eye for the fact that there is no God beyond Christ to whom appeal for any purpose can properly be made. His criticism of orthodoxy is the same. "We stand here before the fundamental error which dominated the doctrine of God of the older theology and which influenced Protestant orthodoxy at almost every point. For the greater part this doctrine of God tended elsewhere than to God's act in His revelation, and for the greater part it also started elsewhere than from there. It is of a piece with this fact that with a surprisingly common thoughtlessness it was usual to begin by deducing the doctrine of the Trinity—theoretically maintained to be the basis of all theology—from the premises of formal logic. In the vacuum which this created, there was no place for anything but general reflections on what God at any rate could be—reflections arising from specific human standpoints and ideas as incontestable data, and then interwoven rather feebly with all kinds of biblical reminiscences."[40]

Orthodoxy has no appreciation of the fact that God is identical with his act of revelation in Christ. Here is the root of its many errors. It did not realize that we either meet God in his act of salvation for all men or we do not meet him at all. It is of God's essence to seek relationship with man. "The fact that we cannot go behind His livingness for a definition of His being means in fact that we cannot go behind this name of His, because in the very revelation of His name there occurs the act which is His being to all eternity."[41]

The work of the Son and of the Holy Spirit in saving men is at once involved in God as identical with his revelation. For revelation is identical with reconciliation.[42] In this relation provision is made for the removal of the sin of man. It is the very nature of God's being to take unto himself the contradiction of man.[43] The whole idea of creation is subordinate to this seeking and realizing of fellowship with man. God wills only one thing, namely, his act of

39. Cf. I:2, pp. 554, 556, 598, 616, 859, 969.
40. II:1, p. 292; Engl. tr. p. 261.   42. *Ibid.*, p. 307.
41. *Ibid.*, p. 306; Engl. tr. p. 273.   43. III:1, p. 436.

fellowship with all men in Christ. He simply is and completes his being by means of his act of redeeming mankind. "As and before God seeks and creates fellowship with us, He wills and completes this fellowship in Himself. In Himself He does not will to exist for Himself, to exist alone. On the contrary, He is Father, Son and Holy Spirit and therefore alive in His unique being with and for and in another. The unbroken unity of His being, knowledge and will is at the same time an act of deliberation, decision and intercourse. He does not exist in solitude but in fellowship. Therefore what He seeks and creates between Himself and us is in fact nothing else but what He wills and completes and therefore is in Himself."[44]

By seeking for a God back of Christ as the act of saving all men, orthodoxy missed coming face to face with the Christ of the Scriptures.

Barth elaborates this point again and again in his discussion of the attributes of God. As orthodoxy failed to see that God is identical with his revelation of grace in Christ, so it failed to see that all the attributes of God are subordinate to the one attribute of love or grace to man in Christ. Traditional theology, including much of Romanism, Calvin and orthodox Protestantism, was largely nominalist in its thinking on the attributes of God.[45] Even when some theologians said that there was some foundation in the being of God for the distinction of attributes that we make, there remained a basic confusion. The attributes of God had to be affirmed *proprie* and yet they could not be.[46]

How shall we escape the nominalism inherent in "the Thomistic and orthodox Protestant tradition?" By doing away with the idea that there is a naked essence of God back of Christ. Involved in all nominalism, as in all non-biblical thinking, is the notion that man must seek for contact with the *nuda essentia* of God above Christ. It is no wonder that men doubted whether they had found the essence of God. The only way to find the essence of God, and with it an objective basis for our faith as believers, is to identify that essence with the revelation of God in Christ. And when we seek for God's essence only in his revelation in Jesus Christ, then we have at the same time the true unity of these attributes. For then this unity is found in the idea of grace that is supreme above all other

44. II:1, p. 308; Engl. tr. p. 275.
45. *Ibid.*, pp. 368-370; Engl. tr. pp. 328-330.
46. *Ibid.*, p. 371; Engl. tr. p. 330.

attributes. In all our discussions of the attributes of God, we are
only repeating the name of Jesus. The multiplicity, individuality,
and diversity of God's perfections are then found within the unity
of his act in saving all men. Only on this basis can it be said that
the attributes of God are identical with his being. Only then do we
have certainty that there is not some false mystery hidden behind
the God we know. And only then can we see the true nature of faith
as the only real possibility for any man.

Of course orthodoxy meant to do all this too.[47] Its instinct on the
subject was right. But in its teaching it did not realize that a "fully
alive doctrine of God's attributes will take as its fundamental point
of departure the truth that God is for us fully revealed and fully
concealed in his self-disclosure."[48] We must realize that we cannot
attribute to this "whole distinction between God in Himself and
God in His relation to the world an essential, but only a heuristic,
significance."[49] The distinction is indeed a valuable one. The fact
that God "is both knowable and unknowable to us, the One who
loves and the One who is free, becomes actually clear to us in this
distinction."[50] God is love in himself. He is free to be this love for us.
And this becomes manifest in his revelation.

With this approach Barth turns to a systematic discussion of the
attributes of God in terms of love and of freedom. He is aware of
the fact that there is no "direct intimation of Scripture" to which he
may appeal.[51] Yet his method is in accord with his general Christological approach. In the nature of the case then grace is the central
attribute of God.

2. Orthodoxy on the Perfections of God

Barth distinguishes between the attributes of divine love and
those of divine freedom. We turn first to what he says on the attributes of divine love.

(a) THE PERFECTIONS OF DIVINE LOVE

Grace and Holiness are the first pair of attributes discussed by
Barth. "God is *vere et proprie gratiosus*. He is so even when He is
for us the unknown and hidden God. He is so even when he is the
God who is denied and hated by us and therefore provoked against

47. *Ibid.*, p. 379.
48. *Ibid.*, p. 384; Engl. tr. p. 341.
49. *Ibid.*, p. 389; Engl. tr. p. 345.

50. *Idem.*
51. 11:1, p. 389.

us. He is so even as the God against whom we sin and who therefore judges and punishes us. We know and rightly understand our sin only when we have realised it to be enmity against the grace of God."[52]

No qualification must therefore be made of this inherently universal nature of grace in terms of the holiness of God. "We now place this concept of the grace of God alongside that of His holiness. This cannot mean that we imply a need either to qualify or to expand what is denoted by the concept of grace. In grace we have characterised God Himself, the one God in all His fulness. We are not wrong, we do not overlook or neglect anything, if we affirm that His love and therefore His whole being, in all the heights and depths of the Godhead, is simply grace."[53]

God's holiness spells his judgment upon sin. God condemns and excludes and annihilates all contradiction against himself. But he does so by expending his judgment upon himself in Jesus Christ his Son. It is only in man's opposition to God that he experiences God's opposition to him. But this opposition comes always and exclusively from the maintenance of God's grace upon men. "God is holy because His grace judges and His judgment is gracious."[54]

The *mercy and righteousness* of God are the second pair of attributes Barth considers. The grace of God expresses itself first of all as mercy to men.[55] God as love is God merciful. And God in himself is what he does.[56] This mercy must therefore precede righteousness as God's grace must precede his holiness.[57] But Protestant orthodoxy was not able, in view of its appeal to a God beyond Christ, to do justice to either the precedence of grace to holiness or of mercy to righteousness. "We have seen that the weakness of the definitions of Protestant orthodoxy in respect of the relationship between God's grace and holiness was that they did not make clear the unity of the divine being. The same is true in this connexion."[58]

Barth mentions Quenstedt, the Lutheran theologian.[59] He mentions Polanus the Reformed theologian. Neither of them properly placed mercy above righteousness. They did not fully realize that God's grace is best exhibited as forgiving grace. "He is merciful as

52. *Ibid.*, p. 401; Engl. tr. pp. 356-357.   56. *Ibid.*, p. 421.
53. *Ibid.*, p. 402; Engl. tr. p. 358.   57. *Ibid.*, p. 422.
54. *Ibid.*, p. 408; Engl. tr. p. 363.   58. *Ibid.*, p. 424; Engl. tr. p. 377.
55. *Ibid.*, p. 414; Engl. tr. p. 368.   59. *Idem.*

He really makes demands and correspondingly punishes and rewards."[60]

It is, of course, the right understanding of what happened for us in Jesus Christ that enables us thus to place grace and mercy above righteousness and holiness. For the meaning of the death of Christ is that he took upon him our sin. Thus it did not happen to us. "What was suffered there on Israel's account and ours, was suffered for Israel and for us."[61] This is the message of John 3:16. Christ died on the cross. He experienced the divine *No*. But Easter follows Good Friday. God's *Yes* presupposes his *No*. "For the terrible thing, the divine No of Good Friday, is that there all the sins of Israel and of all men, our sins collectively and individually, have in fact become the object of the divine wrath and retribution."[62]

This proper view of the substitutionary death of Christ for all men cannot, then, be properly recognized unless we begin by rejecting the idea of a God in himself back of Christ. For it is this idea of a God in himself, taken as a constitutive and not as a heuristic notion, that keeps us from properly subordinating the holiness and righteousness of God to his grace. This point will engage us again. For the moment it must suffice to indicate how deeply Barth considers the rift between himself and orthodoxy to be. Because of its failure to exegete Scripture in a properly Christological fashion, orthodoxy cannot do justice to the objectivity of the substitutionary atonement and therewith the universality of the grace of God.

The *patience and wisdom* of God are the third pair of attributes discussed by Barth. Together with the grace and mercy of God, there is his patience. All three are expressions of his love. Patience is an enrichment of the mercy of God. "We define God's patience as His will, deep-rooted in His essence and constituting His divine being and action, to allow to another—for the sake of His own grace and mercy and in the affirmation of His holiness and justice—space and time for the development of its own existence, thus conceding to this existence a reality side by side with His own, and fulfilling His will towards this other in such a way that He does not suspend and destroy it as this other but accompanies and sustains it and allows it to develop in freedom."[63]

---

60. *Ibid.*, p. 431; Engl. tr. p. 383.
61. *Ibid.*, p. 446; Engl. tr. p. 396.
62. *Ibid.*, p. 444; Engl. tr. p. 395.
63. *Ibid.*, p. 461; Engl. tr. pp. 409-410.

Here then, according to Barth, we have the true basis for human freedom. It is a freedom that exists within and because of the free decision of God's grace towards man. Unbelief is therefore an ontological impossibility. "Polanus and Quenstedt, whom we have so far consulted for the orthodox doctrine of God, fail us at this point."[64]

(b) The Perfections of Divine Freedom

We turn now to a consideration of what Barth says about the *divine* attributes of divine freedom.

The perfections of freedom follow those of love. After discussing the grace, mercy and patience of God we must therefore consider the omnipresence, the omnipotence and the glory of God. Here too at every point orthodoxy fails us, says Barth.

The *unity and the omnipresence* of God are the fourth pair of attributes discussed by Barth. Orthodoxy does not understand the true nature of the unity of God. "If we examine its treatment of the *simplicitas Dei*, we can only be amazed at the way in which orthodox dogmatics entered on and lost itself in logical and mathematical reflections. For the results reached it naturally could not produce a single scriptural proof, and yet this was to form the fundamental presupposition of its whole doctrine of God and therefore finally of its whole Christian doctrine."[65]

What else could be expected from orthodoxy? Its essentially nominalistic approach led it inevitably into speculation on a God in himself apart from and above Christ. Speculating on a God, *a se*, on a *nuda essentia*, is something quite different from regarding the unity of God as the consistency of the expression of his sovereign universal grace in Christ. Of course, when it was too late, orthodoxy said "everything which has to be said if Scripture is the guide." "And the rest of Christian doctrine, too, it tried to present and develop in loyalty to the guidance of Scripture." But this "happy inconsistency did not survive in the teaching of a later period."[66] Orthodoxy lost itself in speculation at this point. "It did not see that the scientific accuracy necessary to present this object requires us absolutely to accept God Himself in His revelation attested in Scripture as the absolutely simple One, the One who is in fact uncomposed and

64. *Ibid.*, p. 479; Engl. tr. p. 426.   66. *Idem.*
65. *Ibid.*, p. 515; Engl. tr. p. 457.

indivisible, and to allow Him to assert Himself as such. God Himself, this God in His reality, is that which is simple, He who is simple. It is He who is incomparably, uniquely simple—infinitely more simple than all the complexities and even all the would-be simplicities of the rest of our knowledge. God Himself is the nearest to hand, as the absolutely simple must be, and at the same time the most distant, as the absolutely simple must also be. God Himself is the irresolvable and at the same time that which fills and embraces everything else."[67]

God is one in his work of creation, reconciliation and redemption. God is this oneness. He is trustworthy. He is this in the inmost core of his being. "And this is His simplicity."[68]

As simple God is therefore omnipresent.[69] But what can properly be understood by the omnipresence of God? Orthodoxy was in no position to understand it. Orthodox theologians took their cue both for the idea of the omnipresence and the eternity of God from the problematics of space and time as these confront the human mind when it thinks independently of Christ. "We can see clearly at this point what is involved when in the definition of the essence of God the starting-point is man rather than God."[70] If one starts with man, one can never solve the problem of the relation of the finite to the infinite. It can then never be settled whether the finite or the infinite is first. "If we find the essence of God in the non-spatiality and timelessness of the basis of the world, this means neither more nor less than that God is drawn into the dialectic of the world's antithesis. But this leaves the way open for Feuerbach's question whether God might not be in man rather than man in God, and to this question there can be no decisive answer. If the only thing which exists is this antithesis which comprehends God, the relativity of the two spheres cannot prevent us from ascribing now to the one and now the other the dignity and function of deity. And this necessarily is what has always happened and will always happen apart from the knowledge of revelation and faith."[71]

It is therefore only if we start with Christ that the true relation of God to both space and to time can be determined. God is inherently coexistent as well as existent.[72] "God's 'infinity,' if we want to use this expression, is true infinity because it does not involve any

---

67. *Ibid.*, p. 515; Engl. tr. p. 458.
68. *Ibid.*, p. 516; Engl. tr. p. 459.
69. *Ibid.*, p. 518; Engl. tr. p. 461.

70. *Ibid.*, p. 524; Engl. tr. p. 465.
71. *Ibid.*, p. 525; Engl. tr. p. 467.
72. *Ibid.*, p. 521; Engl. tr. p. 467.

contradiction that it is finitude as well. For there is no reason why God in His essence should not be finite in the same perfect way as He is infinite."[73] With this Christological view of the unity of God as related to his omnipresence, we have maintained the free and universal nature of the grace of God. The identity of God with Jesus, the man, physically as well as temporally present among men, is expressed in the idea of the spatiality and temporality of God. God's space is the authentic space and God's time is the authentic time. When this is realized, then it is also realized that other men can exist only as participants in the only authentic man Jesus Christ. Orthodoxy was unable to see anything of this.

The *constancy and omnipotence* of God are the fifth pair of attributes discussed by Barth. God is "constantly One and omnipotently omnipresent."[74] The "one whole divine essence, can and must be expressed by recognising and saying that God is constant."[75] The "older Protestant orthodoxy did not display any great felicity in its handling of this matter either."[76] What Polanus said on the immutability of God is in "irreparable conflict with God's freedom, love and life."[77] Polanus was again thinking of God apart from Christ. He was speaking of "the idea of the *ipsum ens,* the *immensitas,* the *primum principium et primum movens.* By definition this is necessarily *immutabile,* and *immutabile* in this sense, which does not correspond in the least with the biblical passages."[78] Surely the constancy of which the Scriptures speak is the constancy of the living God, the God who has a real *Geschichte* with the world he has created.[79] It is the constancy of *Heilsgeschichte.*[80] ". . . . the meaning and secret of the history of salvation *[Heilsgeschichte]* itself is Jesus Christ."[80a] In "Jesus Christ God Himself has become a creature. That is to say, He has become one with the creature, with man."[81] This identification of God with the creature in Jesus Christ is the basis of the fellowship between them. It is God's nature to be thus free in the impartation of itself to his creature. "To sum up, because we have to do with the immutability of the freedom of God, what we have to recognise and acknowledge in Jesus Christ is unalterably

73. *Idem.*
74. *Ibid.,* p. 551; Engl. tr. p. 490.
75. *Ibid.,* p. 552; Engl. tr. p. 491.
76. *Ibid.,* p. 553; Engl. tr. p. 492.
77. *Ibid.,* p. 554; Engl. tr. p. 492.
78. *Ibid.,* p. 554; Engl. tr. p. 493.
79. *Ibid.,* p. 565.
80a. *Idem.*
81. *Ibid.,* p. 578; Engl. tr. p. 514.

the grace of God, but it is also unalterably His will and command and ordinance."[82]

For this divine decision which becomes an ordinance for man, the older theology used the notion of the decree of God.[83] Back of this decree lies the *voluntas Dei beneplaciti*. This may be called "*voluntas antecedens* in that it completely precedes the existence and form of the created world."[84] It is also the *voluntas absoluta*, and *occulta*.

Everything that takes place as a consequence of this absolute will of God "is simply a revelation of it." Yet those who believed in this absolute will also spoke of the "freedom and contingency of the created world."[85] Man was held responsible for sin.

So "this chapter of Reformed orthodox theology" is, at least, in its "embryonic teaching" better than the one on the essence of God. Of the former, in contrast with the latter, it cannot be said "that death is God and God is dead."[86] "The doctrine of the living God does at least begin to emerge; it does at least become possible."[87]

But soon "the doctrine of the simple and immovable essence of God re-emerges. For according to this distinction everything that might be called action in the divine decree belongs to the *voluntas signi* which only improperly can be reckoned the true will of God. In the light of this distinction it appears that it is only provisionally true, only in relation to us, perhaps only from our standpoint, that God is alive and active in the senses enumerated by Wolleb in a hexameter: *Praecipit et prohibet, permittit, consulit, implet.*"[88]

Having started from the Bible as identical with revelation, orthodoxy thus arrived at God as *bare essence*. The counsel of this God is a hidden source of arbitrary action. Thus for orthodoxy death is God and God is dead. Free grace again disappears. "Since it is obscure how far the *voluntas beneplaciti* is God's free grace, it must also be obscure how far the *voluntas signi* is binding on us."[89]

Orthodoxy has, says Barth, an "abstract general doctrine of the essence and relation of God to the world, in other words, a general doctrine of providence."[90] Thus "the creation, preservation and government of the world on the one hand, reconciliation and redemption on the other, and above all the incarnation of the Son of God and

82. *Ibid.*, p. 583; Engl. tr. p. 519.   87. *Idem.*
83. *Idem.*   88. *Idem.*
84. *Ibid.*, p. 584; Engl. tr. p. 519.   89. *Idem.*
85. *Ibid.*, p. 584; Engl. tr. p. 520.   90. *Idem.*
86. *Ibid.*, p. 585; Engl. tr. p. 520.

the existence of Jesus Christ—all form a single series as mere *opera externa* with a common denominator, as specific instances of the *voluntas signi* which has somewhere behind it the unmoved inscrutable *voluntas beneplaciti,* as mere instances of the divine providence."[91] The living Christ of the Scriptures is not found in all this except by inconsistency. In particular the notion of the omnipotence of God is misinterpreted in this way. Thus Quenstedt simply identifies the biblical idea of omnipotence with the idea of omnicausality.[92] This idea was more consistently expressed in Schleiermacher's theology.[93] "The perception that God is the Subject over His works is now lost and God is finally denied as such."[94] "The mistake which appeared in orthodoxy has now become more serious and final."[95] "We can now appreciate the full consequences of the nominalists' doctrine of the attributes, what it means when the identity of the divine attributes is understood as a real *simplicitas,* but not as a real *multiplicitas.*"[96] "The mischief of this view, which first appears in orthodoxy and reaches its full development in the school of Schleiermacher, consists directly in its abandonment of the distinction between what God can do and what He does do."[97]

The *eternity and the glory* of God are the last two attributes discussed by Barth. Just as it is God's nature to be coexistent as well as existent, so God has duration as well as space.[98]

"Eternity is the simultaneity of beginning, middle and end, and to that extent it is pure duration."[99] "God's eternity is itself beginning, succession and end."[100] This Christological view of time enables us to give the truly biblical view of fore-ordination. We must start "from the incarnation of the divine Word in Jesus Christ."[101] "In Jesus Christ it comes about that God takes time to Himself, that He Himself, the eternal One, becomes temporal, that He is present for us in the form of our own existence and our own world, not simply embracing our time and ruling it, but submitting Himself to it, and permitting created time to become and be the form of His eternity."[102]

Starting thus with Jesus Christ, as the *act* of God's identity with

91. *Idem.*
92. *Ibid.,* p. 594; Engl. tr. p. 528.
93. *Ibid.,* p. 595; Engl. tr. p. 529.
94. *Idem.*
95. *Ibid.,* p. 597; Engl. tr. p. 530.
96. *Ibid.,* p. 596; Engl. tr. p. 530.
97. *Ibid.,* p. 597; Engl. tr. p. 531.
98. *Ibid.,* p. 690.
99. *Ibid.,* p. 685; Engl. tr. p. 608.
100. *Ibid.,* p. 689; Engl. tr. p. 611.
101. *Ibid.,* p. 694; Engl. tr. p. 616.
102. *Idem.*

man, we overcome all the static notions of orthodoxy, as above enumerated.

3. *Orthodoxy on Election*

All the evil of the abstract idea of God in himself and of his decree controlling whatsoever comes to pass comes to climactic expression in the orthodox doctrine of election. This point is, for Barth, of basic importance. But we can only touch on it briefly. The criticism on the doctrine of election as held by Calvin, and discussed in the preceding chapter, is repeated in all its essentials when Barth deals with later orthodoxy. Not understanding the fact that Christ is the electing God and the elected man, orthodoxy, with Calvin, does not understand the biblical doctrine of grace. For "the election of grace is the whole of the Gospel, the Gospel *in nuce*."[103] We cannot, therefore, says Barth, follow Loraine Boettner when in his book *The Reformed Doctrine of Predestination* he simply seeks to repeat the classical teaching on predestination. And "it was quite in the spirit of Calvin, and yet quite fatal, when many of the older Reformed dogmaticians thought that they ought to balance against the concept of the election of grace that of an election of wrath."[104]

This fatal parallelism of an election of wrath and an election of grace, it is now apparent, is finally to be traced back to the abstract idea of God as *nuda essentia* and to his absolute counsel as controlling all that comes to pass.

Together with Calvin, orthodoxy was blind to the true imbalance of the gospel. Orthodoxy was unable to subordinate the attributes of holiness and righteousness to God's grace and mercy. For this reason it was also bound to fail to develop a true doctrine of election. "The electing God of Calvin is a *Deus nudus absconditus*. It is not the *Deus revelatus* who is as such the *Deus absconditus*, the eternal God. All the dubious features of Calvin's doctrine result from the basic failing that in the last analysis he separates God and Jesus Christ, thinking that what was in the beginning with God must be sought elsewhere than in Jesus Christ. Thus with all his forceful and impressive acknowledgment of the divine election of grace, ultimately he still passes by the grace of God as it has appeared in Jesus Christ."[105]

103. II:2, p. 13; Engl. tr. pp. 13, 14.   105. *Ibid.*, p. 119; Engl. tr. p. 111.
104. *Ibid.*, p. 16; Engl. tr. p. 17.

The Synod of Dort "repeated, more harshly if anything, the unsatisfactory answer already given by Calvin."[106] The theologians of the *Synopsis purioris Theologiae* too appealed finally to God the Father beyond Christ as the source of election.[107] The election of Jesus Christ is, for them, merely "His election in execution of the decree of the Father."[108] Due to their appeal to an abstract *nuda essentia*, and their appeal to an *absolute decree (decretum absolutum)*, Reformed theologians could not rightly speak of grace.[109] They sought a "Christian and biblical doctrine of predestination."[110] Yet "can there ever be anything more unchristian or anti-Christian than the horror or the peace which is given by the thought of the *decretum absolutum* as the first and last truth from which everything else proceeds?"[111]

"Where the traditional *decretum absolutum* used to stand we must place the *decretum concretum* of the election in Jesus Christ."[112]

When we have thus replaced the idea of an absolute by the concrete decree in Christ, then we obtain a "purified supralapsarianism." A purified supralapsarianism alone does justice to the identification of God and man in Christ as *Geschichte*. It thinks of Christ as the electing God. It also thinks of him as the elected man. It is the second point that is here of basic importance.

As there is no God in general, so there is no man in general. "Supralapsarians, Infralapsarians and mediators all agreed that the controverted *obiectum praedestinationis*, elected or rejected man, must be identified directly and independently with the partly elected and partly rejected individual descendants of Adam, both in the mass and also in detail. The interest of both parties, and of the older Reformed theology as a whole (and indeed of all the older theology), centered exclusively upon these individuals as such. It is in the election of some of these individuals that the man Jesus Christ plays a specific and indispensable part as the first of the elect. With the rejection of the others He has nothing whatever to do. Yet when the question of the *obiectum praedestinationis* arises, then in one way or another He is quickly passed over, and a proper solution is found in the individual *x* or *y*. It may be as *creabilis* or *creatus*, it

---

106. *Idem.*
107. *Ibid.*, p. 120; Engl. tr. p. 112.
108. *Ibid.*, p. 121; Engl. tr. p. 112.
109. *Ibid.*, p. 121; Engl. tr. p. 113.
110. *Idem.*
111. *Ibid.*, p. 172; Engl. tr. p. 158.
112. *Ibid.*, p. 173; Engl. tr. p. 159.

may be as *labilis* or *lapsus,* but this *homo x* or *y* is always the *obiectum praedestinationis.*

"Second, all parties were at one in thinking that in God's eternal decree predestination (and therefore the election or rejection of individuals) implies the setting up of a fixed system which the temporal life and history of individuals can only fulfil and affirm. The doctrine of predestination does not proclaim the free grace of God as glad tidings, but as the neutral impartation of the message that from all eternity God is gracious to whom He will be gracious, and whom He will He hardeneth, and that this constitutes the limit within which each individual must run his course. The Supralapsarian maintains that this system of the eternal election or reprobation of individuals is the system above every other system, being identical with the primal and basic plan of God besides which there is none other. The Infralapsarian allows the existence of another plan or system either alongside or prior to it, in the form of the decree of creation and the fall. But both parties presuppose and maintain that that system is in any case from all eternity, and that it is indeed fixed and unalterable, so that not merely individuals, but God Himself as its eternal author is bound by it in time, and (in relation to that pattern of all things, which is itself thought of as fixed) there can be nothing new under the sun, whether on man's part or on God's.

"Third, all parties were agreed that when God set up this fixed system which anticipated the life-history and destiny of every individual as such, then in the same way, in the same sense, with the same emphasis, and in an exact equilibrium in every respect, God uttered both a Yes and a No, accepting some and rejecting others. In respect of the decree of creation the Infralapsarians do speak in some sense of a general purpose of God in the revelation of His glory, although without attempting to define this purpose more exactly. But when they come to the decree of predestination as such, they too speak of God's purpose in respect of created and fallen man in a way which is absolutely symmetrical. This purpose is to demonstrate His mercy to some and His justice to others. From the general mass of corruption the mercy of God infallibly inclines and guides a certain fixed number of individuals to election, and in the same way the justice of God infallibly inclines and guides a certain fixed number to perdition. There can be no more question of a disturbance or upsetting of the equilibrium of these two attitudes in

God than there can be of any subsequent alteration within the system which has been established by the twofold will of God. The two attitudes together, the one balancing the other, constitute the divine will to self-glorification, and God is glorified equally in the eternal blessedness of the elect and the eternal damnation of the reprobate.

"Fourth and above all—the hidden basis of all other agreement— all parties were agreed in their understanding of the divine good-pleasure which decided between election and rejection and thus determined the concrete structure of the system appointed from all eternity for time. They agreed, then, in thinking that this good-pleasure must be understood wholly and utterly as *decretum absolutum*. It is an act of divine freedom whose basis and meaning are completely hidden, and in their hiddenness must be regarded and reverenced as holy. This *decretum absolutum* is (according to the Infralapsarian view) the divine disposition in respect of *homo creatus et lapsus*, or (according to the Supralapsarian view) the divine disposition in respect of *homo creabilis et labilis*. Behind both these views (at a different point, but with the same effect in practice), there stands the picture of the absolute God in Himself who is neither conditioned nor self-conditioning, and not the picture of the Son of God who is self-conditioned and therefore conditioned in His union with the Son of David; not the picture of God in Jesus Christ."[113]

Thus Barth has *purified* historic supralapsarianism by placing it on "radically new presuppositions." He has placed a Christological foundation underneath the orthodox doctrine of election. He has expunged the idolatrous concept of a *decretum absolutum*. Thinking of Christ as the elected man enables us to see that *in him* God "wills humanity and every individual man and what we may describe as the ideal humanity."[114]

According to the orthodox doctrine of God, death is God and God is dead. The orthodox teaching of an *absolute decree* leads to the same result. So it is natural that, according to Barth, on the old doctrine of supralapsarianism "God threatens to take on the appearance of a demon . . ."[115] It is no wonder that Roman Catholics, Lutherans and Arminians recoiled from such a doctrine.[116]

---

113. *Ibid.*, pp. 143-144; Engl. tr. pp. 133-134.
114. *Ibid.*, p. 152; Engl. tr. p. 141.   116. *Idem.*
115. *Ibid.*, p. 151; Engl. tr. p. 140.

How then can Barth help but be simply *against* orthodoxy? Its principle is for him utterly destructive of the Christological and therefore of the biblical doctrine of revelation, of God, of the decree of God, of creation, of providence, of reconciliation and of redemption. Orthodoxy fails to see the indirect identity of God and man in Jesus Christ as God's act of saving all men.

In conclusion it should be noted that Barth's criticism of orthodoxy is to all intents and purposes the same as is his criticism of Calvin. In both cases the true Christological approach to the exegesis of Scripture is said to be absent. Now it is only in terms of a truly Christological approach to Scripture that Scripture can, in truly Protestant fashion, be placed above the church. If Calvin as well as later orthodoxy hold to the idea of a *decretum absolutum* and therefore to an arbitrary and dark being back of Christ, then they are not, according to Barth, preaching the Christ of the Scriptures. Again, if Calvin as well as later orthodoxy speak of man in himself, having the ability of final unbelief in Christ, then they are not, says Barth, preaching the Christ of the Scriptures. Thus neither of them understands the nature of free, universal grace.

How then can orthodoxy, or how can Calvin really be said to be essentially Protestant in their theology? Barth's Protestantism, like his supralapsarianism, appears to be a Protestantism on "radically new presuppositions," Barth himself being the judge. The spirit of the anti-Christ as discovered by Barth in Romanism appears to be far more active in Calvin and in Reformed orthodoxy than in Roman Catholicism. There is less appreciation for Barth's Christ as act in Calvin and in Reformed orthodoxy than there is in Romanism. Perhaps Han Urs von Balthasar is not far wrong when he says that Barth's *analogia of faith* does not really differ basically from the Roman Catholic concept of being. Perhaps we shall have to conclude that the *dynamic* categories of Roman Catholicism and the act idea of Barth are only gradationally distinct from one another. Do either the dynamic categories of Rome or the activist categories of Barth permit one to submit one's thought captive to the obedience of Christ as he has once for all spoken by the Spirit and through his apostles in the Scriptures? And is it really the voice of God one hears unless one hears it as speaking now directly and clearly in Scripture? The Bible or Speculation, which shall it be?

Chapter VI

Eternity and Time

The question of greatest importance in all that precedes is that of the relation of God to man in terms of Christ as *Geschichte*. For Barth Jesus Christ is both the ground of knowledge and of being for man. He is this as *Geschichte*. And by *Geschichte*, as earlier noted, Barth means the exhaustive Act of interrelationship between God and man.

Barth evaluates every form of theology in terms of his concept of *Geschichte*. Romanism is rejected because in its concept of analogy of being there is no appreciation of Christ as *Geschichte*. The Reformers intended to work with the notion of *Geschichte* but did so only very inadequately. Again and again they fell back on the notion of the direct revelation of God to man in Christ. Again and again they appealed to the false mystery of a God apart from Christ and of a man apart from Christ. Later orthodox theology raised the idea of direct revelation to its first principle. In doing so orthodox theologians virtually prepared the way for the purely immanent theology of modern Protestantism.

If then we are to escape the immanentism inherent in the theology of Schleiermacher, we shall need to eradicate every form of direct contact between God and man in Romanism, in Protestant orthodoxy and even in Calvin as well as in Schleiermacher. A truly Protestant position must challenge all men, within as well as without the church, in terms of *Geschichte*.

As noted earlier, *Geschichte* stands for *indirect* identification of God with man. In the idea of indirect identification alone can we do justice to the idea of sovereign universal grace. In the first place,

90

the sovereignty of grace appears in the fact that, when God is present with man in Christ, he is present as God. God never submits himself to any form of control by man. If God were directly present with man in Christ, then it would no longer be the *sovereign* God who is present. He would then no longer be present in the manner of God. In the second place, the objectivity and universality of grace appears from the fact that, in being present with man in Christ, he is present to all men. Christ is inherently the man for all men. All men are men in him. If God were directly present with man in Christ, there would be neither the objectivity nor the universality of atonement of which the Scripture speaks. God would then be present only to some men, and even they could not be certain that God was present with them. The only theology that is basically Christian and basically Protestant is, therefore, a theology in which God is wholly revealed and wholly hidden in Christ as *Geschichte*. Only such a theology is really a theology of revelation. It alone has a God who speaks "from above." Only such a theology presents Christ as the Victor over Chaos and as such the light of all men and of the whole world.

How can this Christ as the Savior of all men and as the light of the whole world be manifest to men? Surely he must be manifest at one place and at one time. It was in the man Jesus of Nazareth that God was manifest. And Pontius Pilate has a place in the credo. How then can the eternal God be present at this place and at this time among men for the salvation of all men?

As noted in earlier chapters, Barth makes plain that Christ is present among men as *Geschichte*. His presence can therefore not be directly identified with Jesus of Nazareth. To indicate this fact pointedly, Barth, from time to time, says that the facts concerning Jesus Christ do not pertain to *Historie* as such. To identify *Geschichte* with *Historie* would be to commit the great mistake of orthodoxy, namely, to identify history with revelation. *Historie* is, to be sure, an aspect of *Geschichte*. How else could it be maintained that God in Christ is truly man as well as truly God? But since he is truly God when truly man, there must never be any identification of *Geschichte* with *Historie*. Barth therefore makes this distinction between *Geschichte* and *Historie* in the interest of making and stressing his basic principle that God is in Christ always both wholly hidden and wholly revealed among men. If Christ is to be present among men in the manner of God (*in der Weise Gottes*), then we must say that he is indirectly present, present that is in terms of *Geschichte*. *Geschichte* includes *Historie*. Barth constantly uses *Geschichte* in order by means of it to describe the entire transaction between God and man. But when he has particular reason to oppose the idea of direct revelation, he sometimes introduces the distinction between *Geschichte* and *Historie*.

We propose therefore to discuss Barth's concept of *Geschichte* as it relates to his concept of *Historie* more fully than has so far been done. We propose to do so by taking into consideration the whole of Barth's view of the relation of eternity to time. For the idea of *Geschichte* and *Historie* must be seen in terms of the eternal God becoming man in time and temporal man participating in the eternal God. There is no need of a separate discussion of the question of space; it is involved in the discussion on time.

According to Barth, the whole question of the relation of eternity to time is identical with the question of the relation of God to man in Jesus Christ. We are not to discuss the question of how eternity can become time or how time can participate in eternity and after that to ask to what extent Christ is both eternal and temporal. We are rather to begin with the great principle earlier discussed, namely, that Jesus Christ as the fact and act of God's presence with man, and as the act of man's participation in the being of God, is the source of all possibility. It is Jesus Christ as *Geschichte* who is both the ground of being and of knowledge for man in all things. Jesus Christ is the act of reconciliation of all men with God. And that this is true can be known only through him. It can be known through him as the incarnate and risen Saviour. It can be known from the work of salvation accomplished for all men.

1. *The Resurrection of Jesus Christ*

The resurrection of Christ occupies a particularly important place in Christ's work of saving all men. His prophetic work as the light of men comes to particular expression here. Of course, Jesus Christ is priest and king as well as prophet. He is all three at once. But the resurrection lights up his work as priest and king in a striking fashion. The fact that as priest and king Christ is victor over sin for all men is here made fully clear to men. Here it appears clearly that the eternal God is identical with the man Jesus Christ and that all men are men by virtue of their participation with Jesus in this his identification with God. The resurrection is, in short, an event. The

faith of Christians is based on objective facts. There is no parthenogenesis of the faith. This we must maintain in the strongest possible
terms over against Bultmann. On the other hand, the resurrection is
not an event that is directly identical with any fact of *Historie*. Such
identification would take away from the resurrection its true character as the event that lights up all other events. Such identification
would take away the very objectivity in terms of which we wish to
answer Bultmann and all others who rationalize the faith.

To indicate the fact that the resurrection is such an event, Barth
makes the following points:

(a) The resurrection is exclusively the work of God.[1]

From this it immediately follows that it cannot be identified with
a fact in *Historie*.[2] If the revelation of God in the resurrection of
Christ were identical with a fact in *Historie*, then it could not be as
it is and must be the original and exemplary form of the revelation
of God. In the resurrection the disciples are certain of the immediate
presence of God. And the immediate presence of God cannot turn
into the past as it would if it were directly identical with a date on
the calendar. God is *wholly* present to man in the resurrection of
Christ. God comes wholly into time. In being present to man, God's
eternity does not merely touch time as a tangent touches a circle.[3]
God goes into utter estrangement from himself. It is his nature so to
do. His unity is expressed in the fact that he is inherently coexistent
as well as existent.[4] Why should not God be finite as well as infinite
in his perfections?[5] God's eternity itself is pure duration.[6] And pure
duration constitutes divinity.[7] As pure duration God is sovereign
over his being. He has beginning, procession and ending.[8] God's pure
duration begins in every beginning, proceeds in every procession and
ends in every ending.[9] "The eternity of God is itself beginning, procession and end."[10] In Christ God *has* time for us. In Christ God *is*

---

1. IV:1, p. 331. Es geschieht also, ohne dass es von daher verstanden bzw.
missverstanden, gedeutet, bzw. missgedeutet werden könnte. Es geschieht, aber
es geschieht offenkundig, ohne dass man es in jenem Zusammenhang sehen,
ihm also auch einen «historischen» Charakter zuschreiben könnte. Es geschieht
—darin der Schöpfung vergleichbar—als souveräne Gottestat und nur so.

2. *Ibid.*, p. 331.

3. I:2, p. 55—"Sie bleibt der Zeit nicht transzendent, sie tangiert sie nicht
bloss, sondern sie geht in die Zeit ein, nein; sie nimmt Zeit an, nein, sie schafft
sich Zeit."

4. II:1, p. 521.

5. *Ibid.*, p. 526.

6. *Ibid.*, p. 685.

7. *Ibid.*, p. 687.

8. *Ibid.*, p. 688.

9. *Idem.*

10. *Ibid.*, p. 689.

time for us.[11] The triune God is himself the "absolutely real time" (*absolut wirkliche Zeit*).[12]

In the incarnation God therefore submits himself to our time.[13] He could not be wholly present to us without doing so. True eternity includes potentiality for time.[14] We may therefore speak of the "temporality of eternity" (*Zeitlichkeit der Ewigkeit*).[15] This temporality of eternity itself includes pretemporality, supertemporality and posttemporality (*Vorzeitlichkeit, Überzeitlichkeit* and *Nachzeitlichkeit*).[16]

The presence of God to the disciples in the resurrection of Jesus includes all this. Nothing less than this is involved in the pure presence of God. The whole gospel depends upon this fact of God's pure presence with man in the resurrection of Jesus Christ. For only if the eternal God of grace is wholly present with us can our every moment in turn be enveloped in his pure duration.[17] Only if our time is included in God's pure duration dare we recognize God's time in our time.[18]

Here then we already have the heart of the matter. If we are to know that God in Christ is present with us and therewith has saved us, then our time must be enveloped into God's time. We cannot know ourselves as sinners unless we are forgiven of our sins in Christ. This means for Barth that our time must be taken into God's pure duration. But this absorption of our time into God's pure duration requires that this pure duration be present to us. If man is to participate in the pure duration of God, then God must first submit himself to the time of man. There can be no real exaltation of man into participation with the being of God unless there first be participation of God with the state and fate of man. The incarnation must precede the resurrection. But the incarnation must not precede the resurrection temporally. If it did, then the whole meaning of the resurrection as the event of the pure presence of God with man would be cancelled out.

(b) In addition to being an act of God in his pure presence, the resurrection must also be said to be a *new* act of God.

The resurrection is new in relation to the crucifixion that preceded

---

11. *Ibid.*, p. 690. Es ist aber wirklich er selber, der Zeit für uns hat, er selbst ist Zeit für uns, so gewiss seine Offenbarung, so gewiss Jesus Christus wirklich er selber ist.

12. *Ibid.*, p. 694.
13. *Idem.*
14. *Ibid.*, p. 696.
15. *Ibid.*, p. 698.

16. *Idem.*
17. *Ibid.*, p. 704.
18. *Ibid.*, p. 690.

it. In his death Jesus had given himself and with himself all mankind into the Nihil *(das Nichtige)*.[19] God might justly have left mankind subject to the threat of the Nihil.[20] God's act of saving men is something wholly new and undeserved on the part of men. His coming to man in Christ is therefore wholly new. Salvation is of *sovereign* grace.

This sovereign character of grace is expressed in the very notion that God comes to man in visible and tangible form. God comes into space and time and subjects himself to both. He can be seen and heard in it. He appears to his disciples as something "visible, touchable, and that can be heard" *(sichtbares, hörbares, greifbares)*.[21] Is this not evidence enough that Barth does take the resurrection to be a genuinely historical fact? If in his commentary on Romans, Barth said that the resurrection is "not in history at all," does he not now with equal plainness assert that it *is* a fact in history? And is not this in accord with the general difference between Barth's later and his earlier writings? Has he not told us that in his earlier theology he had been too eschatological in his emphasis? If then he said that revelation touches history as a tangent touches a circle, does he not now say that revelation actually comes into history? Has he not opposed the school of consistent eschatology by asserting that in the resurrection the dialectic between the wholly revealed and the wholly hidden has been cancelled out?[22] For in meeting him after the resurrection, the disciples see that, in the man Jesus, the Creator as Lord of time himself becomes time. They now see this in his pure presence.[23] Is not the resurrection for Barth the great exception to the generally eschatological character of the revelation of God in Christ?[24]

The answer to all these questions can only be given in terms of the fact that God in being present with man in time is there present in the "manner of God" *(in der Weise Gottes)*.[25] It is God who is present, and He is wholly revealed. His presence is the presence of his pure duration. And this implies that God is present to man because he allows man to participate in his own eternity.[25a] Thus Jesus ap-

---

19. IV:1, p. 337.
20. *Ibid.*, p. 338.
21. *Ibid.*, p. 339.
22. III:2, p. 537ff.

23. I:2, p. 125.
24. *Ibid.*, p. 126, *cf.* p. 545.
25. III:2, p. 540.

25a. III:2, p. 540. Das von Ewigkeit gesprochene Wort hebt die Zeit, in die es hineingesprochen ist (ohne sie als Zeit auszulöschen), als nunmehr *seine* Zeit hinauf in seine eigene Ewigkeit, gibt ihr Anteil an dem allein wirklichen durch sich selbst bewegten, in sich selbst ruhenden, sich selbst genügenden Sein Gottes.

pears to his disciples in the time which has itself become participant in God's eternity.[26] It is in this time, the time that is real in so far as it is participant in the eternity of God, that Jesus meets his disciples. And only in the fact that they are participant in this time do they meet him. Thus the confrontation between Jesus Christ and his disciples after the resurrection is not all by way of direct revelation in the physico-temporal realm. The confrontation takes place in space and time so far as these have themselves been taken up into participation with the eternity of God.

In putting the matter in this way, Barth is quite true to his own often asserted position with respect to the priority of the man Jesus in relation to other men. Jesus is the only real man because he is the only elect man, the pure grace receiver. The elect in God confront the elected man in Jesus. In him they are identical. There is no confrontation of other men with God except in that they are fellow elect with Jesus. Their faith in him is their own faith, but it is such because they are participants in the universal work of reconciliation accomplished by Jesus.

In corroboration of what has just been said, it must again be pointed out that for Barth the resurrection does not follow the crucifixion, the life of Jesus and his incarnation, in the manner in which days that follow one another are measured by the calendar.

To have the proper perspective on the confrontation of Jesus Christ with his disciples after the resurrection, it is imperative to see the resurrection in its relation to the incarnation.

In dealing with the incarnation, Barth takes up the question of the creed of Chalcedon. In this creed the church was concerned to safeguard both the distinctness and the genuine togetherness of the two natures of Christ. But if the purpose of Chalcedon is to be realized, the incarnation must be actualized. "We have 'actualised' the doctrine of the incarnation, i.e., we have used the main traditional concepts, *unio, communio* and *communicatio,* as concentrically related terms to describe one and the same ongoing process. We have stated it all (including the Chalcedonian definition, which is so important in dogmatic history, and rightly became normative) in the form of a denotation and description of a single event. We have taken it that the reality of Jesus Christ, which is the theme of Christology, is

26. *Ibid.*, p. 541. Jesus appears—"in seiner Existenz in der anderen, der potenzierten, der ewigen Gotteszeit."

identical with this event, and this event with the reality of Jesus Christ."[27]

Unless we thus actualize the incarnation, we simply do not understand the gospel of the saving grace of God. In that case God cannot really become time for man and man cannot really participate in the eternity of God. Only if we actualize the incarnation, do we do justice to the *prima veritas* that in the Christ-Event there is involved the whole essence of God and the whole essence of man. And God is always prior to man. In the act or event of their togetherness, God's humiliation is at the same time man's exaltation.

Since the Christ-Event is a unit, a unit in act, a unit in which the act of God is prior to the act of man, the steps of Christ's exaltation do not follow up the steps of his humiliation in time. Christ's work "cannot be divided into different stages or periods of His existence . . . Where and when is He not both humiliated and exalted, already exalted in His humiliation, and humiliated in His exaltation? . . . We have to do with the being of the one and entire Jesus Christ whose humiliation detracts nothing and whose exaltation adds nothing. And in this His being we have to do with His action, the work and event of atonement."[28]

In the most definite manner Barth thus rejects the traditionally accepted doctrine of the steps of the revelation of God in Christ following one another in history. He does this, moreover, specifically in the interest of the real confrontation of God and man in Christ. The resurrection of Christ, in which this confrontation comes to dramatic and climactic expression is therefore for Barth not at all to be directly identified with a fact that happened *after* the incarnation in terms of calendar time. If the resurrection of Christ is to be, as it must be, a *new* act of God then it must not be *new* on the calendar. The resurrection must add *nothing* to the incarnation in terms of the calendar.

(c) In what has been said Barth laid great stress on the newness of the act of God in the resurrection of Jesus Christ. Grace must be sovereign grace. It must be that which God might have withheld. But it is equally true that grace as new is universal grace. And the resurrection must be evidence of universal as well as of sovereign grace.

27. IV:2, p. 116; Engl. tr. p. 105.
28. IV:1, p. 146; Engl. tr. p. 133.

In speaking of universal grace we speak of our participation in the resurrection of Christ. This is the problem of *Heilsgeschichte*. Both in his death and in his resurrection Christ is our substitute. Together they constitute God's *Geschichte* with us.[29] And to whom does Barth refer when he speaks of Christ as having *Geschichte* for us? Does he refer to one class or group of men for whom Christ died and not to another group of men for whom Christ did not die? Not at all. As noted earlier, Barth thinks it a total misunderstanding of the gospel when Calvin says that Christ died for some and not for all men. Christ is the first receiver of grace.[30] He is this as the elect man. He is this as the only real man. And therefore he receives it for all men who are men precisely because they participate in him as grace-receiver.

Using the language of time and eternity, this means that God has and is time for all men in Jesus Christ. God is therefore present to all men. Why should he not be? He is the Lord of time. He is present to all men in his pure presence. He is present to all men at all times in the one act of his incarnation and resurrection. This one act or event does have in it succession as well as togetherness. The resurrection follows the death of Christ. Yet they are one act. The fact of succession does not break up the togetherness. The togetherness of the incarnation is, to be sure, a temporal togetherness.[31] Even so, this temporal togetherness must not be directly identified with dates on the calendar. What happened on the third day was the lifting up of all previous happenings into the once-for-allness of this one event.

The temporal togetherness of which Barth speaks, therefore, includes or envelops but for that very reason must not be directly identified with anything that takes place in *Historie*. Christ's traveling from Jordan to Golgotha is both God's eternal being and the being of our time each day. *Geschichte* did not become *Historie* (*Seine Geschichte wurde nicht Historie*). The pragmatism of memory, tradition and proclamation can only be viewed as *Epiphenomena* in relation to this *Gottesgeschichte*.[32]

It is therefore from the point of view of their temporal togetherness with Christ as Lord of time that his followers must make all

---

29. *Ibid.*, p. 341.
30. *Idem*. Als erster Empfänger der Gnade Gottes des Vaters.
31. *Ibid.*, pp. 344, 345.
32. *Ibid.*, p. 347.

other distinctions in time.[33] The successive times of the followers of Christ are to be regarded as stages within the one presence of God in Christ who is time for them and has enveloped their time into his time. After the death of Christ comes the period of the forty days.[34] These end with the ascension of Christ to heaven.[35] After that comes the time of the church.[36] Finally, there is the second coming of Christ. But all of these, so far as they are distinct from one another, are so distinct in terms of their participation in the pure presence of Christ.

Finally, the presence of God in Christ envelops even the time of Jesus prior to his resurrection. From the point of view of the resurrection, this fact may be clearly perceived. In Christ God has even been gracious to all men from the beginning. The primary relation of God to all men is that of grace in Christ. Christ is therefore before Adam. He is this in the pure presence of God to all men.

Thus it appears that, not only for the sake of the newness of grace, but also for the sake of the universality of grace, the resurrection of Christ must not be indirectly identified with a fact of *Historie*. If the resurrection were thus identified, then God would be bound. We should have once again the idea of the profane givenness. Again, if the resurrection were thus identified, then the grace of God would be restricted. It could then reach only such as would hear about this fact. God could then not be really present to all men everywhere in terms of grace. He would not really have time for man, for all men.

(d) Barth knows that his readers tend to think in terms of an exclusive contrast between what happened directly as an event in space and time, and myth. But such a contrast, he says, is false. The resurrection did really happen. We must not speak of it in terms of myth. But it did not happen the way other events happen. When the gospels pass on from the passion narratives to the resurrection event, they lead us into an area of history of a different sort *(in einen Geschichtsbereich anderer, eigener Art)*.[37] Historians can make nothing out of such a notion as *Geschichte*. For here we have the divine present. Here we have present *Geschichte*, *Geschichte* that has hap-

---

33. *Ibid.*, p. 356. Eben aus der *Gegenwart* des Gekreuzigten heraus, in der sie, dem Urteil Gottes vertrauend und gehorsam, stehen, strecken sie sich aus nach einer neuen, anderen, vollendenden und abschliessenden Art seiner Gegenwart.

34. *Ibid.*, p. 350.
35. *Ibid.*, p. 351.

36. *Ibid.*, p. 352.
37. *Ibid.*, p. 369.

pened but is not past.[38] As an act of God, the event of the resurrection can therefore not be described. And the "legend" of the empty tomb, as something that goes with the idea of the resurrection, cannot be historically verified any more than the facts pertaining to the resurrection can. What we have in the gospels on the resurrection is full of darkness and contradiction. The apostle Paul assumes a different version than the gospels do. In the *Acts* Paul's Damascus experience is placed on a level with the events of the forty days. Therewith he breaks the scheme of the forty days. Finally, the resurrection appearances take place only in relation to those who were believers in him. It would be impossible to attempt to establish the fact that the resurrection *has happened* by means of appeal to historical science.[39] We simply cannot discuss the matter of the resurrection with the historical concept of *Geschichte* as identical with *Historie*.[40]

For Barth the objectivity of the Christian faith must therefore rest on a *real* event. Our faith must not rest in itself. Objectivity for the gospels rests on real confrontation of the disciples with their risen Lord. But for this very reason the resurrection must not be directly identified with a fact of *Historie*. We have already seen that, if grace is really to be sovereign grace, then the idea of direct revelation must be excluded. So also if grace is to be inherently universal grace, then again direct identification of revelation with any fact in history must be removed. For the same reason, if grace is to be present to man, to all men objectively, and if they are to be able with certainty to rest on it as on a fact that is basic to all other facts, then there must be no identification of the resurrection with a fact of *Historie*. The revelation as *God's* act of grace cannot be present to all men in direct revelation. The revelation as a *new* act of God cannot be present to all men in direct revelation. The revelation of God's new act of grace for *all men* cannot be present to men in direct revelation. The revelation of God's new act of universal grace cannot be *objectively* present to all men in direct revelation. Yet the resurrection must form the basis of the faith of the disciples. For this very

38. *Ibid.*, p. 353. wohl geschehene aber darum nicht vergangene, sondern gegenwärtige Geschichte.

39. *Ibid.*, p. 370.

40. *Ibid.*, p. 370. Es hätte keinen Sinn das zu bedauern: nach Allem, was wir von dem Wesen, dem Charakter, der Funktion der Auferstehung Jesu Christi als Begründung und im Zusammenhang der neutestamentlichen Botschaft gehört haben, kann es gar nicht anders sein, als dass wir mit dem 'historischen' Begriff von Geschichte hier nicht durchkommen.

reason it must not be identified directly with any fact of history. Barth says that we may speak of the resurrection as happening pre-historically *(prähistorisch)*.[41] The gospel has an objective foundation in an event that *happened*. The event of salvation for all men *happened*. Of course it happened. Of course it is objective. The justification of all men depends upon the fact that it happened. But it happened *prähistorisch*.

(e) As that which happened *prähistorisch*, the resurrection is the fact that lights up all other facts. It lights up all the future. It also lights up all the past. In the light of the resurrection, all men are seen to be contemporaneous with Christ.[42] God in Christ has time for us. He subjected himself to our time. In doing so, he took our time into participation with his own eternity. Herewith the indirect and therefore universal character of the grace of God is made apparent. Thus God makes man to participate in his own *Geschichte*. That is the message of the resurrection.

If the resurrection and our justification as based upon it is, therefore, to be properly understood, it must be placed in the widest possible context. We must see more fully how the objectivity of the resurrection as an actual event fits into the idea that the entire relation between God and man is involved in it. We must therefore look backward to the very eternity of God prior to the incarnation, and we must look forward to the participation of all men in the glory of God.

2. *Looking Backward from the Resurrection*

Looking backward from the resurrection, it must constantly be remembered that Jesus Christ is Lord of time. Nothing intelligible can be said about time except in terms of the fact that it participates in Christ as *Geschichte*. In the incarnation God did not assume an already existent human nature. Human nature really came into existence for the first time with the incarnation. So in the incarnation God did not come into an already existing time. Real time came into existence with him. To say anything less, argues Barth, is to speak abstractly. To say anything less is to be docetic.

Men are docetic because they fear that in the incarnation God might really be lost in time. But how can the Lord of time be lost in

---

41. *Ibid.*, pp. 370-371. weil sie als "Historie" offenbar nicht fassbar ist. . . .
42. *Ibid.*, p. 385.

it? When Christ said, "My God, my God why hast thou forsaken me?" it was not merely in some previously existent human nature, assumed by him, that he suffered. It is God himself, as identical with Jesus, who suffers there. There is nothing in the Godhead that keeps him from thus becoming the object of his own wrath in the man Jesus. And only because it is the entire Godhead who, in the man Jesus, suffers is there in that fact real atonement for man. Atonement is an act of *God*, a *new* act of God, and as such cannot be the universally and objectively valid basis of the atonement for all men unless God is identical with Jesus in his suffering. The eternal God without qualifications has become time for man. He has wholly revealed, that is wholly submitted himself, to our time.[43] Without his presence as God suffering for us, we should have no knowledge of our sin. We know our sin in him because as the first and true receiver of grace he is the true Adam. In him therefore we come into existence as men, that is, as fellow-grace receivers. We know our sin through him because we at the same time know that our sins are forgiven through him. All this we know because the crucifixion is seen in the light of the resurrection. And we could not see the crucifixion in the light of the resurrection if the resurrection were directly identified with a fact in *Historie*. The resurrection must follow the crucifixion, but this following must be within the one act of the presence of God with man. This one act is an act of humiliation and, at the same time, an act of exaltation. Without the temporal togetherness of the steps of humiliation and the steps of exaltation in the life and work of Christ, the grace of God would neither be sovereign nor objective and universal. To be really sovereign or new, it must be God's very nature from all eternity to express the whole of his being as grace to man. The relation of eternity to time is not expressed adequately at all, unless God's eternal being is seen to be wholly that of grace, and unless this God of grace decides ever anew to assert this his being in his act of receiving all men into participation with himself in grace.

To see this point still more clearly, we must work back from the resurrection all the way to the attributes of God, and in particular to God's eternity.

Back of the crucifixion then, there is the life of Jesus. It must be seen in the light of the transition from the old to the new age that

---

43. III:2, p. 625. Die Existenz des Menschen Jesus bedeutet aber dies, das Gott Mensch, der Schöpfer Geschöpf, die Ewigkeit Zeit wurde.

takes place in the crucifixion and resurrection. In the light of this transition, fulfilled time must be said to constitute the years 1-30. But we must never turn this about and say that the years 1-30 are fulfilled time, for then we should fail to remember that, while *Geschichte* is a predicate of revelation, this cannot in turn be a predicate of *Geschichte*.[44] Just because the life of Jesus in time is what it is in view of the crucifixion and resurrection at the end of it, there can be no direct revelation in it.

Going back further, we come to the time of the Old Testament. As Lord of time, Jesus Christ is also present in Old Testament time. The time of Jesus, the time of transition from wrath to grace, from death to life, coming to its climax in the crucifixion and resurrection, also envelops Old Testament time.[45] Therefore the difference between Old Testament promise and New Testament fulfillment must not be seen in terms of direct revelation in time. The relation between promise and fulfillment must rather be seen in terms of "spiritual contemporaneity."[46] Back of Old Testament time is creation time. This time is also enveloped in the time of Jesus,[47] for reconciliation precedes creation. In the covenant of grace God is present with man. The Christ-Event therefore envelops creation time into participation with itself. In the death of Christ all men *lose* their sinful time. They *all* lose their sinful time, because in this death God subjects himself to this time. But in his subjection of his eternal self into the sinful time of man, Christ restores to men their original time, their creation time. The total submergence of God's eternal time into created time is at once the comprehensive envelopment of all created time into participation in the pure presence of God.

If then the covenant of grace is the internal ground of creation, and creation only the external ground of the covenant, then the Genesis account of man's origin must not be directly identified with *Historie*. If such an identification were made, then the priority of Christ over Adam could not be maintained. Adam is "only apparently the first. The first is Jesus Christ."[48] Adam is Christ.[49] Sin did not have its origin by way of man's negative reaction to God's direct revelation in history. How could the transition from wrath to grace

44. I:2, p. 64.   46. III:2, p. 579.
45. II:1, p. 698.
47. *Ibid.*, p. 581. Es war dann auch die anhebende Zeit von seiner Zeit umschlossen und insofern *seine* Zeit
48. *Shorter Commentary on Romans*, p. 62 (Cf. Christ and Adam).
49. III:1, p. 229.

take place through the crucifixion and resurrection of Christ if these were direct revelations of God in history? Sin is the futile effort of man to resist the grace of God in Christ. Its defeat is therefore certain in advance. Such would not be the case if sin had taken place in terms of a direct confrontation between God and man in history. In that case there would be no true disequilibrium in favor of God's *Yes* instead of his *No* toward man. In that case the wrath of God might be more than a threat; it might then abide upon some men forever. Faith would then be no more real than unbelief. Unbelief would be something more than an impossible possibility. And the basic biblical truth that the Christ-Event is the act of *God*, the *new* act of God in having all men participate in his own internal *Geschichte*, would vanish as a dream. The idea of direct revelation in Adam is therefore a road-block that would stop the free flow of the grace of God to all men.

But we cannot stop even here. The idea of an historical Adam would destroy the proper idea of the incarnation, inasmuch as it would posit an already existent human nature that Jesus Christ would have to adopt. It would posit the idea of an abstract man, a man about whom we could learn apart from Christ. A still greater obstruction against a proper view of the incarnation lies, however, in the idea of an eternal God in himself prior to his revelation in time, in the man Jesus.

To safeguard the Christ-Event, and to safeguard both the sovereign and the objective universal character of grace, we must therefore work back of creation and remove the idea of a *Logos asarkos*. To maintain the idea of a *Logos asarkos* back of God incarnate in and identical with Jesus is to seek to block the free movement of the grace of God toward man. God does not will to be God without us. He "does not allow His history to be His and ours, but causes them to take place as common history."[50] Of course this common history must not be based on natural theology or on a general anthropology. Then we should have a cheap universality, a universality in which the priority of God over man would be lost.

God and man *must* participate in a common history. But if God is to maintain his priority in this common history, this common participation cannot be by means of direct communication. True commonness between God and man in which God is the sole giver of

50. IV:1, p. 6; Engl. tr. p. 7.

grace and man the sole receiver of grace must be indirect common-ness. It must be commonness in which Jesus Christ, not some *Logos asarkos* back of him, is the sole giver of grace and also the sole or primary receiver of grace.

The message of the gospel is centered in the Christ-Event as the Lord of time. To be the Lord of time, the eternal God of grace had to enter wholly into time. God is therefore identical with his coming into time, his submitting himself wholly unto it in order thus to be Lord over it. God *is* his work of reconciling man through his coming into time and through his making man to participate in his eternity. This entire process of the grace of God for all men would be stopped if we had to think of a pre-incarnate Christ as really existing prior to his work of reconciliation in time. "The second 'person' of the God-head in Himself and as such is not God the Reconciler. In Himself and as such He is not revealed to us. In Himself and as such He is not *Deus pro nobis,* either ontologically or epistemologically."[51] We must not speculate. We must be satisfied with believing that "according to the free and gracious will of God the eternal Son of God is Jesus Christ as He lived and died and rose again in time, and none other. He is the decision of God in time, and yet according to what took place in time the decision which was made from all eternity."[52]

But under the title of a *Logos asarkos* we would pay tribute to a *Deus absconditus* who is not at the same time *Deus revelatus.* We need a God whose eternal being of grace is wholly expressed in the new act of transition from wrath to grace for all men in time. But we should not have such an exhaustive, objective revelation of grace for all men if this revelation were not wholly hidden when wholly re-vealed. If the revelation of God's grace were a matter of direct reve-lation in history, then this grace would be neither sovereign nor universal. And the idea of a *Logos asarkos* involves a God who is wholly hidden prior to and independent of rather than in his revelation.

Once we proceed to speculate upon a *Logos asarkos* back of Christ and a God hidden prior to his revelation, we are driven on to the idea of a God *as such.* This abstract God *as such* is bound to his own being. He is immutable in the sense that he cannot at each

---

51. *Ibid.,* p. 54; Engl. tr. p. 52.
52. *Ibid.,* p. 55; Engl. tr. p. 52. Cf. also IV, i, p. 55: Wir würden unter dem Titel dieses *logos asarkos* doch wieder einem *Deus absconditus* und dann bestimmt einem selbst Gemachten Göttesbild hüldigen.

moment will his being anew. His eternity is then an attribute that prevents him from expressing his whole being in time for the reconciliation of men.

Moreover a God *as such*, being wholly hidden without being wholly revealed in Christ, has a wholly mysterious and arbitrary plan. Orthodoxy, says Barth, has such an absolute God, with an absolute plan prior to and independent of Christ. This means that for orthodoxy Christ is not the electing God. Christ is then merely an instrument for accomplishing the work of the salvation of men. And this Christ as a mere instrument may or may not be sent for the reconciliation of certain men. In fact no man can then be certain that Christ saved him. Thus the resurrection of Christ would not be what Scripture says it is, the objective foundation for the salvation of all men.

This God in himself, who is such an absolute God having such an absolute decree and such an absolute power to condemn as well as to save, has such attributes as holiness which cannot be subordinated to his grace. Unless this God sends Christ to die for certain men, the wrath of God abides upon them forever. The true biblical universalism or disequilibrium by which the *No* of God is penultimate but the *Yes* of God is ultimate toward all men can have no foundation in such a God.

Such a God in himself involves, finally, a doctrine of the trinity which is not taken from the revelation principle but from speculation. Instead of thinking of the trinity as three modes of being in which the God of grace expresses himself in Christ, the speculative notion of the trinity speaks of three persons, one of them the *Logos asarkos*, the others the Father and the Holy Spirit. The absolute decree of God, mentioned above, is, on this speculative view, the fruit of the internal deliberations of these three persons. Their existence and their deliberation is prior to and independent of their revelation of the electing grace of God in Christ.

From this survey backward, it becomes apparent what Barth means when he says that the resurrection is the fact that lights up all other facts. The resurrection must, of course, be interpreted Christologically. The Christ-Event (*das Christusgeschehen*) is self-explanatory and it alone is self-explanatory. All other facts must be interpreted in terms of this one event. All things else get their meaning from it, hence the need of actualizing the incarnation, hence the need of removing all notions of God as anything prior to his revelation of electing grace in Christ. True, the notion of a God in himself may and even must be used. But it must be used, as earlier noted, as a heuristic concept only. And this idea of the heuristic or limiting concept is itself involved in as it is an expression of the idea of God as Act.

To make the resurrection as manifestation of the Christ-Event thus determinative of all that precedes the resurrection is not merely to reject the idea of natural theology and the idea of the analogy of being but it involves also the rejection of the idea of direct revelation of God in Jesus Christ and in the Scriptures. The idea of direct revelation, whether at the point of the resurrection or anywhere else is, for Barth, a pagan idea. The eternal God of grace is always *wholly* present. Therefore he can never be directly present in time. Even when Barth speaks of the resurrection as non-eschatological, he makes plain that it must, none-the-less not be identified with any fact in *Historie*.

From the facts brought out in this and in preceding chapters, it has become apparent that Barth's battle is not merely or primarily with Romanism, nor is it with some of the excesses of orthodoxy. His central attack is on the idea of making revelation a predicate of history. According to Barth, God must always be wholly hidden even when wholly revealed in history. Revelation must become historical but history must never be revelational. Barth has never swerved from insisting on this point. His activist concept of revelation controls all his thinking.

His rejection of the *Logos asarkos*, of the God "in himself," together with all the points mentioned above, and his rejection of the "absolute plan," all spring from his activistic notion of the Christ-Event.

In order to maintain his view of the resurrection, Barth has to empty out every notion of Christ and of God that is not exhaustively expressed in his act of saving all men.

For all his effort to seek some sort of continuity for his thinking with that of the Reformers, and especially with that of Calvin, his thought is, in its basic motif, wholly destructive of theirs. Barth contends that those who do not think Christologically in his sense of the term think nominalistically and therefore subjectively. As a matter of fact, it is, as will be shown, Barth who thinks in nominalistic fashion. It is his position that is subjective and speculative. It is his position that cancels out all the revelation of God in history by the condition that God is wholly hidden even when revealed.

This is the burden of the criticism that G. C. Berkouwer makes in his first book on Barth. Says Berkouwer: "Barth and Occam, between these two there is this difference: what remained practically latent in Occam comes to expression with powerful consistency in Barth, and becomes the foundation on which the whole structure of his theology rests."[53]

Berkouwer's criticism of details is based on this fundamental charge of nominalism. This criticism is basic and to the point. At every point of God's revelation, history, its clarity and dependability, are cancelled out by Barth. On Barth's view, there is no meaning to either the threats or the promises of God. The very life, death and resurrection of Christ become worse than problematic on this basis. Barth's nominalistic principle of discontinuity between God and man leaves us nothing but a wholly meaningless or hidden God. The very objectivity and clarity of God's revelation in the resurrection of Christ is cancelled out by the condition of hiddenness in relation to which all revelation must take place.

The question between Barth and those who believe in the Bible as the clear and dependable word of the Christ who himself appeared in history without being wholly hidden there, is therefore not merely one of exegesis.

To be sure Barth engages in exegesis. And by the sound of words his exegesis may, at points, establish his contention. To be sure, those who today follow Calvin agree with Barth that no abstract God in himself, apart from Christ, elects or does not elect men to salvation. But when Barth rejects the "absolute God" with an "absolute decree" he has in mind the God of Calvin. Barth rejects the God and the Christ of Calvin in terms of the God of Occam, not the God and Christ of Occam in terms of the God of Calvin. Barth wants no God who reveals himself clearly and directly through Christ in history. His exegesis of Scripture is controlled by the *a priori* condition that the Bible *cannot* reveal such a God.

It is well therefore that we engage in exegesis. We shall then agree with Barth that election is inherently election in Christ; Christ is not the mere instrument used for the execution of the election of an arbitrary counsel made by an arbitrary God. But really to agree with Barth on such a passage as Ephesians 1:4 means to agree with him on his entire notion of the Christ-Event. According to Barth, one does not really believe in election in Christ unless one holds to his

53. G. C. Berkouwer, *Karl Barth*, 1936, p. 90.

idea that Christ is the electing God and the elected man as
Geschichte. In other words, the only thing that Ephesians 1:4 can
possibly teach, according to Barth, is that God cannot righteously
punish any man for sin eternally and that the original and only
final attitude of God to all men is therefore that of grace.

3. *Looking Forward from the Resurrection*

But, we must not only look backward from the resurrection of
Christ to its cancellation by Barth as an identifiable fact in history
in the purely nominalist idea of God, for, looking forward, we shall
find a similar cancellation, this time in terms of what is tantamount
to a rationalist or even a realist view of man's relation to God. In
terms of Barth's extreme nominalism, it is God's eternal nature to
come wholly into time. The idea of the immutability of God is thus
interpreted as including the idea that God's being consists of his
choosing himself, and man with himself, anew constantly. God endangers his whole nature in his subjecting of himself to the time of
his creature. This constitutes his humiliation. God is threatened with
non-being. But this humiliation is at the same time man's exaltation.
It is, after all, *God* who endangers himself. His victory over non-
being is therefore assured in advance. And this idea constitutes
Barth's virtual rationalism or realism. With Christ's victory over
non-being, the victory of all those that are "in him" over non-being,
is also assured. As there is no eternal divine nature prior to its manifestation in time in Christ, so there is no human nature prior to its
assumption into participation in the eternity of God. God is, says
Barth, pre-temporal, super-temporal and post-temporal.[54] That is to
say, God's eternity envelops human time. The distinctions just mentioned are within the presence of God. The pre-temporality does not
mean a time when God was not yet present to mankind in the man
Jesus. Christ as the electing God is identical with Jesus, the elected
man. So also the post-temporality of God does not mean that God
will exist without the co-presence of all men in Christ.

The heart of the matter of the relation of eternity and time is the
indirect presence of God and man with one another in Christ. God
is always both wholly revealed and wholly hidden in time. This
notion springs from a nominalist idea of discontinuity and a realist
idea of continuity. Both are present and determine one another. But

54. II:1, p. 698ff.

the nominalist idea comes out most prominently in the backward look from the resurrection to the idea of God's eternal being as the act of grace ever renewing itself in time. The realist idea comes out most prominently in the foreward look toward the absorption of all time into participation in eternity.

As there is for Barth no gradual development of the revelation of grace in past history toward the resurrection, so there is no gradual consummation of the revelation of grace in future history.

The resurrection itself does not follow in time upon the death and the incarnation of Christ. The ascension of Christ to heaven does not follow in time upon the resurrection. The second coming of Christ does not follow the first in time. If there were any direct identification of any of these steps in the exaltation in time then, according to Barth's argument, the whole of the work of Christ would fall to the ground. As any direct identification of any of the steps in Christ's humiliation would have nullified that very humiliation, so any direct identification of any of the steps in Christ's exaltation would nullify that very exaltation. Humiliation and exaltation are, for Barth, always equally present aspects of the free or sovereign and therefore universal presence of God with man. The eternal God, the God of pure duration, is the *Geschichte* of Jesus Christ. As such, God allows temporal man to participate in his own eternal *Geschichte*.

Now, according to Barth, the participation of all men in the eternity of God is at the same time the justification of all men in Christ. The coming of God into the world in time is identical with reconciliation. So also man's participation in the resurrection as *following* the incarnation is also his justification. Christ, as truly God becomes truly man in time. This signifies, for Barth, that God in Christ becomes *the* reprobate man, for all other men. But, as the truly reprobate man, he is also the truly elect, the truly obedient man for all men. Herein lies the fact of the justification of all men in Christ even in advance of their existence.

Truly to believe in election by Christ as the electing God, therefore, immediately involves, in Barth's view, the election of all men in Christ as the elected man. And the election of all men immediately involves their justification. God as Christ has judged and condemned all men in Christ as man. Christ as man has borne the condemnation and offered full obedience to God for all men.

Moreover, sanctification is involved in justification. As the holiness of God is subordinate to his grace, so the Christ as the first and chief receiver of grace secures in himself the participation in his holiness on the part of all men. The real man is the one who as sinner is the fully willing receiver of grace.[55] Man as man, as temporal, is therefore in Christ an elected creature.[56]

Thus the substitutionary death, as it is understood by Barth, is the fact that Jesus Christ is both truly God and truly man. And to be truly God and truly man Christ must wholly appear and wholly disappear to man at the same time. Thus we have a nominalist-realist view of atonement.

Berkouwer points out that it is far from being Barth's intention to minimize the "terribleness of sin."[57] In his earlier book, Berkouwer argued that Barth's nominalist view of God acted as a condition which cancelled out the genuine historic character of the revelation of God. In his later work Berkouwer points out that Barth comes to his notion of the "ontological impossibility" of sin in terms of another condition. This condition comes from the fact that, according to Barth, man is appointed "beforehand" in "the history of victory which Jesus Christ has unfolded."[58] "Sin is ontologically *impossible* because sin means a falling away from grace and it is precisely *God's primordial will* that our unfaithfulness should *not* put to nought His faithfulness."[59] Berkouwer adds: "It is indisputable that Barth's conception of the ontological impossibility of sin (and therewith the 'Christological' goodness of human nature) constitutes a decisive background of his view of the triumph of grace."[60]

Berkouwer says that Barth's notion of the ontological impossibility of sin "is unacceptable because the Bible speaks in a wholly different way about the 'reality' of sin."[61] "The rejection of the 'impossibility' of sin—in whatever form it may be posited—is immediately demanded by the reality of guilt and the alienation which it effects. If sin is ontologically impossible, a transition from wrath to grace in the historical sphere is no longer thinkable. It is clear that *this* transition is excluded when Barth, consistent with his total view, elucidates what he means by the ontological impossibility of sin by saying that sin is essentially a grasping for that 'which has been made impossible for man and against which he has also been secured.' "[62]

55. III:2, p. 36.   56. IV:1, p. 186.
57. *The Triumph of Grace in the Theology of Karl Barth*, 1956, p. 221.
58. *Ibid.*, p. 227—The quotation is from Barth.
59. *Idem.*   61. *Ibid.*, p. 233.
60. *Ibid.*, p. 231.   62. *Ibid.*, p. 234.

"When Barth speaks of chaos, mystery, enigma, shadow and *impossibility*, this last word explains all the others and forms the central category of his doctrine of sin and redemption."[63]

According to Barth, says Berkouwer, "the triumph of grace is emphatically placed *before* sin and for this reason sin is anticipated and intercepted and so made ontologically impossible."[64] But "we do not in the Bible gain the impression that the battle is all 'an emptied matter' in the sense in which Barth speaks of it."[65] "We do not find in Scripture a dimension of chaos which according to its nature is related to creation as a *rejected and not-willed* reality. Such a conception can never find a legitimate place on the basis of the revelation concerning the creation. It bears, rather, the earmarks of speculative thinking wherein the human choice of one possibility, involving the rejection of other possibilities, is transferred to God and is turned into an independent conception from which all kinds of conclusions are drawn."[66]

Barth himself says that Berkouwer is mistaken in this charge of speculation. Barth says that Berkouwer has failed to see that when we speak of grace we speak not of a principle but of Jesus Christ. When we speak of grace as manifest in Christ beforehand for all men, we are not for a moment forgetting that this grace is always an act of God and a new act of God. Is there any inconsistency in thinking of grace in Christ as always both wholly sovereign or new and wholly universal? Not at all. We find it so only if we have not really thought Christologically. The way downward, in which the eternal God is present ever anew in time, and in which the faith of man is therefore also a wholly new decision, moment by moment in time, and the way upward in which the wholly new in God and in man is controlled in advance by the wholly eternal God of grace, involve one another.

There is, to be sure, according to Barth, a disequilibrium in favor of the *Yes* over against his *No*. Barth's is a "purified supralapsarianism." Eternity envelops time, not time eternity. But eternity expresses itself through time. God's *Geschichte* works itself out as world-*Geschichte*. Thus world-*Geschichte* becomes Salvation-*Geschichte*. Man's sinful time, unauthentic as it is, is yet real as participant in God's eternity.

The mutually exclusive character of the idea of Christ and his

63. *Idem.*   65. *Ibid.*, p. 237.
64. *Idem.*   66. *Ibid.*, p. 246.

Word in Scripture as held by a Reformed theologian like Berkouwer, and the idea of Christ and the Scripture as held by Barth, is now unmistakably apparent. Berkouwer represents the traditional Reformed or Reformation view of Christ and the Bible. In the theology of the Reformation, there is a genuine "transition from wrath to grace" in history. We may, for convenience, call this the position of historic Christianity. Barth rejects this position *in toto*. Berkouwer has pointed out in his first book that Barth does this in terms of his nominalism. Berkouwer has pointed out in his second book that Barth does this in terms of his virtual determinism. We may call this realism. We shall do most justice to Barth if we keep in mind that Barth's view of eternity and time and therefore of Christ as *Geschichte*, is, in his latest writings as well as in his earliest, composed of a combination of nominalism and realism. His grace is free and sovereign, primarily in terms of his nominalism. His grace is inherently objective and universal primarily in terms of his realism. But his grace is always both sovereign and universal. This is true because his position is always both nominalist and realist.

Failure to see this nominalist-realist character of Barth's view of grace, that is of Christ as *Geschichte,* tends to make one think that Barth is often inconsistent with himself. We then may wonder why Barth's inherent nominalism or activism can allow for any objectivity or universality of grace at all. Again, we then may wonder why Barth's inherent realism can allow for any reality to the freedom of God and of man in receiving grace at all. But Barth is not inconsistent with himself in any basic way. Barth is fully consistent with himself when he maintains the certainty, the objectivity and the universality of grace while insisting that faith and unbelief are real. Since his objectivity is attained by means of an abstract principle of grace he can, naturally, do nothing else than maintain the reality of man in time in essentially negative terms.

Finally, when Barth's principle of the relation of God to man in Christ is thus seen in terms of the active interaction between an abstract and formal principle of unity and an equally abstract and formal principle of discontinuity, then we can see most strikingly why it is the polar opposite of historic Christianity. On the basis of Barth's theology, there is, says Berkouwer, no transition from wrath to grace in history. No more basic criticism of Barth's theology can be made.

Section Two

Reformed Thinkers Respond

Chapter VII

Reformed Theologians Speak—
General Criticism

It is our purpose now to listen to some of the criticisms that have been made of Barth's theology. In doing so, we limit ourselves in this chapter to Reformed theologians, and, further, we limit ourselves to general criticism. In the following chapter, criticisms on specific doctrines will be discussed.

The criticism made by Reformed theologians may well be said to find its center in the idea that, on Barth's view, there is no transition from wrath to grace in history. The lack of a transition from wrath to grace in history is due to Barth's basically nominalist-realist view of the relation of God to man. In spite of all his efforts to have God speak to man from above, Barth's view remains subjective. In other words, Barth's theology is said, in effect, to reject historic Christianity. The death of Christ on the cross is not that by which he, as our substitute, saves us from the wrath-to-come, for there is no wrath in God that could issue in man's eternal death. The resurrection of Christ is not that event in history by which Christ arises from the dead for our justification; we are already justified in Christ. Thus, there is no place in history where God and man really confront one another.

Naturally, the criticsm on Barth takes its start from the perspective of Scripture as directly identical with the Word of God. It is in this view, as noted, that theologians like Bavinck find the Christ speaking to them. The controversy between Barth and modern Reformed theologians is therefore not merely one of exegesis. To be sure, Barth does not agree with the modern theologians who say that the Bible

merely *contains* the Word of God. He says with the orthodox theologians that the Bible *is* the Word of God. In saying this, however,
Barth does not at all mean what Reformed theologians mean when
they use the same expression. For Barth the Bible must never be
identified with the revelation of God. The Bible is the Word of God,
so far as God allows it to be such, and so far as God speaks through
it. When we say that the Bible is the Word of God we express our
faith in an act of God's redemption of man in the present. The Bible
becomes the Word of God in this event and it is with respect to its
being in this becoming that the little word *is*, in the sentence that the
Bible is the Word of God, refers.[1] Since revelation is an event, any
record of it given in the past is, according to Barth, of necessity in
itself no more than a human witness to that event. Reformed theologians realize therefore that even though Barth says that the
Bible *is* the Word of God, this very expression must be seen in the
light of his activist view of revelation.

That the Reformed view of Scripture is itself imbedded in and is
an expression of Reformed theology as a whole was well expressed
by Herman Bavinck and by Abraham Kuyper. When Bavinck speaks
of Scripture, he is well aware of the "human factor" that is present
in it. Human beings with various backgrounds and gifts are its
writers. But for Bavinck this does not spell necessary error. Is not
man made in the image of God? And though he be sinful and prone
to repress the truth, has not Christ given his Holy Spirit to prophets
and apostles to guide them into all truth? And Christ himself, as
truly man and truly God, can he not speak to us in the language of
man and yet guarantee it to be the very Word of God? Christ is the
Way, the Truth, and the Life. All things were made by him. He
rules over all things. His word, the Bible, is therefore the final court
of appeal for all human speech. The inspiration of Scripture is merely
the climax of God's immanent working of the Spirit of God in the
world.[2] "In inspiration revelation reaches its climax."[3]

It is therefore from the Bible as identical with revelation that we
must begin our interpretation of all the facts of the world.

Because the Bible "is a writing down of the revelation of God in
Christ, it is bound to arouse the same opposition that was aroused
by Christ himself."[4] "The Scripture is the maid servant of Christ.

1. I:1, p. 113.
2. *Gereformeerde Dogmatiek*, I, 2 de druk, p. 449.
3. *Ibid.*, p. 451.   4. *Ibid.*, p. 465.

She shares in his disgrace. She stirs up the hostility of sinful man."[5] As for the believer, his trust in Scripture increases with his trust in Christ. He too has this hostility to Christ and Scripture by nature. For it is the mark of the "psychical man" thus to be hostile to Christ and his word. But by the grace of God the believer has learned to accept the Scripture as the Word of God even as he has learned to accept the teachings of Christ in it. He has learned to accept the inspiration of Scripture "not because he understands the truth of it, but because God tells us of it."[6]

The believer must therefore ask other men together with himself to lead all their thoughts captive to the obedience of Christ as he speaks in Scripture as his revelation. "A Christian does not believe because everything manifests God's love, but in spite of all that leads to doubt."[7] This is the proper starting-point for a Christian theory of knowledge.[8]

Abraham Kuyper presents essentially the same view as that of Bavinck. Belief in the infallible Scripture is for him, as for Bavinck, not the conclusion of a process of reasoning but the premise on which all reasoning rests.[9] God speaks directly to us in Scripture. This is true of the Old Testament as well as of the New. He who embraces Christ with all his benefits dare not reject his assertion with respect to the Old Testament that it is the Word of God.[10] With Calvin we must hold that nature must be read in the light of Scripture. The Christian cannot permit this his premise to be tested by the premise of the unbeliever. The believer interprets all things in the light of Scripture as the very Word of God. The unbeliever starts from himself as the final judge of all things, including Scripture. The two positions are mutually exclusive. The one spells light, the other darkness.

It is in the light of this background that one can understand the concern of recent Reformed theologians with Barth's view of Scripture. They would like to think of him as one who, against the subjectivism of Schleiermacher and his many followers, proclaims the Christ of the Scriptures. Does not Barth with them seek to interpret all things in terms of revelation, in terms of the Christ of God? When the consciousness-theologians thought of God as a projection of their

---

5. *Ibid.*, p. 466.
6. *Ibid.*, p. 462.
7. *Ibid.*, p. 467.
8. *Ibid.*, p. 461.
9. *Encyclopaedie der Heilige Godgeleerdheid*, II, p. 517.
10. *Ibid.*, p. 508.

own minds, was it not Barth who called upon them to be still and listen to the voice that comes from above? Was it not Barth who rejected all natural theology in order to listen to Christ alone? Was it not Barth who refused to speak even of a negative, let alone a positive, point of contact for the gospel of Christ within the autonomous consciousness of man? And was he not in all this professing to build upon Luther and Calvin and with them calling men back to the Word of God?

But herein was a strange thing. Kuyper and Bavinck said that hostility to the Scriptures as the Word of God written springs from hostility to the Christ of that Word. Barth says that if we truly love Christ then we must reject the Scriptures as the direct revelation of God. If God in Christ is to be the subject of revelation, then, Barth argues, this revelation can never be a product of and in history. Revelation must, to be sure, be historical, for Christ does really enter into history. But nothing historical can be identified with revelation!

When God is wholly revealed in history he is still wholly hidden in it. If therefore we listen to the words of the Bible as though they were, as such, directly the words of Christ we should not hear the true Christ at all. There must be no givenness of revelation (*Offenbartheit*). What Bavinck and Kuyper regarded as the highest expression of the work of the Holy Spirit, Barth speaks of as the "profane given."

Try as they would, Reformed theologians could not limit the dispute between themselves and Barth to a question of exegesis. Barth might well have the correct exegesis on certain passages of Scripture, and Reformed theologians may well have given a wrong exegesis of certain passages of Scripture. Even so, between historic Reformed theology and Barth there lies a basically different approach to the whole idea of Scripture. And with it there is a basically different idea of the Christ of the Scripture. For all his insistence that revelation must come straight down from above, has Barth really any objective revelation at all?

1. G. C. Berkouwer

As far back as 1932, Dr. Berkouwer came to the conclusion that in spite of his noble effort to outreach the subjective approach of many nineteenth and twentieth-century theologians, Barth's basic starting-point is the same as theirs.

Summing up his description of Barth's view of the relation of faith to revelation Berkouwer says: "The controlling motif in his concept of revelation is the antithesis to all direct revelation and all revelation as '*Offenbartheit*,' which finds its expression in the subjectivity of God. His faith concept corresponds to this. In order to maintain the subjectivity of God, God himself is regarded as the subject of faith-knowledge, and the effort is none-the-less made to maintain faith as an act of man. In this manner he hopes to arrive at pure objectivity—what amounts to the same-exclusive subjectivity of God, which is a victory over all subjectivism."[11]

This point is of basic importance. It will engage us again. If the human subject as it believes, is virtually absorbed by the divine subject believing in it, then the objectivity that results is bought at the expense of the authentic existence of man. We shall speak of Barth's constant seeking for objectivity by the idea of faith as itself participant in the revelation of God as his realistic or rationalistic tendency. This realist or rationalist tendency corresponds to his nominalist tendency in view of which he says that God is always wholly hidden in his revelation.

The question at issue here is a basic one. By subjectivity is meant not merely the fact that truth must have reference to a believing subject. The necessity of this is readily granted by all. But the question of subjectivism is identical with the question of where the norm of truth is to be found.[12] Subjectivism therefore signifies the idea that the believing subject finds the ultimate norm of truth in itself rather than in God.

Many modern theologians have sought to escape the charge of subjectivism in this sense of the term. They realize that with the acceptance of the pure subjectivity of the norm of truth the very idea of truth would be without meaning. Modern Protestant theologians have therefore sought for an objective norm in their various views of Christ. Romanism had charged all Protestantism with being subjective. This charge, the modern theologian feels, cannot be met in terms of a Christ speaking in an infallible Bible. This charge of Romanism must rather be met in terms of a Christ who is objectively present to man in spite of a fallible Bible. "We may therefore posit as a general principle that the absoluteness of the authority of Scripture is dropped in the whole of modern German theology."[13] We do indeed find among these theologians a very high appreciation of the

---

11. *Geloof en Openbaring in de Nieuwere Duitsche Theologie*, p. 124.
12. *Ibid.*, p. 135.   13. *Ibid.*, p. 140.

Scripture as a record or witness of God's revelation.[14] But they will not speak of an absolute authority of Scripture-revelation. "Not the question whether through the Scripture (as record or as witness) we can listen to God's revelation, but, whether in it we possess the infallible Word of God, which cannot be submitted to human criticism is the question here at issue . . ."[15] The reasons given for the rejection of an infallible Scripture are various. Scripture itself, we are told, does not speak of itself in this way. The facts of Scripture belie such a view. The contradictions in Scripture, we are told, make it impossible to hold such a view. But back of all these and similar objections is the point that this idea of Scripture is said to be in conflict with the evangelical faith.[16]

In what way then could the modern Protestant theologians find objectivity? Was not Bavinck right when he asserted that, if Scripture falls, then, for the Protestant, all authority in religion also falls? Every effort to go back of Scripture, says Bavinck, to the person of Christ, to the church, to religious experience, to reason or to conscience ends in disappointment.[17]

In seeking for objectivity in Christ without believing in the Bible as identical with his word telling of himself, the modern theologian has a difficult problem on his hands. The revelation of Christ must come into history, and yet it must not be identified with anything in history. How shall we know anything about such a Christ? "Where is the real revelation so that in spite of our dropping of the Scripture and the church we may none-the-less overcome our doubt and uncertainty?"[18]

Berkouwer says that this was a basic question for the Ritschlian theologians. Ritschl sought to overcome the subjectivism of Schleiermacher's theology. He wanted an objective revelation of Christ in history, not merely a Christ of experience. Even so, the Christ of Ritschl is largely controlled by the value judgments of the subjects believing in him.[19] So his position remains subjective still.

Later theologians in turn sought to overcome the "latent subjectivism" of Ritschl. They did so again in the interest of the "evangelical faith." They wanted again to give a true expression to the principle of the Reformation.[20] Faith must not be a mere intellectual assent to the revealed truth of God.

14. *Ibid.*, p. 141.   18. *Ibid.*, p. 143.
15. *Idem.*   19. *Ibid.*, p. 144.
16. *Idem.*   20. *Ibid.*, p. 142.
17. *Ibid.*, p. 142.

Is not this a praiseworthy endeavor? Did not Bavinck also assert the religious nature of faith against Romanism? Faith, says Bavinck, involves an attachment of the believer to the person of Christ. Is it not this that modern theologians also say when they speak of *evangelical faith*?[21] Do they not, as well as Bavinck, reject a mere intellectualist concept of faith? Are they not, as well as Bavinck, rejecting the Romanist view of faith because they believe in the principles of the Reformation?

Berkouwer soon makes plain that for all the striking similarity of words between Bavinck and the theologians of which he speaks, there is a basic difference of meaning between them. The modern theologians seek to determine the nature of revelation from the nature of faith. For them the subject therefore largely controls the object.[22] Faith is trust; revelation must therefore be that which produces trust. That, says Berkouwer, is in general the view of many modern theologians. And this, he adds at once, involves the rejection of the traditional view of Scripture. The traditional or orthodox view of Scripture is deemed to be destructive of the correlation between faith and revelation. The contents of the Bible as a whole cannot, it is said, be an object of trust. To hold the orthodox view of Scripture would therefore be, according to these modern theologians, to fall back into the intellectualist view of faith held by Romanism. We must therefore think of Scripture as a witness to the revelation that lies behind it. We must, in short, trust in an act of God in Jesus Christ that lies back of Scripture.[23] Berkouwer mentions the names of Ritschl, Herrmann, Haering, Stephan, Franck, Wobbermin, and Ihmels in this connection. With their best efforts, they cannot, says Berkouwer, give the proper place to Scripture. For these modern theologians, the correlation between revelation and faith takes place in virtual independence of Scripture.

Berkouwer seeks to do full justice to the efforts of modern theologians whereby they seek to attain to objectivity. He therefore speaks of a *latent* subjectivism in their case.[24] But these men attempt to overcome subjectivism without the idea of the inspiration of the sacred Scriptures. And this entails the subjectivization of the idea of revelation. There is no escape from this.[25]

Having come to this point, Berkouwer reviews the position of

21. *Ibid.*, p. 152.
22. *Ibid.*, p. 155.
23. *Ibid.*, p. 157.
24. *Ibid.*, p. 159.
25. *Idem.*

those theologians who speak of a religious *a priori*. He mentions Rudolph Otto and says that in his theology external revelation has no proper place.[26] The same is true of Bousset. Otto speaks of a "wholly other." He sets this "wholly other" *(neuter)* off against the reality that can be understood by rational categories. He wants to do justice to the irrational elements in the idea of God. But an appeal to an irrationalist view of God does not help to relieve the subjective nature of theology.[27] Troeltsch no less than Otto must be classed with the subjectivists.[28] The root error of every form of subjectivism is that it seeks in a more or less idealist sense to attribute to faith a power of control over revelation.[29]

There is no escape from subjectivism, says Berkouwer, other than by a return to the idea of the verbal inspiration of Scripture. So long as the subject of faith is thought of as having a productive and creative function, no justice can be done to the idea of revelation. And the more one thinks of the subject as creative, the more one becomes subject to the criticism of illusionism. This criticism was strikingly voiced during the nineteenth century by Ludwig Feuerbach. Feuerbach boldly claimed that all theology is basically anthropology. Theologians attempted to answer this charge. But, so long as they held to an idealist view of the subject as inherently creative, they could not be said to have a revelation that is more than a projection of the subject.[30] Illusionism can be overcome only if the subject who believes submits himself to the revelation of God as found in Scripture. In support of this position, Berkouwer here quotes F. W. Grosheide, who says that the ultimate question is as to who shall be the final authority in this world. Shall it be God, who gave his Word in this world, or shall it be man?[31]

Thus it is that Berkouwer, with Grosheide, holds to a view of Scripture similar to that of Kuyper and Bavinck. Only if one holds to this view of Scripture does one have the true Christ. Only if one holds to this view of Scripture does one have a truly objective revelation. Only if one holds to this view of Scripture can one escape subjectivism, projectionism, and therefore illusionism.

Berkouwer devotes a separate discussion to the theology of Karl Heim. Heim seeks to outreach the charge of subjectivism by a new conception of the subject of faith. He would replace the entire

26. *Ibid.*, p. 161.
27. *Ibid.*, p. 167.
28. *Ibid.*, p. 168.

29. *Ibid.*, p. 173.
30. *Ibid.*, p. 178.
31. *Ibid.*, p. 181.

subject-object scheme of many former theologians. We need a new ego, says Heim, one that stands wholly beyond the categories of human experience. "The solution of Heim is this, that the non-objectifiable ego is identified with God and that thus God himself is the subject of faith."[32] Thus the subject can participate in the essence-insight *(Wesensschau)* of the non-objectifiable Ego. "The subject participates in the self-consciousness of God."[33] Thus faith is an act of God. Heim admits his indebtedness to dialectical theology on this point.[34] However inconsistent he may have been at points, the main thrust of his position in his book on the problem of certainty is that the human subject must be absorbed by the divine subject.[35] According to Heim, the relation of faith to revelation must finally be interpreted in terms of the subjectivity of God. At bottom there is for Heim only one being, God, and only one ego, only one person, namely God.[36]

What then, on this view, must be said about Christ? As far as the life of Jesus is concerned, it is subject to the laws of relativism. Revelation cannot be directly identified with anything in history. Faith must therefore attach itself to Christ as above the relativities of history. Thus faith itself has a "wholly irrational nature."[37] Faith is therefore a gift of grace.

From his own point of view, Berkouwer regards Heim's idea of the absorption of the human subject by the divine Ego as a new falling back on subjectivism. And this is due to Heim's denial of the "direct revelation of God in Scripture."[38]

The question now is whether in the dialectical theology we can really speak of faith and revelation. The dialectical theologians speak much of revelation and of faith. But the question is whether the "ground-structure of their theology" permits them to give a biblical meaning to these words.[39]

Limiting ourselves now to what Berkouwer says on Barth, the following points must be mentioned. Barth wants to maintain the priority of God in relation to man. This cannot be done, he thinks, if revelation is thought of as producing a permanent and given result in history. With the idea of a *given* revelation, thinks Barth, God's priority over man is lost, for we then have an interchangeable rela-

32. *Ibid.*, p. 184.
33. *Idem.*
34. *Ibid.*, p. 185.
35. *Ibid.*, p. 186.
36. *Idem.*
37. *Ibid.*, p. 188.
38. *Ibid.*, p. 192.
39. *Ibid.*, p. 195.

tion between God and man. Man then can regard himself as in possession of a permanent and static relation to God.[40] According to Barth, a given or direct revelation involves the worst kind of subjectivism. It is a subjectivism that leads directly into illusionism.[41] Every form of a "static polarity" between God and man must, says Barth, be rejected. This can only be done in terms of the subjectivity of God.[42] Thus the essence of Barth's view of revelation appears negatively in his opposition to every form of revealedness (*Offenbartheit*), for if revelation could be found in a "given fact in our world," then revelation would be an object among objects. Faith would no longer be determined in its nature by revelation. Faith would then be determined in its nature *partly* by itself and *partly* by revelation.[43]

We must therefore think of revelation as in "another dimension than that of the given."[44] A given or direct revelation cannot be true revelation because it cannot be truly present to us. "Against this direct, given revelation Barth stresses the absolute actuality of the speaking of God."[45] Only in terms of the absolute actuality of revelation can we really speak of revelation as coming from God.[46] The idea of a direct or given revelation makes us think of the gift of God but not of God himself.[47] Is this charge correct? "On this question," says Berkouwer, "lies the cardinal difference between Reformed orthodoxy and 'dialectical theology.' . . ."[48] Barth's idea of God comes to expression in his actualistic notion of revelation. And, as in every other theology, Barth's view of God is all important. Barth's view of Scripture and of Christ is based upon, as it gives expression to, his view of God.[49]

As Barth holds to the pure subjectivity of God, so he holds to an activistic relation of God to the world.[50] Barth's actualist concept of God, and his consequent actualist concept of the relation of God to the world, excludes every form of direct revelation. "A true 'given' historical revelation is no more possible than a direct identity of the Word of God with Scripture . . . Christ no less than the Scriptures stands beneath the '*Vorbehalt*' [condition] of the speaking of God."[51]

40. *Ibid.*, p. 202.
41. *Idem.*
42. *Ibid.*, p. 203.
43. *Idem.*
44. *Ibid.*, p. 207.
45. *Idem.*

46. *Idem.*
47. *Idem.*
48. *Idem.*
49. *Ibid.*, p. 210.
50. *Ibid.*, p. 212.
51. *Ibid.*, p. 213.

God would, according to Barth, no longer be God in the face of a revelation that is given *(Offenbartsein)*.

Berkouwer's criticism of the dialectical view of Scripture therefore leads him into a discussion of the entire actuality concept from which it springs.[52] This actuality concept, says Berkouwer, is speculative in character. It introduces an idea of the relation of the creator to the creature that is not derived from Scripture.[53] On the one hand, it is said that God cannot be known except through his revelation, and, on the other hand, this revelation is construed in purely speculative terms.[54] In this Barth and Heim resemble one another. "The speaking of God in Scripture which is always a concrete speaking is pushed into the background through a dimensional speaking about the divine reality."[55] This is essentially the way of negative theology. All this is expressed in the idea of the freedom of God. It is in terms of the freedom of God that the attack is made on the idea of given revelation. But to make an attack on direct revelation in the interest of the freedom of God is in reality to deny the true character of this freedom. The denial of a 'given' revelation is nothing less than the denial of the freedom of God to give such a revelation.[56] "Not the idea of the freedom or sovereignty of God to reveal himself is incorrect, but the mistake is, that this sovereignty concept is employed, for the purpose of exchanging the absolute binding character of a 'given' revelation for an 'arbitrary' revelation of God. It seems to us to be undeniable that there is here a connection between 'actualistic' and Occamistic nominalism."[57]

With an actualist notion of revelation, there goes an actualist notion of faith. For faith must, according to Barth, be interpreted in terms of the subjectivity of God.[58] This being the case, the entire correlation between revelation and faith falls outside empirical reality. There is no more possibility of a faith as an empirical experience than there is of a revelation directly identified with Christ or the Scriptures. And here the full significance of the actuality concept that controls dialectical theology appears. "For now that no given revelation nor a human subjective possibility of revelation can be accepted the result is that one can in no sense speak of revelation, which would remain revelation *extra usum*."[59] For Barth the polarity

52. *Idem.*
53. *Ibid.*, p. 214.
54. *Idem.*
55. *Idem.*

56. *Ibid.*, p. 215.
57. *Idem.*
58. *Ibid.*, p. 217.
59. *Ibid.*, p. 220.

between revelation and faith falls outside the empirical realm. "The subject of faith-knowledge lies wholly outside the empirical subject. It is the Holy Spirit himself, who speaks *and* hears. The circle is closed. God can be known by God only."[60]

To be sure, Barth does not intend this speaking and hearing of God in an intertrinitarian fashion. Even so, the only possible result of the idea of the subjectivity of God, and of the actualistic concept of revelation, is that faith cannot be really said to be an act of man.[61] Barth does indeed say that "faith is our faith." But, when we hear Barth use such language, it is imperative that we always recall the basic condition in terms of which he speaks. Thus faith as a human act is again said to take place in the Holy Spirit. "God himself is and remains the subject of faith . . . The actualistically interpreted *con* in *concreata* has sublated the *creata*."[62]

Finally when Barth qualifies his statement about God as the subject of faith by the idea of participation, he does this lest the whole correlation between revelation and faith should be taken in intertrinitarian fashion. Without the idea of man's participation in God, the correlation between revelation and faith would be reduced to mere identity. And, to the extent that man after all has faith that is not wholly supra-empirical, we have not escaped the subjectivism he was so anxious to avoid.[63]

Thus the threat of illusionism faces all theologians who reject the finished given revelation of God in Scripture.[64] Barth's theology is therefore a new form of modern subjective theology. Barth and Brunner as well as Heim have worked out their conception of God apart from his concrete revelation in Scripture.[65] "Therefore here too the problem of Scripture is the central problem."[66] With the rejection of Scripture as the direct revelation of God goes a reinterpretation of the testimony of the Holy Spirit. That testimony is regarded as taking place beyond the experience of the empirical man.[67]

From this survey of Berkouwer, it appears clearly that for him the rejection of Scripture as the direct, given and infallible revelation on the part of Barth as well as of many other modern theologians, springs from, as it is the expression of, an actualistic concept of the relation of God and man. It is clear that the rejection of Scripture as a given and direct revelation involves, and leads to as it is the ex-

60. *Ibid.*, p. 221.
61. *Idem.*
62. *Ibid.*, p. 222.
63. *Idem.*

64. *Ibid.*, p. 228.
65. *Ibid.*, p. 232.
66. *Idem.*
67. *Ibid.*, p. 237.

pression of, subjectivism. That is, the rejection of Scripture springs from an idealist view of the human self as having determinative significance for the kind of revelation this self will accept. The inevitable consequence of such subjectivism is helplessness in the face of the charge of illusionism. One who rejects the Bible as the direct revelation of God in Christ can find no objective basis for his faith. Barth as well as Heim sought objectivity by means of the virtual absorption of the human self by the divine self. Man's faith in revelation is said to be by way of participation in revelation. But the very idea of participation is based on the principle of identification. To obtain full objectivity, Barth would need to say that it is the Holy Spirit as God who believes for man and within man as God. To the extent that in the idea of participation it is said that man himself believes, to that extent Barth falls back on the sort of subjectivism he was seeking to overcome.

In 1936 Berkouwer published a book entitled *Karl Barth*. In it he again conjoins the question of revelation in Scripture with the actualistic principle of Barth's theology. He points out that the theme of Barth's theology is that of "the freedom, the sovereignty and actuality of God in his revelation."[68] And what is the nature of the sovereignty concept of Barth? It is such as to be a "threatening background" for the idea of God's revelation in history. Occam still appealed to the direct authority of the church. Barth no longer does so.[69] Barth's concept of the freedom of God is controlled by the idea of actuality. And this implies for him the rejection of every form of a given revelation of God to man.[70] Thus "God's revelation is deprived of its meaning, when over against all that is 'given' reference is made to a deeper 'reality' of the hidden God. Respect for divine sovereignty cannot consist in our submission to the *condition* of the final revelation of God, but herein, that we honor him in the acceptance of his *given* Word."[71]

Berkouwer sets Barth's nominalist view of revelation over against that of Calvin. In Barth's view, the whole of positive revelation is "uprooted and given over to an actualist, unapproachable reality of God."[72] But such is not at all Calvin's view. Calvin has no nominalist view of God.[73] Calvin does teach that men must not seek beyond the

68. Berkouwer, *Karl Barth*, Kampen, 1936, p. 75.
69. *Ibid.*, p. 80.
70. *Ibid.*, p. 91.   72. *Ibid.*, p. 92.
71. *Ibid.*, p. 93.   73. *Ibid.*, p. 87.

expressed will of God for a reason of his doings. But for Calvin the sovereignty of God never becomes a threat that hangs above his given revelation.[74] On the contrary, the Occamist view of God with its idea of "absolute power" is for Calvin the fruit of useless pagan speculation.[75] The contrast between Calvin and Barth is complete. Calvin's idea of God is taken from the Scriptures as absolutely trustworthy. Barth has no trustworthy Scripture because he has a nominalist view of God. Barth has, says Berkouwer, a formalist view of the sovereignty of God. Through the one theme that reappears in every subdivision of his work, Barth's theology has "become the opposite of a biblical dogmatics, that is to say, a dogmatics in which there is no condition of any sort with respect to the revelation of God that is given us in Scripture and in which all dualism in the idea of God is rejected."[76]

In 1938 Berkouwer published a large work on *The Problem of Scripture Criticism.*[77] The approach in this book is similar to that of his earlier works. He again points out the fact that modern theologians have rejected the idea of a given or direct revelation in the interest of what they speak of as *evangelical faith.*[78] In this book Berkouwer discusses more fully than he did in his first work the theology of Erich Schaeder. Schaeder's work on *Theocentric Theology* marks, says Berkouwer, a high spot with respect to the discussion of Scripture. Schaeder was out to counteract the immanentism of modern theology. But to find a proper place for a God-centered theology he too found it necessary to reject the Scripture as the infallible norm for faith.[79]

Paul Althaus holds views that are similar to those of Schaeder. Althaus too engages in Scripture criticism but not primarily because he thinks that the factual situation with respect to Scripture requires it. Rather, his more basic reason is that the living Word of God could not be given us in an infallible Scripture.[80] The revelation of God cannot be directly known. There can be no clear, univocal revelation in history. Revelation comes to man in servant-form. Corresponding

---

74. *Ibid.,* p. 89.
75. *Ibid.,* p. 87. Berkouwer quotes from Calvin (*Institutes,* III:23, 2) at this point. Says Calvin, Neque tamen commentum ingerimus absolutae potentiae: quod sicuti profanum est, ita merito detestabile nobis esse debet.
76. *Ibid.,* p. 97.
77. *Het Probleem der Schriftkritiek*—Kampen, no date given.
78. *Ibid.,* p. 18.
79. *Ibid.,* p. 21.   80. *Ibid.,* p. 23.

to this view of revelation, is the idea that faith is a choice, not an acceptance of clearly revealed fact. Revelation in Scripture may, from one point of view, be regarded as characterized by contingency and error. But faith sees through and beyond this contingency and error and finds the Word of God behind the Scripture.[81] "To objectify the Scripture and to think of it as a given or direct revelation would be to deny the freedom of God, to destroy the paradoxical relation between revelation and hiddenness and between *praesens* and *perfectum*."[82]

With the phraseology employed here by Althaus, we have entered upon the question of the *existential* relation of God to man. Althaus and others sought to escape the subjectivism found in previous experience theology.

Barth thinks in terms of this existential relation between God and man.[83] More definitely than those before him, Barth therefore rejects the idea of revelation as objectified and made into a "thing" (*Verdinglichung*).

Even in the introduction to the first edition of his work on *Romans*, Barth rejoiced in the fact that he could look beyond historical critical problems to the Spirit of Scripture. This is the eternal Spirit.[84] In the introduction to the third edition of *Romans*, Barth asserted that he agreed with Bultmann with respect to the relativity of all human words, including those of Paul the Apostle.[85]

In the Scripture then, we have the words of those who are erring men like ourselves. But this fact need not in the least interfere with our idea that we must stand under the revelation that comes through the apostolic word. All the human spirits that speak in the Bible are somehow subject to the divine Spirit.[86]

Berkouwer speaks in this connection of a sharp dualism between Barth's view of Scripture and of the Word of God. There is for Barth the historical dimension and there is also the dimension of faith. Divine infallibility and human fallibility are combined in Scripture. In the volume of the *Church Dogmatics* published in 1938, I:2, Barth reaffirms this fact.[87] The infallible Word of God must be heard through the fallible witness of erring men. No systematic harmony must be sought between the historical and the

81. *Ibid.*, p. 25.
82. *Ibid.*, p. 26.
83. *Ibid.*, p. 27.
84. *Ibid.*, p. 28.

85. *Ibid.*, p. 29.
86. *Idem.*
87. *Ibid.*, p. 31.

faith aspects of revelation. To think of the Bible as a direct revelation of God would be to deny the "essence of the Word of God."[88] Barth opposes every form of "stabilization" of the Bible. The idea of a given revelation is for him an evidence of docetic thinking. The idea of a given revelation in Scripture, moreover, does injustice to the idea that the believer must participate in the revelation of God through faith.[89] Through faith we must become participant in inspiration as a continuation of the original inspiration.[90] When therefore Barth speaks of his belief in verbal inspiration, it is to be remembered that he actualizes this concept and thus fits it into his "system."[91]

For Berkouwer it is of great importance to note that, according to Barth, the idea of Scripture criticism "stands in the closest relation to the motif of the existential and actual relation between man and the revelation of God."[92] The motivation for Bible criticism that springs from scientific considerations is subordinate to that which springs from the idea that revelation is inherently an act of God. This motif "is absolute, inasmuch as it is founded in revelation itself."[93] Faith in the Bible does not exclude but includes Bible-criticism.[94]

Of special interest in this connection is Berkouwer's discussion of Barth's view of *saga* and *myth*. This involves the question of the relation of faith to the science of history. Barth rejects Bultmann's notion of myth. To speak of the biblical witness to revelation as myth is, says Barth, to cut all connection with the true idea of revelation.[95] To speak of the Bible narratives as myths is to think of them as illustrations of eternal truths.

Stressing the act character of revelation requires Barth on the one hand to reject the idea of direct revelation and, on the other hand, to reject the idea of myth. He does not object to the use of the terms saga and legend as indicating the events of revelation. For in these terms one only indicates a rejection of the direct identification of revelation with history. The use of saga and legend indicates that revelation is a special kind of history.

As for Berkouwer's evaluation of Barth's idea of a special as over against ordinary history, it is simply to the effect that it "tears apart

88. *Ibid.*, p. 32.
89. *Ibid.*, p. 33.
90. *Idem.*
91. *Idem.*

92. *Ibid.*, p. 35.
93. *Idem.*
94. *Ibid.*, p. 37.
95. *Ibid.*, p. 79.

the idea of historical revelation."[96] He says that Barth is still caught in the confusion between historical revelation and the knowability of that revelation from the point of view of unbelieving neutrality. And the problem of the relation between historical criticism is insoluble on this basis. Barth does not reject unbelieving criticism based as it is on false presuppositions. He rejects it only when this criticism takes the extreme form of dealing with the scriptural witness as a myth. Barth does not determine the meaning and useability of the ideas of saga and legend from Scripture itself.[97] He is only concerned to defend the possibility and reality of a history between God and man *(Geschichte Gottes mit dem Menschen)*.[98]

Barth has in this case again in principle broken the bond between history and revelation. He has in principle opened the way for a neutral science to reject everything that it cannot fit into its idea of an historical continuum.[99] "It speaks for itself that it is principally impossible to open the way for atheism in the historical approach to the Scriptures and then to seek to limit this atheism at a certain point *on grounds based upon a wholly different territory*."[100] Barth is quite inconsistent when he rejects the idea of myth once he has accepted the idea of saga and legend.[101] It is impossible to give over the Bible to historical criticism and still maintain the content of the Christian faith.[102] It is no marvel then that in Barth's exposition of the Apostolicum we have a striking instance of a reinterpretation *(Umdeutung)* of the virgin birth of Christ.[103] Berkouwer here refers to his book on *Karl Barth*.[104] In that work we are told that on Barth's view "there is no real connection *in* the person of Christ between the incarnation and the virgin birth."[105]

Berkouwer inserts his reference to the virgin birth merely as an illustration of the principle of *Umdeutung*. That principle applies to the other articles of the Christian faith as well as to the virgin birth.[106]

In his concluding chapter Berkouwer makes a general comparison between the position of Kuyper and that of Barth. There is a great distance between what Kuyper wrote about the servant-form of the Scriptures and what Barth writes about the *essential* prop-

96. *Ibid.*, p. 80.
97. *Ibid.*, p. 81.
98. *Idem.*
99. *Ibid.*, pp. 81-82.
100. *Ibid.*, p. 82.
101. *Ibid.*, p. 83.
102. *Idem.*
103. *Ibid.*, p. 110.
104. *Ibid.*, p. 123.
105. *Karl Barth*, p. 63.
106. *Het Probleem der Schriftkritiek*, p. 124.

erty of the Word of God, namely, that God himself hides himself and thus reveals himself *(Gott selbst sich verhüllt und eben damit sich enthüllt).*[107] "With Barth everything is controlled by the dialectical tension between revelation and hiddenness, while Kuyper speaks of revelation *pro mensura humana.*"[108] So also when Bavinck speaks of the servant-form of Scripture, this is in no wise meant to detract from the divine character of revelation. Christ too appeared in servant-form. Yet he was sinless. So the Scripture, for all the presence of the human factor, is none-the-less the perfect Word of God.[109]

It appears then that according to the arguments of the three books discussed, Barth's rejection of the traditional Reformed doctrine of Scripture entails his reinterpretation along activistic lines of all the articles of the Christian faith. In these works it is the nominalistic character of Barth's theology that is stressed. Nominalism cuts the nerve between revelation and history in any form. It cuts the nerve between revelation and the human nature of Christ. For the same reason it cuts the nerve between revelation and Scripture. Such is Berkouwer's main contention.

But his criticism is not limited to the nominalist character of Barth's theology. Criticism of what we have called the realist aspect of Barth's theology is not lacking even in these earlier works. Barth's vain search for objectivity by means of virtual absorption of the human subject into the divine subject is but a futile effort to escape from the consequences of a consistently applied nominalism into the abstract unity of Platonic realism. Here again the nerve between revelation and history is cut.

The fact that this is the case is brought to the fore in Berkouwer's later book on Barth, *The Triumph of Grace in the Theology of Karl Barth.* Only one all-important illustration of this criticism can here be cited. It pertains to the question of sin and its nature in relation to the all conquering grace of God in Christ. According to Barth, it is a foregone conclusion that sin cannot in the case of any man lead to eternal punishment. Says Berkouwer of Barth's position on this point: "Our being in Adam stands in advance *(zum vornherein)* in the light of the fact that we are in Christ."[110] "Only *apparently* can we recognize Adam as our head." The triumph of grace is therefore of an *a priori* nature. It is correlative to the ontological impossibility of sin. "This impossibility is *raised above all*

---

107. *Ibid.*, pp. 360-361.
108. *Ibid.*, p. 361.
109. *Ibid.*, p. 355.
110. *De Triomf der Genade* etc., p. 80.

doubt in the pre-figuration of the creation triumph."[111] Again the nerve between revelation and history is cut. We are here "confronted with ideas that lie on a totally different plane from that of Scripture when it tells us what God is not."[112] On Barth's view of impossibility, "there is no transition from wrath to grace in historical reality."[113]

In concluding this section on Berkouwer, it is well to contemplate afresh the serious nature of his criticism on Barth's theology.

In modern German theology, Berkouwer contends, the subject of faith has been thought of as having a productive and a creative function. This led to subjectivism and illusionism. In refusing to return to the Bible as the direct and infallible Word of God, Barth's position too is subjectivist. His effort to find objectivity by the idea that faith itself participates in revelation did not help matters in the least. To seek for objectivity in this fashion is virtually to pay tribute to an identity philosophy. It is only by an inconsistency, that is, by saying that man's faith *merely participates in* but is not identical with revelation, that Barth escapes the identification of the human subject with the divine.

Berkouwer speaks a good deal of the nominalist view of Barth's concept of revelation. He speaks of its actualist character. He speaks of the dualistic distinction Barth makes between the realm of history and the realm of faith. He says that Barth thinks in terms of an existential relation between God and man. It is not our purpose now to seek to relate these points to one another. Suffice it to note that for Berkouwer they all rest on the basic point of subjectivism which leads to illusionism. In the last analysis, one must take his idea of revelation in Christ from Scripture as the direct expression of that revelation or one has to project his Christ from his own self-sufficient self-consciousness.

It is therefore in line with Berkouwer's criticism to say that two mutually exclusive views of Scripture involve two mutually exclusive views of Christ, and therewith of God and of man. And only the Christ of the Scriptures rather than the Christ of Barth can save us from subjectivism and illusionism. With all due credit to the influence of the Scriptures and of the Christ of the Scriptures upon Barth's work, it must still be set diametrically over against the Scriptures and the Christ of Reformed theology and of historic Christianity.

111. *Ibid.*, p. 82.
112. *Ibid.*, p. 215.

113. *Ibid.*, p. 228.

2. Klaas Runia

Klaas Runia wrote his doctoral dissertation on *Theological Time in Karl Barth*.[114] He deals more particularly with Barth's anthropology.

Runia's approach to Barth's theology is similar to that of Berkouwer. After giving a broad survey of the theology of the *Church Dogmatics* and its general teaching, Runia remarks about its magnificence and its newness. On account of these we might be tempted to be carried away with it, or again, we might be tempted simply to reject it. But there is really only one thing that we can do. We must measure the dogmatic results of Barth's thinking by the "message of Scripture."[115]

Runia begins with Barth's view of the resurrection of Christ. The resurrection of Christ is, according to Barth, not a step that follows upon the death of Christ in time. But, says Runia, in Scripture the resurrection is precisely that. In denying that the resurrection is a second step, namely, a step of exaltation which begins at this point, Barth does injustice to the succession of God's works of redemption in history. Barth reduces the resurrection to the final moment of a revelational dialectic, a moment in which this dialectic has come to rest because it is sublated.[116]

The Bible speaks of a revelational history in which the redemptive acts of God follow one another. Barth's discussion of the resurrection is "too timeless." We must reject Barth's "unscriptural construction" of the resurrection.[117] This unscriptural construction of the resurrection springs from Barth's concept of revelation. Can we escape the impression that in Barth's theology revelation stands dualistically over against time?[118] Does revelation, according to Barth, really enter into our time, i.e., datable time?[119]

How about Barth's view of original time? In connection with it, Barth speaks of unhistorical history *(unhistorische Geschichte)*. This kind of history can be spoken of only in terms of saga. "Here a contrast is posited that is not found in Scripture. The Bible speaks constantly of creation as an historical happening, indeed incomprehensible to our thought, but none-the-less 'historical,' as the begin-

114. *De Theologische Tijd by Karl Barth*, Franeker, 1955.
115. *Ibid.*, p. 39.
116. *Ibid.*, p. 44.
117. *Ibid.*, p. 46.
118. *Ibid.*, p. 49.
119. *Ibid.*, p. 48.

ning and source of later history."[120] Barth simply excludes the *"status integritatis* as historical reality."[121]

We may also ask about Barth's view of revelation time, the time of Jesus Christ. Barth does, indeed, say that this time includes ordinary time. But he immediately adds that revelation time differs from all other time. Revelation time is prior to all other time. It is God's time.

Can we then, asks Runia, still call this *real* time? When Barth says that this revelation time is both God's time and our time he again engages in a dialectical construction that finds no support in Scripture. And this dialectic involves reality as well as knowledge.[122] Barth claims that in the *Church Dogmatics,* if not in his *Romans,* he has done justice to the apostle John's statement that the Word has become flesh. But, says Runia, we have the impression that the man Jesus is really taken out of time and eternalized.[123] In the end we see only "eternal time which has absorbed ordinary time, even though the latter is formally maintained."[124] In contrast with this, Runia argues, in the Reformed view of the incarnation time is not taken up into eternity. On the Reformed view the Son of God adopts time and fills it with divine redemption.[125]

Controlled as he is by his unbiblical view of revelation, Barth does not hesitate when it suits him to make Scripture say exactly the opposite of what it actually says. So in Galatians 4:4, Paul speaks of the fulness of time *"as an objective event,* which is the condition of the sending of the Son by the Father." Runia quotes Grosheide on this point. Grosheide says: "Paul wants to call attention to the fact that Christ came when according to the plan of God the time for this had come."[126] Paul therefore does not at all say that "in the time of the man Jesus time *as such* became fulfilled time. . ."[127] When Barth discusses the time of the man Jesus he uses the notion of contemporaneity. But the New Testament knows of no such idea.[128]

Again and again Runia's criticism of Barth is to the effect that Barth's dialectical view of the relation of revelation to time is not seen in the biblical perspective of the history of salvation.[129] Barth

120. *Ibid.,* p. 52.
121. *Ibid.,* p. 53.
122. *Ibid.,* p. 54.
123. *Idem.*
124. *Ibid.,* p. 55.

125. *Ibid.,* p. 59.
126. *Idem.*
127. *Ibid.,* p. 60.
128. *Ibid.,* p. 70.
129. Cf. the whole of Chapter II.

has a *Christo-monistic* vision. And "every *Christo-monistic* conception involves a principial mis-forming of the biblical message. It does injustice to the theocentric starting-point (creation) and to the theocratic purpose (the Kingdom) of the history of this world."[130]

In terms of Barth's notion of revelation, Scripture cannot tell us of a direct revelation of God at any point in history. Sin cannot be the transgression of a direct revelation of God in history. Through his idea of the Nihil, sin is made much more of a riddle than it was before. On the other hand, an "illegitimate relativizing" of sin takes place because it is thought of as overcome in Christ.[131]

In short, Runia's criticism of Barth, dealing more directly and exclusively with the problem of the relation of eternity to time, is essentially the same as that of Berkouwer. There is, on the one hand, Barth's emphasis on the hiddenness of revelation in time. There is, on the other hand, the idea that when God is revealed he is wholly revealed. This finds expression in the grace-objectivism in which man with his time is taken up into the eternity of God.

We have here, as in Berkouwer, both the charge of virtual nominalism and the charge of virtual realism. Berkouwer charged Barth with holding to a nominalism that cancels out the actual presence of God with man in history both by way of commandment or by way of promise. Runia does the same. Berkouwer charged Barth with holding to an objectivism that would, if carried through consistently, lead to an identity philosophy. In effect, Runia does the same.

In criticizing this type of theology, Runia assumes that the Bible is and gives a direct revelation of God in history. His entire notion of redemptive history as identified with events in datable history presupposes the idea of Scripture as direct revelation. The idea of Scripture as direct revelation and the idea of redemption directly identifiable with facts of history stand or fall together. Barth's Christo-monism constructed from both nominalist and realist materials requires the rejection of both.

Runia no less than Berkouwer seeks to place the best possible construction on many passages of Barth. Even so, both find that, according to Barth, there can be no transition from wrath to grace in history, and that the Bible does not, because it cannot, tell us that there is such a transition.

130. *Ibid.*, p. 221.   131. *Ibid.*, p. 137.

3. Klaas Schilder

On the question of Scripture and its relation to Barth's theology in general, the name of Klaas Schilder cannot be omitted. Schilder died March 23, 1952. At the time of his death he was engaged in the writing of a detailed exposition of the Heidelberg Catechism.[132] In the first three volumes and in the incompleted part of the fourth volume Schilder deals in a penetrating fashion with many modern theologians. And among them none has received more attention than Barth. One thing is central in this work, as in all of Schilder's other works, namely, that the deepest line of division in theology lies at the point where some believe and others do not believe in Scripture as a direct revelation of God. And with it goes the fact that those who believe in Scripture at the same time and in the same act of believing hold to direct, factual revelation of God through Christ in history.

There is nothing that Schilder stresses more than that those who are Christians hold their position by faith. And the object of this faith is Christ as he speaks directly to them in the Scripture. Everything that confronts man in this world must be seen in the light of one's faith.[132a] Says Schilder: "In the last analysis everything depends on the trustworthiness of Scripture."[133]

There are, Schilder says, two views of the significance of wrath and grace; there is the biblical and there is the mystical view. The biblical view sees God and man as standing in person-to-person confrontation everywhere in history. It is the view of the covenant. Adam was created perfect. He loved God above all else. But he wilfully sinned against God and was driven out of paradise.[134]

Mystics have a totally different view. Sin and grace, the fall and the resurrection, and life and death are no longer questions of right relations of the creature to God. On the mystic view they are questions of power and of moral strength.

At this point Schilder discusses the "theology of the cross." This theology of the cross, or dialectical theology, has nourished itself upon such movements as mysticism and existentialist philosophy.[135] Thus it is not likely that the dualism found in these positions will be

---

132. *Heidelbergsche Catechismus*, Goes, 1947 (This work will be referred to by volume number only.)

132a. I, p. 196.

133. *Ibid.*, p. 205.

134. *Ibid.*, p. 206.

135. *Ibid.*, p. 213.

overcome by it in the near future.[136] By this dualism Schilder refers to the idea that the world is not created and controlled by God and therefore allows for no renovating influence through redemption by God. In accordance with this dualistic relation of God and the world, Christ's coming into the world was not necessitated by the historical fall of man. By the term Christ this theology means only that there is above the dimension of space, time and death, a higher dimension of life and revelation. This higher dimension does not depend on the historical appearance of Jesus Christ; on the contrary, the historical appearance of Jesus Christ depends on it.[137]

We must, says Schilder, set a biblical theology over against the "theology of the cross" as well as over against mysticism and existentialism. We do so not on philosophical grounds. We do so by the prejudice of faith (geloofsvooroordeel).[138] "We simply believe in the historicity of the paradise because the Bible speaks of it as an historical reality."[139]

In holding to the historical character of paradise, and therefore of the fall of man, we can also believe in an actual or real restoration of the world by the victory of Christ over Satan. This work of Christ is then a real "breakthrough" of victory in the world in which we live. In denying the historicity of the fall, the theology of the cross also devaluates with it the work of redemption.[140] He who destroys the biblical doctrine of creation has also, in effect, destroyed the true view of sin and redemption. All heresies flow together in a common rejection of the biblical view of creation and the fall, and, with it, in a common rejection of the biblical view of redemption. On these points Barth and those whom he opposes meet one another.[141] We must hold on to the simple biblical statement which declares that when God *had* created all things he said that they were *very good*. Therefore we must have no Manicheanism, no gnosticism and no theology of the cross.[142]

It is well known that Barth speaks of orthodox theology as a theology of possession. Orthodoxy, argues Barth, claims to have a direct revelation of God and therefore claims to control God. Orthodoxy is, according to Barth, in effect, an attack on the freedom of God.

136. *Idem.*
137. *Ibid.*, p. 212.
138. *Ibid.*, p. 215.
139. *Idem.*

140. *Ibid.*, p. 219.
141. *Ibid.*, p. 220.
142. *Idem.*

Schilder rejects this charge. We must indeed look, back of creation and the fall, to God and his plan. But we do not do this in terms of philosophy. We must look upon the eternal counsel of peace because Scripture as the "clear" revelation of God tells us to do so.[143] Our very idea of the Christ as mediator must be taken from Scripture as the clear revelation of God and therefore lead back to the counsel of peace. If we did not do this, then, as Calvin said, God would have played a game with us.[144] The very constitution of the mediator between God and man is rooted in the counsel of God the Father, God the Son, and God the Spirit.[145] To fail to find this constitution of the mediator in God's counsel is to construct a mediator of our own devisings. A mediator taken from Scripture as the direct revelation of God reveals God directly and clearly. The mediator taken from Scripture, and only such a mediator, brings atonement through satisfaction.[146] For only this mediator can take the place of man without displacing man.

The reader will note how, according to Schilder, the Christ of the theology of the cross and the Christ of the Scripture cancel each other. In this immediate context Schilder speaks of Brunner rather than of Barth, but the ideas of a theology of the cross are common to them. They are expressed in the notion that God is wholly hidden in Christ even when he is wholly revealed in him. And this Christ, Schilder says, is not according to the Scripture.[147] Do we want absolute indirectness? Schilder answers: "No . . . absolute directness."[148]

If we are to know who either God or Christ is, we need to have the direct revelation of Scripture. The same holds true for man. What man is is determined by the creative and directing will of God. And we can learn about this, not from a speculative study of man, but only from the direct revelation of God in Scripture. From it alone do we learn of God's address to man. From it alone we learn of the covenantal relation in which man stands to God.[149] God determines the nature of every creature with reference to the task in history that he has for that creature.[150]

If we are to understand the mediator to be true God and true man, and if we are to understand the nature of his work as mediator, we must learn about man as well as about God from the direct

143. II, p. 111.
144. Idem.
145. Idem.
146. Ibid., p. 123.

147. Idem.
148. Idem.
149. Ibid., p. 132.
150. Ibid., p. 150.

revelation of Scripture.[151] The mediator must be both true God and true man, and he must also be righteous man. In the work of atonement, God must be the subject throughout. *Christ* reconciles us, not because he takes the initiative over against God, nor do we reconcile ourselves with God, but it is God who reconciles us with God, and he does this in Christ.[152] God plans and elects the mediator. As true man, the mediator must therefore be spotless and pure. Only thus can he be the substitute for other men, and bear for them the wrath of God, as well as merit for them eternal life. No beginning of the work of salvation could be made for men without such a righteous as well as such a true man.

Moreover, only when we take our idea of God and of man from the direct revelation of Scripture can we see that the mediator between God and man constitutes a simple unity. And only then can we see that his work of reconciling man is not a piecemeal affair. Reconciliation is the work of the person of the mediator everywhere and all the time.[153] Thus God, who alone is the subject of reconciliation, reconciles man to himself through the mediator constituted as true God and true man by himself. And only thus can we see that while the plan of reconciliation is eternal with the triune God, the constitution of the mediator is reality in history.[154] Thus also we can see that the shedding of his blood on Calvary for the remission of the sins of his people is the climax and conclusion of his work of reconciliation.[155]

Schilder sets forth his view of Christ as the true God-man and of his work of reconciliation in conscious opposition to Barth. He stresses again and again the truth that the facts of the history of redemption can be seen for what they are only in the light of the direct revelation of Scripture. We dare not first conceive an idea of the history of redemption and then read the Bible in the light of it. Facts do not explain one another. Facts of one series do not explain facts of another series.[156] We need to go to Scripture as the direct revelation of God to hear about God, about man, and about the God-man and his work. If we do not thus go to Scripture, then we have another God, another man, and another God-man. Such is Schilder's argument throughout. Forsake the direct revelation of Scripture and you also have a false idea both of the first and of the

---

151. *Idem.*
152. *Ibid.*, p. 167.
153. *Ibid.*, p. 184.

154. *Ibid.*, p. 211.
155. *Ibid.*, p. 229.
156. *Ibid.*, p. 264.

second Adam. Follow Scripture and the second Adam is as "reportable" as is the first. Christ is the second Adam as being reportable.[157] One can only speak of Christ as the second and as higher than Adam if both are placed in the same level of history.[158] Of course, to see this requires faith.[159] Only by the power of the Holy Spirit can we accept the Christ of the Scriptures and the Scriptures as the Word of Christ. The promises of the gospel in the Old Testament and the fulfillment of those promises in the Christ of the New Testament take place in the same dimension, the dimension of ordinary history. They take place in history as itself under the direction of God through Christ his Son.

Again, only on this view of Scripture and of Christ do we have the proper idea of the sovereignty of grace.[160] For then we do not, with Barth, subordinate the righteousness of God to his grace.[161] Due to his unbiblical subordination of the righteousness of God to grace, Barth also virtually rejects the biblical idea of sin.[162] He virtually denies that there is a "seed of the serpent." He does so in the interest of a preconceived idea of universal love. O shades of Schleiermacher![163]

Schilder's idea of the clarity of Scripture and of the teachings it contains is anything but a deductive system.[164] God's speech is one. There is one message in the Scripture. It is the message of the grace of God to sinful men. But our understanding of that message is quite another matter. In the nature of the case, we cannot fathom the depth of the simplicity of God. Reformed theologians have therefore not attempted a definition of God which was supposed to help man understand this simplicity. But, just because of their principle of direct revelation in Scripture, they have been quite harmonious in rejecting every speculative view of Christianity. If we are to say something positive about the simplicity of God, then we must do this on the basis of the direct revelation of God through Christ in the Bible. Over against this, Barth speaks of God's simplicity in dialectical or speculative terms.[165]

In effect, Schilder is here making the charge of nominalism against Barth. To say, as Barth does, that we can say nothing positive about

157. *Ibid.*, p. 337.
158. *Ibid.*, p. 338.
159. *Ibid.*, p. 339.
160. *Ibid.*, p. 392.
161. *Ibid.*, p. 399.

162. *Idem.*
163. *Ibid.*, pp. 399-400.
164. III, p. 52.
165. *Ibid.*, p. 88.

God even on the basis of his direct revelation in Scripture is, in effect, to seek to penetrate the essence of God by telling us what God cannot be. Thus the foundation is taken away from every true revelation of God to man in history through Christ. Such a position involves the notion that God is free to cancel the laws and promises that he himself has given to men.[166] Creation has for Barth, says Schilder, little more than a limiting significance.[167] He rejects the idea of any, even a Christian world-view.[168] With his theory of limit, Barth has taken every possible *real border* from us.[169] Barth has disallowed the possibility of a direct revelation of God. This disallowance is based on his dualistic distinction between the world of revelation and the world of history. Thus he has left us with a "symposium of tautologies."[170]

But if Barth is virtually a nominalist, can he help but be also virtually a realist in his view of God? In Barth's view, the *Nihil* has an independent, albeit negative, power over against God. Schilder means that for Barth sin did not come into the world by the disobedience of Adam as a perfect creature of God, for the Nihil is something apart from such a rebellion. In consequence, the freedom of God is not complete with respect to it.[171] God's election is, on Barth's view, no pure action but in part reaction.[172] His whole idea of election is therewith reduced from the ethical to the metaphysical level. Neither reprobation nor election any longer means anything like what Scripture says they mean.[173] Rejecting the orthodox idea that God has a plan with the world, Barth now virtually makes God subject to a program or universal principle that is above himself.[174] Barth takes up the Nihil into a "process of unity."[175] In all this, Barth will not submit himself to the true mystery of the plan of God in relation to creation and evil.[176] We hold to the biblical view of the mystery of God for no other reason than that Scripture teaches it.[177] The wisdom of God is unfathomable to men, just because they *find* a situation. We must have no God who *finds* a situation. We must have no God who is confronted with a mystery that surrounds him as well as man.[178] The God of Scripture is the source of all possibilities; he is not subject to abstract possibility above him.[179]

166. *Ibid.*, p. 90.
167. *Ibid.*, p. 283.
168. *Idem.*
169. *Ibid.*, p. 285.
170. *Ibid.*, p. 283.
171. *Ibid.*, p. 371.
172. *Idem.*

173. *Ibid.*, p. 373.
174. *Ibid.*, p. 375.
175. *Idem.*
176. *Ibid.*, p. 379.
177. *Ibid.*, p. 437.
178. *Ibid.*, p. 476.
179. *Ibid.*, p. 477.

The general approach of Schilder's criticism on Barth's theology is therefore the same as that of Berkouwer and Runia. It is to the effect that once one forsakes the idea of direct revelation of God in Christ and therefore in Scripture, one is left with a speculative reduction of the main biblical teachings. The real transaction between God and man then does not, according to Barth, take place in history at all. History becomes a mere appendage to some vague spiritual realm of free personality. And objectivity must be sought by means of the virtual absorption of the human person or subject into the divine subject. Schilder adds that the divine subject is itself subordinated to an abstract principle above itself. Barth's theology is basically a non-biblical theology because its very doctrine of the Bible is constructed in terms of a concept of revelation that is itself a false philosophical construct.

Chapter VIII

Reformed Theologians Speak—
Special Doctrines

In the previous chapter, three outstanding modern Reformed theologians were allowed to express their basic criticism with respect to the problem of Scripture and its chief message. In the present chapter, these and other Reformed theologians will be cited in their criticism of Barth on certain specific doctrines of Scripture. The difference of approach in the two chapters is not absolute. Even in the previous chapter, certain doctrines were discussed. So, in the present chapter, differences with Barth on special doctrines will be expressed because they are found to be unscriptural. The fact, however, that the idea of Scripture cannot be discussed without a discussion of special doctrines and vice versa is clear indication of the fact that the rift between Reformed theology and Barth's theology is basic.

1. Revelation

Barth's view of revelation has come up for discussion from time to time in the previous chapters. The idea that when God is revealed to man he is wholly revealed and that in this exhaustive revelation of himself God is at the same time wholly hidden is in itself a seemingly baffling notion. Light has been thrown on its meaning by the fact that this view of revelation was found to be opposed to the traditional Protestant view of the direct revelation of God in history. Yet, how explain the fact that it is precisely by his

146

activist view of revelation that Barth seeks to oppose Romanism? Must we with Barth reject the idea of direct revelation in order effectively to oppose natural theology?

a. A. D. R. POLMAN

In a four-volume work on the Belgic Confession Dr. A. D. R. Polman, professor of Dogmatics at the theological seminary in Kampen (Oudestraat), the Netherlands, discusses the question of revelation. Let us examine his comments with respect to the second article of the Belgic Confession of Faith, which article reads as follows:

"We know him by two means: First, by the creation, preservation, and government of the universe; which is before our eyes as a most elegant book, wherein all creatures, great and small, are as so many characters leading us to contemplate *the invisible things of God,* namely, *his eternal power and Godhead,* as the apostle Paul says (Rom. 1:20). All which things are sufficient to convince men and leave them without excuse. Secondly he makes himself more clearly and fully known to us by his holy and divine Word, that is to say, as far as is necessary for us to know in this life, to his glory and our salvation."[1]

Is this article written in the spirit of Calvin? Must we hold to it in the face of modern theology, and especially in the face of the theology of Barth?

Polman answers the first question by briefly setting forth the view of Calvin on revelation. Calvin, he says, lays great stress upon the self-evident clarity of the revelation of God in his works. These works include not only nature in the narrower sense of the term but also the maintenance and government of the world. God shows his grace and mercy in history. The fact of God's providence is patent in the world. The revelation of God, moreover, is as clearly present within the constitution of man himself as it is in the facts of his environment. Even after the fall of man, God's revelation to him is clear. Polman quotes Calvin on this point. Says Calvin, "It must be acknowledged, therefore, that in each of the works of God, and more especially in the whole of them taken together, the divine perfections are delineated as in a picture, and the whole human race thereby invited and allured to acquire the knowledge of God, and,

---

1. *Onze Nederlandsche Geloofsbelijdenis,* Franeker, no date. Vol. I, p. 144.

in consequence of this knowledge, true and complete felicity."[2] According to Calvin, there is a direct and clear revelation of God in every fact of the universe. Man cannot excuse himself by holding that this revelation is hidden. The fact that man does not respond to this revelation properly is due to his ethical perversion. Though the world be a theatre in which God's face stands before man ever so clearly, man is so perverse that he sees in the world only the face of man-made deities.[3] The natural or non-regenerate man seeks to suppress the truth of God as it stands before him. By the use of his reason, apostate reason that is, as he exercises it upon the revelation of God, the natural man never comes to the knowledge of God. Man is spiritually estranged from God. Standing in the middle of light, he does not see.[4]

Since then the sinner reads nature and history so mistakenly, the only means by which he can learn to know God effectively and existentially is through Scripture. Scripture, says the confession, reveals God, "yet more clearly and more fully" than does nature. Fallen man needs Scripture with its message of redemption through Christ even in order to understand general revelation in nature and providence aright. This is not due to lack of clarity in general revelation. It is due to the darkness of the human mind. This darkness can only be removed by Christ and his Holy Spirit.

If then the second article of the Confession is read in the light of the theology of Calvin, it can be seen not to contain any natural theology at all. There is great stress in Calvin on the clarity of both general and biblical revelation. There is also a great stress in Calvin's theology on the blindness of the mind and the hardness of the heart of all men as the result of their fall into sin. These points together exclude the Romanist notion of natural theology altogether. Calvin met Romanism in terms of the idea of a clear revelation of God which is misread by the natural man because he has become blinded through his sin. Romanism posits a lack of clarity in revelation. According to Romanism, there is no self-evident clarity found in it. This gives man a measure of excuse if he does not find God there. On the other hand, if he does find God there, it is to man's credit since he has done well in the reading of revelation about him.

In a book entitled *The Dogma of the Church*, each of a number of Reformed theologians writes an article on one of the doctrines

---

2. *Institutes*, I:v:10. Henry Beveridge translation.
3. Polman, I, p. 149.   4. *Ibid.*, p. 152.

of the Christian Faith. Polman contributes an article on "The Revelation of God."

In this article he first speaks of *fundamental revelation*. All revelation is by a voluntary act of God. The God of the Bible has nothing in common with philosophical constructions, such as the Absolute, the One, Being or the Eternal.[5] In contrast to them all God reveals himself to man. Of course, God does not exhaustively reveal himself to man, since man is finite. But though God is not exhaustively comprehensible to man, he is truly known by man. There is an ability in man to observe the eternal majesty and power in the works of God's hands. The object of knowledge, God's revelation, and the subject of knowledge, man the knower, are adapted to one another. Yet, no natural man truly reads the revelation of God. This is due to his sinful blindness.[6] Man may and does indeed have some vague notions about God's presence round about and within his own constitution.[7] If man is to have a true knowledge of his sin, he needs to know about the Christ of the Scripture. Yet the revelation of God through Christ in Scripture builds upon the revelation of God in his works of nature and providence. He who denies the clarity of the general revelation of God undermines at the same time one of the great presuppositions of the gospel.[8] Special revelation builds upon this fundamental revelation.[9]

At this point Polman informs his readers about Barth's violent rejection of what he calls fundamental revelation.[10] Among many other points, Polman deals with Barth's exegesis of Romans 1. According to Barth, this chapter does not teach "what the church has always read in it."[11] According to Barth, Paul did not teach the presence of a revelation among men before Christ. In reply to all of Barth's criticism of fundamental revelation, Polman says: "We cannot accept this criticism. It stands in plain conflict with what God himself reveals to us." So in Romans 1 "the difference between Paul and Barth is plain."[12] With the apostle, the revelation of God through his works, the vague knowledge thereof by every man, the repressing of this truth in unrighteousness, and the judgment of wrath, precede the revelation in and through Christ.[13] Barth rejects

5. *The Dogma of the Church*, p. 32. Groningen, 1949, p. 82.
6. *Idem.*
7. *Ibid.*, p. 83.
8. *Ibid.*, p. 84.
9. *Idem.*
10. *Ibid.*, p. 85.
11. *Ibid.*, p. 86.
12. *Idem.*
13. *Idem.*

the idea of a fundamental revelation in the works of God's hands. He confuses natural theology and fundamental revelation. "These two must not," as Barth constantly does, "be identified."[14] To hold to fundamental revelation in no wise commits one to the idea of synergism. The history of mankind begins with paradise. We have torn ourselves loose from God. But God continued to do us good and to reveal himself to us. Everything about us and within us continues to speak of him. But we have ignored his voice. When God in Christ draws us back and receives us as his children again, then he is not an Other. God then opens his heart to us as never before. "Barth knows not this progress. He wrings everything into a Christo-monism (God reveals himself alone in Christ), which does not do justice to the facts of Scripture."[15]

From this point on, Polman then sets forth the Reformed view on special revelation. This special revelation finds its completion in the Scriptures. "Many times revelation and the writing down of the same coincide."[16] Jesus accepted the Old Testament as one unity and as having one message, namely, that pertaining to himself. He makes no distinction between historical and religious ethical truths. His whole attitude toward Scripture is that he submitted himself to it as he did to God.[17] "The Spirit of the Lord does not accept our faults, ignorance, mistakes, and errors. The Bible is truly a human book, but this does not include fallibility."[18] At this point Polman returns to Barth and says: "With holy determination, therefore, the view of Barth—to limit ourselves to him—with respect to Scripture, must be rejected."[19]

Having thus set the Reformed doctrines of revelation and of Scripture over against the false views of Barth, Polman makes a final remark about the closing of the canon. This brings him to the question of the relation of God's providence to his revelation as given in Scripture. Barth holds that, though for God the canon of Scripture is closed, we as men must allow that possibly writings not now found in the Bible should eventually be added to it. Says Polman on this: "Over against this we place with the fathers of the days of the Reformation the idea that God himself in his fatherly care has so directed that all which in reality belongs in the canon has actually been taken into it."[20]

14. *Idem.*
15. *Idem.*
16. *Ibid.,* p. 91.
17. *Ibid.,* p. 93.

18. *Ibid.,* p. 102.
19. *Idem.*
20. *Ibid.,* p. 109.

Summing up, it may be observed that Polman has briefly brought out the following points:

(1) The Reformation principle, as set forth by Calvin, involves the idea of direct and clear revelation of God in all the facts of the universe.

(2) It is man's sin that makes him unable to perceive this revelation for what it is. These two points exclude rather than include the Romanist idea of natural theology.

(3) Man needs special revelation through Christ and the Scriptures on account of the fact of his sin against God, whom he has already met. And this special revelation builds upon the fact of fundamental revelation.

(4) The Scriptures form the climactic expression of the special revelation of God in Christ. To interpret all things in the light of Christ is therefore to interpret them in the light of the final direct revelation of God in the Bible.

(5) The providence of God itself, now interpreted in the light of Christ and the Scriptures, must be regarded as making available to man the direct revelation of God in Christ.

These points are, of course, involved in one another. They are meaningless unless taken together. And taken together they stand squarely over against Barth's view of revelation and of Scripture. These in turn are but the expression of the whole of Barth's point of view.

b. G. C. BERKOUWER

In his series of dogmatic studies, Berkouwer has a book on *General Revelation*. In it he speaks of Barth's offensive against the idea of natural theology. Involved in the idea of natural theology is that of "the reality and the character of the revelation of God."[21] It is well known, says Berkouwer, that Barth's approach to the question of revelation is Christo-centric.[22] According to Barth, revelation takes place only in the pure presence of God in Christ's work of reconciliation.[23] Revelation comes to man, says Barth, through "Christ alone." When we examine what he means by this, then it appears not to be unfairly described as Christo-monism.[24]

According to Barth, the "main line" of teaching in Scripture is

---

21. *Algemene Openbaring*, Kampen, 1951, p. 14.
22. *Ibid.*, p. 15.
23. *Ibid.*, p. 18. 24. *Idem.*

revelation in Christ. Is there also, asks Barth, a second or secondary line of teaching in Scripture?[25] Certainly not in the sense that there is previous to Christ a revelation of God in the cosmos. When Psalm 19 tells us that the heavens declare the glory of God, this idea is read into the cosmos. In itself the cosmos is dumb.[26]

For a moment we might think, says Berkouwer, that Barth means the sort of thing that Calvin means when he compares special revelation with glasses through which general revelation must be read. But we soon discover that the two are not at all the same. Calvin holds to an objectively present revelation of God in the works of his hands, which man does not perceive properly because of his sin.[27] With Barth the situation is entirely different. An objective knowability of God through created reality which, according to Calvin, always bears the traces of its Creator, is rejected by Barth. But for Calvin this knowability exists.[28] Calvin refuses to determine the nature of revelation from the point of view of the subjective reaction.[29] Calvin speaks of man's blindness and deafness, but this does not for him detract from the reality of the revelation.[30] The guilt of man's ignorance of God appears precisely from the fact that he is confronted with an actually present revelation.[31] Barth's exegesis of Romans I is basically different.[32] His "offensive against natural theology is at the same time a denial of 'general' revelation."[33]

From Barth's point of view, the idea of general revelation, as well as the idea of natural theology, constitutes an attack on the exclusiveness of the grace of God in Christ.[34] "For Barth *general* revelation and *natural* theology are inseparably united. The root idea of Barth's violent attack lies in the fact that he considers them to be on the same plane."[35]

Berkouwer points out in this connection that it is because of this identification of natural theology and general revelation that Barth is violently opposed to the second article of the Belgic Confession.[36]

From what we have learned from both Polman and Berkouwer, it is clear that, in effect, Barth rejects the Reformation principle of direct revelation as vigorously as he rejects the Romanist view of

25. *Ibid.*, p. 21.
26. *Ibid.*, p. 22.
27. *Ibid.*, p. 23.
28. *Ibid.*, p. 23; Engl. tr. p. 23.
29. *Idem.*
30. *Idem.*

31. *Idem.*
32. *Idem.*
33. *Ibid.*, p. 25; Engl. tr. pp. 32-33.
34. *Ibid.*, p. 25.
35. *Ibid.*, p. 26; Engl. tr. p. 33.
36. *Ibid.*, p. 25.

natural theology. This analysis is in accord with the earlier analysis given by Berkouwer of Barth's activist or nominalist view of God. This fact corroborates the general statement of Berkouwer, earlier recorded, that the basic principle of Barth's theology is opposed to the basic principle of Reformation theology. The Reformation view of direct revelation is, according to Barth, destructive of the grace of God in Christ. Finally, this analysis corroborates the earlier conception of Berkouwer's to the effect that Barth's position starts, after all, with the human subject as ultimate. Earlier, Berkouwer said that, despite all of Barth's efforts to escape the subjectivism of modern theology, he is a subjectivist still. In the present connection, Berkouwer again points out that Barth determines the nature of revelation from the point of view of the subject. In the former case, Barth's subjectivism was shown to lead to illusionism; in the present case, it is shown to be opposed to Reformation theology, and with it to the true biblical idea of revelation.

2. Providence

The question of general revelation leads on directly to that of providence. According to Calvin, it is in the works of nature and history that the general revelation of God appears.

a. G. C. BERKOUWER

In 1950 Berkouwer published a book on *The Providence of God*. In it he points out that a bliblical doctrine of providence is not natural theology.[37] We must obtain our doctrine of providence from Scripture. It is only through faith in Scripture that we can have full assurance of the fact that God through Christ rules over all in the works of his hands.[38] This, says Berkouwer, was really the position of both Bavinck and Kuyper.[39]

But the fact that our knowledge of providence must from the beginning be tied to our knowledge of Christ through the Scripture must not lead us to accept Barth's approach. Barth says that there is no revelation of God except in the period of the years 1 to 30. But whoever says this subjects the Scripture to prejudicial notions and cannot escape a "Christo-monistic theology."[40] When in Romans 8

37. *De Voorzienigheid Gods*, Kampen 1950, p. 39.
38. *Ibid.*, p. 54.
39. *Ibid.*, pp. 44-47. 40. *Ibid.*, p. 51.

Paul speaks of God's providence, there is no condition or threat that overhangs God's promises.[41]

Barth rejects the Christ who speaks directly to man either in the works of nature or in Scripture. To believe in this Christ, is, according to Barth, in effect, to believe in natural theology and in a self-constructed Christ.

Rejecting direct revelation in the interest of his Christology, Barth gives an allegorical interpretation of Genesis 1 and 2 in its account of the creation of the world.[42] He therewith does injustice to the sinless creation of the world.

Barth's allegorical interpretation, furthermore, of origins fits in with his Christo-monistic theodicy. Barth seeks to explain the idea that God permits sin. In doing so, he does not respect the impenetrable mystery of the acts of God.[43] Barth speaks of the justification of creation without recognizing the distinction between what was true before and what was true after the historical fall of man.[44] All creation must, according to Barth, be seen from the beginning in the light of the death and resurrection of Christ.[45]

It is clear, says Berkouwer, that Barth's theodicy is quite different from that which Scripture gives. According to Scripture, the wrath of God is manifest in the world because of the sin and guilt of man.[46] This fact can be understood only from the point of view of the forgiveness of sins that those who are in Christ enjoy. Christ bore the curse of God for them. From the point of view of the actual forgiveness of sins through what Christ did for them on the cross, it is impossible to construct a theodicy in abstract terms.[47] Men seek to flee the judgment of God by their speculatively constructed theodicies.

As for Barth's theodicy, though it is not to be identified with that of Leibniz and others, it is nonetheless quite different from that which is found in Scripture. Barth is not concerned with the confrontation of the world with the righteousness of God. He wants to see the world "in the light of the *love* of God."[48] We therefore have to trace his view of theodicy back to his teaching on the attributes of God. "In this teaching the love of God dominates in a peculiar

41. *Idem.*
42. *Ibid.,* p. 65.
43. *Ibid.,* p. 167.
44. *Ibid.,* p. 290.

45. *Ibid.,* p. 291.
46. *Ibid.,* p. 314.
47. *Ibid.,* p. 312.
48. *Ibid.,* p. 316.

way over righteousness and grace over wrath."[49] "In so doing Barth *seems* to be doing justice to the biblical message of grace as given in Scripture. But the manner in which Barth speaks of the yes and the no of God, which led him to such dangerous consequences in his doctrine of election, shows that he speaks differently about God's grace than Scripture does. Barth is concerned with a new order of grace which has been raised up among men through the reconciliation and election in Christ and in which all men participate. Unbelief is then nothing but the folly of the denial of this unexpected "factum of the *universal love* of God."[50] Barth's doctrine of providence is bound up with his doctrine of election. Therefore everywhere that he speaks of judgment, this is always "merely the *reverse* side of grace."[51] Berkouwer brings out here what he has elsewhere spoken of as the Christological rather than the natural goodness of man. In cutting his theodicy loose from the historical fall of Genesis, he arrives at a theodicy which is anti-Scriptural. "Barth's speculative theodicy is in complete contrast with that of Scripture."[52] "The message of reconciliation is *proclaimed* in the world not as an objective communication of a new *state of affairs* but with appeal to faith."[53]

What Berkouwer asserts here is in accord with what he said under the heading of general revelation. There he showed that the Reformation view of objective revelation in history is, from Barth's point of view, a denial of the grace of God in Christ. What Berkouwer says here is also in accord with what he said before, namely, that there is in the theology of Barth no transition from wrath to grace in history. The two conceptions of grace, the one held by Reformation theology and the other held by Barth, stand over against one another. The Reformation view is based on the objective facts of Christ's death and resurrection in history and on the objective interpretation of those facts by the Christ of history as he speaks by his Spirit in the Scripture. Barth can find no evidence of God's wrath in history. He makes certain that there can be no such wrath by his purely speculative subordination of the righteousness of God to his grace. After that he has clear ground for his universal salvation in Christ.

Berkouwer points out, of course, that Barth seeks to qualify his

49. *Ibid.*, p. 317.
50. *Idem.*
51. *Idem.*

52. *Idem.*
53. *Ibid.*, p. 316.

universalism. This does not take away the fact that Barth's view of providence, and his view of theodicy involved in it, is, in the judgment of Berkouwer, destructive of the historic Christian view.

3. Creation

a. A. DE BONDT

Another writer who compares the Reformed and the Barthian views of divine providence is Dr. A. de Bondt. He does so in an article on "Creation and Providence" in *The Dogma of the Church*.

A biblical view of providence, says de Bondt, goes with a biblical view of creation. And a proper view of creation cannot be obtained unless we think of the Genesis account of origins as telling us what really happened. Man can of himself know nothing of the origin of all things, but God tells him about it in his revelation.[54] "God revealed his own work. This revelation he had written down. We find this in Genesis 1 and 2."[55] "Genesis 1 and 2 does not give us human phantasy, but divine revelation."[56]

According to Barth, however, Genesis 1 and 2 do not report history at all.[57] According to Barth, Genesis does not speak of an actually existing condition.[58] The Chaos of which Genesis speaks is, thinks Barth, only a *possibility* which God *passed by*.[59] God intends to produce a certain type of reality. Accordingly, he rejects every possibility which conflicts with this reality.[60] Genesis tells us, says Barth, about the Chaos which God passed by because it conflicted with the reality he intended to produce. God rejects the impossible world of the absurd. In Christ God liberates the world from this Chaos.

All this, says de Bondt, is the fruit of speculation, not of exegesis. Genesis does not speak of a shadow that falls upon the created world. Barth wants to make Genesis say something other than what it really says.[61] Genesis speaks of an actually existing Chaos, while Barth speaks of a mere possibility.

54. *The Dogma of the Church*, Groningen, 1949, p. 198.
55. *Idem.*
56. *Idem.*   59. *Idem.*
57. *Ibid.*, p. 197.   60. *Idem.*
58. *Ibid.*, p. 220.   61. *Idem.*

4. Sin

a. A. DE BONDT

Dr. de Bondt discusses the problem of sin immediately after that of creation. Again he assumes that only from Scripture as the direct revelation of God can we obtain information on this point.

What is sin? It is man's rebellion against God-imposed limits. Sin is lawlessness.[62] Sin leads away from God and leads toward destruction. Man was created as the image of God. But this image of God was lost through sin.[63] Genesis 3 gives us the sad story of the entrance of sin into the world.[64] De Bondt takes the narrative of the fall, as well as the narrative of creation in Genesis, as an account of what really happened in history. De Bondt then takes up Barth's view of the image of God in man. On Barth's basis, man has not lost the image of God for the reason that he never possessed it.[65] Barth begins with the man Jesus. Only in communion with Jesus can other men be said to be made in the image of God.[66] Therefore, against Barth, we must maintain that Adam was the image of God.[67] God did not create man as a neutral being. Man was created good. This is, says de Bondt, the basis of the biblical idea of grace in Christ. Barth lacks this foundation for the biblical view of grace.

b. G. C. BERKOUWER

Berkouwer works out Barth's Christological interpretation of man more fully than does de Bondt in his book, *Man as the Image of God.*[68]

According to Barth, says Berkouwer, Christ does not participate in an already existing human nature. We participate in human nature because Christ first participates in it.[69] In Jesus it appears what being a man really means. It means being together with God. Therefore, other men exist as men in their participation with the man Jesus. Accordingly, men cannot sin and in spite of that still quietly retain their manhood.[70] Godlessness would destroy manhood. But

---

62. *Ibid.*, p. 269.
63. *Ibid.*, p. 270.
64. *Ibid.*, p. 267.
68. *De Mens het Beeld Gods,* Berkouwer, 1957, J. H. Kok, Kampen, 1957.
69. *Ibid.*, p. 94.

65. *Ibid.*, p. 271.
66. *Idem.*
67. *Ibid.*, p. 272.
70. *Idem.*

God cares for man. Since manhood is togetherness with God, it is impossible that godlessness should separate man from God.

But the particular point to note here is that man's essence is what it is through the "a priority of grace." Manhood is retained in man through grace.

What is to be said about this? Is it wrong to say, as Barth does, that we must not seek to understand man apart from his relation to God? Of course not. Barth's criticism on the idea that man is an "animal *ratione praeditum*" is quite to the point.[71]

Berkouwer's point here is similar to what he and others have made with respect to natural theology. Of course Barth is right in rejecting natural theology. Reformed theology also rejects natural theology. Berkouwer is quite willing to reject the idea that man has certain qualities apart from his relation to God in Christ. But Barth's negative criticism on the idea of man's existing independently of his relation to God proceeds from a positive foundation. This positive foundation rests ultimately in his Christology.[72] According to Barth, we participate in the human nature of Jesus. He does not participate in ours but we in his.[73] That is the important starting-point. But if we read such passages as Philippians 2 and Hebrews 2, we see that the reverse is maintained. Scripture speaks from the point of the actual fallen estate of man. It then speaks of the astounding fact that the Word became flesh among sinful men.

Barth, on the contrary, formulates his doctrine in the opposite direction.[74] He says that we receive our nature wholly from Jesus. Barth puts the matter this way because he wants to maintain that man's nature is what it is primarily because of the grace-relation that it sustains to God through Jesus.[75] "The essence of man is to be exclusively seen in the light of the a priori triumph of grace."[76] And since the image of God in man is expressed in this relationship of grace in Christ, it cannot be destroyed.[77] "The 'essence of man' is his standing in grace."[78]

At this point Berkouwer contrasts Calvin's and Bavinck's method of determining the nature of man as the image of God with that of Barth. Calvin and Bavinck deal with the incarnation from the point of view of the guilt and fall of man. Thus they remain within the

71. *Ibid.*, p. 95.
72. *Ibid.*, p. 96.
73. *Ibid.*, p. 98.
74. *Idem.*

75. *Idem.*
76. *Idem.*
77. *Idem.*
78. *Ibid.*, p. 99.

limits of biblical thinking. By way of contrast, Barth begins with Jesus of Nazareth. This leads him with inner necessity into ways of speculation. He then thinks of the relation of man to God as inherently and immediately a relation of grace.[79] It is this relation that forms the background and content of Barth's anthropology. It is the same concept which leads him to hold that the law is a form of the gospel and wrath a form of grace.[80]

Earlier in this chapter, it was shown that, according to Berkouwer, Barth rejects the idea of general revelation because he thinks it virtually constitutes an attack on the inclusiveness of the grace of God in Christ. In the present work, Berkouwer shows that, according to Barth, the belief in the historical fall also constitutes an attack on the true idea of grace in Christ. The difference between Calvin and Bavinck, on the one hand, and Barth, on the other hand, is again shown to be one as deep as is possible. These are two mutually exclusive views of grace competing with one another. And this difference rests upon a basic difference in the view of God implied in both of these positions. For Calvin and Bavinck, God reveals himself directly in history. All history is a direct revelation of God. In the beginning of history, man was created perfect. Then, at a date in history, man fell into sin. He was after that subject to the wrath of God, and this wrath will lead him into eternal perdition. But God sends his Son into the world to bear the wrath of sinners for them. Those who by his Spirit, which is also the Spirit of Christ, believe in him will be saved forever, and those who refuse to believe will be under the wrath of God forever.

For this biblical approach, Barth substitutes the idea that there is no wrath of God resting upon man as the consequence of his disobedience to a directly revealed will of God. Thus there is no guilt that is the consequence of the disobedience of man to the will of God before the coming of Christ. In consequence, grace and forgiveness of sin is not given to men on the basis of what Christ Jesus suffered and did directly in history. Grace is rather something that is built into the very nature of man. Sin is therefore, for Barth, an ontological impossibility. We have earlier seen that Berkouwer characterizes this view of sin as involved in Barth's idea of grace as speculative and as involving the fact that there is on that basis no transition from wrath to grace in history.

---

79. *Ibid.*, p. 100. 80. *Idem.*

Barth's view of sin as something that is in advance destroyed by the grace of God requires the rejection both of the biblical view of sin and of the biblical view of grace. There is no transition from sin to grace in history in Barth's theology. And his views of both sin and grace are, it becomes increasingly clear, imbedded in and in turn permeate the whole of his theology.

5. Election in Christ

In the preceding section, it appeared that Reformed theologians object to Barth's view of sin as an ontological impossibility. In rejecting this view of sin, they also reject Barth's view of grace as that which in advance virtually makes sin to be of no effect. And this idea of grace has its foundation in Barth's view of man's election in Christ. Let us briefly note what some Reformed theologians have to say about Barth's view of election in Christ.

a. K. G. IDEMA

In *The Dogma of the Church,* Dr. K. G. Idema discusses this question. He does so in a section that forms a sub-division of an article on "The Counsel of God."

God's counsel is free, says Idema.[81] It is the source of all created things. As free, this counsel is unchangeable.[82] Does this spell determinism? It does not.[83] God made man a responsible being. Man and man alone is responsible for sin. Even so, this sin does not take place independently of the counsel of God. Acts 2:23 teaches that the crucifixion of our Lord happened according to the determinate counsel and foreknowledge of God. Yet those who crucified him are said to be wicked men for having done so.[84] Can we understand the relationship of the will of man to the counsel of God? Not at all. We simply confess what Scripture teaches.

At this point, Idema goes on to bring Christ and his work in relation to the counsel of God. Of course, everything that he has said so far was based on the word of Christ in the Scripture. But now he points out that, according to Ephesians 1:9, 10, God plans to bring all things into unity through Christ Jesus. The purpose of God's counsel lies in that which he intends to do in Christ Jesus. To believe

81. *The Dogma of the Church,* K. G. Idema, p. 162.
82. *Idem.*
83. *Ibid.,* p. 163.   84. *Ibid.,* p. 164.

in the counsel of God is therefore not an abstract belief in God's control over all things. It is from the outset a belief in the electing grace of God in Jesus Christ.[85]

It is as such that the doctrine of election may be said to be the heart of the gospel. It is at this point that God's truth appears in its deepest incomprehensibility. Yet here faith finds its final rest.[86]

With what adoration believers repeat the words of Paul from Ephesians 1:1-12. They rejoice in the fact that they have been elected in Christ before the foundation of the world unto good works.[87] With deepest awe, they listen to Paul as he bewails the fact of the stubborn unbelief of his fellow Israelites. But even human unbelief cannot make the promises of God which are in Christ Jesus of no effect. If it could, then the whole of God's electing grace in Christ would disappear. For all men have sinned. For that reason, the decree of God includes the idea of reprobation. And the decree of election and that of reprobation are one decree of God's sovereignty.[88] The Lord Jesus himself, in the same act in which he proclaims the gospel of the kingdom and the love of the Father, fulfills the judgment of hardening on the unbelieving Jews by hiding himself from them.[89] Scripture teaches that there will be an eternal blessedness and an eternal damnation. Believers realize that they are saved for eternal life because their sin, their unbelief, is overcome through the electing grace of God in Christ. And if this fact of the grace of God in Christ is to stand, the reverse side is also true. The final destiny of all men is ultimately in the hands of God.[90]

Idema is quite willing to admit that Reformed theologians have sometimes spoken too scholastically about election and reprobation. "Election was sometimes separated too much from Christ and from the promises of the gospel. Then it would be considered too much as something by itself, as an eternal fixed decree of God with respect to election on the one hand and reprobation on the other hand."[91] When that was done, believers did not simply rely on the promises of God's grace in Christ but reasoned deductively about their belonging or not belonging to God from the idea of election in the abstract. The result was discouragement, pride and passiveness.[92]

When Barth therefore stresses the fact that all election is election

85. *Ibid.*, p. 165.
86. *Ibid.*, p. 166.
87. *Idem.*
88. *Ibid.*, p. 167.

89. *Ibid.*, pp. 167-168.
90. *Ibid.*, p. 168.
91. *Ibid.*, p. 171.
92. *Idem.*

in Christ, we can only agree with him. We want no scholasticism of any sort. But whether this agreement is one that pertains merely to words or also to content, remains to be seen.

At this point, Idema reviews briefly the main features of Barth's "purified supralapsarianism." According to Barth, God's election of grace is his act of self-determination. God wants to be *for* his creatures. His election is the beginning of all God's ways and works. All God's works are therefore *per se* works of grace. This is true of creation, of reconciliation and of redemption. This is also true of sin, death, the devil and hell. These too are works of God, that is, of his negative or denying will.[93] Through all the stadia of creation, sin and atonement, God realizes one all-inclusive act of governance. There is no break in history that is due to sin. The whole of history stands in the sign of the struggle between sin and grace and of the victory of the latter over the former.[94] In Christ God takes his own reprobation upon himself and gives his creatures his election of grace. The glad message of salvation that must be proclaimed to all men is therefore "God has in Christ taken your rejection upon himself and has elected you."[95] Through unbelief man can bring the threat of eternal punishment upon himself but not eternal punishment itself.[96] The destiny of the reprobate therefore lies not in his own reprobation but in the fact that he is a witness of the reprobation that has been borne for him by Christ.

In his final evaluation of Barth's view of election in Christ, Idema does full justice to Barth. Many biblical emphases, he says, have come to expression in Barth. Barth is against the view of the Remonstrants. He is theocentric and Christocentric. He has rightly stressed that we must not separate our own election from Christ. Barth is right in saying that there must be no coordination between election and reprobation.[97] For a moment we might be tempted to accept Barth's purified supralapsarianism. But when all is said and done, we must none-the-less reject Barth's view entirely. If we accepted it, we should set ourselves above the simplicity of Scripture. Using the language of Scripture, Barth none-the-less says something wholly different from Scripture.[98] Barth speaks of a self-distinction in God that obtains form in space and time. This is not biblical language; it is speculation. Barth says that God cannot reveal him-

93. *Ibid.*, p. 173.
94. *Idem.*
95. *Ibid.*, p. 174.

96. *Idem.*
97. *Ibid.*, pp. 175-176.
98. *Ibid.*, p. 176.

self without evil also coming to expression. This is in direct contra-diction to the simple sense of Scripture when it says that God saw all that he had created, and behold it was good. Barth seeks to give a sort of explanation of sin. Since sin is, according to Barth, necessarily involved in the revelation of God, he cannot accept a state of rectitude in the simple historical sense. In his doctrine of election Barth uses scriptural terminology but teaches anti-scriptural meaning.[99] Barth's view of election in Christ is no election at all, for it pertains universally to man as man. Even reprobation is, according to Barth, in Christ. In contrast with this, Scripture says that many are called but few chosen; he who does not believe is judged al-ready. And that these words are laden with the absolute weight of eternity, of that Jesus, and the epistles of the apostles, as well as the revelation of John, give earnest witness. According to Scripture, reprobation means to be outside Christ, and this totally, subjectively and objectively. Scripture knows nothing of a reprobation that stands under the control of election. "To be sure God uses both sin and the hardened sinner in the service of the counsel of his grace but the sinner himself stands outside this grace. Jesus speaks of Judas as the son of perdition, who was lost, a devil, and that it had been better if he had not been born or had sunk into the depth of the sea."[100] Barth takes away the seriousness of such words.

Involved in his denial of the biblical teaching of everlasting pun-ishment is Barth's identification of the promises of salvation with the decree to save. Thus the promise is the proclamation of the decree that God elects the reprobate and that his election triumphs over reprobation.[101]

Of special interest at this juncture is what Idema adds on the question of Barth's universalism. According to Barth, the election of God is not a definite and final determination of the lot of his creatures. In the last analysis, it is not a question of men being elected but of God's act of electing. The question is not one of a definite effect of the will of God. It is rather a question of the mani-festation of the will of God.[102] But Scripture speaks of God's will as producing certain effects. It does not leave us in the dark on the question whether all men shall be saved. It is certain, according to God's decree, that there will be an eternal salvation and an eternal woe. Moreover, from eternity God knows those who are his and

99. *Ibid.*, p. 178.
100. *Ibid.*, p. 181.
101. *Ibid.*, p. 185.
102. *Idem.*

from eternity he has not known others. Barth does injustice to the teaching of eternal damnation.[103] "It is fantastically unscriptural to say that 'pre-destination' does not indicate a separation between men, but rather their deepest union."[104] Barth makes a "titanic effort to think as God." He therewith overreaches his own power and sets aside the revelation of God.[105]

b. C. TRIMP

In 1954 the Reverend C. Trimp published a book dealing with the question of Christian comfort.[106] In this book Trimp dealt first of all with a publication of Dr. J. G. Woelderink on the subject of pre-destination. In doing so, Trimp also took up Barth's doctrine of election.

Woelderink accepts the central point of Barth's doctrine of election and defends it as scriptural.[107] Barth is said to be the great rejuvenator of Reformed theology with his idea that Christ is both the electing God and the elected man.[108]

In not making Christ the subject of election, Reformed theology has, says Woelderink, often torn God and Christ apart. And since Jesus is the elect man, all men are elect in him.[109] God has rejected himself and so man cannot be rejected.[110]

Here Trimp, like Idema, brings out the point that Barth does not want to teach universal salvation as the inevitable effect of the election of all men in Christ. Men are simply to witness to what happens in Christ. Trimp calls this entire construction a gigantic effort to use Reformed terminology in order to express wholly unreformed ideas.[111] We have in Barth's view a "monstrous emptying-out of all Reformed teaching."[112]

In Barth's doctrine we hear nothing of the scriptural teaching that Christ Jesus came to shed his blood for his people. We hear nothing of the sheep whom the Son has received from the Father and whom no one can pluck out of his hand. In Barth's theology, the passage of Acts, that as many believed as were ordained to eternal life, is meaningless. Here the power of the high-priestly prayer of Christ for his own and not for the world is lost in theory. Here we have no

103. *Ibid.*, p. 186.   105. *Idem.*
104. *Ibid.*, p. 189.
106. C. Trimp, *Tot Een Levendige Troost Zijns Volks*, Goes, 1954.
107. *Ibid.*, p. 22.   110. *Ibid.*, p. 28.
108. *Ibid.*, p. 23.   111. *Ibid.*, p. 29.
109. *Ibid.*, p. 26.   112. *Ibid.*, p. 32.

room for the words of John 3, "He that believeth on him is not condemned: but he that believeth not is condemned already, because he believed not in the name of the only begotten Son of God."[113]

Election and reprobation are but pawns in Barth's game of dialectically related concepts.[114] When Barth says that his views are Christological, we ask him what he means by the term Christ. And then we discover that his Christ is nothing more than a concept by means of which he gives a Christological color to his "philosophical operations."[115]

Woelderink's mistake in seeking to combine the Barthian and the Reformed view of election springs from his failure to see the scheme of Barth's theology as a whole.[116] He should have tested Barth's basic concepts and rejected them instead of merely guarding himself against the more extreme consequences of his view.[117]

Does this strong condemnation of Barth's doctrine of election derive from one who himself holds an extreme view? Does Trimp perhaps believe in an abstract God of absolute power who elects and reprobates men apart from Christ? Does he perhaps think of Christ as simply the instrument through whom the absolute counsel of an absolute God is brought to execution? Does Trimp wish to ignore the promises of grace in Christ and appeal directly for his comfort to a God beyond Christ? Nothing of the sort.

Trimp exegetes Ephesians 1:4 and satisfies us on these points. The decree of election, he says, in no sense takes place apart from or prior to Christ.[118] Nor do we know anything of the decree or counsel of peace except through Christ. Paul tells us that the election of God takes place within the relationship of Father, Son and Holy Spirit (Eph. 3:11). In Christ God purposed the gathering together of all things in Christ (Eph. 1:10). Trimp refers here to the exegesis of S. Greydanus. Greydanus says that God's sovereign and gracious election took place before the foundation of the world, that is, in eternity. But it took place then not apart from but in the closest possible relation to Christ, and those who are elect in Christ and will be purified and saved by him are from eternity elect with him.[119] "We may not separate in any wise between Christ and

113. Idem.
114. Ibid., p. 33.
115. Ibid., p. 34.
116. Ibid., p. 35.

117. Idem.
118. Ibid., p. 42.
119. Ibid., p. 43.

those that are given him of the Father."[120] Christ is the mid-point of everything. In him the counsel of God has its coherence, its root and its goal.[121]

For Trimp the difference is therefore not at all in that Barth wants to stress the idea of election in Christ and he himself does not. Both men stress the central and controlling place of Christ in election. But Trimp says that the Christ of Barth is a Christ of human construction, while the Christ he is setting forth is the Christ of Scripture. These two Christs are exclusive of each other. The Christ of the Scriptures saves men from the wrath of God and from eternal punishment. For Barth there is no wrath of God except as a form of grace, and so his Christ saves no one from eternal punishment. The Christ of the Scripture, however, does not save all men from eternal punishment. The Christ of Barth, if he may be said to save any man at all, saves all men to participation in himself.

As was the case with Idema, so it is also with Trimp. Trimp too is willing to admit the fact that some Reformed theologians have separated the election of and in Christ from the counsel of peace preceding it. Ephesians 1:4 does not justify any such distinction.[122] Election is an act of the Father, the Son and the Spirit, in their internal communication with one another.[123] But Barth does not thus bring Father, Son and Spirit together in the counsel of peace. He thinks of the idea of the counsel of peace as being nothing more than mythology.[124]

The Reformed doctrine of election has no God of "absolute power" which arbitrarily elects certain men and rejects others apart from Christ.[125] The truth is quite otherwise. It is Barth's Christ that is the product of construction rather than of biblical exegesis. The Synod of Dort had no nominalist notion of a will of God to which a second decision of God had to be added in order to connect election properly with the love of Christ.[126] On the contrary, it is only in the idea of the counsel of peace that a truly Christ glorifying doctrine of Christ finds its root. Denying the Christ of the Scriptures, the Christ who saves men from the wrath of God to come, Barth naturally also rejects the counsel of peace which gives the foundation of the salvation that Christ effects for men.

120. *Idem.*
121. *Ibid.*, p. 44.
122. *Ibid.*, p. 47.
123. *Ibid.*, p. 48.
124. *Ibid.*, p. 49.
125. *Ibid.*, p. 61.
126. *Ibid.*, p. 62.

c. G. C. Berkouwer

In 1955 Berkouwer published a book on *The Election of God*. In this work, he makes plain that Calvin rejected the idea of absolute power, *"potestas absoluta,"* as the source of election. Calvin rejects the idea of *potestas absoluta* as being of scholastic origin. But to reject the idea of an arbitrary power is not to place a law above God himself.[127] God's power must not be separated from his righteousness and holiness. In the idea of God's sovereignty, Calvin expresses the idea that the righteous and holy God is a law unto himself. Calvin maintains the perfection of all of God's properties.[128]

Bavinck follows Calvin in this respect. We must not, argues Bavinck, seek beyond the will of God for the ground of all things. But this does not mean that with Duns Scotus and especially with Occam we hold to a merely formal idea of freedom, one in which the will of God is separated from all his perfections.[129]

If one has a merely formal, that is, a nominalist idea of the freedom or sovereignty of God, then one cannot understand the simple biblical statement that God cannot deny himself.[130] On the basis of this formal idea of the power of God, the certainty and the dependability of his revelation is jeopardized.[131] Paul tells us that neither height nor depth can separate us from the love of God which is in Christ Jesus our Lord. This is the depth of the *wisdom* of God. The idea of pure contingency is utterly opposed to this.[132]

In his work on *Karl Barth*, as earlier noted, Berkouwer pointed out that Barth's nominalism was much more extreme than that of Occam. The point of particular importance for Berkouwer was that Barth's nominalism cancelled out the dependability of God's revelation of grace to man in history.

In the work now under discussion, Berkouwer asserts that Calvin is anything but nominalistic in his view of the will of God. Calvin learns about the will of God from the Scripture as the dependable revelation of God to man.

Thus Calvin and Barth stand squarely opposed one to another. There is, of course, a formal similarity between them. For both the will of God is the last court of appeal for man. But Barth interprets

127. Berkouwer, *De Verkiezing Gods,* Kampen, 1955, p. 61.
128. *Ibid.,* p. 62.
129. *Ibid.,* p. 63.   131. *Ibid.,* p. 66.
130. *Ibid.,* p. 64.   132. *Ibid.,* p. 70.

this will of God in nominalist fashion. As he has, in the first place, not taken his teaching about the will of God from the Scripture as the dependable Word of God, so this will of God in turn cancels out the idea of Scripture as a dependable revelation of God. In opposition to this, Calvin has taken his teaching on the will of God from Scripture as the dependable revelation of God. Accordingly, the will of God, in Calvin's case, in turn establishes the idea of Scripture as the dependable revelation of God.

In a nominalist view of the will of God, Berkouwer points out, the whole of the work of salvation in history is threatened.[133]

But to reject a nominalist view is not to accept a realist view. The will of God is not arbitrary, but neither is it subject to a law above him. There is a third way, a way that avoids both nominalism and realism. This third way is the way of revelation.[134]

Berkouwer also speaks about the hiddenness of the revelation of God. About this too we dare not speak in speculative fashion.[135] In Scripture the hiddenness of God is never set over against revelation. There is no contrast between a *"deus absconditus"* and a *"deus revelatus."*[136] God is not fully comprehensible to man. He dwells in light that no man can approach unto. His revelation to man does not remove his incomprehensibility. Rather, revelation presupposes this incomprehensibility.[137] It is therefore the incomprehensible God who reveals himself to man in his works. And he can and does also hide himself in these works. But this hiding never conditions or cancels the dependability of the promises of God.[138]

If therefore with Calvin we follow the way of revelation in Scripture, then we have no metaphysical or speculative idea of God at all. Then we are therewith set free from a God who, apart from the idea of revelation that presupposes his incomprehensibility, wholly reveals himself. And then we are also free from a God who, apart from his revelation, wholly hides himself. The New Testament never speaks of a conditioning of the revelation of God from the point of view of the hiddenness of God.[139]

We must therefore not allow the promises of grace in Christ as they are offered in Scripture to be relativized by a nominalist view of God.[140] The Reformation principle of the direct revelation of

133. *Ibid.*, p. 93.
134. *Idem.*
135. *Ibid.*, p. 132.
136. *Ibid.*, p. 133.

137. *Ibid.*, p. 135.
138. *Ibid.*, p. 138.
139. *Ibid.*, p. 140.
140. *Ibid.*, p. 148.

God through Christ has saved us from every nominalist view of the promises of God.[141]

At this juncture, Berkouwer refers to his work on *The Triumph of Grace in the Theology of Karl Barth*. Berkouwer is concerned in both works with the question as to whether Barth's view of election can in any wise be said to be similar to that of Calvin. In particular, he is concerned to compare the two men on the question of what it means when they say that men are elect in Christ.

Berkouwer has established firmly that Calvin's view of election in Christ is not based on a nominalist view of God while Barth's view of election is. Berkouwer has also established that Barth's idea of general and special revelation, together with his view of Scripture, springs from and is expressive of his nominalist view of God. Berkouwer has established that Barth's view of revelation and his view of man as the image of God is subjectivist in character and leads him on to illusionism. On all these points, Barth stands, according to Berkouwer, opposed to Calvin. And on all these points Calvin holds to the biblical view while Barth holds to a speculative one.

What then of Barth's claim that Calvin and his followers have not given a proper place to Christ in the question of election?

Berkouwer says that Barth's reading of the history of the doctrine of election is mistaken.[142] Barring exceptions, the classic-reformation did seek to do justice to Ephesians 1:4.[143] What is behind Barth's mistaken reading of history on this point is his basic view that Christ is the subject of election. Any one who does not agree with Barth in thus making Christ the subject of election does not, according to him, attribute a proper place to Christ at all.[144]

Since for Barth Christ is the subject of election, "there is no creature which does not have its origin and existence in this grace."[144a] According to Barth, election in Christ "is the joyful message, the miracle which God has worked among men, among all men."[145]

It is no marvel that Barth's view of election constitutes what he thinks of as an "incisive correction" of the Reformation view.[146] But Berkouwer in turn points out that Barth's view of election involves his idea of the ontological impossibility of sin, and this in turn is the product of a speculative effort to explain sin.[147] Barth's view of elec-

---

141. *Ibid.*, p. 180.
142. *Ibid.*, p. 180.
143. *Ibid.*, p. 179.
144. *Ibid.*, p. 181.

144a. *The Triumph of Grace*, etc. p. 90.
145. *Ibid.*, p. 92.
146. *Ibid.*, p. 99.
147. *Ibid.*, p. 221.

tion, and with it that of sin, may be said to involve the Christological goodness of human nature.[148] And this leads to Berkouwer's basic criticism of Barth's theology earlier noted, namely, that it excludes the transition from wrath to grace in history.[149] "We do not in the Bible gain the impression that the battle is all 'an emptied matter' in the sense in which Barth speaks of it."[150]

Even the idea of substitutionary atonement comes to be an emptied matter on Barth's view of election. On Barth's view the atonement merely realizes the fact of universal election. How then can faith or unbelief mean anything?

In concluding this chapter, two remarks may be made. In the first place, note may be taken of the fact that, in discussing the doctrines mentioned, Reformed theologians found it necessary to point out constantly that their views are biblical and Barth's views are subjective or speculative. This fact brings corroboration to the discussion of the previous chapter. In the previous chapter, it was found that the idea of Scripture as the direct revelation of God at once involved the idea that God confronts man directly in history. The point of this mutual involvement of the doctrine of Scripture and of the doctrines of Scripture centers around the Christ of the Scriptures. If the human mind will not submit itself to the Scriptures in order there to find its Christ, it is because it has already constructed a Christ of its own independently of Scripture. Such is the case with Barth.

The second remark is that the criticisms made by various Reformed theologians may be said to fall into two classes. There is first the constantly repeated charge that Barth's actualist view of Christ and his work is based upon a nominalist view of God and his relation to the world. On the basis of this nominalism, with its anti-biblical contingency idea, the revelation of God becomes mere factuality without connections.

There is, second, the not so often mentioned but no less important charge, that Barth's view of Christ is based upon a virtually realist view of God and his relation to the world. Two important aspects of this charge may again be called to mind. In the first place, Berkouwer pointed out that the only way Barth had of escaping the subjectivism of modern theology was by having the human subject subsumed under the divine subject. But that involved the virtual

148. *Ibid.*, p. 231.
149. *Ibid.*, p. 233.   150. *Ibid.*, p. 237.

loss of the human subject itself in the divine subject. Corresponding to this attempt on the part of Barth to rescue the idea of revelation by the virtual absorption of the human subject into the divine subject, is his attempt to rescue the objectivity of the substitutionary atonement by absorbing it into the idea of man's election in Christ. These two aspects are brought together in what Runia calls the "grace-objectivism" of Barth. This "grace-objectivism" involves the absorption of the fact of the atonement as an historical fact into an eternal principle.

So far then as God's grace in Christ is said to be sovereign, this sovereignty itself becomes, to speak with Berkouwer, a merely formal principle allowing pure contingency. And so far as this grace of Christ is objective, it becomes again a formal principle, this time leading to abstract identity.

Chapter IX

Christian Philosophers Speak

In the previous two chapters, note was taken of the fact that Reformed theologians charge Barth over and over with interpreting Scripture in terms of non-Christian speculation. Christian philosophers assert the same thing. But they do it for a somewhat different purpose. They do it in the interest of protecting their own project. This project is that of reforming philosophy.

These Christian philosophers seek to reform philosophy by removing from it all speculative elements. A truly Christian philosophy, they say, must take its basic presuppositions from the Scriptures. The Christian philosopher, as well as the Christian theologian, must be himself subject to Word-revelation. The Christian philosopher frankly makes a religious commitment. This commitment is pre-theoretical. It is basic to the proper function of theoretical thought. Only if theoretical thought works on the ground-motive of Scripture expressed in the ideas of creation, fall, redemption and salvation through Christ, and applied by the Holy Spirit, can it really discover the true states of affairs about the world and man.

The reader will at once realize that the Christian philosophers of whom we speak are not Roman Catholics. On the contrary, they are Protestants. More specifically, they are Reformed Protestants, for they are convinced that only on a Reformed view can one hold to a really Christian philosophy. They speak of Romanist thinking as a synthesis view. In seeking to combine the Greek and the Christian points of view, they assert, Romanism does radical injustice both to a true Christian philosophy and to a true Christian theology.

A true Christian theology and a true Christian philosophy stand side by side in common subjection to Word-revelation. Romanism does not even subject theology to Word-revelation in any proper way. For Rome the Scripture is not the sole and final authority for men even in theology. Much less does Rome subject philosophy to Scripture. And, on its basis, philosophy is made subject to theology just because neither is subject to Scripture.

Is there then for these Reformed philosophers no difference between theology and philosophy? Is philosophy then only an undercover theology? A glance at the works of the philosophers of which we speak will convince one of the opposite. These philosophers discuss all the problems that have been discussed in the history of philosophy elsewhere. Moreover, they discuss all these problems with non-Christian philosophers themselves so far as this is possible. And, in speaking with non-Christian philosophers, these Christian philosophers are holding conversation with themselves. There is no attitude of superiority in the method of their approach. They know that only by grace have they themselves been saved from the attitude of apostacy that underlies all non-Christian philosophy. But now that they have been saved by grace, they can see that they have been saved from all false speculation, that is, from all false metaphysics. They now seek simply to search out the order of the cosmos as God has placed it there. Thus they are kept from falling into the antinomies of speculative thought and discover the actual states of affairs of the universe though never exhausting their meaning.

The Christian philosophers referred to thus far have their center of activity at the Free University of Amsterdam. The leaders of the group are Dr. D. H. Th. Vollenhoven and Dr. Herman Dooyeweerd. But they have many fellow-workers and followers. These men are all Reformed in their religious convictions. Some of them are theologians as well as philosophers. But all of them are endeavoring to develop a philosophy that shall not depend upon theology, for theology too is the work of men. On the other hand, this philosophy does not wish to lord it over theology. Each must do its own work, in its own field, as both are subject to Scripture.

The question now is as to what interest these Christian philosophers might have in the theology of Barth. Has not Barth asserted over and over again in recent times that he wants to keep his theology clear of all contact with philosophy? And has he not, on the

other hand, asserted that he is more than willing to permit philosophers to do their work in their own way?

1. Herman Dooyeweerd

Let us listen first to Dooyeweerd as he seeks to have converse with
the Barthians. In 1951 Dooyeweerd wrote an article[1a] on "The
Philosophy of the Cosmonomic Idea and the 'Barthians'." The title of
this article itself needs explanation. Dooyeweerd argues that God is
the law-giver and man the law-receiver. Non-Christian philosophy
does not recognize this fact. It is therefore to be spoken of as immanentistic philosophy. The failure to recognize the fact that God is
man's law-giver springs from failure to recognize the significance of
the fall of man. "By the fall of man, human thought ($\nu o \hat{v} s$), according
to St. Paul's word, has become $\nu o \hat{v} s \ \tau \hat{\eta} s \ \sigma a \rho \kappa \acute{o} s$, the 'carnal mind'
(Colos. 2:18), for it does not exist apart from its apostate religious
root. And thought includes its logical function."[1]

A Christian philosophy, therefore, is known by the fact that
through grace it owns the proper borderline between God and man.

This grace is in and through Jesus Christ. "To the ultimate transcendental question: What is the 'Aρχή of the totality and the
modal diversity of meaning of our cosmos with respect to the cosmonomic side and its correlate, the subject-side? It answers: the
sovereign holy will of God the Creator, who has revealed Himself
in Christ."[2]

Here then is a Christ-centered philosophy. It is also a philosophy
that takes its religious presuppositions from the inscripturated Word.
In being a Christological philosophy, it is anything but realist or
nominalist. With Calvin, it does not subject God to a law above him.
On the other hand, God is not without law. He is a law unto himself.
"Calvin's judgment: 'DEUS LEGIBUS SOLUTUS EST, SED NON
EXLEX,' ('God is not subject to the laws, but not arbitrary') touches
the foundations of all speculative philosophy by laying bare the
limits of human reason set for it by God in His temporal world-
order. This is the alpha and omega of all philosophy that strives to
adopt a critical position not in name but in fact.

1a. Dooyeweerd, "De Wysbegeerte der Wetsidee en de 'Barthianenen'" in
Philosophia Reformata.
1. Dooyeweerd, *A New Critique of Theoretical Thought,* (Pres. and Reformed Pub. Co., 1953, Vol. I, p. 100).
2. *Ibid.,* p. 101.

"I have laid all emphasis upon the transcendental character of authentic critical philosophy, because I wish to cut off at the root the interference of speculative metaphysics in the affairs of the Christian religion. An authentic critical philosophy is aware of its being bound to the cosmic time-order. It only points beyond and above this boundary line to its pre-supposita. Its task, worthy of God's human creation, is great; yet it is modest and does not elevate human reason to the throne of God."[3]

Dooyeweerd requests the "Barthians" to re-evaluate their attitude toward Romanist or scholastic philosophy. Pope Pius XII condemned existentialist philosophy. And Dr. K. H. Miskotte, as a Barthian, rejoices in the fact that Barth is not thus exclusivist in his attitude toward existentialism. Barth expressed his solidarity with the concerns of existential thought.[4] His discussion of the philosophy of the French existentialist Sartre is the clearest evidence of this fact.

Miskotte then argues that there are certain philosophers who are not as generous as Barth but who think of faith as a new birth "which makes another man of us" and brings with it "another logic." These could not express such a sense of solidarity with existential thought as Barth expressed.[5]

What is Dooyeweerd's reaction to this? It is to the effect that only a philosophy that takes its religious presuppositions from the divinely inscripturated Word-revelation in Christ can truly profess solidarity with every form of apostate thought. Christian philosophers know that they, as well as all other men, are creatures and sinners. But Christian philosophers also know that in Christ they are, in principle, set free from sin. They do not think according to new laws of thought. But they do think of themselves as subject to the temporal cosmic order which presents them with the law of God. They therefore hold to the possibility of a Christian philosophy and science. In the development of such a Christian philosophy, use can be made of the discoveries of non-Christian philosophers.

In contrast with this, Barth holds that philosophical reflection is inherently and properly independent of Word-revelation.[6] For him philosophical reflection is inherently autonomous. And, with this view, we have returned to a basically scholastic standpoint.[7]

To be sure, Barth's view is not Thomistic scholasticism with its

3. *Ibid.*, p. 93.
4. *Philosophia Reformata*, 1951, p. 148.
5. *Ibid.*, p. 148.

6. *Ibid.*, p. 150.
7. *Ibid.*, p. 151.

notion of natural knowledge as the preamble to grace. But Barth's rejection of a truly Christian philosophy springs from a "nominalistic scholasticism of the school of William of Occam, which denies every point of contact between a 'natural' knowledge and a 'supernatural' truth of revelation and rejects every metaphysic."[8]

The reader will note that the point here made is essentially the same as that which Berkouwer and other theologians made earlier. The Christian philosopher no less than the Christian theologian is anxious to protect the idea of the direct revelation of God against its cancellation by Barth's nominalist or activist idea of revelation.

The reader will also note that the Protestant philosopher, as well as the Protestant theologian, opposes the natural theology of Romanism. Both do so by means of the idea of the direct revelation of God through Christ in Scripture. Barth, on the other hand, opposes the natural theology of Romanism and the direct revelation of Calvin by being more consistently nominalist even than Occam. Occam did still allow, however inconsistently, of a direct revelation of God in history. Barth's idea of the freedom of God, and with it the idea of the freedom of revelation as act, destroys every form of direct revelation in history. It would destroy the entire idea of the temporal cosmic order as Dooyeweerd teaches it.

Someone might think of all this as oversimplification. How can one speak of the thought patterns of such a genuinely modern theology as that of Barth in terms of nominalism? Dooyeweerd's answer is simple. The old thought-forms of nominalism find a very new because very modern expression in the theology of Barth. This is not unimportant. But the main point is that Barth's thinking is still to be characterized as a "Christian scholasticism." As such it is but another form of the nature-grace scheme of medieval scholasticism.

Medieval scholasticism was composed of a pseudo-synthesis of Greek metaphysics and Christian thought. Why should there not be a pseudo-synthesis between Christian thinking and the nature-freedom scheme of modern thought?[9]

Such a pseudo-synthesis does take place when the kingdom of God is placed antithetically over against an irrationalist and activist concept of temporal reality.[10] In a truly Christian philosophy, there is no dialectical relation between creation and sin or between fallen creation and the Word-revelation in Jesus Christ. It is here, says

8. *Idem.*   10. *Idem.*
9. *Ibid.*, p. 151.

Dooyeweerd, that we must look for the basic difference between dialectical theology and ourselves.[11]

Barth's discussion of Sartre's existentialism may illustrate this point. Sartre works according to the nature-freedom scheme of modern thought. In his *Critique of Theoretical Thought,* Dooyeweerd shows that this nature-freedom scheme is, though different, still basically the same as the form-matter scheme of Greek thought. This form-matter scheme is composed of an irrationalist principle of discontinuity and a rationalist principle of continuity. In Plato's philosophy, form had, to be sure, the primacy of position over matter. Even so, form was correlative to matter and empty without it. On the other hand, nothing can be said about matter except in terms of form. Matter was brought into contact with form through *participation* in it.

On this dialectical view, sin is not a transgression of the law of God. Dialecticism cannot allow for sin in the integral, radical sense that it has in Scripture. Paul says there is no sin without law, and in dialectical thinking this law is lacking.

On a biblical basis, even Satan is a creature of God. He was created good but fell away from God. On a pagan basis, evil stands over against the good as an independent force. This is true even if, as in Zoroastrianism, good is made to triumph over evil.[12] So also, godless men cannot escape their creation-structure. Their sin, like that of Satan, is an effort to suppress the law of God. Godless men finally place their trust in "free creating man" himself.

This free and creating man absolutizes some aspect of the created universe. When this is done, then this absolutized relative calls for a correlative. Thus we have the form-matter scheme of Greek thought and the nature-freedom scheme of modern thought.

And as Romanism compromised Christianity by incorporating the form-matter scheme into its view of nature, so dialectical theology compromises Christianity by incorporating the nature-freedom scheme into its view of the temporal world.

What is gained, asks Dooyeweerd, when Barthian theology rejects Greek metaphysics and then allows Sartre to have his full say?[13]

Does modern philosophy any more than Plato think of sin as a transgression of the law of God? Even Plato's principle of evil is not merely negative. The *wandering cause* of the *Timaeus* is more than

11. *Ibid.,* p. 152.
12. *Ibid.,* p. 153.

13. *Ibid.,* p. 155.

an ontological negation. Plato's principle of matter has indeed an independent power of opposition to the good. This is something quite different from the optimist view of Leibniz.[14] But Plato is not able to speak of sin in its radical-scriptural sense because he does not know the integral and radical creation-motive of Word-revelation.[15] And, so long as we speak of evil as a power that is not to be traced back to the fall of man, we have not the biblical view of sin. Sin without the radical and integral sense of creation is meaningless.[16]

Barth has failed to understand the biblical view of man. Had he understood it, it would have meant the end of dialectical theology. Dialectical theology lives from the basic dualism in its ground-motive. The result is bound to be a denial of the radical unity of human existence. While Thomas saw man in the pseudo-synthesis of form and matter, dialectical theology can discover nothing but man in contradiction.[17]

In his doctrine of creation, Barth introduces a view of the *Nihil* that gives it independent power. Therewith he was already in the grasp of the Greek form-matter scheme, which works itself out in a sharp metaphysical-ontological dualism. The *wandering cause* of Plato is accommodated to the revelation about the fall into sin as revealed in the Word of God.[18]

Barth rejected the idea of the analogy of being, but not because the Greek form-matter scheme to which it gave expression allowed no place for the biblical view of creation.[19] On the contrary, Barth rejects any view that holds to or is based on the possibility of a truly Christian or Reformed view of created temporal reality.[20] Instead of returning to the biblical view of creation, Barth declares his solidarity with Sartre's existential philosophy. In this philosophy, independent human thought is set over against the "wholly other" of the Word of God.[21]

All this proves that Barthian theology is still deeply imbedded in the scholastic ground-motive.[22] But again it is the late scholastic view of nominalism, not Thomism, that Barthian theology resembles. If we are to overcome scholasticism, we shall need to return to the

14. *Idem.*
15. *Idem.*
16. *Ibid.*, p. 156.
17. *Idem.*
18. *Idem.*

19. *Ibid.*, p. 157.
20. *Ibid.*, p. 158.
21. *Ibid.*, p. 157.
22. *Ibid.*, p. 158.

idea of the priority of propositional Word-revelation. We shall need to hold that, even before the entrance of sin into the world, man was directed toward Word-revelation. The rejection of this Word-revelation on the part of man implied the basically apostate nature of the interpretation of the revelation of God in creation.[23]

Barth is therefore radically mistaken when he thinks that his view is essentially the view of the Reformation and that in terms of it medieval scholasticism can be effectively opposed. Reformation thought is based upon the idea of Word-revelation as basic to a proper interpretation of created reality. Only on this basis is it possible to have a unified notion of man and his relation to the world. The rejection of Word-revelation is apostasy from God. It was apostasy from God that made man grasp for a dialectical method of interpreting himself and the world. The Greek form-matter scheme and the modern nature-freedom scheme are alike manifestations of the dialectical method of apostate man. Medieval scholasticism is a pseudo-synthesis of the Christian religion with the Greek form-matter scheme. Barthianism is a pseudo-synthesis of the Christian religion and the nature-freedom scheme of modern thought.

Dooyeweerd concludes his discussion with the Barthians by asking them to submit their thinking to the test of the revelation of God in Scripture. They will need to show that the radical view of creation, sin, and redemption, is not biblical. They will need to show that the ground-motive of the Bible itself contains a hidden dualism that justifies their dialectical approach. So long as this is not done, the radically integral view of Scripture and its teaching will threaten all forms of theoretical dogmatism, including that of dialectical theology.[24]

2. S. U. Zuidema

We listen next to Dr. S. U. Zuidema. Zuidema is both a philosopher and a theologian, and a professor of philosophy at the Free University of Amsterdam.

In the 18th volume of *Philosophia Reformata* (1953), Zuidema has an article on "Theology and Philosophy in the *Church Dogmatics* of Karl Barth." To the 20th volume of the same magazine (1955),

23. *Idem.*   24. *Ibid.*, p. 161.

Zuidema contributed an article on "The Revelation Concepts of Karl Barth and Martin Heidegger."

Zuidema begins the first article by saying that though Barth has no doubt changed his views on many things, the impelling motif of his theological and philosophical thinking has remained the same.

Barth has given his heart to the idea of the freedom of the revelation of God.[25] Involved in this is the idea that no philosophy must place itself as judge above revelation. Therefore, the Christian faith may not be subjected to the notion of the general religiosity of men. Revelation must simply announce itself as fact.[26] Revelation creates faith in itself. The fact that man does not of himself know God cannot be learned from agnostic philosophy. The unknowability of God is itself to be learned from revelation.[27]

Zuidema stops to point out the importance of Barth's view of the hiddenness of revelation. By means of it, Barth wants to outreach every form of philosophical agnosticism. Barth finds his answer to the principle atheism of Feuerbach and the relativistic skepticism of Overbeck in the idea of the revelation of hiddenness.[28] Revelation in its hiddenness is simply beyond the reach of all human speculation. "The hiddenness of God is philosophically hidden."[29] The work of skeptical philosophy, such as that of Sartre, must not be employed in the service of theology. But, despite this, it can be useful in demonstrating that all philosophy is innerworldly.[30]

Over against such a useful agnostic philosophy, there is the would-be Christian philosophy. Such is the philosophy of the *Analogia Entis* idea. Here philosophy enters upon the field of theology. Let the children of the Reformation beware. The idea of the analogy of being attacks the notion of the hiddenness of revelation. For this reason, it is deadly to the idea of revelation and to faith in revelation.

Thus, in Barth's view, an agnostic philosophy is usable up to a point. But philosophy becomes wholly unusable when it does not allow itself to be relativized by theology.[31] Any philosophy that refuses to hold to the wholly hidden character of the revelation of God is utterly unusable.[32]

Barth finds it unavoidable to speak of philosophy and its proper task. He has to do so in order to safeguard his theology of the God

25. *Philosophia Reformata*, 1953, p. 77.
26. *Ibid.*, p. 79.
27. *Ibid.*, p. 80.
28. *Idem.*

29. *Idem.*
30. *Ibid.*, p. 81.
31. *Ibid.*, p. 83.
32. *Idem.*

who is wholly hidden in his revelation.[33] If Barth is going to protect his theology, no form of Christian philosophy is to be tolerated. On the other hand, Barth not only tolerates but needs an atheistic philosophy. The sort of philosophy that Barth needs is one that proceeds from the Renaissance dogma of free and autonomous man.[34] Only such a philosophy does not interfere with the idea of God as wholly hidden in his revelation. There is no law of God that controls such a philosophy. Therefore such a philosophy, and only such a philosophy, does not disturb the hidden character of God and of his work. Only a philosophy that does not even believe in general revelation can fit onto the theology of Barth. The atheistic character of such a philosophy is no hindrance to Barth's theology, for atheism can be relativized by the idea of the hidden revelation of God.[35]

From his point of view, Barth must therefore reject not only the natural theology of Rome but also the idea of natural knowledge and of general revelation as Calvin teaches it.[36] Barth's basic thesis is that God can be known by God only. Any idea of direct revelation in history would be destructive of this basic thesis of his. But an atheistic philosophy such as that of Sartre corroborates, even if only indirectly, the main thesis of Barth. An anthropocentric subjectivism in philosophy can be used by Barth as an analogy of the idea of the revelation of hiddenness and of the hiddenness of revelation.[37]

Zuidema here points out that in all this Barth outranges Scripture, faith in Scripture, and scriptural revelation. According to Barth, it is the fool who says in his heart that God exists. According to Scripture, it is the fool who says in his heart that God does not exist.[38] Involved in Barth's attitude toward philosophy is the rejection of an apologetics based on the direct revelation of God in general and special revelation. But Barth's own theology is, in effect, an apologetics for another type of revelation. Barth's dogmatics is from this point of view "the most speculative apologetics that has ever been produced in the Christian Church. In this respect it runs completely parallel to his speculative theological theodicy."[39]

That such is the case may be seen from a comparison of Barth's idea of the hidden God with the existentialist idea of the hidden man.[40] Karl Jaspers hurls his *No* against every form of departmental

33. *Idem.*
34. *Idem.*
35. *Idem.*
36. *Ibid.*, p. 84.

37. *Idem.*
38. *Idem.*
39. *Idem.*
40. *Idem.*

science in the interest of the purity of his idea of human self-revelation. Barth similarly hurls his theological *No* against every form of
human self-knowledge.[41] Barth's *No* is hurled not only against
Brunner, but it is also hurled against Jaspers' existentialist philosophy
and its doctrine of self-transcendence. It is hurled against Heidegger
and Sartre's doctrine of the *Nihil*. It is this *No* against every philosophy that constitutes Barth's theological apologetics. For Barth the
best defensive is an offensive. He expresses his offensive in his universal negative against every philosophy except such a one as allows itself to be wholly relativized in terms of his *No*.[42]

The correlative to this *No* of God is his *Yes*. And again this *Yes* of
Barth's theology is similar to the *Yes* of existential philosophy.
Jaspers asserts the positive freedom of man. But he asserts this as
that which proceeds wholly from man himself. This freedom is lit
up exclusively in terms of itself. Man's self-existence in freedom is
something that only the self can reveal. And when this freedom is
revealed, it still remains wholly hidden. If it did not remain hidden,
then it would not be true freedom. Similarly, God's freedom is revealed to God alone and to the man to whom God by grace reveals
himself in his hiddenness.[43] Those who receive the grace of God are
therefore participants in the archetypical self-knowledge of God.[44]
Thus man transcends himself in this his participation in the self-
knowledge of God. And because this self-transcendence is the gift
of God, it remains hidden in man. Consequently, this idea of self-
transcendence and of participation of the human subject in the
divine self-knowledge meets the requirement, and is at the same
time an expression of the idea, that God is wholly hidden in his
revelation.

So far then, the following results appear in the article of Zuidema.
First, on Barth's view, every form of Christian philosophy must be
rejected. Barth's *No* is absolute against such a philosophy. Second,
any atheist philosophy is innocent just to the extent that it is really
atheist. It may then even be indirectly useful in pointing up the fact
that only in terms of the hiddenness of revelation can God be
known. Third, when Barth seeks to go beyond such men as Sartre,
Heidegger and Jaspers in the interest of his idea of revelation, he
does so by means of a negation that goes deeper than any of their
negations in order then to reach an affirmation that goes deeper than

41. *Ibid.*, pp. 84-85.   43. *Idem.*
42. *Ibid.*, p. 85.   44. *Idem.*

any of their affirmations. As noted earlier, Berkouwer pointed out that Barth's idea of revelation is more nominalist than is the nominalism of Occam. In similar fashion, Zuidema points out that Barth's *No* outreaches that of Jaspers and other existentialist philosophers. When Jaspers asserts the self-lighting freedom of man, Barth asserts the self-lighting freedom of God. To maintain this freedom in its self-contained character, its absolute hiddenness in history must be maintained.

But when this is done, then the way is open for a wider affirmation than is made by existentialist philosophers. For then it is possible to take man up into participation with the self-existence and self-knowledge of God. This makes man essentially a grace receiver. He is what he is through his participation in God's knowledge and being, but he is this through grace. Thus, grace is both free and universal.

In setting forth such views, Zuidema says, Jaspers and Barth are thoroughly consistent with themselves. Barth is not inconsistent with himself when, as the correlative of his *No* by which he seems to cut man wholly loose from God, he places his *Yes* by which man is virtually absorbed into God.

This point is of utmost importance. We have heard a great deal, not only from Berkouwer but also from the other theologians and philosophers mentioned, about Barth's virtual nominalism. In terms of this nominalism, everything that is done by means of human nature is cancelled out. But correlative to this deeper *No* is Barth's deeper *Yes*. And this deeper *Yes* rests upon his "objectivism" by which man and his faith are virtually absorbed in God, as the final subject both of revelation and of human faith.

If every expression of the "*humanum*" is cancelled out in terms of pure nominalism or irrationalism, then this same "*humanum*" must be re-established by some form of realism. In other words, objectivity must then be sought by the idea of man's participation in God. The very idea of revelation of God *to* man then requires that this man participate in this revelation. Man's very faith by which he *receives* revelation must itself participate in the revelation it receives. If there is to be room for revelation and for the knowledge of God in man, that is, if there is to be room for a "pure" theology of faith, such knowledge must be a participation in the archetypical self-knowledge of God.[45] "Only as participation in divine self-knowl-

45. *Ibid.*, p. 86.

edge is theology possible. Our ectypical knowledge of God is in essence identical with God's archetypical self-knowledge."[46]

Zuidema points out here that, in saying this, Barth does not at this point follow Occam. In opposing the *analogy of being*, Barth does not, as did Occam, return to the idea of the equivocation of being. On the contrary, Barth here asserts, in the manner of Duns Scotus, the *univocation* of being *(Univocatio Entis).*[47]

Barth's *No* reaches deeper than that of Occam. It reaches deeper also, Zuidema has pointed out, than that of existentialism.

It is wholly consistent with this, says Zuidema, that Barth, more consistent here too than Occam, follows Duns Scotus in holding to man's essential unification with the being of God. Barth's pendulum swings wider than that of Occam. Being more irrationalist he is, quite consistently, also more rationalist than was Occam. It is for this reason that grace is for Barth both free and universal.

It is this greater irrationalism and this greater rationalism that Zuidema finds expressed in Barth's idea that God is wholly revealed and wholly hidden in his revelation. Barth opposes all positive theology and philosophy in the interest of the hiddenness of revelation. But absolute hiddenness by itself is the death of the whole idea of revelation. Barth is interested in revelation, not in hiddenness as such. He wants revelation in hiddenness. But the only proper form of revelation that can, according to Barth, retain the true hiddenness or freedom of God is a revelation in which God is wholly revealed. And God is wholly revealed only to himself. Thus, if man is to receive revelation at all, a revelation that maintains the hiddenness of God in itself, then man must participate in the revelation of God to himself. Only God can know God. In knowing God, man must participate in the self-knowledge of God. It is for this reason, says Zuidema, that Barth rejects the idea of the analogy of being and substitutes for it the idea of the univocation of being. Man must transcend his creatureliness and participate in deity. "The *'divinity'* of man in this self-transcendence above the limits of its own creaturely humanity is then the final conclusion."[48]

Zuidema here refers to the section of Barth's Anthropology in which he speaks of Jesus as the man for God.[49] In this section, Barth gives his Christological grounding of anthropology. A truly biblical anthropology, Barth argues, must start from Christ. It is

46. *Idem.*   48. *Idem.*
47. *Idem.*   49. *Kirchliche Dogmatik,* Vol. III:2, pp. 64ff.

not that Christ must participate in human nature, but that human nature must participate in him.[50] And human nature must participate in Jesus as identical with his work. "His being as man is his work."[51] Still further, this work is the salvation of all men. "As the *Geschichte* of the divine salvation of all and every man is wholly and completely and exclusively he, so he is wholly and completely and exclusively the *Geschichte* of the divine salvation of all and every man."[52] The man Jesus, as *Geschichte*, is the coming kingdom of God, nothing more, nothing less, even as the kingdom of God is, without any condition, this man.[53] Jesus is therefore the created being "in whose existence God's act of salvation of all men is a reality *(Ereignis)*."[54] "The ontological destiny of man is grounded in the fact that in the midst of all other men one is the man Jesus."[55] And therefore sin is "not a possibility, but the ontological impossibility of man."[56] All other men than Jesus are fellow-elect with him.[57] It is thus that God's lordship over man is accomplished. And, in the lordship of God, the creature exists in "identity with the divine Subject."[58] In the *Geschichte* of Jesus, the "creator is creature and the creature is creator."[59]

"Jesus is, of course, the only one of whom it can thus be said that in him the creator is the creature and the creature is creator."[60] For Christ is what he is in his act, that is, his *Geschichte* of saving all men. There is, of course, only one *"Urgeschichte."*[61] But the existence of other men is *Geschichte* in a secondary, derivative and mediated sense. Their existence is *Geschichte* in or with *(an oder mit)* the *Geschichte* of Jesus.[62] Men in general must therefore be sought nowhere else but in the *Geschichte* founded by Jesus.[63]

Jesus, the only real man, is identical with God. Other men participate in the being of Jesus, and thus they outreach their creaturely limitations.[64] This is Barth's argument. And, in using this argument, says Zuidema, Barth is not using the idea of the equivocity of being. He is rather using the idea of the univocity of being. He is following Duns Scotus rather than Occam.

50. *Ibid.*, p. 69.
51. *Idem.*
52. *Ibid.*, p. 81.
53. III:2, p. 80.
54. *Ibid.*, p. 158.
55. *Idem.*
56. *Ibid.*, p. 162.
57. *Ibid.*, p. 163.

58. *Ibid.*, p. 81.
59. *Ibid.*, p. 190.
60. *Ibid.*, p. 192.
61. *Ibid.*, p. 193.
62. *Idem.*
63. *Idem.*
64. *Ibid.*, p. 222.

Occam's nominalism was useful to Barth when he sought first to break down the philosophical idea of the analogy of being. But when he wanted to establish his "pure" theology on a positive basis, then he reached for Scotus' idea of the univocity of being. Then he argued that God is the subject of our faith, and that our believing is a predicate of God.[65] It is by this univocity of being that Barth's *Yes* outreaches that of Existenz philosophy. Existenz philosophy also sought for a transcendence idea, but this transcendence idea was after all a human possibility. A true transcendence idea, according to Barth, realizes that man's theological being is in advance "in the Word of God."[66] "Our theological existence 'in the Word of God' is divinity, nothing less, nothing else. And the authentic being of existing man is identical with this theological existence."[67]

The necessary correlative of this idea of man's participation in divinity is the idea that created existence is as such atheistic.[68] Philosophy, itself atheistic, deals with this atheistic reality.[69] In philosophy, even in existential philosophy, there is no place for the real self-transcendence of man. The divinization of man is not an extension of man's humanity. It is a gift of grace to him. There is no point of contact for true self-transcendence in the creatureliness of man. This self-transcendence is a gift of grace. It is thus that Barth uses the weapons of existentialist philosophy. He uses them by first transforming them into weapons of grace.[70] His Christological founding of anthropology is accomplished by means of the idea of the univocity of being as correlative to the idea that the man and his world are dumb.

Zuidema here points out the basic similarity between Barth's relation of grace to nature and the nature-grace scheme of Thomas Aquinas. In Karl Barth, the Protestant scholasticism of the twentieth century has found its master. Whatever the difference may be between Barth and Thomism, and especially neo-Thomism, the similarity between the Roman Catholic and the Barthian conceptions is deeper than the difference.[71]

Zuidema also takes due note of the fact that in his later works Barth distinguishes more clearly than he did formerly between creation and the fall.[72] Even so, he points out, this does not imply a

---

65. *Philosophia Reformata*, 1953, p. 87.
66. *Ibid.*, p. 87.
67. *Idem.*
68. *Idem.*

69. *Idem.*
70. *Ibid.*, p. 88.
71. *Ibid.*, p. 90.
72. *Ibid.*, p. 94.

return to anything like a biblical idea of creation. Barth's view of the created world, says Zuidema, is more irrationalist than is that of Romanism.[73] Barth uses a notion of contingency similar to that of modern existentialism. In fact, so far as Barth differs from Thomism, he differs because his thinking is affiliated with the thinking of modern irrationalism.[74] It is Kierkegaard, the father both of existentialism and of dialectical theology, who must be taken into account at this point. The conceptual apparatus of Barth's *Church Dogmatics* is borrowed from modern irrationalism and in particular from existentialism.[75]

In fact, Barth goes beyond existentialism. He subordinates the concepts of existentialist philosophy in the interest of his doctrine of grace, of revelation, of faith and of God.[76] In existential philosophy, the essence of human existence is act, self-constituting act. Similarly, in Barth the essence of God is his self-constituting act.[77] In Jaspers' existential philosophy, man is man in communion. So for Barth, God is God in communion. The triune God is identical with his relation.[77a] In existential philosophy, the act of man expresses itself in the contingent world, while it yet remains uncommitted in relation to that world. Similarly, in Barth's theology, God's activity in the world is not to be seen in any permanent results. God's act remains free and uncommitted in relation to the world.

In existential philosophy, the spoken word does not reveal but rather hides its source in existential man. In similar irrationalist fashion, Barth teaches that God's spoken word in the Christus Incarnatus, in Scripture, and in preaching, does not betray its source in God.

In existential philosophy, man is history. So in Barth's theology, God is history. But this history of man and of God must be set over against the history of the historians or the history spoken of in Scripture.[78]

Thus it appears that the categories of "humanistic existential-philosophy" have become the basic categories of the Barthian theology of revelation.[79] Thus the "*being*" of grace and of revelation is God's history, and the same holds for the "*being*" of faith. From the

73. *Ibid.*, p. 95.
74. *Idem.*
75. *Ibid.*, p. 96.
76. *Idem.*

77. *Idem.*
77a. *Ibid.*, p. 97.
78. *Ibid.*, p. 97.
79. *Ibid.*, p. 98.

time of *Romans* to and inclusive of the *Church Dogmatics* Barth
maintains this basic motive.[80]

In saying this, Zuidema is fully aware of the fact that, according
to Barth, faith is an act of man himself, not only of God. Even so, it
remains true that in the act of faith, as the gift of God, man transcends his creaturely limitations.[81] In all existential philosophy, the
idea of human self-transcendence is indispensable. Barth uses this
idea, and with the help of the idea of analogy of faith, makes it the
foundation of his Christological anthropology. "The idea of self-
transcending is the crux of the whole of Barth's theological anthropology."[82] And having used the basic categories of existential philosophy for the construction of his theological anthropology, this
theology is as strong or as weak as is existential philosophy. The
categories of existential philosophy are not to be considered as an
innocent apparatus. These categories determine the entire structure
of Barth's theology. Without the concepts of existential philosophy,
the whole of Barth's theology would fall to pieces as a house of
cards.[83]

The reader will observe that Zuidema is here, in effect, asking
whether with his idea of man as participant in the *Geschichte* of
God Barth can escape subjectivism and illusionism. Let us, says
Zuidema, take first the philosophical idea of analogy. This is familiar
to us. We shall call it A. Then we take the theological idea of analogy
of faith. It is unknown to us. We shall call it X. What then is the
relation between A and X? "According to Barth God in his grace
makes A analogical to X. This is well. But is A thus made analogous
to X and therewith also made unknowable? Or is X made analogous
to A and therewith also made philosophically knowable."[84] It is apparent, says Zuidema, that on the one hand A is made usable for X
and, on the other hand, A is said to be unusable in itself for X. Thus
the analogy idea which is supposed to mediate between the analogy
idea of philosophy and the analogy idea of theology is at the same
time both philosophical and theological as well as neither philosophical nor theological. In this way the theology of Barth is made
an intellectual game. That is to say "the analogy which God creates
between the philosophical and the theological ideas of analogy is
itself *ambiguous* and *antinomic* in nature. Theologically it is un-

80. *Idem.*
81. *Ibid.*, p. 99.
82. *Idem.*

83. *Idem.*
84. *Ibid.*, p. 109.

knowable but usable; philosophically, it is knowable but unusable while yet it must apparently fulfill the function of being knowable and usable as a philosophical-theological function."[85]

In reality, this theology is worse than a game. If Barth is going to make his theological *X* known to us, he must do so in terms of philosophy. In that case, we have a new kind of natural theology. Then modernism has gained the victory over Barth's theology.[86] On the other hand, if a theology of the Word is to prevail, then it must use the utterly unfit materials of the world as means of the revelation of God. Then that which is nature is turned into a supernatural medium of revelation. "Jesus of Nazareth *becomes* the Son of God, the Bible *becomes* the Word of God, preaching *becomes* God's Word, our theology *becomes* . . . God's theology and *Barth's Dogmatics becomes* God's own Dogmatics. Our truths *become* God's truth, taken into his service."[87] Thus the miracle of *indirect identification* takes place.[88] Nothing remains dark in man. He is completely revealed in his theological, teleological destination.[89] Evil is overcome because God takes the contradiction of it against himself into himself.[90] Good and evil are tensions within God. They have their source in God. And evil is defeated in God.[91]

In this "speculative theological ontologism, Barth's thinking reaches its climax, as well as its lowest point. It estranges him more than any of his other basic ideas from the revelation of Scripture and from the only true God."[92]

In his later article in *Philosophia Reformata*[93] and in the *Free University Quarterly*, Zuidema makes a detailed comparison of the structure between the revelation concept of Barth and that of Heidegger. In a note, Zuidema emphasizes the fact that he is dealing with the *pattern*, not with the contents of the two systems of thought that he compares with one another.

We must note the difference between the two patterns of thought. The last word of Barth's *Church Dogmatics*, says Zuidema, is *Er* (i.e., He, God). The last word of Heidegger is *Es* (i.e., It, Itself). "The difference between them is the difference between 'He' and

85. *Ibid.*, pp. 109-110.
86. *Ibid.*, p. 111.
87. *Ibid.*, p. 112.
88. *Ibid.*, p. 117.
89. *Ibid.*, p. 126.
90. *Ibid.*, p. 135.
91. *Idem.*
92. *Ibid.*, p. 136.
93. *Philosophia Reformata*, 1955, pp. 162ff., and the *Free University Quarterly*, Vol. 4, pp. 70ff.

'It'."[94] But then comes the similarity. Both Barth and Heidegger deal with mystery. "He" is the mystery of Barth; "It" is the mystery of Heidegger. In both cases, revelation is revelation of a mystery which remains mystery in its very revelation. Revelation is revelation of mystery. It is this fact that places a limit on revelation. Man himself is determined by this mystery.

Both men think and speak of the limit of man as eschatological. But Barth has now advanced beyond this point. He now speaks of the elevation of man's being into the divine mode of being.[95] "So the eschatology retains its critical function, but is subservient to the central idea of the triumph of grace, which does not only throw the light of the revelation of the Mystery as mystery on man, but which let(s) man partake of the mystery of Being, and includes man in this mystery."[96] While Heidegger remained a pure eschatologist, in Barth pure eschatology gives way to the idea of consummation, "because he moved forward the borderline into God's being, with the aid of a speculation *upon the trinity*."[97]

Zuidema here makes the same point which he made in his earlier article, when he spoke of Barth's employment of Duns Scotus' idea of the univocation of being. The triumph of grace in the theology of Barth is accomplished by virtual absorption of man into deity.

Kant separated between the theoretical and the practical reason. He limited the former for the sake of allowing room for the operation of the second. In similar fashion, says Zuidema, Barth sets his idea of revelation, into which man is virtually absorbed, over against and above the area of natural being.[98]

And Heidegger's thought pattern at this point is the same as that of Barth. Both men insist that revelation carries with it its own criterion. For revelation does not enter into the sphere of human experience, or if it does, it does so in disguise. "The history of human experience goes on within the horizon of the limited humanity. Both of them render anything within this horizon to the revelation-less reason and (or) existence. The 'History' within the sphere of experience, accessible to the professional historian, to their opinion, is quite different from '*Geschichte*' (happening) of the revelation of Mystery. Thus rationalism and subjectivism have free play in the former sphere. They think it does not matter, because revelation is

---

94. *Free University Quarterly*, p. 70.   97. *Idem*.
95. *Ibid.*, p. 72.   98. *Idem*.
96. *Idem.*

beyond the grasp of reason anyway. Though both of them are very anti-rationalistic, they don't attack the rationalistic, and the underlying Renaissancistic, preconceptions as far as this limited sphere is concerned."[99] "Consequently, both hold that the Bible as such is not the Word of God. If this were so it would smash both Barth's and Heidegger's ideas of revelation. So it cannot be. In both concepts the idea of revelation has such force that the Bible *cannot* be the Word of God. Essentially the Bible rests within the sphere of the dominion of man, of his little existence, and of his degenerated reason; it is *at his disposal.*"[100]

Zuidema here points to an "extremely important parallel in their pattern of thought."[101] For both the essence and revelation of being are Unique, Surprising, Unexpected and Unpredictable. "According to Barth God is so much special that even his unknowableness may only be imparted to us by his revelation."[102] The case is similar with Heidegger on the question of being. As in S. Kierkegaard's system the category of the Individual, so with Barth and Heidegger the category of the Special, as being the Exclusive, plays a dominant role.[103] "Barth's as well as Heidegger's idea of revelation must be grasped from this anti-rationalistic and irrationalistic way of thought. They may be summarized in the one word, Special. But they are special in a special sense, in an exclusive sense surpassing any idiomatic scope, and applying the word special in such very special sense that it cannot be but a mere pointer, and one that points deficiently for all that, to the essential sense of this specialty. Revealing revelation, here, becomes the transcendent marginal idea of this 'special theology' (of Barth) and of this special theory of Being (of Heidegger)."[104] In both of his articles, then, Zuidema's criticism is similar to that of Dooyeweerd. Zuidema, as well as Dooyeweerd, finds that Barth's essential nominalism is in his later thinking overbalanced by an essential realism. And in this essential realism, man is said to be real only to the extent that he is sublated and absorbed into deity.

The point here made is the same as that made in his earlier article, when Zuidema spoke of man's elevation to participation in the being of divinity. "According to Barth, 'I am,' to have some sense, must follow from 'God is' and should be equally special as God's

99. *Ibid.*, p. 74.
100. *Ibid.*, p. 75.
101. *Ibid.*, p. 77.

102. *Idem.*
103. *Ibid.*, p. 78.
104. *Ibid.*, p. 79.

being and revelation are."[105] "That is why Barth makes our knowledge of faith, granted to us through revelation, to be something like a flash, degrading to worthlessness the next moment, for conceived as achievement it would constitute an unacceptable contrariety to revealing revelation. Consequently, knowledge of faith should be made eschatologic and dynamic."[106]

Barth and Heidegger are both anti-subjectivist. They are opposed even to the subjectivist point of view of Jaspers. For Heidegger "it is self-evident that he must consequently break away from Christianity too, at least from the Christian onto-theology, and above all from the Reformation with its interest in subjective, personal security of salvation.

"To Barth it is self-evident that, doing so, he opens up a way to a real reformational theory of revelation, as opposed to Renaissance, Roman-Catholicism, and Protestant orthodoxy."[107]

3. E. G. van Teylingen

At this point, we turn to an article by Dr. E. G. van Teylingen. The title of it is, "About the Philosophical Background of Dialectical Theology."[108] Van Teylingen first turns to the second part of Volume I of the *Church Dogmatics*. There Barth discusses the proper place of philosophical thought in relation to theology. Everybody approaches the Bible with certain philosophical presuppositions, says Barth. This is true because to read the Bible at all requires conceptual activity on our part.[109] The point of importance is that when we employ our thought schematism in reading Scripture, we do so self-consciously. We must be aware of the fact that though we can think idealistically or realistically, we cannot think in any special Christian way.[110]

This point, says van Teylingen, is basically important. The reader will recall that, according to Zuidema's analysis, this point involves, for Barth, that the Bible cannot as such be the Word of God. A Christian philosophy, it was noted by Zuidema and also by Dooyeweerd, is for Barth tantamount to an attack on the hiddenness of revelation and therefore on the only truly Protestant form

105. *Idem.*   107. *Ibid.*, p. 84.
106. *Idem.*
108. *Philosophia Reformata*, 1945, pp. 2ff.
109. *Ibid.*, p. 3.   110. *Idem.*

of revelation. If the freedom of the Word of God is to be maintained, then the thought schematism by means of which Scripture is read must itself be controlled by the idea of revelation.[111]

Barth recognizes the fact that he did not from the beginning of his career follow the same procedure that he now follows. In *Romans* he had worked, he says, in part with a crust of Kantian-Platonic concepts.[112] He now feels no longer bound to them.

Van Teylingen then points out that in *Romans* Barth showed agreement with Kant in the place that he assigned to the practical reason.[113] For his understanding of Kant, Barth asserts that he has learned a great deal from his brother, Heinrich. He says that he has also been influenced by Eduard Thurneysen's book on Dostoevsky.

It appears clearly, says van Teylingen, that in his work on Romans Barth makes use not merely of a crust of ideas borrowed from Kant and Plato, but, "on the contrary; in that exposition it appears over and over that Paul has been pushed aside by Kant and Plato and I may add by Kierkegaard."[114] The movement of thought in Heinrich Barth's main work, *The Philosophy of the Practical Reason*, proves this point.[115]

Heinrich Barth follows Kant in his statement of the problem of philosophy. Kant's distinction between the theoretical and the practical reason he simply accepts as unassailable.[116] Karl Barth was especially intrigued with his brother Heinrich's concept of history. This idea of history is controlled by the central notion of Heinrich Barth's theology, namely, that of the "idea as crisis of reality."[117]

In order to have an idea of history that is formed by the "idea as crisis of reality," we must turn back from Kant to Plato. The idea must have merely regulative, not constitutive control, in our thinking. After that we must go beyond Kant to Kierkegaard in order to find a guarantee for the primacy of the practical over the theoretical reason. This must be done in order to have a proper concept as *Source* in the ethical sense of the term. Kant was not formal and critical enough in his concept of the categorical imperative. For that reason he, after all, confused idea and reality, heaven and earth.[118]

If we are to have proper knowledge of ourselves, we must think of ourselves as grounded in the ethical *Idea*. "Who 'is' then the

111. *Ibid.*, p. 4.
112. *Ibid.*, p. 5.
113. *Ibid.*, p. 6.
114. *Idem.*

115. *Ibid.*, p. 7.
116. *Idem.*
117. *Idem.*
118. *Ibid.*, p. 9.

practical Subject? It is the concrete willing I, grounded in the transcendental Idea of pure Willing."[119]

Heinrich Barth guards himself at this point against the charge of advocating an Identity-philosophy.[120] Does not the *I* of whom he speaks seem to be absorbed by the Idea? Heinrich Barth replies that all ethical reality implies decision. Man's relation to the idea is therefore one of ethical decision. There is here no identity-philosophy at all. The ethical approach to philosophy is the enemy of all speculation.

The problem of evil must be solved in terms of ethical decision.[121] Every ethical decision is relative.[122] The idea criticizes and relativizes all reality. The resolution of the duality of life lies beyond life in the ordering of the Idea. The final relation of the Idea to human life is, however, not negative. There is in the negative a pointer to the Idea.[123]

Looking at Heinrich Barth's argument, we note that Plato's influence is paramount in it. This is evident from the basic antithesis between Idea and reality. But Plato's dualism is itself taken up into a "post-Kantian subjectivist nominalism, a combination of motifs frequently found in the history of philosophy."[124]

Heinrich Barth's opposition to subjectivism is only apparent. In his notion of the Idea as actively critical of reality, he absolutized the logical-ethical subject-function of human thought. This itself indicates the rationalist character of this thought. The fact that he includes the irrationalist thought of Kierkegaard into his "system" does not disprove the essentially Platonic nature of his thought, for Kierkegaard himself is employed as the great defender of the qualitative distinction between time and eternity. On this point Plato, Kant and Kierkegaard are in basic agreement.

Now it is the same Platonic-Kantian-Kierkegaardian motifs that control Karl Barth's early theology. The idea of the death-line as separating the world of Idea and reality points up this fact. Man's relativity is his sin, his not being absolute.[125] Even so, in man's existence as under the judgment of God, there is a pointer to his unity with his Source. But the initiative of redemption is with God. "Insofar as man is creature, he is reprobate, insofar as he receives

---

119. *Idem.*
120. *Idem.*
121. *Ibid.*, p. 10.
122. *Idem.*

123. *Ibid.*, p. 11.
124. *Idem.*
125. *Ibid.*, p. 13.

grace he is elect. It is God who elects and rejects, but he rejects in order to elect."[126]

In Jesus Christ, man's rejection by God becomes apparent. But this revelation of rejection is itself what it is because revelation is always, in the last analysis, revelation of redemption.[127] In redemption the human subject is, as it were, destroyed. God alone is the actual subject in his relation to man. God's entering into history from above the death-line spells the sublation of the crisis and therewith the end of history.

In this theology of judgment, we note the similarity with Heinrich Barth's philosophical thought.[128] It is no marvel that Karl Barth, as well as Heinrich Barth, was charged with holding to a form of identity-speculation. If redemption is thought of as the removal of a qualitative difference between God and man, what else but a final identification of man with God can result?[129]

But how about Barth's later publications? Did he in them still hold to a basic dualism which is overcome by a more basic monism? Did not Barth confess to the fact that he had earlier served false gods but that he was now turning away from all philosophy?[130]

In looking into the *Church Dogmatics*, we soon discover that he is again using Kantian categories. This is particularly so with respect to the question of time. Though using more biblical terms than formerly, he still sets time and eternity dualistically over against one another. The time which God has for us, the time of revelation, is still another time than the time in which we as human beings live.[131]

Again, in his opposition to Brunner, Barth makes an absolute contrast between God and cosmic reality. Cosmic reality is still thought of as wholly unfit for the reception and transmission of revelation.[132] Everything in this world is at most a sign of the presence of revelation. This is true of Scripture in relation to the Word of God, of the human nature of Christ in relation to the Son, of the virgin birth in relation to the incarnation, of the church in relation to the kingdom of God, and of love of neighbor in relation to the love of God.[133] Thus, the entire reformatory confession and theology are pressed

126. *Idem.*
127. *Ibid.*, p. 14.
128. *Idem.*
129. *Idem.*

130. *Ibid.*, pp. 16-17.
131. *Ibid.*, p. 17.
132. *Ibid.*, p. 21.
133. *Idem.*

into this thought schematism. His dogmatical exegesis is made to serve this schematism.[134]

It appears that Van Teylingen's criticism of Barth is similar to that of Zuidema before him. In Van Teylingen's view, Barth's thought structure is similar to that of modern existential philosophy. Barth's essential agreement with Kant's primacy of the practical reason leads him to hold a principle of discontinuity and a principle of continuity that are together destructive of Reformation theology.

4. M. P. Van Dyk

The last man to be considered in this chapter is M. P. Van Dyk. He published a book with the title *Existence and Grace* in 1952.

He who wants to understand Barth, says Van Dyk, must realize that Barth wants to think theologically not philosophically.[135] In particular, Barth has sought to liberate himself from existential philosophy. He wants no general concept of existence. He wants to learn what existence means by listening to revelation.[136] We must therefore impress no philosophical schematism on his theology unless we are compelled to do so. In particular, we can no longer think of Barth's thought as being centrally expressed in the idea of the transcendence of God. Barth now teaches the immanence as well as the transcendence of God. Barth must therefore be thought of as desiring to proclaim the grace of Jesus Christ. This is his basic aim. He seeks to make the concept of existence subservient to this purpose.[137] Did Barth succeed in his purpose of deriving the concept of existence from revelation?[138] This is the question Van Dyk seeks to answer in his book.

His answer is unequivocallly in the negative. Doing full justice to Barth's intentions to have grace rule over existence, we must, none-the-less, he says, conclude that in his theology a general philosophical idea of existence rules over that of grace.

It is impossible to follow Van Dyk in the details of his argument. But his central contention is readily made clear. It is to the effect that both Barth's idea of God and that of man are interpreted, ultimately, by the notion of existence. In Barth's thinking, there is not a

134. *Ibid.*, p. 22.
135. M. P. Van Dyk—*Existentie en Genade*, Franeker 1952, p. 23.
136. *Ibid.*, p. 10.
137. *Ibid.*, p. 9.   138. *Ibid.*, p. 11.

divine next to a human being. There is only "divine act with human act taken up into it. There is only divine movement which calls up human movement, divine transcendence which calls up human transcendence. Looking at this concept of God and with it this concept of man, we come to the conclusion that in Barth's thinking, quite consistently and unavoidably, *both poles* of the relation between God and man have disappeared and that nothing but relativity and existential movement remains."[139] "God has disappeared and man has disappeared. The divine as well as the human being are reduced to the vague notion of act. *God is his coming to man and man is his coming to God.* The man who answers does not exist, he is the answer even as God is his word. Thus man is related to God, or rather, thus man is not related to God, *for this man is not.*"[140]

Van Dyk does not come to this severe judgment except after due examination of the evidence. Barth's theology, he says, is now a theology of grace. It is no longer merely that of the contrast between time and eternity. But grace does not come to man without judgment. Even the sign of grace in the world therefore always stands under the judgment of God. This revelation of grace can never be identified with anything in time. As a man Jesus Christ no doubt had his historical time, but this historical time, even though it was that of Jesus of Nazareth, is not as such revelation. God's revelation is always *"jenseits."*[141] Our time falls apart into past, present and future. For that reason, it cannot be directly identified with revelation. "Historical time is the hiding sign of divine revelation."[142] To be sure, in Jesus Christ God adopts our time. Even so, though adopting our time, God is hidden in it. "Thus *geschiedenis (Geschichte)* stands over against *historie, (Historie)* thus *geschiedenis* though it adopts *historie,* is still its judgment."[143] God's revelation comes as condemnation upon the sign of it, because this sign is not *in the Word.*[144] How then can we know that we have been speaking of divine revelation at all?[145] Barth can give no answer to this question.

In consequence, his theology must be said to be subjective. "Objective in appearance the thought of Barth is none-the-less in reality subjective."[146] Barth will not allow that we have in Christ and in the Bible a direct revelation of God. His whole dialectical approach

---

139. *Ibid.,* p. 132.
140. *Idem.*
141. *Ibid.,* p. 35.
142. *Ibid.,* p. 36.

143. *Idem.*
144. *Idem.*
145. *Ibid.,* p. 42.
146. *Ibid.,* p. 45.

requires him to reject the only objectivity that exists. In this respect, his thought resembles the thought of the ninenteeth century
in general. Together with modern thought in general, Barth has
built doubt into his very system. The *Yes* of his grace rests on the
bottom of pure subjectivity.[147] Together with Berkouwer, says Van
Dyk, we must hold that Barth has made all objectivity in revelation
relative to the human subject.[148] According to Barth, revelation disappears when faith in it disappears. As the result of the application
of the idea of existence, revelation is made dependent upon the believing subject. Thus we have the disappearance of God and his
revelation because the idea of existence is applied to him.

Man too is made to disappear by the application of the idea of
existence. For faith is nothing else than a being taken up into revelation.[149] The whole existence is one of relation.[150] Barth rejects natural theology by means of the existential idea of man's readiness
for God as enveloped in the readiness of God.[151] God is free. But
his freedom is freedom in love to man.[152] God's whole being is the
act of grace, and this act of grace includes the election of all men.
God is not free to condemn men, for he would be denying himself
if he did. God's holiness is nothing but the freedom of his grace.
Thus even Christ could not suffer absolute dereliction. He suffered
only the *No* which God in his grace speaks to men together with his
Yes.[153] It is this universalistic and monistic idea of grace which is
really the sustaining and moving force in the world. God is love.
The entire existence and continued existence of the world, including
the punishments and judgments with which God judges sin, find in
love their ground and explanation.[154] The whole idea of the covenant of grace is explained by Barth in this existentialist fashion.[155]
By applying the idea of existence to God, Barth, in fact, loses the
personality of God.[156] Similarly, using the idea of existence the destination of man is wholly determined in advance by the grace of
God.

On this existential interpretation of the relation of God to man,
there is no real condemnation at Golgotha.[157] Barth's doctrine of the
attributes of God excludes any such thing.[158] Barth has no room in

147. *Ibid.*, p. 46.
148. *Ibid.*, p. 47.
149. *Ibid.*, p. 51.
150. *Idem.*
151. *Ibid.*, p. 54; 11: 1, 143.
152. *Ibid.*, p. 63.

153. *Ibid.*, p. 65.
154. *Ibid.*, p. 67.
155. *Ibid.*, p. 68.
156. *Ibid.*, p. 71.
157. *Ibid.*, p. 81.
158. *Idem.*

his theology for justice except as a judgment of grace.[159] Christ did not accomplish atonement through satisfaction.[160] Barth has roundly declared that it is unnecessary that God should be reconciled to man.[161] God is already reconciled. Christ merely subjected himself to the judgment of God's grace. Thus, the idea of reconciliation itself is interpreted in terms of the idea of existence.[162] The dualism between the world of revelation and that of history is finally overcome by the monism which assures universal salvation of all men in advance in Christ.[163] Sin is sin only against grace.[164] In his deepest existential existence, man cannot say *No* to the grace of God.[165] Man's existential freedom is freedom only to choose for God.[166] Thus, the being of man is really nothing but movement, transcendence toward God.[167] The man Jesus is as being "in the Word."[168] The divinity of Jesus is the act of God for the reconciliation of the world. And the humanity of Jesus is the obedience to this saving work of his divinity.[169] Now God comes to other men in Jesus Christ. Their being is determined by the fact of the act of Jesus in saving them. The existence of other men consists in their participation in what God does for him in the act of salvation.[170] The incarnation is the act of God's grace, and we as men are included in this happening. As men, we are created in this event of incarnation and we are related to it; our whole being as men rests in it. "The being of man is being in the incarnation, or rather, it is happening in the incarnation. . ."[171]

In all this, it is apparent that such concepts as transcendence, revelation and *Geschichte,* are in Barth's theology controlled by the idea of existence.[172] And herewith we have returned to the basic contention of Van Dyk, mentioned earlier. The entire concept of man and the entire concept of God, he says, are controlled by the existentialist principle.[173] Consequently, just as there is on this basis no real bearing of the wrath of God on Golgotha, so there is no place for real recreating grace.[174] When we allow Scripture to speak to us, we shall have to reject the theology of Barth as a whole in its

159. *Ibid.,* p. 101.
160. *Ibid.,* p. 105.
161. *Idem.,* Cf. II:2, p. 826.
162. *Ibid.,* p. 106.
163. *Ibid.,* pp. 99, 112.
164. *Ibid.,* p. 111.
165. *Ibid.,* p. 115.
166. *Ibid.,* p. 118.

167. *Ibid.,* p. 122.
168. *Ibid.,* p. 125.
169. *Idem.*
170. *Ibid.,* p. 126.
171. *Ibid.,* p. 127.
172. *Idem.*
173. *Ibid.,* pp. 130, 131.
174. *Ibid.,* p. 153.

ground structure. This is not to deny the elements of truth that may be found in it. But even in these elements of truth, the false existentialists ground-structure appears.[175] If we do not accept the Bible as the dependable Word of God, then a confrontation between God and man will be artificially constructed.[176] The deepest desire of Barth is no doubt, Van Dyk repeats, to proclaim grace. And the biblical elements in his thought will act as brakes upon his existentialist pattern of thought. But the existential pattern of his thought has led him to a relinquishing of those truths that are central in the revelation of God.[177] The Bible knows nothing of a dropping of the person behind the deed. Where does the Bible speak of God as identical with his coming, with his saving, or with his redemption? On the contrary, everywhere the person of God is presupposed in all these events. He is not identical with his sending, but he sends his Son into the world.[178] The Bible does not hesitate to speak of God as the object of our faith. Barth's idea that the Scriptures are only the witness to revelation, but not identical with revelation, springs from a point of view that itself destroys the true idea of revelation. If God has the freedom to reveal himself directly in history, and therefore in the Bible, then the entire analysis of Barth's theology will have to proceed from this point. And, beginning with this point, the whole of the structure of Barth's theology is to be condemned.[179]

175. *Ibid.*, p. 183.   178. *Ibid.*, p. 185.
176. *Idem.*   179. *Ibid.*, p. 186.
177. *Ibid.*, p. 184.

Section Three

Dialecticism

Chapter X

Medieval Dialecticism

In the remainder of this work, it will be our task to evaluate the theology of Barth more definitely for ourselves. This examination will fall into two main parts. Section three will indicate that, together with Romanism and modern Protestantism, the theology of Barth is dialectical rather than biblical in character. Section four will show that, because of this dialectical character of Barth's theology, it is not in accord with Reformation principles at all but is essentially a speculative theology. As such it resembles Romanism and New Protestantism, and, as such, it cannot escape the charge of illusionism.

The great divide is between those who do and those who do not assume that God has actually acted for and spoken to man in Jesus Christ, and through him in the Scriptures of the Old and New Testaments in final form. Neither the Roman Catholic Church nor the followers of Schleiermacher are willing to do the former, and Barth stands with them in their common opposition to the Reformation principle. The differences between Barth on the one hand, and Romanism with New Protestantism on the other hand, are differences that take place within the framework of a common assumption. This assumption is that there is no such God as can reveal himself to man in history in such a way as to challenge man with his presence.

The informing principles of Romanism as well as the two forms of Protestantism with which we are concerned are those of apostate thought. All three of these forms of theology assume the autonomy of human thought at one point or another. This assumption involves them in a dialectical view of reality as a whole. That is, it involves them in a purely rationalist principle of continuity and a purely irrationalist principle of discontinuity.

Parmenides gave expression to the rationalist principle of continuity when he said that only that can exist which man can consistently think of as existing. Spinoza expressed the same view when he said that the order and connection of things is identical with the order and connection of ideas.

It is this rationalist principle of continuity which underlies the idea that, if God is to be revealed in or to man at all, then he must be wholly revealed. Only if God is *wholly* revealed will his revelation be wholly within the control of man's powers of logical manipulation.

But only an outspoken identity-philosophy can seek for a direct and complete identification of God with man. Accordingly, those who adopt the rationalist principle of continuity frequently also adopt as its correlative a wholly irrationalist principle of discontinuity.

This is especially true of modern thinking since the time of Kant. Even Greek philosophy has its irrationalist principle of individuation. Its notion of pure matter expresses it. And the form-matter scheme of Greek philosophy expresses the idea of correlativity between a purely rationalist principle of continuity and a purely irrationalist principle of discontinuity. Even so, in Greek philosophy the ideal of the actual control of the irrational by the rational principle was kept alive. But, in modern thinking since Kant, this ideal has been given up. Kant said that time and therefore contingency or discontinuity are as ultimate as are the logical principles of continuity. All truth is therefore *de facto*. Rationality is, therefore, nothing in itself. It is what it is for man only as a formal organizing principle of the raw stuff of experience.

It is this irrationalist principle of discontinuity which underlies the idea that, if God is wholly revealed, he must be, at the same time, wholly hidden. On this view, it is only if God is wholly hidden that man is wholly free and God wholly sovereign.

If the abstract rationalist principle of continuity were to be taken by itself, it would obviously destroy all individuality and all history, and therewith all human predication. To prevent this calamity, apostate thought employs the irrationalist principle of discontinuity. By means of it, as correlative to form, the reality of time, of change and therefore of history, is supposed to be preserved. But if the principle of pure discontinuity were employed by itself, it would destroy all rational connection between the facts of time. And human predication would cease once more.

To prevent the calamity of the destruction of human predication by the exclusive use of either the principle of *pure* form or *pure* matter, the two principles are put into correlativity with one another.

Will this idea of the correlativity between an abstract or formal principle of continuity, and an equally abstract principle of discontinuity, save human predication? The answer must be in the negative. Each of the two principles are, in the nature of the case, destructive of one another. Each claims the whole of reality exclusively for itself. Nowhere can the contact between them be that of supplementation. On the contrary, any contact must always be that of a death-struggle.

Accordingly, a God who reveals himself *wholly* must reveal himself to himself alone. And then the idea of revelation no longer has any meaning. And a God who is *wholly* hidden must also be wholly hidden to himself alone. And then the idea of hiddenness no longer has any meaning.

Yet the entire idea of dialecticism is built upon the idea of the correlativity of a purely formal principle of continuity and a purely abstract principle of discontinuity. The assumption is that a purely static or formal principle of continuity can supplement and be supplemented by a principle of discontinuity based upon the notion of pure chance. It would be easier to combine fire and water.

An objection may be raised at this point. It may be urged that no one holds to the correlativity of pure staticism and pure dynamism. It may be urged that, in the idea of analogy, dialectical thought ascribes priority to the principle of continuity over that of discontinuity. But, in reply to this, it is to be urged that such an ascription of priority to rationality over irrationality can be made only by purely arbitrary decree. If any priority is to be given to the principle of continuity or rationality, this must be done on the basis of this principle alone, and exclusively in terms of itself. That is to say, if analogy is to be analogy at all, it must be such because of the principle of identity that operates in it. And the principle of identity, as earlier noted, does not operate at all but it is purely formal. If it is to "operate," it must do so by becoming correlative to pure discontinuity. And how can abstract identity *become* correlative?

Thus, on the assumption of apostate or dialectical thought, a purely formal staticism in logic seeks in vain to make contact with a non-being composed of pure chance.

It is the apostate man that has brought himself into the impasse just now described. Assuming himself to be autonomous, he has no tools with which to explain either himself or his world except by the two mutually destructive principles of interpretation mentioned.

The principle of dialecticism employed by the would-be autonomous man has appeared in two forms. There is first the form-matter scheme of Greek thinking, and there is second the freedom-nature scheme of modern thinking. The latter is really only the modernized form of the former. Thus, we may speak of all apostate thought as starting from the common assumption of the autonomy or self-sufficiency of man and of his attempt to interpret himself and his world by the mutually destructive principles of pure staticism and pure dynamism.

Now Roman Catholic thinking has tied Christian teaching onto the Greek form-matter form of apostate dialectical thought. Its doctrine of analogy is the expression of this combination. In it there is the combination of pure equivocism or irrationalism and the idea of univocism or pure rationalism. There is assumed to be an imbalance in this idea of analogy. This imbalance is in favor of the idea of univocism. The absolute correlativity that would result from an equal ultimacy of pure equivocism as over against pure univocism would provide no basis for the primacy of God and of Christ that Romanism requires. Rome holds that all being is inherently good. Therefore God must have more being than man. Only then can he be the source of the eventual victory of goodness over evil in man and in creation as a whole.

The idea of the chain of being or the fitness of things gives expression to the imbalance of the Romanist dialectical principle. God draws all men and all things to himself so far as the fitness of things allows. The function of Christ in this Romanist scheme is to help the upward movement of finite and evil reality to the eternally good being which is God. Here then we have a Christological interpretation of man and of his goal of participation in God as good.

New Protestantism and Barth have tied Christian teaching to the nature-freedom scheme that springs from Kant's notion of the primacy of the Practical Reason. The idea of the primacy of Christ, as maintained by Schleiermacher and Ritschl as well as by Barth, is built upon some form of the Kantian motif of the primacy of the Practical Reason. Barth, no less than Schleiermacher and Ritschl, assumes the legitimacy of autonomous theoretical thought in the field of science and in the field of philosophy. Barth, no less than these men, therefore holds to a wholly irrationalist principle of discontinuity and to a wholly rationalist principle of continuity. In fact, the Kantian principle of discontinuity is, if possible, more irrationalist than its Greek counterpart. So also the Kantian principle of continuity is, if possible, more rationalist because more formal than its Greek counterpart. For this very reason, the correlativity between the two principles is the more absolute. And for this reason the imbalance between the two principles in favor of the principle of continuity is also the more absolute. If therefore there is a basically universalist tendency in Roman Catholic thought, this basically universalist tendency is even more in evidence in the two forms of modern dialectical theology. And Barth's theology being most consistently irrationalist, it is therefore also the most consistently rationalist. If he maintains the *sovereignty* of grace, he equally maintains its *universality*.

It is from this point of view that the Reformed theologians and philosophers discussed in the preceding chapter have criticized Barth. They found his principle of discontinuity expressed in his nominalism. And this nominalism, they asserted in unison, constitutes a threat to the biblical idea of the actual saving power of God in history. There can be no actual atonement in history through the work of Christ for man, and there can be no regeneration and faith in the believer whereby he can say with Paul that there is now no condemnation for him. As God's wrath cannot be manifest in history upon man's disobedience, so his grace cannot be his possession. But if Barth's nominalist principle of discontinuity is inherently destructive of the idea of the triumph of God's grace through Christ in history, this is no less true of his realist or rationalist principle of continuity. Barth's purely formal principle of continuity is but the correlative of his principle of pure discontinuity. According to his principle of continuity, Barth virtually absorbs the human subject into the divine. And the divine subject is itself formalized till nothing remains of it but an abstract principle of goodness. On this view, it is indeed possible for man to sin, but only in the sense that a child can disobey his parent. Man cannot sin in such a way as to require his being driven forth from the father's house.

Barth's idea of analogy therefore is not basically different from that of Romanism. Both express a Christianized humanism or theodicy.

According to both, nature is inherently open for grace, and grace is the expected consummation of nature. According to Kant, man's theoretical reason knows nature but not nature's God. But according to Kant's practical reason, man postulates a God who has a purpose with nature. It is thus that pure rationalism and pure irrationalism are combined. It is thus that science and religion are "harmonized." And the primacy is given to morality and religion. The theology of modern Protestantism and the theology of Barth have followed in this track. And for this very reason their theology is a far cry from historic Protestantism and is basically similar to the theology of Romanism. And since such a theology works with a God and a Christ that is a projection of man's practical reason, this theology leads back to, as it has sprung from, the human subject as sufficient to itself. It will be our business in the remainder of this work to show more fully that the Reformed theologians and philosophers cited were not mistaken in the criticism they made.

But our concern is with the theology of Barth, not with his personal faith. When Dr. F. W. Grosheide recently wrote an essay on the writing of history, he referred to Rudolf Bultmann and his method of demythologizing the message of the New Testament. The writings of Bultmann teach us what one will think of biblical history if he does not approach the question from the point of view of faith. But, in saying this, he assures us that he is not dealing with Bultmann as a person.[1] Our attitude to Barth is similar to that of Grosheide in relation to Bultmann.

Our attitude toward Barth is also similar to that of M. P. Van Dyk as we have heard him express it in the preceding chapter. Van Dyk takes for granted that Barth wants to think theologically, not philosophically. Barth wants to learn what existence is by listening to revelation. But though it is Barth's deepest intention to have grace rule over existence, in the end it is, says Van Dyk, existence that rules over grace. With this judgment we agree. Again with Berkouwer we gladly note the great influence that Scripture has had on Barth's formulation of his theology. But we also agree with Berkouwer when he asserts that for all that there is no transition from wrath to grace in Barth's theology. How could there be, since his theology is dialectical in character?

1. *Gereformeerd Theologisch Tijdschrift*, Vol. 56, p. 19.

A further remark must be made here. Our first concern is not with the effects of Barth's writings. Some of these effects have been good. Barth has called attention to some defects in historic Protestant thinking, which has not always been truly Christological and biblical. The Romanist principle of natural theology has, to a considerable extent, influenced Protestant theology throughout its history. This is true of Reformed as well as of Lutheran theology. Recent Reformed theologians are seeking to be more truly Christological and more truly biblical than some of their forefathers were. This may be due, at least in part, to the stimulation of Barth. Liberal or modernist theologians too have turned to a renewed study of Scripture. Through Barth the Bible has had more influence on at least some of them than it formerly had. Moreover, a number of church people, other than theologians, have learned to have a new respect for the Bible as in some sense the Word of God. For all this, who can help but be grateful to Barth and to God?

But we cannot stop here. What does Barth mean when he says that he wants a truly Christological theology? For Schleiermacher too "everything is related to the redemption accomplished by Jesus of Nazareth."[1a] But now listen to what Barth says about Schleiermacher's Christology. "Schleiermacher's Christology has as its summit the indication of a quantitative superiority, dignity and significance in Christ as opposed to our own Christianity. This is as much as to say that just because the point with Christ is that he has only an incomparably greater quantity of that which we see in ourselves as our Christianity, this indication is ultimately linked with the assertion, the self-assertion, of our own Christianity. The two foci of the ellipse draw relentlessly closer to one another, and how is the dissolution and disappearance of the objective moment in the subjective to be prevented? *The Word is not so assured here in its independence in respect to faith as should be the case if this theology of faith were a true theology of the Holy Spirit.* In a proper theology of the Holy Spirit there could be no question of dissolving the Word. Here, quite seriously, there is a question of such a dissolution."[2]

Barth recognizes the fact that Schleiermacher renounced a purely speculative Christology.[3] He recognizes the fact that Schleiermacher

1a. *The Christian Faith,* New York, 1928, p. 52.
2. *Protestant Thought from Rousseau to Ritschl* being the translation of eleven chapters of Die Protestantische Theologie IM 19. Jahrhundert; New York, 1959, p. 352.
3. *Ibid.,* p. 349.

too wanted to build upon the principles of the Reformation.[4] Yet he finds that in Schleiermacher's theology Christ has not really been given the priority over man. In Schleiermacher's thinking, the superiority of Christ is only a quantitative one. On such a basis, the dissolution of "the objective moment in the subjective" can scarcely be presented. Therefore, in the theology of *The Christian Faith* it is the Christian rather than the Christ who comes first. Schleiermacher's theology is after all written from an anthropocentric point of view. By thinking of faith and of Christ as two foci of an ellipse, "Schleiermacher turns the Christian relationship of man with God into an apparent human possibility."[5] "The great formal principle of Schleiermacher's theology is at the same time its material principle. Christian pious self-awareness contemplates and describes itself: that is in principle the be-all and end-all of this theology."[6]

Inasmuch then as Schleiermacher's basic starting-point is the human self-consciousness, Jesus Christ gives him a great deal of trouble. "He obviously gives Schleiermacher, the professor and preacher, a great deal of trouble! But nevertheless he is in fact there. And the professor and preacher goes to this trouble, swims ceaselessly against his own current, and wishes under all circumstances, and be it at the cost of certain artifices and sophistries, to be a Christocentric theologian. Whether he really is, who can say? Perhaps in fleeing from one kind of philosophic speculation he became all the more deeply embroiled in another. Perhaps after all he avoided the offence of a real Christology."[7]

Schleiermacher wanted in his Christology "to proclaim Christ." "And the fervour with which he did it, as a dogmatician and preacher, is also beyond all doubt in the minds of all who know him. If anyone was most deeply in earnest in this matter then it was Schleiermacher. That cannot of course be regarded as a last word upon the subject; the theological question of truth must remain open here as everywhere, even in the face of the greatest personal sincerity."[8]

Our question with respect to Barth resembles that of Barth with respect to Schleiermacher. Is his theology perhaps, for all its serious intent to make Christ come first, still an ellipse theology? Is Christ really first in the theology of Barth? Or is his theology of the Word a consciousness-theology after all?

4. *Ibid.*, p. 354.
5. *Ibid.*, p. 344.
6. *Ibid.*, p. 338.
7. *Ibid.*, p. 313.
8. *Idem.*

In asking this question, it is imperative that we ask it first of ourselves. Are we not all subjective? Can anyone escape his self-awareness as a Christian? And must not faith, to be genuine faith, be *our* faith? Was this perhaps all that Schleiermacher meant by his idea of the Christian self-consciousness. Not at all, says Barth. And we may well agree. For the question of subjectivity in theology is a quite different one. It is a religious question. It is the question whether the human subject regards itself as the ultimate or final reference point in all that it says about itself and its relation to Christ. Calvin realized this fact full well. It is the starting-point of his *Institutes*. The questions of creation, of sin and of redemption, are immediately involved in the question of self-consciousness. Proper self-awareness is awareness of the proper relation of the self to Christ. As noted earlier, Barth says that he agrees with Calvin on this point. He only seeks to make Calvin's meaning somewhat more precise.

But Barth makes Calvin's meaning "more precise" in terms of his own Christology. And in Barth's Christ, God is wholly revealed and at the same time wholly hidden. It is only if we have this Christ, so runs Barth's argument, that we can really do full justice to what Calvin started out to say.

And herewith the question is asked where the Christ is to be found? It is the problem of the relation of faith to history. Did Christ appear in history? Barth affirms with Calvin that he did. Barth wants no Christ that is a mere projection of the human consciousness. Again, does Christ speak by his Spirit in the Scriptures? Must we say that the Bible *is* the Word of God? Barth is again in agreement with Calvin that we must. But is his agreement with Calvin more than a formal one? Is Barth's insistence on the idea that, while revelation is historical history, it is not revelational, consistent with Calvin's basic concept of revelation? It does not seem to be.

If we are to have more than a consciousness-theology, we must have Christ, the Son of God, coming to us directly in history and speaking to us in history through the Scriptures. We look in vain for Christ if we do not hear him speaking to us directly in the Bible. A truly Christological approach is a truly biblical approach. A Christ-centered theology is a theology of the Word.

Finally, only by having a Christ-centered and a Bible-centered theology does one have a proper theology of grace. As over against Rome with its synergism, Barth follows the Reformers in affirming this point too. In fact, he is against any form of synergism and of natural theology wherever it is found, in Protestant as well as in Romanist theology. With great erudition and with great consistency, Barth searches out every form of consciousness-theology, and with it any form of synergism, in order to set it under the judgment of Christ, of the theology of the Word and of grace. But being *against* synergism in itself means very little. We must ask what the positive foundation is for Barth's opposition to Rome. That positive foundation, as already noted, is his activist view of the relation of God to man. And it is Barth's basic activism that allows for neither general nor special revelation in the Reformation sense of the term.

Those who are interested in Reformation theology today cannot fail, therefore, to take note of Barth's qualifications and corrections with respect to Calvin's view of Christ and Scripture. In the most vigorous fashion, Barth rejects Calvin's theology of grace as being really no theology of grace at all. The reader will recall this fact from what was earlier said about Barth's view of election.[9] According to Barth, Christ is the electing God and the elected man. As such, he is the ontological and epistemological basis of the believer's faith. Only if we have this view of election, says Barth, do we understand the scriptural meaning of grace. In terms of Christ as the electing God and the elected man, grace is both sovereign and universal. Not having such a view of election, Calvin has no eye either for the sovereign or for the universal character of grace. Grace is Christ as the act of saving all men. But Calvin does not regard him as such. He has a God back of Christ who does the electing of men. Calvin has no eye for the fact that men, to be truly men, are such as they receive the grace of God in Christ.

Barth rejects with utmost clarity Calvin's doctrine of grace and of Christ. He is less outspoken in his rejection of Calvin's view of revelation. At this point, it is later orthodoxy that must bear the brunt of his attack. It is orthodoxy that is said to work with static notions of revelation. It is orthodoxy that does not see that Scripture cannot be identified with revelation. It is orthodoxy's notion of revealedness *(Inspiriertheit)* that is utterly destructive of the idea that Christ is the act of saving all men.

It would have been more consistent with his own view of Christ and of grace if Barth had also charged Luther and Calvin directly with holding to a static view of revelation. Barth gives no evidence to prove that, though Calvin held to anything but a truly activist

9. II:2, p. 119.

view of grace and of Christ, he yet held to an activist view of revelation. In fact, when he says that Calvin's statement on man's relation to God needs to be made more precise he, in effect, destroys it altogether. He brings about "precision" by means of his Christology. And, in terms of his Christology, God is wholly hidden even when wholly revealed. Calvin taught no such thing. For him God is directly revealed in history. This point will engage us again.

Barth's view of revelation is wholly in accord with his view of Christ and of grace. He asserts plainly that Scripture *cannot* teach anything but free and universal grace in Christ. The idea that God is wholly revealed in Christ, and, when wholly revealed he is at the same time wholly hidden, is but the expression in the realm of revelation of his idea of the free and universal grace of Christ.

1. *The Christ of Barth Cannot Be Found*

If we are to evaluate fairly Barth's view of Christ, we must ask again where his Christ may be found. One point is plain. It is that, according to Barth, Christ cannot be found to be directly identified with anything in history. Christ cannot even be directly identified with Jesus of Nazareth. Yes, indeed, Barth says that God is identical with Jesus. He lays the greatest possible stress on this identification. For him everything depends upon it. Without this identification, he argues, there would be no divine-human encounter at all. It is on this identification that the fact of the reconciliation of all men in Christ rests. Only through this identification do men have saving contact with God at all. But then this identification of God with Jesus must be *indirect*.

If the identification were direct, then the revelation of God in Jesus would be subject to the relativities of human experience. Then too this Jesus, and with him God's revelation, would lose its uniqueness. Jesus would then be in a class with other men, and the revelation of God through him would be in a class with revelations through other men. Such a revelation, says Barth, would be no revelation at all.

Moreover, since the revelation of God cannot, according to Barth, be directly identified with Jesus of Nazareth, so also the Scriptures cannot be directly identified with revelation. For Barth the Bible *is* the Word of God but this does not for him indicate direct identification. The idea of a given revelation is from Barth's point of view a pagan idea. In the case of Scripture, as well as in the case of Jesus Christ, the identification of God must be indirect. God's communication with man is indirect communication always. When God is wholly revealed to man, then he is wholly hidden in this very revelation.

The reason for Barth's rejection of the idea of direct identification of the revelation of God with anything in history, either in Jesus Christ or in the Scriptures, can perhaps best be illustrated from his idea of the resurrection of Christ. In the fact of the resurrection, we have, argues Barth, the climax of the revelation of God to man. It is the fact of the resurrection that lights up all other facts, past, present and future. For in it God is wholly revealed. It is Jesus Christ as the electing God, beyond whom there is no God and no counsel of God, who has wholly revealed himself in the incarnation. And the fact that God is wholly revealed in the incarnation appears most clearly in the resurrection. According to Barth, the resurrection does not follow in ordinary time *(Historie)* upon the event of the incarnation. As noted before, the steps of Christ's humiliation and the steps of his exaltation are, for Barth, always co-present with one another. Even so, they have their own internal succession. And therefore the resurrection stands in a special sense for the completeness of God's revelation. It must be spoken of as a fact that is the objective basis for the faith of the apostles. Barth stresses this "objectivity" of the resurrection over against Bultmann's idea of faith as producing its own objectivity. The whole of Christianity, its objectivity as a revelation of God's reconciliation of all men, depends for Barth upon the factual character of the resurrection. In the resurrection, God is as a *fact* wholly present to man.

But precisely because of the need for absolute identification of God's entire being with the fact of the resurrection, Barth cannot tolerate the idea that this resurrection should be directly identified with any fact of ordinary history. The facts of ordinary history, he says, have no objectivity in them at all. To be sure, the resurrection must also *(auch)* be a fact of ordinary history. In the incarnation the eternal God submits himself to our human time. Even so, there must never be direct identification of any sort. Just because God must be *wholly* revealed when revealed at all, he must be wholly hidden in his revelation. God could not be wholly revealed and as such identified in history.

The question that confronts us now is whether on Barth's theory of indirect communication it is possible to find Jesus Christ at all. If God can be wholly revealed to man in Christ, is he then really more than man? If faith has for its object this wholly revealed God, what else then is faith but revelation itself? And what else then is revelation but revelation of God to himself? And is such a God anything more than a Platonic idea wholly beyond the reach of man?

We are not forgetting that, according to Barth, God is also wholly hidden in his revelation. But does this fact make Christ any easier to find? Why does God have to be wholly hidden? Is it not because to reveal himself at all God must wholly reveal himself? The meaning of the idea that God is wholly hidden is determined by the fact that revelation, to be revelation at all, must be exhaustive revelation. But the idea of exhaustive revelation destroys the whole distinction between God and man. On its basis God is wholly lost in man and therewith God is wholly hidden to himself as well as to man.

To be sure, Barth does not want any identification of God with man or of man with God. He spurns the thought that his idea of revelation springs in any sense from an identity philosophy. But what means does he have of keeping his theology from being an identity philosophy? The only means he has is that of the idea of the wholly hidden character of God's revelation. But if God is wholly hidden, then the confrontation between God and man is lost once more. For in that case both God and man are wholly hidden to themselves and to one another. A God who can be wholly hidden to man is also wholly hidden to himself. Such a God is no God at all. He has no self-contained character. And a man who exists by virtue of his participation in this wholly hidden aspect of the revelation of this wholly hidden God is also wholly lost to himself. Zuidema's articles have taught us this much unmistakably.

It will be objected at this point that Barth does not take either the idea of exhaustive revelation or the idea of the wholly hidden character of revelation by itself. This is true. It would be utterly unfair to Barth to judge his idea of revelation by either the idea of exhaustive revelation or by the idea of the wholly hidden character of revelation. For him everything depends upon these two being kept into correlative relation with one another. The idea of indirect communication itself depends upon the correlativity between the idea of revelation in which God is wholly manifest and wholly hidden at the same time.

But our difficulties with finding the Christ of Barth are not alleviated by this fact. The correlativity idea itself is based upon the assumption that there is no irreducible difference between God and man. For the distinction between total revelation and total hiddenness is in the last analysis a distinction within God himself. It is God who is wholly revealed and at the same time wholly hidden. But to whom is he wholly revealed and wholly hidden? He is wholly hidden to man indeed, but it is to man as one who participates in God in this dual type of revelation. Man is what he is by participation in the only fully real or authentic man, namely, Jesus Christ. Man is real to the extent that he participates in Jesus Christ as the act of revelation of God. And this act of revelation consists of God's being wholly revealed and wholly hidden. In other words, man is real only so far as he participates in the internal self-distinction within God. Any sort of reality that man may think he has prior to or independent of this participation is no reality at all. Moreover for Barth revelation is at the same time reconciliation. Thus reconciliation is also a matter of internal self-distinction for God. And man's reconciliation with God turns out to be a matter of his participation in God's self-reconciliation through Christ as reprobate and elect.

2. *The Reformation View of Christ*

Barth's view of Christ does not seem to be anything like the Reformation view of Christ. The Christ of Reformation theology is simply and directly identical with the Jesus of Nazareth of history. This Christ can be known, after he has returned to heaven, from the Scriptures only. Jesus promised his Spirit in order to lead the apostles into all truth. He had already sent his prophets before him to tell of his coming into the world. Thus the whole Bible, the Old and New Testament, is the direct revelation of God given to man to tell about Christ and his redeeming grace.

Time and again the Reformed theologians who were mentioned in the seventh and eighth chapters of this work stress the fact that this Christ is accepted by faith alone. This Christ must be taken at his word. We believe him to be what he is because he tells us what he is. He says he is the bread of life. So we believe that he is the bread of life. He tells us he is the way, the truth and the life. So we believe that he is the way, the truth and the life. And why do we need redemption? Christ Jesus tells us that we are sinners. He tells us himself, and through his apostles and prophets, that we have become sinners at the beginning of history through our first representative, Adam (Rom. 5:12). And he tells us that he has been sent by the Father to bear the penalty due us for our sins and to bring us into his presence forever.

Expressed a little more fully, the following picture emerges. Scripture tells us about the origin of ourselves and the world. It tells us of a task assigned to man. The historical character of the Genesis narrative must be maintained. It must be maintained over against those who would, like Philo and Origen, allegorize what Genesis teaches on origins.[10] The Genesis account tells us about the fall of man at the beginning of history. It speaks of the far-reaching and terrible results of the fall.[11] Everywhere about us, we see the evil consequences of this fall. The true nature of evil about us and within us is seen only if regarded in the light of the narrative of the fall as an historical occurrence. The event of the fall is of such great significance that the whole of Christianity stands or falls with it.[12] Christ himself confirmed the witness given in Scripture with respect to it. And no marvel, for the fall is a necessary component of the history of redemption.[13]

On Barth's view, this simple picture of the biblical view of sin and its origin as presented by Bavinck, falls away. His view of revelation as indicating both the fact that God is wholly revealed and wholly hidden leads him to reject the direct confrontation of God and man in history at every point. He is particularly outspoken in his rejection of the historicity of the Genesis account of the origin of man and of sin.[13a]

Having told us of the origin of sin, Scripture also tells us of its nature. Its nature is the transgression of the holy law of the love of God. And the nature of grace comports with the idea that sin is transgression of the law of God.[14]

Does this mean that we have been given a rationally penetrable insight into the question of the origin or nature of sin? Not at all. We must assert of sin that "we know not whence nor what it is."[15] We believe that it is what Christ in his Word says it is. We believe and realize deep in our being that we as men, not God, are responsible for it. Sin makes us guilty before God.[16]

Eternal punishment with Satan would be the just desert of every

10. Bavinck, *Gereformeerde Dogmatiek*, Kampen, 1918, III, p. 12.
11. *Ibid.*, p. 13.   13. *Ibid.*, p. 16.
12. *Ibid.*, p. 15.
13a. Barth, *Church Dogmatics*, III:1, p. 84ff.
14. Bavinck, *op. cit.*, pp. 138-139.
15. *Ibid.*, p. 143.   16. *Ibid.*, p. 174.

man. "As all men have sinned in Adam, lie under the curse, and are [deserving of] eternal death, God would have done no injustice by leaving them all to perish and delivering them over to condemnation on account of sin, according to the words of the Apostle (Rom. iii.19), 'that every mouth may be stopped, and all the world may become guilty before God;' (vs. 23) 'for all have sinned, and come short of the glory of God;' and (vi. 23), 'for the wages of sin is death.' "[17]

"But 'in this the love of God was manifested, that he sent his only-begotten Son into the world,' 'that whosoever believeth on him should not perish, but have everlasting life' (1 John iv.9; John iii.16)."[18]

". . . God mercifully sends the messengers of these most joyful tidings to whom he will, and at what time he pleaseth; by whose ministry men are called to repentance and faith in Christ crucified. 'How then shall they call on him in whom they have not believed? And how shall they believe in him of whom they have not heard? And how shall they hear without a preacher? And how shall they preach, except they be sent?' (Rom. x.14, 15)."[19]

"The wrath of God abideth upon those who believe not this gospel . . ."[20]

"That some receive the gift of faith from God, and others do not receive it, proceeds from God's eternal decree. 'For known unto God are all his works from the beginning of the world' (Acts xv.18; Eph. i.11). According to which decree he graciously softens the hearts of the elect, however obstinate, and inclines them to believe; while he leaves the non-elect in his just judgment to their own wickedness and obduracy. And herein is especially displayed the profound, the merciful, and at the same time the righteous discrimination between men, equally involved in ruin; or that decree of *election* and *reprobation,* revealed in the Word of God, which, though men of perverse, impure, and unstable minds wrest it to their own destruction, yet to holy and pious souls affords unspeakable consolation."[21]

"Election is the unchangeable purpose of God, whereby, before the foundation of the world, he hath, out of mere grace, according to the sovereign good pleasure of his own will, chosen, from the

---

17. *The Canons of the Synod of Dort,* First Head of Doctrine, of Divine Predestination, Article I.
18. *Ibid.,* Article II.   20. *Ibid.,* Article IV.
19. *Ibid.,* Article III.   21. *Ibid.,* Article VI.

whole human race, which had fallen through their own fault, from
their primitive state of rectitude, into sin and destruction, a certain
number of persons to redemption in Christ, whom he from eternity
appointed the Mediator and head of the elect, and the foundation of
salvation.

"This elect number, though by nature neither better nor more
deserving than others, but with them involved in one common
misery, God hath decreed to give to Christ to be saved by him, and
effectually to call and draw them to his communion by his Word
and Spirit; to bestow upon them true faith, justification, and sanctification; and having powerfully preserved them in the fellowship of
his Son, finally to glorify them for the demonstration of his mercy,
and for the praise of the riches of his glorious grace: as it is written,
'According as he hath chosen us in him before the foundation of the
world, that we should be holy and without blame before him in love;
having predestinated us unto the adoption of children by Jesus
Christ to himself, according to the good pleasure of his will, to the
praise of the glory of his grace wherein he hath made us accepted
in the Beloved' (Eph. i.4-6). And elsewhere, 'Whom he did pre-
destinate, them he also called; and whom he called, them he
also justified; and whom he justified, them he also glorified'
(Rom. viii.30)."[22]

It is apparent even from these quotations that, according to the
Synod of Dort, election is "the fountain of every saving good"[23] and
that, according to this Synod, it should be taught "for the glory of
God's most holy Name, and for enlivening and comforting his
people."[24] For in the doctrine of election the sovereign grace of the
triune God, Father, Son and Holy Spirit appears. Sin is so heinous
a thing that all men, on account of it, deserve eternal punishment.
God is free according to his justice not to redeem any man. Therefore he is free, by his grace in Christ, to save some men from the
"common ruin" and to pass others by.

But God is thus free in his act of election, not by subordinating
his holiness and righteousness to grace and love. He is free in his
act of election because he sends his Son into the world to satisfy
divine justice. "God is not only supremely merciful, but also supremely just. And his justice requires (as he hath revealed himself
in his Word) that our sins committed against his infinite majesty

22. *Ibid.*, Article VII.   24. *Ibid.*, Article XIV.
23. *Ibid.*, Article IX.

should be punished, not only with temporal, but with eternal punishments, both in body and soul; which we can not escape, unless satisfaction be made to the justice of God."[25]

How was satisfaction to be made to the justice of God? Through Christ Jesus "who was made sin, and became a curse for us and in our stead, that he might make satisfaction to divine justice on our behalf."[26]

"The death of the Son of God is the only and most perfect sacrifice and satisfaction for sin; is of infinite worth and value, abundantly sufficient to expiate the sins of the whole world."[27]

It is thus through the death of Christ in history that God's sovereign purpose of election in Christ was accomplished in history. "For this was the sovereign counsel and most gracious will and purpose of God the Father, that the quickening and saving efficacy of the most precious death of his Son should extend to all the elect, for bestowing upon them alone the gift of justifying faith, thereby to bring them infallibly to salvation: that is, it was the will of God, that Christ by the blood of the cross, whereby he confirmed the new covenant, should effectually redeem out of every people, tribe, nation, and language, all those, and those only, who were from eternity chosen to salvation, and given to him by the Father; that he should confer upon them faith, which, together with all the other saving gifts of the Holy Spirit, he purchased for them by his death; should purge them from all sin, both original and actual, whether committed before or after believing; and having faithfully preserved them even to the end, should at last bring them free from every spot and blemish to the enjoyment of glory in his own presence forever."[28]

It is this story of man's creation in paradise, his fall into sin, and his sovereign redemption through Christ, of which the Scripture tells us. It is Christ himself telling his people what he has done and will do for them in his sovereign grace. God binds himself by oath that, notwithstanding man's apostasy and unfaithfulness, he will, in Christ and by his Spirit, grant man eternal life.[29] From all eternity the Father, the Son and the Holy Ghost, wholly free and self-conscious in their covenant relation to one another, plan the work of salvation to be accomplished in history.[30] "The work of salvation

---

25. *Ibid.*, Second Head of Doctrine. Of the Death of Christ, and the Redemption of Men thereby. Article I.

26. *Ibid.*, Article II.

27. *Ibid.*, Article III.

28. *Ibid.*, Article VIII.

29. Bavinck, *op. cit.*, p. 211.

30. *Ibid.*, p. 222.

is a work of the three persons, in which all work together and in which each performs his own task."[31] Thus the covenant of grace realized in time has its foundation in the eternal counsel of peace.[32] Thus the covenant of grace which is revealed in time "rests on an eternal unchangeable basis."[33] The covenant of grace is certain of realization because of the triune God and his counsel back of it. It is first of all God, not man, who acts in the covenant of grace. "But it is again the triune God who, after having conceived the work of redemption, brings it to realization."[34] "It is not as though God first made his covenant with Adam and with Noah, with Abraham and Israel and at last with Christ. But the covenant of grace lies ready from eternity in the counsel of peace of the three persons and is realized at once after the fall through him. Christ does not begin to work for the first time after his incarnation, and the Holy Spirit does not commence his work for the first time with his outpouring at Pentecost. For as the work of creation is a trinitarian work, so the work of redemption is from the first moment a work of the three persons. All grace which, after the fall, pours into creation, comes to it from the Father through the Son in the Holy Spirit. Immediately after the fall the Son arose as Mediator, as the second and last Adam, who took the place of the first, and restores and completes what he destroyed and neglected. And the Holy Spirit at once arose as Comforter, as the one who applies the salvation which was to be procured by Christ . . . The Father is eternally Father, the Son eternally Mediator and the Holy Spirit eternally Comforter. For this reason the Old Testament is to be regarded as one in essence and substance with the New Testament."[35]

It is in this manner that we can see something of the nature of the triumph of grace as Reformed theologians, following Calvin, have seen it. This grace is free or sovereign. The three persons of the trinity are from all eternity equally involved in its conception and in its execution. The triune God creates freely. There is therefore no power of any sort that stands over against him to resist his work. Creation was perfect when it came into existence. Even the devil was at the first a good angel. There is no power of evil which is original. There is no non-being that stands over against being as a reactionary force. There is no wandering cause that gives trouble to the gods that be as they fashion the world according to ideals of

---

31. *Idem.*
32. *Ibid.*, p. 223.
33. *Idem.*

34. *Idem.*
35. *Idem.*

the good, the true and the beautiful above them. There is no *Nihil* that has independent power over against God.

It is the act of free creation that furnishes the basis of the free act of God's redemption. If creation were not free in this absolute sense, then grace would not be free either. Free grace can be built upon creation just because creation itself is free. Even from the beginning the free activity of the three persons of the trinity is expressed in the work of creation, so this work of creation is the foundation of the work of redemption, and redemption is in turn the crown of creation.

The true universality as well as the true sovereignty of grace is thus established. The first promises of grace as they come from the mouth of God to Adam and Eve are universal in nature. "In the fulness of time Jew and Gentile are reconciled in the one man; humanity gathers itself about the cross; and the church, chosen out of this humanity, stands in the most intimate connection with it."[36] Luther was not wrong when he spoke of the "gracious, happy punishment" that was pronounced by God upon the serpent, the woman and the man after the fall. For grace was intermingled with this punishment. Mercy speaks through it even more than wrath. And, on the basis of this mercy, the victory of mankind is assured.[37]

It must be noted in particular how centrally Christ is placed in this biblical story. There is not an act in eternity or in time but he is there and is the center of it. "The whole of the covenant is from beginning to end committed to him; in him alone does it have solidity; as the father has ordained the kingdom to be his, so he ordains it for them who are given him; the blessings procured by him he gives to them as an inheritance."[38] It is all important, says Bavinck, to hold that neither in the counsel of peace nor in the covenant of grace must Christ even for a moment be thought of as separate from his own. In both it is the *Christus mysticus*. Christ as the second Adam appears as the acting party.[39] In his work of creation and in his ordaining of the covenant of works, God already had the Christ and the covenant of grace in mind. They are all related to one another in his counsel. Even the breaking of the covenant of works does not take place independently of the counsel of God.[40]

It is this Christ who speaks in the gospels and says that no one comes to the Father but by him. In the whole of his person and in

36. *Ibid.*, p. 224.
37. *Ibid.*, pp. 224-225.
38. *Ibid.*, p. 240.

39. *Idem.*
40. *Idem.*

all of his work he is a manifestation of the love of God.[41] He came to do the will of God. He was obedient to the will of God. He was made under the law (Gal. 4:4). He came to give his life a ransom for many (Matt. 20:28). "For he hath made him to be sin for us who knew no sin; that we might be made the righteousness of God in him" (II Cor. 5:21). Paul had seen nothing but scandal in the cross of Christ. But when it pleased God to reveal his Son in him, then this cross became all his glory. Then he wrote to the Corinthians: "But of him are ye in Christ Jesus, who of God is made unto us wisdom, and righteousness, and sanctification, and redemption: that, according as it is written, He that glorieth, let him glory in the Lord" (I Cor. 1:30, 31).

As it was always the desire of Christ Jesus to do the will of God, therefore in his suffering he made satisfaction for his own to the Father. This was a vicarious satisfaction; for they had broken the will or law of his love and were therefore under his wrath. He fully bore the punishment for sin as announced in Genesis 3.[42] In this vicarious satisfaction, the objective historical foundation for the salvation of his people is found. And this vicarious satisfaction in turn rests upon the counsel of peace. In the person and in the work of Christ, God maintained himself as God and brought his virtues, that of righteousness as well as of love, to manifestation. While Christ was truly God, it can be said that God himself through the cross reconciled all things to himself[43] (II Cor. 5:18, 19). "In the καταλλαγή God himself stands forth as subject. In giving Christ as ἱλαστήριον, he brings about a relation of peace between himself and the world. He shows wrath no longer; what made him to be our ἀντίδικος, namely, sin, is covered in the sacrifice of Christ."[44]

"This καταλλαγή is the content of the gospel; all is finished, God is reconciled . . ."[45] Nothing further remains to be done by us. In one word: the whole of recreation, the entire restoration of the world as laden with guilt, is the fruit of the work of Christ. "Objectively, principally, in the sphere of justice he has brought recreation to be realized through his cross. The καταλλαγή between God and the world was established then."[46]

Christ had to suffer in order after that to enter into his glory. The

41. *Ibid.*, p. 404.
42. *Ibid.*, p. 459.
43. *Ibid.*, p. 507.

44. *Ibid.*, p. 508.
45. *Idem.*
46. *Ibid.*, p. 510.

resurrection followed in history upon the crucifixion. And the ascension to glory followed the resurrection. From heaven he will come again to judge the living and the dead. "He was declared to be the Son of God with power, according to the spirit of holiness, by the resurrection from the dead . . ." (Rom. 1.4). He himself said to his apostles when parting from them: "All power is given unto me in heaven and on earth" (Matt. 28:18). The powers of hell cannot prevail against the kingdom that he came to establish. Through his shed blood we have redemption, even the forgiveness of sins. He is the "image of the invisible God, the firstborn of every creature." Through him and for him all things were created. He it is that is "the head of the body which is his church." He is the "firstborn from the dead; that in all things he might have the preeminence." "It pleased the Father that in him all fulness should dwell and having made peace through the blood of his cross, by him to reconcile all things unto himself; by him I say, whether they be things in earth or things in heaven" (Col. 1.15-20).

In barest outline, we have now touched on the highlights of the person and work of Christ. The reader will note even from this brief sketch that we have given a Protestant view of Christianity. Our whole purpose is to indicate that the self-identification of Jesus as the Christ and the idea of the Scriptures as his word of direct revelation to man are involved in one another.

If we were to go into further detail, differences between the Reformed and the Lutheran view of Christ and his work would appear more fully. But our main purpose now is to note that the Protestant view of Christ cannot be maintained unless in the plainest and simplest fashion the self-identification of Jesus of Nazareth as truly God and truly man, and as speaking directly in history, and as heard speaking after his departure to heaven through the Scriptures, be held fast.

3. Romanist Subjectivism

Barth's views of the person and work of Christ are, at every point, the antipodes of this historic Protestant view. His Christ cannot be identified in history. The work of his Christ does not take place directly in history. Barth's view of Christ as *Geschichte* allows for no transition from wrath to grace in history.

It is of particular import to note that it is from the historic Protestant point of view alone that Romanism and its idea of analogy of being, as well as the whole of Romanist theology, can be properly evaluated. Between Romanism and Protestantism the primary problem was that of truth and therefore where truth may be found. Rome anathematized those who did not seek it in the church as the final authority on earth. She paid lip service to the idea of an infallible Scripture. She may even at times appeal to its authority over against modern forms of subjectivism. But these modern forms of subjectivism spring, according to Rome, from the principle of Protestantism. This principle itself is, Rome says, that of subjectivism. It is this because according to Protestantism the individual believer does not need to take his final authority in the interpretation of the Bible to be the Church.

To make a proper reply to this, argues Berkouwer, it must be realized that a merely formal statement to the effect that the Scriptures are infallible is not enough. The question is rather whether in practice there is complete submission to Scripture.[47] No appeal to the Church as infallible or to the Holy Spirit on the ground that the Scripture is in itself a dead book is anything like a justifiable reason for failure to submit one's thoughts captive to the obedience of Christ as he speaks in Scripture.[48] The Reformers had the courage to reject the idea that under the influence of the Holy Spirit independently of Scripture there has been a proper development of dogma.[49] He that is of the truth hears the voice of him who is the truth. And in the Bible we have the words of Christ given to us by the guidance of his Spirit. In the last analysis, the question as between Rome and the Reformation is as to who really is willing to listen to the voice of Christ.[50]

Paul anathematizes any one, including himself, who should bring another gospel than that which Christ in his Word has given unto men. That there is no effective way of replying to the charge of subjectivism by Rome except it be made on the basis of Scripture is shown by Berkouwer by means of three examples.

In 1923 Friedrich Heiler published a book in criticism of Romanism.[51] But the foundation on which Heiler stands when he criticizes Romanism is not that of Scripture. Therefore he does not

47. *De Stryd om het Roomsch-Katholiek Dogma*, Kampen, no date, p. 100.
48. *Ibid.*, p. 102.   50. *Idem.*
49. *Ibid.*, p. 204.
51. *Der Katholizismus, Seine Idee und Seine Erscheinung*, München.

really raise the question of where the norm of truth may be found. Between him and Romanism it is not a "conflict with respect to truth."[52] It is simply a question of whether the empirical reality of the church answers to what Heiler thinks is the proper idea of the church. But he does not draw the lineaments of such a proper idea of the church from Scripture. All knowledge of God, says Heiler, is purely symbolical. Thus he loses the norm for his own religion and cannot call the Romanist church back to the revelation of God in Christ.[53]

A second critic of Romanism mentioned by Berkouwer is Karl Heim. He too is interested in confrontation with Romanism in his work on *Das Wesen des Evangelischen Christentums*. In this instance too it is the failure to start from the direct revelation of Christ in Scripture that spells impotence in the way of effective criticism of Romanism. Heim starts out well enough. The heart of the difference between Romanism and evangelicalism, says Heim, is found in a difference of vision with respect to Christ.[54] Both Romanism and Protestantism deal with the drama that centers round the person of Christ, but they differ on the unfolding of this drama. Romanism thinks that, with the resurrection of Christ, we have the decisive turning point in history. Since then Christ has all power in heaven and on earth.[55] Evangelicalism, on the other hand, says Heim, holds that the power question will not be solved till the return of Christ.[56]

In stating the difference between Romanism and Protestantism in this way, the question as to where God may be found is again the background. In the Romanist view of Christ, God is found to be speaking through the infallible church. This church stands above the consciences of men. For Heim, on the contrary, God may and must first be found in the human conscience.[57] From the point of view of true Protestantism, this is a subjective position. Berkouwer has pointed out the subjective character of Heim's theology fully in his book on *Revelation and Faith in Recent German Theology*, as earlier noted. When Heim states the question as between Romanism and Protestantism to be one of power and conscience, he too has suppressed the question of truth. He too cannot call Romanism back to the truth so long as he does not stand upon the truth.

The third instance of a criticism of official Romanism is that of

52. Berkouwer, *op. cit.*, p. 58.
53. *Ibid.*, p. 62.
54. *Ibid.*, p. 64.
55. *Idem.*
56. *Idem.*
57. *Ibid.*, p. 66.

Reform-Catholicism. In 1937 a book appeared with the title, *Der Katholizismus Sein Stirb und Werde*. The writers of this work had as their main interest the ideal of having Romanism recognize the full import of modern science. Rome is therefore not called back to the obedience of Scripture but to the obedience of the results of science.[58]

The general conclusion at the end of this review of these three efforts at criticism of Rome is expressed in the following words: "Every criticism which attacks Rome, but which in such an attack relativizes and restricts the revelation of God in Scripture is doomed to unfruitfulness."[59]

The reason for this conclusion needs scarcely to be elaborated further. Romanism is itself subjective to the extent that it will not in all its thought and practice submit to Scripture. But the positions of Heiler, of Heim and of the Reform-Catholics are, if anything, more subjectivist than that of official Romanism.

The significance of all this for our main argument may now be indicated. Berkouwer has pointed out to us, as indicated above, that Barth's basic position is fundamentally subjective. His argument is that, for all his effort to reach a position more objective than that of Heim and many other modern theologians, his basic starting-point is not based on the direct revelation of God in Scripture.

The deepest line of demarcation between all the types of theology that present themselves is therefore that which separates those who do and those who do not base their work upon the self-identifying Christ of Scripture. Both Romanism and Barth profess belief in an infallible Scripture. But for both this is not followed by a practical submission to the truth as taught in Scripture. Thus the difference between them is in practice the difference between two forms of subjectivism. And, of the two, Romanism is often less subjective than is Barthianism, for in Romanist thought there is at least some measure of recognition of the direct revelation of God in history. This is no longer the case with Barth. He is, says Berkouwer, more Occamistic than was Occam.

4. Christian Philosophy

The Protestant vision of Christ is, as is apparent from what has just before been said, a comprehensive one. The Christ of the Scriptures speaks about the whole of human history. He speaks

58. *Ibid.*, p. 74.   59. *Ibid.*, p. 75.

about the beginning and the end of time, and he speaks about all the extent of space. By him all things were created, and by him all things consist. All power in heaven and earth is given unto him. In the new heaven and the new earth, no sickness, sorrow and death shall make their entrance. The powers of darkness have been in principle destroyed by him. He is King of kings and Lord of lords. He will at last deliver up the kingdom to God, even the Father, when he shall have put down all rule and all authority and power (I Cor. 15:24).

All proper human activity is therefore activity within the kingdom of the Christ. Philosophy no less than theology must be actively engaged in working for and under Christ. There cannot be an absolute separation between the field of theology and the field of philosophy. In the most basic sense, they both deal with all reality, God and the world. Both deal with Christ and what he has done *(das Christusgeschehen)*. There is, of course, a relative difference between the work of theology and that of philosophy. This may readily be seen from the writings of theologians and from the writings of Christian philosophers. But our concern at the moment is that both are subject unto Christ and his infallibly inscripturated Word while they engage in their respective labors. Christ is to be found as presupposed in science and philosophy if he is to be found in theology.

The Christian philosophers mentioned earlier therefore speak frankly of the pre-theoretical presuppositions which they have taken from the Scriptures as the Word of Christ. These presuppositions are the facts of creation, the fall, and redemption through Christ, applied to the hearts of men by the Holy Spirit, the Spirit of Christ. In thus taking their basic presuppositions from the Bible, these philosophers are subjecting themselves in their hearts to Christ their redeemer.

From this point of view, they must, in the nature of the case, regard all philosophy which is the product of the thought activity of those who do not thus subject themselves to Christ, as apostate philosophy. Apostate philosophy is marked by the fact that the human person, and therefore the human mind that produces this philosophy, does not subject itself to Christ and his Word. In apostate philosophy, the human subject does not subject itself to the law or ordinances of God in Christ. In particular, such apostate philosophy does not realize that in its theoretical thought activity it is really making man, rather than the creator-redeemer, the source of what is possible and actual.

Accordingly, apostate philosophy constitutes a virtual attack on the Christ of the Scriptures. Such a philosophy brings the creator-redeemer down into the universe itself, or it lifts the created universe into participation with the being of the triune God. All apostate philosophy is immanentistic. Paul says that there are those who worship and serve the creature, and there are those who worship and serve the Creator. Apostate or immanence philosophy is creature worship.

Barth has spoken of the Romanist notion of the analogy of being and of its natural theology in severest terms. But if the Reformed theologians and philosophers who were quoted in the foregoing chapters are right, then Barth did not at all see into the real nature of the disease of Romanist theology. This disease is due to the fact that Rome has made an alliance with apostate philosophy. To call Rome back to the obedience of the gospel of Christ, it must be asked to forsake its alliance with apostate philosophy, and then to subject all its thought captive to the obedience of the written Word of Christ.

Barth cannot thus challenge Romanism to forsake its deepest error. The reason for this, in the last analysis, is that Barth himself holds to the same error as does Rome on this point. At no time has he challenged apostate philosophy to forsake its autonomy. At no time has he urged any philosophy to take its pre-theoretical presuppositions from the Scripture. On the contrary, he frankly allows the legitimacy of autonomous philosophy. To be sure, he wants to restrict the field of its operation. He wants to keep philosophy from making pronouncements about God and Christ. He therefore favors a philosophy of the sort that Sartre develops over any form of "Christian philosophy." But he fails to see that any and every form of immanentist philosophy speaks by implication about God. To assume that any fact of human experience can be properly interpreted without placing it in its true relation of subordination to Christ is, in effect, to reject Christ. Sartre assumes that, if man is to be in any wise intelligible to himself, he must be so in terms of himself as autonomous. In such an attitude, there is a virtual exclusion of God and of Christ. Such a philosophy is anti-Christian. Yet Barth allows the legitimacy of its procedure. He does not challenge its apostasy at the root. How can he then be said to challenge Romanism in any proper way? The philosophy with which Romanism has made its alliance is no more and no less anti-Christian than is the philosophy of Sartre or of any of the modern existentialists. The

only way in which Barth could really have challenged the root error
of Romanism would be if he had asked Romanism to take its pre-
theoretical assumptions from the Word of Christ as found in Scripture. But how could he do this so long as he does not even wish to
submit his own thinking in theology to the direct revelation of God
in Christ? So long as Barth wants to go beyond Romanism in terms
of his Christ as *Geschichte,* so long will he be unable to challenge
Romanism in the way the Reformers challenged it. For it is precisely
this notion of Christ as *Geschichte* in terms of which Barth so violently rejects the Reformation idea of the direct revelation of God
in and through the Christ of history as he speaks to us in Scripture.
The fact that Barth is against Romanism, and that as orthodox
Protestants we are also against Romanism, does not prove that
Barth and we oppose Romanism in terms of the same Christ.

5. The Form-Matter Scheme

A proper estimate of the Romanist synthesis between Christianity
and apostate philosophy involves, as noted at the beginning of the
chapter, an analysis of the form-matter scheme of Greek philosophy.
For it is Greek philosophy, and more particularly Aristotelianism,
that has had great influence on Romanist thought. Romanist thinkers consider the method of Aristotle's philosophy to be basically
right when used for the interpretation of the world of space and
time.

Dooyeweerd has traced the development of the Greek form-
matter scheme in great detail in his work on *Reformation and
Scholasticism in Philosophy.*[60] The pre-Platonic period of Greek
philosophy has been treated very fully by Vollenhoven in his *History
of Philosophy.*[61] But we turn to the more readily available work of
Dooyeweerd quoted earlier, namely, his *A New Critique of Theoretical Thought.*

Dooyeweerd speaks of the "integral and radical character of the
central ground-motive of the Christian religion in its biblical sense,
*the motive of creation, the fall into sin, and the redemption through
Jesus Christ in communion with the Holy Ghost.*"[62] "As the Creator,
God reveals Himself as the Absolute and Integral Origin of the

60. *Reformatie en Scholastiek in de Wysbegeerte,* Franeker, 1949, Vol. I.
61. *Geschiedenis der Wysbegeerte,* Franeker, 1950, Vol. I.
62. *A New Critique of Theoretical Thought,* Dooyeweerd, Vol. I, p. 173.

'earthly world,' concentrated in man, and of the world of the angels. In the language of the Bible He is the Origin of heaven and earth. There is no original power which is *opposed to* Him. Consequently, in His creation we cannot find any expression of a dualistic principle of origin."[63]

The opposition between the biblical and the Greek view of origins is at once apparent at this point. "This Christian view cut off at the very roots the religious dualism of the Greek motive of form and matter, which came to a head in anthropology in the dichotomy between a material body and a theoretical rational substance of a pure *form*-character. Moreover, the creation implies a providential world-plan, which has its integral origin in the Sovereign Will of the Creator. We have indicated this world-plan in the transcendental Idea of the cosmic temporal order."[64]

This question of "religious dualism" is of the greatest importance. This religious dualism characterizes every form of immanentist philosophy. It is that which replaces the distinction between the creator and the creature.

In Scripture Christ tells us about the introduction of this religious dualism into the world. It came into the world when Satan suggested to Adam and Eve that they consider themselves and him on a par with God, or, what amounts to the same thing, that they consider God on a par with themselves and him as to the ultimacy of being. The Creator-creature distinction, Satan suggested, in effect, was not basic. God and man and Satan were all of one being. Man did not need to obey God's command. God was in no position to command. Was not God, as well as man and Satan, surrounded by a factual situation over which no one had any control? Why then should God usurp authority over man? Authority lies in personality wherever it is found, in man as well as in God. All personality is a law unto itself. God is not the law-giver and man is not the law-receiver. Does God pretend to be testing man as to his love for his maker? God is not man's maker and cannot be the object of man's love. Man must love personality, himself first and his God afterwards. Sin is not the transgression of the law of love as given to man by God. Sin is rather the yielding to the forces of evil somehow surrounding both God and man.

When Adam and Eve listened to this Satanic philosophy of life,

63. *Ibid.*, pp. 173-174.   64. *Ibid.*, p. 174.

they became apostate from the triune God. They turned from the love of God to the love of themselves. They declared their independence from God. They no longer recognized the ordinances of God as extending over the created universe. They changed religions. It was not because they had theoretically understood themselves and their relation to God. Their theoretical efforts were wholly subordinated to their pre-theoretical religious commitment. They broke the ordinance of love that God had given them; they became covenant-breakers.

But is their position now *dualistic* as well as religious? Is it not rather monistic? Are not God and man reduced to oneness of being? Is not the Creator-creature distinction now subsumed under a general idea of being? And did not Dooyeweerd tell us that all apostate thought is immanentistic in character? Do we not evince the fact that we have not cleared ourselves of apostate thinking so long as we are willing to speak of *being* without at the outset introducing the distinction between Creator-being and creature-being?

All this is true. But the dualism of which Dooyeweerd speaks is a substitute for the Creator-creature distinction. This dualism presupposes that the Creator-creature distinction has been removed and the general monistic idea of being put in its place. The dualism of which Dooyeweerd speaks indicates a distinction *within* this general being. The need for such a distinction on the immanentist view is apparent. Man knew that he had not always existed. The fact of change impressed itself upon him every waking hour. Instead of taking time and all its products as having back of it and controlling it the counsel of the triune God, man now conceived of the cosmic world order as ultimate. Thus evil was virtually identified with temporal plurality.

From this time forth, man set himself a false theoretical problem. He set himself the problem of seeking for a unity that should make the eternal, now identified with the abstract good, to prevail over the temporal, now identified with evil.

On the basis of this dualism, the eternal and the temporal are really correlative to one another. But to soothe his conscience for having insulted his Creator, man now projects an ideal of eternal goodness and strives, in thought and action, to make it prevail over temporality as evil. His ideal becomes that of participation of himself as temporal and evil with his projected God as eternal and good.

But who is he now, this one that did not wish to be told by God who he is? How can he now identify himself? He refused to be told who and what he was by the God who had identified himself in terms of himself. In order to assert his own autonomous personality, he had depersonalized his God. Wishing to assert, control and direct himself, he submerged God with himself into an impersonal environment. This implied his own depersonalization too. He could actually identify himself and live only if God had first identified him as the image of God. Denying his God, apostate man denies himself as the image of God. Thus in seeking himself out of his proper relation to God, apostate man has lost himself. Seeking his authentic personality and freedom outside the framework of God's plan for him, apostate man explodes, or tries to explode, the airplane on which he is traveling.

What has been said must not be directly attributed to Dooye-weerd. But it seems to be similar to what he expresses when he speaks of the biblical motive of creation "being superbly expressed in the 139th psalm" and then adds: "This is certainly the radical opposite of the Greek dualism of the form- and matter motive. In the revelation that God created man according to His image, He discloses man to himself, in the religious radical unity of his created existence, and in the religious solidarity of mankind, in which was integrally concentrated the entire meaning of the temporal cosmos."[65]

Now the Greeks, like all men, were descendants of Adam. Adam was the representative head of all mankind. All men have therefore received from him their basically apostate attitude of heart and mind toward God (Rom. 5:12). For this reason, the form-matter scheme is, from the biblical or truly religious point of view, used by apostate man in order, by means of it, to excuse himself for his sin.

All apostate thought has reduced the radical nature of sin as an insult to the love of God to a dialectical struggle between two equally ultimate principles, one of good and one of evil, over which man ultimately has no control and for which he is not responsible. Says Dooyeweerd: "Both the Greek and the Humanistic oppositions do not touch the religious root of human existence, but only the temporal branches of human life. They are only absolutized here in a religious sense. Their concept of guilt, in consequence, is of a merely dialectical character. It consists of a depreciation of an

65. *Ibid.*, p. 174.

abstract complex of functions of the created cosmos over against an
other abstracted and deified complex. In its revelation of the fall,
however, just like in that of creation, the Word of God penetrates
to the root, to the religious centre of human nature. The fall is the
apostasy of this centre, of this *radix* of existence, it is the falling
away from God. This was spiritual death, because it is the apostasy
from the absolute source of Life. Consequently the fall was radical.
It involved the whole temporal cosmos, since the latter had its religious root only in mankind."[66]

In the form-matter scheme of Greek thought, we have the first
major expression of a well worked out religious dualism that is
apostate in nature. In this form-matter scheme, the biblical teachings with respect to creation and the fall of man have been set
aside. In it God cannot identify himself to man and man could not
hear God if God did speak to him. The cosmic world order is not
the expression of the will of God. Man cannot sin either against the
word or the order of God. There is neither word nor order of God.
On this view history is not governed by the providence of God.
Creation implies a providential world-plan, which has its integral
origin in the Sovereign Will of the Creator.[67] But in Greek thought
there is no room for the idea of divine providence as there is no
room for the idea of creation. With the divine word the divine order
of the world has also disappeared.

It is to be expected that in this situation any reconciliation that
man would think of would be dialectical in nature. It would be an
attempt to invent a deity who would help man somehow to realize
his ideal of goodness over evil. But in the teaching of the Bible "sin
is not dialectically reconciled." It is *"really* propitiated."[68] "And in
Christ as the new root of the human race, the whole temporal
cosmos, which was religiously concentrated in man, is in principle
again directed toward God and thereby wrested free from the power
of Satan."[69]

On the basis of the form-matter scheme, there is no room for the
actual triumph by the grace of God over sin. For there is then no
real transition from sin to grace in history. The principle of evil is,
on this basis, in the last analysis as ultimate as is the principle of the
good. And, being only a principle, the good has no power of any
sort by which to overcome evil. Therefore "if the central ground-

66. *Ibid.*, p. 175.
67. *Ibid.*, p. 174.
68. *Ibid.*, p. 175.
69. *Idem.*

motive of creation, the fall and redemption is to have the above-sketched reforming influence upon philosophical thought, this motive must, as we have shown in our transcendental critique, determine the content of our cosmonomic Idea and must exclude all *dialectical motives* which lead thought in an apostate direction."[70]

It is at this point that the true nature of Roman Catholic thought appears. Even Augustine had not been able to break away from Greek thought entirely. But he did break away from the Greek idea of time as this is inherent in the form-matter scheme. Thus he laid the groundwork for a truly Christian philosophy of history.

But "the situation became quite different when the dialectical ground-motive of nature and grace made its entry into Christian scholasticism. This occurred in the period of the Aristotelian Renaissance, in which, after a bitter struggle, the Augustinian-Platonic school was pushed out of the dominating position that it had hitherto enjoyed. Roman Catholicism now strove consciously to effect a religious synthesis between the Greek view of nature (especially the Aristotelian) and the doctrines of the Christian faith. This synthetic standpoint found its most powerful philosophical and theological expression in the system of Thomas Aquinas. The two foundational tenets of this system were the positing of the autonomy of natural reason in the entire sphere of natural knowledge, and the thesis that nature is the understructure of supernatural grace."[71]

It is in the acceptance of the idea of the autonomy of reason, even though it was supposed to be restricted to the sphere of "natural knowledge," that Romanism makes its alliance with the religious dualism of the Greek form-matter scheme. In consequence, the "Biblical creation-motive was deprived of its original integral and radical character."[72] "Creation is proclaimed to be a natural truth, which can be seen and proven by theoretical thought independent of all divine revelation." And "the five ways of this proof presupposed the axioms of the Aristotelian metaphysics, and especially the Aristotelian idea of God as 'pure Form' opposed to the principle of 'matter.' This signified, ultimately, the elimination of creation in its Biblical sense as the *religious motive* of theoretical thought."[73]

Dooyeweerd continues: "The Greek form-matter motive in all its different conceptions excludes in principle the Idea of creation in

70. *Ibid.*, p. 177.   72. *Ibid.*, p. 180.
71. *Ibid.*, p. 179.   73. *Idem.*

its Biblical sense. *The sum total of Greek wisdom concerning the Origin of the cosmos is: 'ex nihilo nihil fit' (from nothing nothing can originate)*. At the utmost, Greek metaphysical theology could arrive at the Idea of a divine demiurge, who gives form to an original matter as the supreme architect and artist. Therefore, the scholastic accommodation of the Aristotelian concept of God to the Church-doctrine of creation could never lead to a real reconciliation with the Biblical ground-motive. The unmoved Mover of Aristotelian metaphysics, who, as the absolute theoretical *nous*, only has himself as the object of his thought in blessed self-contemplation, is the radical opposite of the living God Who revealed Himself as Creator. Thomas may teach, that God has brought forth natural things according both to their form and matter, but the *principle* of matter as the principle of metaphysical and religious imperfection cannot find its origin in a pure form—God."[74]

Romanism also attempted to combine the Aristotelian view of man with that of Scripture. This too proved to be a fatal mistake. "Nor could the Aristotelian conception of human nature be reconciled to the Biblical conception concerning the creation of man in the image of God. According to Thomas, human nature is a composition of a material body and a rational soul as a substantial form, which, in contradistinction to Aristotle's conception, is conceived of as an immortal substance."[75]

Finally, so far as the form-matter motive was employed by the scholastics, the "redemption in Christ Jesus can no longer have a relation to the very religious root of the temporal cosmos, but it can only bring nature to its supra-natural perfection."[76] Jesus Christ is, in effect, reduced to an exhibition of the cosmic process.

It is to be remembered, of course, that there is a supernatural as well as a natural theology in Romanism. Rome wants to use the method of Aristotle for the natural realm only. But the supernatural has on this basis no longer a proper relation to the natural. By the method of natural theology only a god that is reduced to pure form can be allowed to exist. Such a God is not the creator of the world. "As pure actual form the deity can be accepted as the origin of the motion which proceeds from matter toward form as its goal. However, there is no way in which the deity can be considered as the

74. *Idem*.   76. *Ibid.*, p. 181.
75. *Idem*.

origin of the principle of matter, with its blind arbitrary ἀναγκή."[77] Thus the supernatural realm is placed above the natural as standing on a higher level.[78] The result of the scholastic procedure was an artificial synthesis between the Greek and the Christian world of ideas.[79]

The Greek form-matter motive was based upon the assumption of the autonomy and self-sufficiency of human theoretical thought. In this sense it must be said to be subjective. The human subject determines by means of its logical capacities what can and cannot exist in reality. Its philosophy is a consciousness-philosophy. Therefore the Romanist idea of revelation can never be a revelation of the Creator-redeemer in the biblical sense of the term. The form-matter scheme of Greek thought does not allow for a Christian idea of revelation to be superimposed upon itself. This scheme involves an idea of God as well as an idea of the world. In other words, the Greek scheme of thought is a view of the totality of being in every form. Christianity too is a totality view. And these two totality views are built upon mutually exclusive principles.

Yet Romanism seeks to combine these two mutually exclusive totality views. The Romanist idea of the relation of the natural to the supernatural orders of being cannot allow for the simple self-identification of Christ in history. According to it, history belongs, in part at least, to the natural realm. Here the dualistic notion of form and matter is at least in partial control of the situation. And these are always inherently destructive of one another even as they supplement one another. Even the concept of substance as the central category of being cannot unite the two, "because it lacks a real starting-point for this synthesis."[80]

So far as substance is form, it is universal and therewith form. So far as substance is matter and therewith individual, it is utterly isolated from form. Rome does not realize that there can be no self-identification in history by the Son of God unless through the Son all things have been created. The Christ identifies himself as the one by whom all things consist.

Naturally, as there is no self-identifying triune God who speaks to man at the beginning of history, so there is no self-identifying Christ who speaks clearly to man in the redemptive work of history. There cannot be, on the Romanist basis, influenced as it is by Greek

77. Ibid., p. 182.
78. Ibid., p. 183.
79. Idem.
80. Ibid., p. 182.

philosophy, a once for all and finished work of Christ that is itself interpreted once for all in finished form through Scripture. All is reduced to process. And this process is itself an artificial combination between a static notion of abstract form and an equally abstract notion of pure contingency.

The Reformation sought to set Christianity free from any form of alliance with apostate philosophy. It called men back to the God and the Christ of the Scriptures and therefore to the Scriptures as the direct revelation of this God and this Christ. Only thus, the Reformers knew, could they identify themselves as creatures and as sinners and find assurance of salvation through the grace of God in Christ. Only thus could they have forgiveness of sins through the merits of the Redeemer through his death on the cross. Only thus could there be a transition from wrath to grace in history. Only thus could they rest assured that God, the ruler of the world order, would be victorious over sin and evil. Only thus could there be a true triumph of grace.

It is in the interest of subjecting all of human thought to the Word of God in Christ that the reformation of philosophy along truly Protestant lines was undertaken by Vollenhoven and Dooyeweerd. The reformation of philosophy, as much as the reformation of theology, meant first of all the subjection of the believer in his inmost being to the direct revelation of God to man in Christ. A reformation philosophy, no less than a reformation theology, must cut itself loose from all forms of apostate thinking. And there is not likely to be a full reformation of theology unless there is, next to it, a reformation of philosophy.

But Barth did not object to Romanist theology because of its alliance with apostate philosophy. To be sure, Barth rejects any form of philosophy that seeks by the method of reason to attain to a concept of God. But he does not do this in the name of the God who speaks to man directly through Christ in the Bible. On the contrary, and this point is basically important, those who find God by listening to him in the direct revelation of Christ in the Scripture are by Barth placed in the same class with those who find him by the Roman method of natural theology.

Barth rejects the dialecticism of the Romanist synthesis in terms of a deeper dialecticism than that of Rome. He wants to overcome Romanism by a deeper rejection of any form of direct revelation than is found in Romanist thinking. He wants to go beyond Romanism in terms of his Christ as *Geschichte*. But this Christ of *Geschichte* can not be identified in history. He cannot be found anywhere. The God who speaks to man in terms of this Christ is therefore a form that is more formal, if possible, than the form of Greek philosophy. And the man who listens to God in terms of this Christ, cannot hear this Christ or, if he does hear him, is lost in the Christ.

Meanwhile, full note must be taken of the fact that Barth deliberately seeks to set himself free from every form of philosophy, modern as well as ancient. Is there any way of really doing that short of the way of the Reformers? Can Barth really hold that his theology is free from alliance with immanentist philosophy, and therewith from consciousness-theology, so long as he himself commits himself as radically as ever to the idea of Christ as *Geschichte?* We have already seen earlier in this chapter that there is no possible confrontation of God and man in Christ unless one frankly accepts this confrontation in terms of the direct revelation of God in the Christ revealed directly in history and in the Bible. The modern consciousness-theology of Schleiermacher and his followers has made alliance with modern dialectical philosophy. And is there any way of challenging either this modern or the ancient form of dialecticism except by means of the self-identifying Christ of Scripture as historic Protestantism has presented him?

Is Barth's view *less* speculative than that of Rome? The answer is that it is *more* speculative. Barth is outspoken in his rejection of the direct revelation of God in history. His idea of Christ as *Geschichte* is more obviously anti-scriptural than is the Romanist idea of the analogy of being. Barth's idea of God as wholly revealed and wholly hidden to man in Christ is, as the Christian philosophers have shown, a secularization of Christianity by means of the modern philosophical scheme of freedom and nature. This scheme is itself but the modern expression of the form-matter motive of all immanentistic philosophy. Barth's compromise with apostate philosophy is deeper even than that of Romanism.

Chapter XI

Modern Dialecticism

In the previous chapter, we dealt with ancient dialectical philosophy and its influence on Romanist theology. In the present chapter, it will be our concern to study modern dialectical philosophy and its influence on modern theology. But our study of both ancient and modern dialecticism is made only in the interest of understanding and evaluating the theology of Barth. Barth rejects with vigor the natural theology of Rome, based as it is upon the Aristotelian idea of the *analogy of being*. But he does not do this in the interest of calling men back to the direct revelation of God through Christ in history and therefore in Scripture. And this fact, we found, is of the greatest possible significance, for there is only one truly Christian way of rejecting any synthesis theology. It is the way of asking men to confront God where alone he can be found, namely, in the direct revelation of himself through Christ in Scripture. It is there and there alone that his voice can be heard. It is there and there alone that Christ identifies himself in terms of himself and man in terms of his relation to Christ. The pathway of Greek natural theology led to God as an abstract form. The Greeks started their thinking about "reality" with the apostate assumption that man is somehow autonomous. Starting from this assumption, they naturally used the method of abstraction and negation when they wished to speak about "god." For on their assumption of human autonomy, God must not be like anything in the spatial-temporal world, while yet he must be the "creator" of it. The result was that nothing could be said about God. Or, if anything was said about "him," it had to be done by repersonalizing the form, the *it*, he had become by the method of negation employed in his construction. But when thus repersonalized, this God together with man was confronted with an environment over which he had no control. Thus this God turned out to be a demiurge. This demiurge sought to impress the form of rationality, pure form upon pure matter. This is the nature of dialectical thought. It is the thought of apostate man. It is always immanentistic in character in that it assumes the distinction between God as creator and man as creature to be of a secondary or derivative nature. This apostate immanentistic thinking will not submit itself to the ordinances of God deposited in the created universe. Having rebelled at the beginning of history, man assumes that he himself by means of his intellectual capacity, his logical function, must for the first time introduce distinctions of order into an inherently chaotic world.

Scholastic theology adopted the method of this apostate thought in its philosophy and in its natural theology. It did so in order to make the Christian religion appear reasonable to the natural man. Scholastic thought sought to limit the activity of philosophy to the "natural realm." But this was impossible. The method of Aristotle was itself as much the product as the source of the theory that he held of reality as a whole. The form-matter scheme was a method, and, at the same time, a theory of reality and a theory of knowledge. The method of dialecticism based upon the assumption of the autonomy of man could not produce the idea of God as man's creator and law-giver. God as a pure form was the inevitable result of the method of Aristotle, as this method was in turn itself based upon the assumption of human autonomy. And this assumption was in the nature of the case pre-theoretical or religious in nature.

We turn now to the modern form of dialectical thought. In doing so we shall again depend to a considerable extent upon the analysis given of it by Dooyeweerd.

It was the nominalism of William of Occam, says Dooyeweerd, that turned against the "artificial compromise between Christian and pagan lines of thought in the Thomistic system."[1] "The Thomistic cosmonomic Idea required the realistic-metaphysical conception of the Aristotelian 'substantial forms.' As soon as this conception would be abandoned, the whole Thomistic-Aristotelian Idea of the natural order, as an understructure of the supranatural order of

1. Dooyeweerd, *A New Critique of Theoretical Thought*, Vol. I, p. 183.

grace, was doomed to break down. And the same holds good in respect to natural theology as an understructure of the sacred theology of revelation."[2]

Nominalism denies that universal concepts have any foundation in reality *(fundamentum in re)*. By this nominalist view the "realistic metaphysical concept of truth" was destroyed.[3] Back of the nominalist position with respect to universal ideas was an arbitrary notion with respect to the absolute power of God *(Potestas Dei Absoluta)*. And expressed in it all was the idea of the primacy of the will as over against the Thomistic doctrine of the primacy of the intellect.[4] Did this nominalist view of universals prepare the way for a return to the idea of the direct revelation of God in history? Not at all. To be sure, Occam himself did not want to reject such a revelation. But his philosophical view did imply a denial of it. It prepared the way for modern philosophy and its peculiar notion of pure contingency. The service of nominalism to the Christian religion was, in consequence, a negative one. It showed the artificiality of the synthesis between the Greek form-matter scheme and Christian thought.[5]

By breaking up the artificial synthesis of scholastic thought, nominalism prepared the way for modern humanism. There was, to be sure, a period of transition between the break-down of scholastic thought and modern humanism. Nominalist thought at first, to some extent, subjected itself "in a positivistic faith to the dogma of the Church."[6] But this subjection was itself an artificial matter. Inherently, the principle of nominalism was that of an even greater stress on the autonomy or freedom of man as over against the law of God than had been found in medieval realism. And the modern course of philosophy was set on its way by this principle of man as wholly autonomous and free.

As earlier noted, Dooyeweerd speaks of modern philosophy as being controlled by the freedom-nature motive. The basic idea in this freedom-nature motive is that of human autonomy or freedom. This was the basic idea also, as already observed, of the Greek form-matter motive. The modern freedom-nature motive and the ancient form-matter motive are expressions of the same underlying idea of human autonomy. Both make the pre-theoretical assumption

2. *Ibid.*, pp. 183-184.
3. *Ibid.*, p. 185.
4. *Idem.*

5. *Ibid.*, p. 187.
6. *Ibid.*, p. 188.

of man's ultimacy. But the freedom notion of modern thought is even more consistently anti-Christian than the ancient freedom notion was.

Ancient philosophy still recognized the "objective" existence of law above itself. The free man of Greek philosophy was even seeking to accommodate himself to the reality of such laws. But the modern notion of freedom, when brought to consistent expressions, allows for no objective existence of law at all. Even law is said to proceed from man himself.

To be sure, modern man must and does recognize the existence of something outside and independent of himself. Even the most extreme existentialist does that. But modern man assumes that the order or form which exists in nature is ultimately derived from the activity of man. In the Renaissance period of modern thought, free man sought to dominate nature. He thought he could do so since he had discovered, as he thought, that God does not dominate it. The idea of a law of God controlling nature is thought to be a universal that has no foundation in reality.

Using the methods of mathematics, modern man began to think that he could give an exhaustive interpretation of nature. "All of reality should be construed in terms of this new method. To this end, all modal structures of individuality, which are grounded upon the divine order of creation, must be methodically demolished. Autonomous theoretical thought will now recreate the cosmos by means of the exact concepts of mathematical natural science."[7]

But herewith modern man had created an artificial combination between man and nature. The free man was seeking to understand himself by the method with which he sought to understand nature. In fact, he sought to understand himself as included within nature. But, when he sought thus to understand himself, he lost his freedom. The method of modern science was no less determinist in its tendency than was the method of the realism of Aristotelian philosophy. But the antinomy involved in the modern freedom-nature motive is more glaringly apparent than it was in the Greek form-matter motive. Modern man thinks of himself as no longer controlled by any objective laws at all. And yet he creates for himself laws that are fully as determinist as were the supposedly objective laws that he had rejected. Thus the antinomy is shown to be within man himself. The free man is caught in the net that he has laid for himself.

7. *Ibid.*, p. 193.

It is at this point that the apostate character of all dialectical thought appears in its clearest form. If man is to maintain his freedom as he conceives of it, he needs not only to declare himself independent of every law of God, but he needs also to declare himself independent of any law of nature, even when he himself is the source of such a law. He must therefore stand in essentially negative relation over against anything that appears to have any form of universality in it. God must be wholly hidden to man in nature. God must also be wholly hidden to him even in his own experience. If God were anywhere known by man, then man would no longer be free.

1. *Immanuel Kant*

It is this humanistic-freedom motive that is the driving force of "the modern religion of human personality."[8] Human personality regards itself as self-dependent. It wants to dominate nature. But to dominate nature spells determinism. And this determinism tends to envelop man. Thus there is a basic antinomy within the modern idea of free personality. Modern personality finds itself in the situation that, having rejected God as its creator and Christ as its source of freedom, it has lost itself.

The "religion of human personality" finds its first major expression in the philosophy of Immanuel Kant. Kant is often called the philosopher of Protestantism. Did he not limit science in order to make room for faith?

There are radically different answers given to this question. There is first the answer of the consciousness-theologians. They, of course, do look upon Kant as their chief source of inspiration. For them Kant has set the human consciousness free from the bondage of laws that come to it from without. Their theology is consciousness-theology precisely because they, together with Kant, assume that the general human consciousness of man is sufficient unto itself. It can and does create its own religious ideals and creates its own means for the realization of these ideals.

But there is, second, the answer of those who interpret the human consciousness and its activities in terms of the biblical motive of creation, sin, and redemption through Christ in the way that Dooyeweerd speaks of it. Says Dooyeweerd: "Kant is not the philosopher

8. *Ibid.*, p. 190.

of the evangelical idea of freedom; his philosophy is separated from
the Biblical spirit of the Reformation by the irreconcilable cleft between the Christian and Humanistic ground-motives. Naturally this
does not exclude the fact that Kant has been *historically* influenced
by Puritanism and Pietism in his ethical and theological conceptions. But the very spirit and transcendental ground-Idea of his
critical idealism is ruled by the Humanistic motive of nature and
freedom. And the latter cannot be reconciled to the genuine Biblical
ground-motive of the Reformation. All attempts at synthesis are
born out of a lack of insight into the religious foundation of Kant's
philosophy, and into the integral and radical character of the Biblical ground-motive."[9]

Consciousness-theologians call themselves Protestants. But if they
are to be called Protestants, then Protestantism must itself be taken
to mean the idea that the consciousness of man is autonomous, and
historic Protestantism believed in no such thing. According to
modern consciousness-theologians, Kant wrought deliverance from
the idea of external authority. He gave men freedom to interpret
the facts of nature and of history in accordance to their moral worth
as this moral worth is established by the aspirations of man himself. Was not this deliverance similar to the deliverance accomplished by Luther? "Instead of assent to human dogmas Luther had
the immediate assurance of the heart that God was on his side. And
what is that but a judgment of the practical reason, the response of
the heart in man to the spiritual universe? It is given in experience.
It is not mediated by argument. It cannot be destroyed by syllogism.
It needs no confirmation from science. It is capable of combination
with any of the changing interpretations which science may put
upon the outward universe."[10]

There is here a basic misconception of the method and position of
Luther and the Reformers in general. The Reformers, as already
observed, did not reject Romanism with its natural theology in the
interest of the idea of the human subject as autonomous. On the
contrary, they rejected Romanism just because it did not require
the human consciousness to place itself under Christ as he speaks
in the Scriptures. The modern religion of man as free, that is, as
autonomous, does find its major inspiration in Kant. But Kant's idea

9. *Ibid.*, p. 327.
10. Edward Caldwell Moore, *An Outline of the History of Christian Thought
Since Kant*, p. 44.

of human freedom has, as was indicated above, its roots, not in the Reformation, but in the Renaissance view of man. And this Renaissance view of man in turn had its background in medieval nominalism.

Moore is quite right, of course, when he says that Kant rebelled against the Protestant orthodoxy of his day. But, on the position of man as subject to revelation, the position of Protestant orthodoxy is not essentially different from that of the Reformers. Protestant orthodoxy simply followed the Reformers when they listened to Christ directly speaking in the Scriptures. According to Protestant orthodoxy, and no less according to the Reformers, the real confrontation between God as Creator and man as creature and sinner takes place in Christ alone as he is mediated to man through his Word as the direct revelation of Christ.

The radical character of Kant's rejection of the Reformation position may now be more fully described. Kant, we are told, limited science in order to make room for faith. How did he do this?

2. Ethical Dualism and Ethical Monism

In the ultimate sense he did this, as noted, by carrying forth the apostate idea of autonomy of man to far greater consistency than had been done before. For Kant God is not the creator of man. God is not the law-giver to man. God cannot reveal himself to man through nature or through man's own constitution as the image-bearer of God. Man can know nothing of God. Man's free personality therefore rests not upon his basic relation to God as creature and as sinner redeemed by Christ. First of all man's freedom is wholly a negative something. To have any relation to God or to nature, man must project them both. And Kant does project both nature and God.

For him nature is projected by man in the sense that its order is derived from himself. By means of his logical prowess, the free man of Kant imposes order upon nature. For him the facts of nature are *taken* as much as they are *given*. They are given only in the sense that there must be a world of pure contingency as raw stuff which the formalizing activity of the mind of man uses for the purpose of constructing a universe that is subject to him.

Kant projects God as well as nature. But he does so by the method of indirect or negative control. He says that the intellect of man makes no positive assertions about God. Man cannot know God in the way that he knows nature. If man were to know God in the way he knows nature, then God would be an object of nature. As such he would not be God at all. To be truly God, he must be wholly other than nature. Such a God can be posited by the practical reason only. The practical reason is the reason of the whole man. In it the will of man is central. This practical reason deals with the question of good and evil, even as the theoretical reason deals with the question of the true and the false. Each has its own realm. The realm of the practical reason is higher than the realm of the theoretical reason. Man has no knowledge of the higher realm. The realm of the practical reason is higher than the realm of the theoretical reason because the free man places it there. The free man postulates the idea of the ultimate supremacy of the good over evil in the realm of the practical reason. And he even finds indications in nature of its subordination to the realm of the practical reason. Having rejected the teleological argument for the existence of God in its theoretical form along with the other arguments, Kant restores the idea of teleology in terms of the practical reason. It is thus that Kant makes room for faith. He does so first by positing what Richard Kroner calls an ethical dualism.[10a] By means of this dualism, he rejects the traditional theistic proofs as these were developed by Thomas Aquinas. He rejects natural theology by limiting the idea of knowledge to the realm of nature. Man knows this realm of nature because he is himself an original contributor to it. And man cannot thus control the whole of infinite reality. He must therefore recognize the idea of ultimate mystery or contingency as surrounding him. The dualism between man and nature is therefore an *ethical* dualism. That is to say, it is a dualism in which the will of man as act considers itself the ultimate source of the distinction between good and evil.

Though Kant disclaims knowledge of the supersensible realm, he nonetheless makes, to all effects, a universal negative statement about it. He is certain that the God who lives in that realm cannot be man's creator and law-giver. To hold to such a God would be against the principles of theoretical reason. Thus theoretical reason, while with seeming humility abstains from making any pronouncement about the realm of the practical reason, nevertheless makes

10a. Richard Kroner, *Kant's Weltanschauung*, Engl. tr. by John E. Smith, Chicago, 1937.

sure for itself that only a certain kind of God *can* exist there. It is a
God who makes no demands on man. It is a God against whom man
could not sin and therefore has not sinned. Accordingly, man's radical evil is not so radical as to need atonement by any sacrifice provided by God himself. Salvation is a matter of character.

After making sure that no Creator-redeemer God in the biblical
sense of the term can exist in the realm of practical reason, Kant
projects into this realm a God who is good by human standards.
And this good God is then said, somehow, to cause the good to prevail even in the natural realm.

Thus the ethical dualism is developed in the interest of an ethical
monism, that is, in the interest of having what man considers good
to prevail over what he considers evil.

Moore celebrates the declaration of independence that modern
man has made through Kant as its chief spokesman. He rejoices in
the reinterpretation that has been given to Christianity by means of
Kant as a modern Luther. Before Kant, Moore says, the Reformation had gone back to the old scholastic position. "It had rested
faith in an essentially rationalistic manner upon supposed facts in
nature and alleged events of history in connection with the revelation. It had thus jeopardised the whole content of faith, should these
supposed facts of nature or events in history be at any time disproved. Men had made faith to rest upon statements of Scripture,
alleging such and such facts and events. They did not recognise
these as the naive and childlike assumptions concerning nature and
history which the authors of Scripture would naturally have. When,
therefore, these statements began with the progress of the sciences
to be disproved, the defenders of the faith presented always the
feeble spectacle of being driven from one form of evidence to another, as the old were in turn destroyed."[11]

There were of course the true, pious souls who knew all the while
that Christianity is not a matter of externals. "But they were unable
to prove that they were right, or even to get a hearing with many of
the cultivated of their age. To Kant we owe the debt, that he put an
end to this state of things. He made the real evidence for religion
that of the moral sense, of the conscience and hearts of men themselves. The real ground of religious conviction is the religious experience. He thus set free both science and religion from an embar-

11. Moore, *op. cit.*, p. 44.

rassment under which both laboured, and by which both had been injured."[12]

The free man was now in control of both realms. He could therefore keep them at peace with one another. "According to Kant, it is as much the province of the practical reason to lay down laws for action as it is the province of pure reason to determine the conditions of thought, though the practical reason can define only the form of action which shall be in the spirit of duty. It cannot present duty to us as an object of desire. Desire can be only a form of self-love. In the end it reckons with the advantage of having done one's duty. It thus becomes selfish and degraded. The identification of duty and interest was particularly offensive to Kant. He was at war with every form of hedonism. To do one's duty because one expects to reap advantage is not to have done one's duty. The doing of duty in this spirit simply resolves itself into a subtler and more pervasive form of selfishness. He castigates the popular presentation of religion as fostering this same fault. On the other hand, there is a trait of rigorism in Kant, a survival of the ancient dualism, which was not altogether consistent with the implications of his own philosophy. This philosophy afforded, as we have seen, the basis for a monistic view of the universe. But to his mind the natural inclinations of man are opposed to good conscience and sound reason. He had contempt for the shallow optimism of his time, according to which the nature of man was all good, and needed only to be allowed to run its natural course to produce highest ethical results. He does not seem to have penetrated to the root of Rousseau's fallacy, the double sense in which he constantly used the words 'nature' and 'natural.' Otherwise, Kant would have been able to repudiate the preposterous doctrine of Rousseau, without himself falling back upon the doctrine of the radical evil of human nature."[13]

Thus, according to Moore, from Kant's thinking a new concept of revelation is born. "Revelation is experience, not instruction. The revealers are those who have experienced God, Jesus the foremost among them. They have experienced God, whom then they have manifested as best they could, but far more significantly in what they were than in what they said."[14]

When the theological construction of the nineteenth century be-

12. *Ibid.*, p. 45.
13. *Ibid.*, p. 47.

14. *Ibid.*, p. 50.

gan, much use was made both of the ethical dualism and of the ethical monism of Kant. Theologians, to be sure, went beyond Kant. His religion was too moralistic for them. Again, it was too individualist. By means of the religious imagination, they added the religious dimension to the moral dimension of Kant. But even this religious dimension, as added to the moral, presupposed Kant's ethical dualism and his ethical monism. There is always the affirmation that human knowledge is limited to the realm of nature, that is, the realm of the phenomenal. This realm is the realm of science. It is here that the intellect of man legislates. For it is here that this intellect has imposed its intellectual categories upon the raw material of experience. This phenomenal realm is the realm of cause and effect. It is impersonal. And then above this realm of nature, the realm of the intellect, is the realm of the will and of faith. From this realm comes the Christ as the Saviour of men. He comes from God. But God is himself a postulate or projection of the religious consciousness.

In going beyond Kant, many modern theologians built upon the insights of the idealist philosophers who followed Kant. These idealist philosophers too had builded upon, even as they went beyond, Kant. Fichte works out the concept of revelation as it was inherent in the critical principles of Kant's philosophy. He makes use of Kant's ethical dualism in that he first denies that God can directly reveal himself in the realm of nature, for, if God did so reveal himself, then he would become an object among the objects of nature. Fichte then makes further use of the ethical monism of Kant by saying that God is "to be understood as subject, as the real subject, the transcendent thinking and knowing subject, indwelling in the world and making the world what it is, indwelling in us and making us what we are."[15]

Thus man, assuming himself to be the ultimate or autonomous subject of predication, projects a God in order then to participate in the "being" of this God. Thus his faith is faith in that it is participation in the revelation of this God to himself. And the human subject is absorbed in the process of divine self-revelation.

Schelling too made his contribution to the idealist development that went beyond Kant. He contributed the idea that nature is "the progress of intelligence toward consciousness and personality."[16] Nature is "personality in the making."[17] With such a concept of na-

15. *Ibid.*, p. 58.   17. *Idem.*
16. *Ibid.*, p. 61.

ture, all nature itself becomes, through man, participant in the being of the great Subject which is God.

As for Hegel, he "saw clearly that God can be known to us only in and through manifestation. We can certainly make no predication as to how God exists, in himself, as men say, and apart from our knowledge. He exists for our knowledge only as manifest in nature and man. Man is for Hegel part of nature and Jesus is the highest point which the nature of God as manifest in man has reached."[18] And Hegel, true to the idea that there can be no direct revelation of God through nature and history, also clearly saw that "Scripture is only the record of God's revelation of himself in and to men."[19]

To be sure, much of what these idealist philosophers said was rejected when the process of reconstruction in theology began. For the followers of Schleiermacher, Hegel was too rationalistic and metaphysical. Even so, fully in line with Hegel, they held that the human subject must participate in the divine subject by faith. According to the consciousness-theologians too, the Christian religion must itself be reinterpreted in terms of this idealist notion of God as Subject or Spirit.

3. *Friedrich Schleiermacher and Consciousness-Theology*

According to Schleiermacher, it is only in interpreting Christianity in accord with the principles of Kant's idea of the primacy of the practical reason that the proper place can be assigned to Christ. And surely Christ must be made central in any Christian theology. Christ was made central in Schleiermacher's *Christian Faith.* "In a very real sense," says Moore, "Jesus occupied the central place in Schleiermacher's system. This centralness of Jesus Christ he himself was never weary of emphasising."[20]

Schleiermacher "accords to Jesus an absolutely unique place in revelation."[21] In his system of theology, Jesus is spoken of as "the sole redeemer of men." He is "their only hope." Their dependence upon him is "described as absolute."[22]

If in this view of Christ, Schleiermacher goes beyond Kant, he is still, in a basic sense, operating in accordance with Kant's principle of ethical monism. For when he says that Jesus is the sole redeemer

18. *Ibid.*, p. 69.
19. *Idem.*
20. *Ibid.*, p. 82.

21. *Idem.*
22. *Ibid.*, p. 83.

of men, he does not refer to anything unique that happened in the history of Jesus Christ. "Every external, forensic, magical notion of salvation, as something purchased for us, imputed to us, conferred upon us, would have been utterly impossible to Schleiermacher. It is within the soul of man that redemption takes place. Conferment from the side of God and Christ, or from God through Christ, can be nothing more, as also it can be nothing less, than the imparting of wisdom and grace and spiritual power from the personality of Jesus, which a man then freely takes up within himself and gives forth as from himself. The Christian consciousness contains, along with the sense of dependence upon Jesus, the sense of moral alliance and spiritual sympathy with him, of a free relation of the will of man to the will of God as revealed in Jesus. The will of man is set upon the reproduction within himself, so far as possible, of the consciousness, experience and character of Jesus."[23]

The sin from which man is to be delivered is therefore by Schleiermacher said to be the "dominance of the lower nature in us, of the sense-consciousness."[24] And the Scriptures are for him a "record of the Christian experience of the men of the earlier time. To us it is a means of grace because it is the vivid and original register of that experience. The Scriptures can be regarded as the work of the Holy Spirit only in so far as this was this common spirit of the early Church. This spirit has borne witness to Christ in these writings not essentially otherwise than in later writings, only more at first hand, more under the impression of intercourse with Jesus. Least of all may we base the authority of Scripture upon a theory of inspiration such as that generally current in Schleiermacher's time. It is the personality of Jesus which is the inspiration of the New Testament."[25]

It was in this way that Schleiermacher "opened men's eyes to the fact that the great work of Christ in redemption is an inward one, an ethical and spiritual work, the transformation of character. He had said, not merely that the transformation of man's character follows upon the work of redemption. It is the work of redemption. The primary witness to the work of Christ is, therefore, in the facts of consciousness and history."[26]

"None since Kant, except extreme confessionalists, and these in diminishing degree, have held that the great effect of the work of

---

23. *Idem.*
24. *Idem.*

25. *Ibid.*, pp. 86-87.
26. *Ibid.*, p. 93.

Christ was upon the mind and attitude of God. Less and less have men thought of justification as forensic and judicial, a declaring sinners righteous in the eye of the divine law, the attribution of Christ's righteousness to men, so far at least as to relieve these last of penalty."[27]

Here then in Kant and his followers there stands before us, a new synthesis of dialectical thought and Christianity. The nature-freedom scheme is, as noted, composed of the same ingredients that composed the form-matter scheme of Greek thought. Basic to both is the assumption that man is his own law-giver. Man's theoretical thought is therefore assumed to operate autonomously. It needs merely to be supplemented by the pronouncements of the Practical Reason.

The basic similarity between the modern freedom-nature scheme and the form-matter scheme can best be seen from this, their common assumption. Their methods appear on the surface to be quite different from one another. The Greek view appears, on the surface, to be much more pretentious. Does it not claim to be able to prove God's existence by reason? And does not Thomas claim that, in addition to proving God's existence, reason can ascertain at least something of the nature of the divine being? On the other hand, does not Kant disclaim for the theoretical intellect any knowledge of God as well as of freedom and immortality whatever?

When this difference between the ancient and the Kantian theory of knowledge is considered, it may well seem to explain why Protestant theologians, who rejected the Romanist synthesis of Christianity with the form-matter scheme of Greek thought, were quite ready to make a synthesis composed of Christianity and the freedom-nature scheme. In this scheme, human freedom seems to be given its rightful place, while yet science too is protected as independent in its field. Here we seem to speak of God in a truly religious manner. We do not audaciously determine anything about the nature of God by reason. We do not even prove his existence. We allow him to announce both his own existence and the nature of his being. Thus the *that* and the *what* of things in the phenomenal world are determined by man, and the *that* and the *what* of things in the noumenal world are determined by God himself.

Above all, the place seems to be prepared for the proper apprecia-

27. *Ibid.*, pp. 93-94.

tion of the relation of the higher realm, the realm of practical reason, to the lower realm, the realm of theoretical reason. When God announces his presence in the lower realm in the way of incarnation, he remains free in doing so. Man cannot lay his hands on him as though he were an object among other objects. God's presence in the lower world is ethical and therefore intellectually incognito. That he is intellectually incognito is not due to the fact that he has not fully revealed himself. In the nature of the case, he has fully revealed himself. He is not revealed at all unless he is exhaustively revealed. For, from the ethical point of view, the character even of the realm of nature is wholly what it is because of its relation to God. Thus, what was at first sight only ethical dualism, turns out to be what Kroner calls ethical phenomenalism, and what Moore calls monism. That is to say, the phenomenal world is said to be properly, that is, ethically, subordinated to the noumenal realm. It is proper that this position in which the lower realm is subordinated to the higher realm should in the end be called monistic. But it must always be recalled that we have here an *ethical* monism. There is here no intellectual identity philosophy such as that of Spinoza.

Kant's ultimate aim in his *Critique of Pure Reason* was the finding of a foundation for his deep moral and religious convictions.[28] He saw that metaphysical being cannot be proved to be necessary from the principle of contradiction as this is used by the theoretical reason.[29] He could not agree with Spinoza that the order and connection of things is identical with the order and connection of ideas. He concluded that a distinction must be made "between space and time as synthetic apriori forms of sensory intuition and the apriori pure concepts of understanding."[30] "As long as space and time were subsumed under the creative apriori concepts of logical thought, there lurked the constant danger that the relations discovered between spatial things would be transferred to the 'mundus intelligibilis.' This would result again in a domination of the mathematical science-ideal within the realm of the free and autonomous human personality."[31]

The problem now was how on Kant's view the world of time and space or the world of sense *(mundus sensibilis),* was to be brought into renewed relation to the other world, the higher world *(mundus intelligibilis).* The world of space and time must by all means be

28. Dooyeweerd, *op. cit.,* p. 330.   30. *Ibid.,* p. 345.
29. *Ibid.,* p. 335.   31. *Idem.*

thought of as lower than the world of intelligence. The world of sense is therefore said to be phenomenal only. The things themselves appear somehow in the phenomena but are never identical with these phenomena.[32]

Thus in his *Critique of Pure Reason* and in his *Critique of Practical Reason*, says Dooyeweerd, Kant breaks the cosmos "asunder into two spheres, that of sensory experience and that of supersensory freedom."[33] He is, of course, seeking to reach a unified interpretation of the whole of human experience. And he wants his moral experience, that is, his experience of freedom, to be unhampered by the determinism that is inherent in the physical and mathematical interpretation of the sensible world. So the dualism between his two worlds is definitely in the interest of an eventual supremacy of the realm of the moral, the realm of the good, over the realm of the spatio-temporal.

But how shall a supremacy of the moral and spiritual world over the realm of physics and mathematics be accomplished? For the diremption between the two worlds seems to have its source in man himself. The answer is that Kant makes the "transcendental logical subject" the lawgiver of nature, and he makes the "transcendent subject of autonomous moral freedom" the "lawgiver of human action." Thus "natural necessity and freedom, causal law and norm, in their relationship to each other become antinomic species of laws which cannot find any deeper reconciliation in Kant's dualistic cosmonomic Idea."[34]

Moreover, there is antinomy even within his world of sensibility. "In spite of the proclamation of logical understanding as the lawgiver for nature, the sovereignty of theoretical thought is seriously threatened, because sensibility as a purely receptive instance, imposes insurmountable limits upon it. The understanding (*'Verstand'*) is the sovereign lawgiver only in a *formal* sense. Only the universally valid *form* of natural reality originates in the 'transcendental cogito.' The *material* of knowledge, remains deeply a-logical, so that at this point the problem of the *'Ding an sich'* behind the phenomena of nature arises again in a dangerous fashion. In the traditional metaphysical way, Kant permits the purely receptive sensibility to be affected by the *'Ding an sich'*."[35]

Kant cannot unify the two worlds by means of the categories of

32. *Ibid.*, p. 348.
33. *Ibid.*, p. 357.
34. *Ibid.*, p. 359.
35. *Ibid.*, p. 360.

the intellect. He cannot even unify elements of the sense world internally by means of the categories of the intellect. He can therefore conceive of the noumena only in a negative sense.[36]

Dooyeweerd expresses the predicament in which Kant finds himself as follows: "At every point this ground-Idea implies 'purity' in the sense of the unconditionedness of 'theoretical reason.' Consequently, the cleft between the ideal of science and that of personality *may* not be eradicated in an actual transcendental self-reflection. But it *must* be eradicated, since actually the Idea of the autonomy of pure theoretical thought, in the deepest sense, is entirely dependent upon the Idea of the autonomous freedom of personality!"[37]

Kant finally seeks to overcome the antinomies involved in his dualistic concept of the relation of the two worlds to one another by his idea of Deity as the postulate of the practical reason,[38] "which in this practical function is nothing but the idol of the Humanistic ideal of personality."[39] "The kernel of the Humanistic ideal of personality in the typical form which it assumes in Kant's transcendental ground-Idea is the freedom and autonomy of the ethical function of personality in its hypostatization as 'homo noumenon.' As we have formerly seen in another context, it is essentially the hypostatization of the merely formally conceived moral law itself which is identified with the 'homo noumenon,' as 'pure will.' "[40]

At this juncture the relation between the medieval synthesis of theology with the form-matter scheme of Greek thought and the modern synthesis of theology with the freedom-nature scheme can be readily observed. Says Dooyeweerd: "The entire *theologia naturalis* with its speculative rational proofs for the existence of God must be destroyed by the '*Critique of Pure Reason*,' because the ideal of personality can no longer find its veritable Idea of God in absolutized mathematical thought, but only in the hypostatized moral function of free and autonomous personality. To this end even the theoretical Idea of God must be *depreciated*."[41]

It appears then that the difference between the medieval or scholastic and the modern or Kantian synthesis cannot be a basic one. In both cases theology makes an alliance with a philosophy in which man is assumed to be ultimate. Kant does not reject natural

36. *Ibid.,* p. 362.
37. *Ibid.,* p. 369.
38. *Idem.*

39. *Ibid.,* p. 372.
40. *Ibid.,* pp. 372-373.
41. *Ibid.,* p. 372.

theology because it does not give the proper place to God in the biblical sense of the term. He rejects natural theology because in it the free, autonomous personality would not really be autonomous and free. The only way he had of setting human personality fully free, given his assumption of the ultimacy of human personality, was to increase the area of pure contingency. And this can only be done by formalizing the function of theoretical thought. The material of knowledge is made deeply alogical as the unity of knowledge becomes more formal. But what becomes of the free personality itself in this process? Is it now really free?

The answer is that in all its effort to find its freedom, the free personality has lost itself. "The transcendental concept of freedom considered in itself is merely negative (freedom from natural causality) and is to acquire a positive sense only through the principle of autonomy, in the sense of the absolute sovereignty of Human personality as the highest legislator. But this 'autonomy,' too, lacks as such a meaningful content. It is in itself only a formal principle. The religious ground-motive which finds its expression in Kant's transcendental freedom-Idea implies the *self-sufficiency* of the *homo noumenon* and it is this very divine predicate which makes any moral autonomy of man meaningless."[42]

And as for the God of practical reason by which Kant sought so desperately to find unity between his two worlds, he is in his system of thought as meaningless as he is in his idea of free personality. This God must be for Kant the combination of virtue and blessedness.[43] But how, on Kant's view, can virtue and happiness be united? So far as human experience goes, the world of the moral will, of virtue, is distinct from the world of sense and of happiness. And man cannot prove logically that there is a God who, as the highest good, combines virtue and blessedness. Nor can man prove logically that such a God is the creator and ruler of the world. Accordingly, such a God must be the postulate of the practical reason. This postulate must serve to bring about a unified relation between the two worlds. Man somehow wants the good to conquer over evil. When he can no longer prove the existence of a God whose providence rules all things, he postulates him. "Thus Kant finally felt compelled to accept a coherence between 'nature' and 'freedom' in order to escape the antinomical consequences of his hypostatization (and

42. *Ibid.*, p. 375.   43. *Ibid.*, p. 382.

consequently logicistic formalization) of moral personality. The acceptance of such an intelligible Creator of nature (the Deity) cannot be rationally proved, but it is a *postulate* of pure practical reason that makes possible the realization of the highest good. This postulate consequently, does not rest upon a theoretical knowledge, but just as the two other postulates of pure practical reason (freedom in a positive sense and immortality), it rests upon a universally valid and necessary reasonable faith in the reality of a supra-sensory, noumenal world and in the possibility of the realization of the highest good."[44]

"Kant's Idea of deity as postulate of 'pure practical reason' is the final hypostatization of the ideal of personality."[45]

In having absolutized itself, this would-be autonomous personality is finally broken up beyond repair. On the one hand, it possesses the faculty of understanding, and, on the other hand, it possesses the faculty of reason. The two are antithetical to one another. Each produces its own world. And these worlds stand antagonistically over against one another. In his *Critique of Judgment*, Kant made a final effort to bring understanding and reason together in order thus also to bring their two worlds together. But it was a foregone conclusion that such an effort should be a failure. There can be no internal harmony between the various aspects of human personality, and between the various aspects of his world, unless it be through the Creator-redeemer of Scripture. The two worlds of Kant were set in opposition to one another because each was the product of an absolutized function of the human consciousness. Now the *Critique of Judgment* has no other means than a third and equally absolutized function of human consciousness with which to bind the former two together. In the introduction to his *Critique of Judgment*, Kant says: "The Understanding legislates *a priori* for nature as an Object of sense—for a theoretical knowledge of it in a possible experience. Reason legislates *a priori* for freedom and its peculiar causality; as the supersensible in the subject, for an unconditioned practical knowledge. The realm of the natural concept under the one legislation and that of the concept of freedom under the other are entirely removed from all mutual influence which they might have on one another (each according to its fundamental laws) by the great gulf that separates the supersensible from phenomena.

44. *Ibid.,* p. 383.   45. *Ibid.,* p. 384.

The concept of freedom determines nothing in respect of the theoretical cognition of nature; and the natural concept determines nothing in respect of the practical laws of freedom. So far then it is not possible to throw a bridge from the one realm to the other."[46] Here then we have the ethical dualism of Kant expressed finally and fully in his own words. But now the judgment is, after all, to bridge the gap between understanding reason and their two worlds. The *Critique of Practical Reason* had furnished the notion of "causality through freedom." And "now, according to Kant, the faculty of judgment is supposed to furnish us with the mediating concept between the concept of nature and that of freedom, and this in the concept of a teleology in nature: 'because through the latter is understood the possibility of the final end which can only be realized in nature and in accord with its laws.' "[47]

It is thus that Kant seeks to provide for the idea of "the effects of the supersensible upon the sensible."[48]

Kant thinks that the theoretical reason need not complain that in this idea of free causation, this idea of an effect produced in the world of sense by the world of pure freedom, in any wise transgresses any of its laws. For this effect in the natural world "is to take place in the world according to its formal laws."[49] Thus the triumph of grace or personality can be accomplished.

Meanwhile, the would-be autonomous free personality that stands back of the creation of the world of sense, and of the world of practical reason, and back of their unification, cannot identify itself. The *homo noumenon* "is nothing but an absolutizing of the moral aspect of human existence, which is lifted out of the cosmic temporal coherence of the modal law-spheres by means of a false analysis, and is thus logically formalized. And in this logical formalization it destroys itself."[50]

How can man identify himself unless he does so in subjection to God who has in Christ first identified himself to man? Having rejected the Creator-redeemer as self-identifying God in relation to which man must identify himself, man loses himself in the abyss of the unrelated. He must then relate his two worlds in terms of a form-matter scheme. Greek philosophy used the notion of a primary sub-

46. *Kant's Kritik of Judgment,* translated by J. H. Bernard, D.D. London: MacMillan & Co., 1892, p. 38.
47. Dooyeweerd, *op. cit.,* p. 392.   49. *Idem.*
48. *Kant's Kritik of Judgment,* p. 38.   50. Dooyeweerd, *op. cit.,* p. 393.

stance in order to relate these two worlds. This notion of substance was inherently at odds with itself. As far as it had any individual content, it was irrational. And as far as it had contact with the world of form, it was itself absorbed by form. Kant spurns the Greek idea of substance as a means by which to unify his two worlds. He substitutes for it the idea of the free act of man. But this concept of the free act of man is subject to the same criticism which he himself applies to the notion of substance. The notion of free personality in Kant's thinking is once more a combination of a purely formal or abstract notion of rationality and a purely irrational notion of individuality and content.

Thus Kant must be said to be anything but the philosopher of Protestantism. In Protestantism man identifies himself by subjecting himself in covenant obedience to his maker and redeemer. He has unity in his personality, not because he understands himself exhaustively, but because both he and the cosmic order in relation to which he has his spatio-temporal content have their common origin and salvation in Jesus Christ as he speaks directly to man in history.

It was because the consciousness-theologians made their basic alliance with this Kantian approach that they must be spoken of as *New* Protestantism. They are Protestants who have secularized the principle of Protestantism. In historic Protestantism, man is indeed free from the authority of men. But man is free only in so far as he subjects himself to the authority, to the self identification, of God through Christ in the Scriptures. In contrast with this, the position of New Protestantism is subjective. New Protestant theologians find their final reference point with Kant in the human subject. At the same time, this position, in being subjective, is also illusionistic. When man loses his proper environment, the environment provided for him in his creation and redemption through Christ, he loses himself.

It has already been pointed out that Barth did not reject the medieval synthesis in order that men might return to the self-identifying God of Scripture. Barth rejected the medieval synthesis in terms of his Christ as *Geschichte.* In doing so, Barth virtually placed himself on the side of those who interpret the whole of human life and experience from the point of view of man as autonomous. By not calling the Romanist theologians back to the Bible as the direct revelation of God, Barth virtually took the immanentist or dialectical view of reality as this is involved in the apostate

notion of the autonomy of man. All non-biblical thought is dialectical. Dialectical thought expresses itself in the form of a religious
dualism. There are assumed to be two ultimate principles, the one
of temporal plurality and with it of evil, and the other of eternal
being which is a form and is good.

So far as the intellectual contemplation on these two realms is
concerned, they can never be brought into unity with one another.
So, for instance, Plato first has apostate man determine the difference between good and evil in terms of his own moral consciousness. Then he adds that, since God is good, he is the source of the
good. And, since God is good, he can have no manner of connection
with evil. There must, therefore, argues Plato, be an independent
source of evil. If there is to be a triumph of the good over the evil,
then we must therefore *posit* a Good that is above the principles of
good and evil that were found by logical derivation. Thus the idea
of the Good as above and therefore triumphant over evil is a matter
of projection.

Even the God of Aristotle, though his existence is said to be logically proved, is proved by the process of negation. Accordingly, this
God turns out to be a pure form. Aristotle's god is not a person. He
is an *it*, a principle. And this principle is correlative to pure potentiality. So here too we discover a religious dualism. And the monism
that Aristotle seeks as much as Plato has again to be seen in terms
of vision.

However much then Barth seeks to call men away from Romanism, his own methodology is also dialectical. Barth does not reject
the dialectical character of Romanism. On the contrary, he rejects
the Christ who identifies himself directly in history. He does so in
the name of a dialectically constructed Christ. However vigorous
Barth may be when he casts out the medieval synthesis, his own
theology is therefore still a synthesis theology. It can only differ in
degree from the Romanist approach.

Herewith we approach the problem of Barth's relation to the
modern synthesis theology that is found in the consciousness-theologians. The synthesis theology of the consciousness-theologians
consists of an alliance of Christianity with the modern form of
dialectical philosophy. This dialecticism owes its formative principles to Kant.

At first sight, the methodology of Kant's thinking might seem to
be attractive to Christian theologians. He denies that man can say

anything about God. He rejects all natural theology. This may encourage us greatly. For if man can say nothing about God, then will not God be given a real opportunity to speak to man? If philosophy in true modesty keeps to the realm of the phenomenal, the spatio-temporal realm, then may not theology listen to God as he speaks from the noumenal realm? Is the way not open now for a real confrontation between God and man? Will not God now really speak straight down from above, and will not man simply listen in obedience to the voice of God? It is no wonder that Christian theologians were attracted to the Kantian theory of knowledge. Here truly seemed to be the philosopher of Protestantism as Aristotle was the philosopher of Roman Catholicism.

It must be said, however, that the idea of man as independent of God is as deeply imbedded in Kant's philosophy as it is in that of Aristotle. Kant's assertion of the free moral person as self-sufficient, and as therefore independent of the law of God, is basic to his dualistic relation between the world of the theoretical and the world of the practical reason. Kant says that he limits theoretical knowledge to the world of nature. He says that man cannot know anything about God. The most important consequence of this approach is that on its basis God cannot in any sense identify himself to man. Nothing can be said about God by man, because God cannot say anything about himself to man. If God is not made first in human interpretation, then he is not God at all. But he is not made first if the world of space and time is not created and redeemed by him. If the laws of the realm of nature spring in the last analysis from the organizing activity of the autonomous man, then God cannot speak to man through them. If the act of creation, providence and redemption is not back of man himself, as well as back of nature, then there is no possible confrontation of man with God. All that remains then is that man projects a God who is an echo of his voice.

Any consciousness-theology, in making an alliance with the Kantian dualism, will be an essentially negative theology. In this it will resemble the theology of Romanism. So far as Romanism was influenced by Greek thought, it too was a negative theology. All dialectical theology is negative theology. It can be nothing else, since it is based on the idea of human autonomy. The God of a negative theology is always a projected god, a god who says nothing of himself. He will speak what the moral or religious consciousness of man has decided that he should speak.

4. Barth's Ethical Dualism and Ethical Monism

It is not thus that Barth has analyzed the consciousness-theology against which he reacted when he began his work. To be sure, Barth says that the consciousness-theologians made a god in their own image. He says that he himself wants a God who really speaks from above. But as Barth did not signalize the basic fault of medieval synthesis theology, so he does not signalize the basic fault of modern synthesis theology. In all that he says about the necessity of having God speak to man, he fails to do so in terms of the self-identifying Christ of Scripture. His criticism of the modern synthesis theology, like his criticism of the medieval synthesis theology, is in terms of his Christ as *Geschichte*. He has made his basic choice with the apostate principle of immanence over against the Protestant principle of the revelation of God through Christ in history. Barth is critical of the modern synthesis as he is of the medieval synthesis. But he goes beyond both in terms of a deeper dialecticism than that of Thomas or than that of Schleiermacher.

Barth himself informs us that, in his exposition of Paul's epistle to the Romans, he made some use of the Platonic-Kantian method. Just what he means by these words may be doubtful. But the fact that he did employ the notion of a religious dualism similar to that of Plato, and more particularly similar to that of Kant, is plain. The Kantian form of religious dualism is more dualistic than that of Plato. Dooyeweerd has pointed out that the influence of medieval nominalism has been great on the humanistic motive of the freedom of man. Berkouwer has shown that due to his nominalism Barth's actualistic theology is more destructive of the idea of the revelation of God through Christ in history than was the view of Occam. Zuidema has indicated that Barth's idea of the absolute hiddenness of revelation conditions everything that he says about God and Christ. In other words, when Barth wants a God and a Christ who speak from above, he finds such a God by the help of the idea of pure negation.

At this point, Barth's thought runs true to the pattern of Kant's idea of the limits of human knowledge. This idea seemed to be destructive merely of the idea of natural theology. In reality it was destructive of the idea of the revelation of God in nature and history. Whereas Calvin says that God speaks to all men everywhere in

all the facts of the created universe, Barth says that God speaks nowhere in nature and history or in human experience because man
has first spoken there. Yet Barth tries to combine Kant and Calvin.
His chief alliance is with Kant.

In his commentary on *Romans*, Barth's religious dualism is plainly
apparent.

The book of Romans, says Barth, "moves round the theme (i:16,
17) that in Christ Jesus the *Deus absconditus* is as such the *Deus
revelatus*. This means that the theme of the Epistle to the Romans
—Theology, the Word of God—can be uttered by human lips only
when it is apprehended that the predicate, *Deus revelatus,* has as its
subject *Deus absconditus.*"[51] God remains hidden even in his revelation. "God is pure negation."[52] God "must never be identified with
anything which we name, or experience, or conceive, or worship, as
God."[53] It is this theme that Barth works out with great ingenuity.

"The word of Paul," Barth says, "and the word of Theology has
done its work when men are driven by it to ask of God why it is
that His Word stands written in no book—not even in a 'table of
contents'—and has been attained by no man."[54]

"In Jesus, God becomes veritably a secret: He is made known as
the Unknown, speaking in eternal silence."[55]

The apostle who speaks must speak of God as "pure negation." A
true apostle is, therefore, one who, in speaking of the God of "pure
negation" is himself an "impossibility." Paul realized this and was
therefore a good apostle.

The preacher in turn following the apostle must realize that "the
final justification of the Church consists in its perpetual collapse,
just as Pharisaism is justified by its power of self-destruction."[56]
The preacher must speak of God's concern for the individual, but
the individual is, strictly speaking, ineffable.[57]

Finally, those who hear the preacher must realize that they catch
hold of nothing but the unknown God. The hearer must not seek to
obtain any content either positive or negative. "Genuine faith is a
void, an obeisance before that which we can never be, or do, or
possess; it is devotion to Him who can never become the world or

51. *The Epistle to the Romans*, tr. by Edwyn C. Hoskyns, London, 1933,
p. 422.
52. *Ibid.*, p. 141.   55. *Ibid.*, p. 98.
53. *Ibid.*, p. 331.   56. *Ibid.*, p. 406.
54. *Ibid.*, p. 422.   57. *Ibid.*, p. 352.

man, save in the dissolution and redemption and resurrection of everything which we here and now call world and man."[58] "Faith is the predicate of which the new man is the subject,"[59] and this new man exists only on the other side of the death-line. "The point where faith and unbelief part company can be defined neither psychologically nor historically."[60] "Faith and its power is invisible and non-historical."[61]

In such words as these, Barth's nominalistic irrationalism is apparent. In this respect Barth resembles Kant's basic approach to philosophy. Kant insisted, more consistently than anyone before him, that the material of knowledge is alogical. Only by conceiving this material as utterly illogical could he ascribe to the categorical action of the subject of knowledge the ultimacy that he desired for it. If the free man is to be really free, then he must not be confronted with an ordered universe.

Barth's principle of individuation is as irrational as is that of Kant. And this is true of the pre-dialectical period of his thinking no less than of his dialectical period.

Barth's theological training was in large part given him under Ritschlian influence. At an early period, Barth began to realize that there was no true gospel in the teaching of Ritschlian theology. But he was at the same time convinced that he could not return to orthodoxy and its idea of direct revelation.

He seeks therefore to go beyond Ritschlianism. And, in going beyond Ritschlianism, he seeks also to go beyond Kant, for Ritschlian theology is largely true to a Kantian theory of knowledge. Yet he seeks to go beyond Ritschl and beyond Kant by means of a God constructed by a more consistent application of Kantian, that is, critical principles. Barth too wants to start from the idea of pure or brute factuality. And Barth too speaks of a world of values that is formal and impersonal.[62]

When then Barth is beginning to break himself loose from his

58. *Ibid.*, p. 88.　　　　　　60. *Ibid.*, p. 150.
59. *Ibid.*, p. 149.　　　　　　61. *Ibid.*, p. 152.
62. Article on *Moderne Theologie und Reichsgottesarbeit* in *Zeitschrift für Theologie und Kirche*, 1909, pp. 317ff.
Article on *Noch einmal: Moderne Theologie und Reichsgottesarbeit, ibid.*, p. 406.
Article on *Zum dritten Mal: Moderne Theologie und Reichsgottesarbeit, ibid.*, pp. 475ff.
Article on *Antwort an E. Chr. Achelis und D. Drews, ibid.*, pp. 479ff.

Ritschlian teachers, the principles of a critical philosophy are still axiomatic for him.

It is these same principles that guide him in his work on *Romans*. The God of "pure negation" is the God of critical philosophy. It is the God who is wholly hidden.

But hiddenness by itself is meaningless. Barth is concerned with the *revelation* of his *Deus absconditus*. But how could he construct the idea of revelation from the idea of pure negation? The answer is that Barth does not build his idea of revelation upon that of negation. He had his idea of revelation as soon as he had his idea of negation. They are only aspects of one idea.

Kant conceived his idea of man's philosophical knowledge of the world of sense at the same time that he conceived his idea of man's complete ignorance of the world of the spirit.

In Kant's scheme, the knowing subject provides the categories which order the raw stuff of the realm of pure contingency. To the extent that man knows, he, therefore, knows exhaustively. For knowledge pertains precisely to the formal relations of the world. And these formal relations originate from man himself.

If then the wholly unknown God is to be known at all, he must be wholly known. And, as wholly known, God becomes wholly under the control of man. But a God who comes wholly under the control of man is, properly speaking, no God at all.

So Barth first counterbalances the idea of the God who is wholly unknown with the idea of the God that is wholly known, and then he counterbalances the idea of the God who is wholly known with the idea of the God who is wholly unknown. And Christ as *Geschichte* is the pinpoint of interaction between the God of pure negation and the God of pure affirmation.

If therefore we are to do justice to Barth, it is necessary to see that from the beginning, and especially in his commentary on *Romans*, Barth did not only think of God as the God of pure negation, but that, correlative to this idea of pure negation, of pure irrationalism, is the idea of pure rationalism.

In consequence, Barth's "ineffable" individual, who disowns all rationality and universality outside itself, produces it from within. On the one hand, faith is said to receive no content at all. On the other hand, when he says that "faith is, as it were, creative of divinity," he is speaking as a rationalist.[63] The individual who be-

63. *Romans*, p. 143.

lieves must be thought of as "beyond the death-line." The subject of faith, as we have already noted, is said to be super-historical. Abraham, the father of the faithful, as the "recipient of the promise," is said to stand "outside every historical and particular company of men."[64] Faith is something that takes place in no historical person. Through what we are not, we participate in divinity.[65] By faith we are found with Abraham beyond the "line of death."[66] This "invisible relationship" that David speaks of, in the thirty-second psalm, constitutes "the whole fullness and significance of human personality."[67] All this is, in effect, to say that it is really God who believes through us, or that when we believe we are divine. The Holy Spirit, says Barth, is "the subject of faith."[68] It is God who through us believes in himself.

Berkouwer was therefore quite right when in his first book on Barth he insisted on the strongly nominalist character of Barth's view of revelation. He was equally right when in his second book on Barth he said that even in *Romans* it was Barth's purpose to speak of the triumph of grace. Sin is, accordingly, for Barth an "impossible possibility." These two ideas have always gone together in Barth. With a nominalist stress on the wholly hidden character of God's revelation goes a realist or rationalist stress on the idea that man is what he is by virtue of his virtual absorption into deity.

It is thus that Barth has from the beginning spoken of grace as free and as universal. As God's revelation is not identical with any point in history, so faith is "possible for all."[69] "There is no man who ought not to believe and who cannot believe."[70] Consequently, it is possible to affirm that faith takes place "on the border-land of the philosophy of Plato, of the art of Grünewald and Dostoevsky, and of the religion of Luther."[71] In fact, "the possibility of hearing the Gospel is as universal as is the responsibility to hear it, and as is the promise vouchsafed to them who do hear it."[72]

Still further, faith is not only possible for all but is potentially present in all. In truly idealist fashion, Barth argues that the possibility of its denial presupposes its presence. "Though men may never have heard the name of God, though, having heard it, they may have blasphemed it; yet, in the midst of the horror they have of them-

64. *Ibid.*, p. 139.
65. *Ibid.*, p. 121.
66. *Ibid.*, p. 120.
67. *Ibid.*, p. 124.
68. *Ibid.*, p. 158.

69. *Ibid.*, p. 99.
70. *Ibid.*, p. 40.
71. *Ibid.*, p. 141.
72. *Ibid.*, p. 40.

selves, stands clearly the new man, born into a new world."[73] It may therefore be said that "that by which men are justified by God is discovered in them." The "memory of eternity" breaks in upon their minds as well as upon the minds of those that are in the church. The "New Day," the "day of Jesus Christ," has nothing to do with calendar dates or the country of Palestine. It is rather "the Day that ushers in the transformation of all time into eternity."[74] Thus all the children of time are saved for all eternity. All men find the "absolutely Other" in themselves. As in the case of Kant's criticism, so in the case of Barth's, it is the autonomous man who accepts only that which has been produced by himself. "When we rebel, we are in rebellion not against what is foreign to us but against that which is most intimately ours, not against that which is removed from us but against that which lies at our hands. Our memory of God accompanies us always as problem and as warning. He is the hidden abyss; but He is also the hidden home at the beginning and end of all journeyings. Disloyalty to him is disloyalty to ourselves."[75]

As to Barth's later theology, only the following points may be made in this chapter.

Barth's thinking still operates within the framework of immanentistic dialecticism, as we have earlier defined this. There is no indication of any sort in Barth's later writings that he wants to return to the historic Protestant idea of the direct revelation of God through Christ in history. His notion of the freedom of God, so central to the theology of his *Church Dogmatics,* is fully as nominalist and actualist as is his concept of revelation in *Romans.*

To be sure, Barth no longer thinks of the incarnation as merely touching history as a tangent touches a circle. He even claims to be more orthodox than the orthodox in his view of the incarnation. Orthodoxy, he says, is docetic. It does not believe that in the incarnation God has been wholly revealed. One is not really sound on the doctrine of the incarnation unless one thinks of God as wholly submitting himself to the conditions of the creature.

But for this reason, all the more, there can be for Barth no question of direct revelation. There simply can be no revelation at all, for Barth, unless it be wholly hidden. According to Barth, the world is not created in the biblical sense. It is, therefore, in the material aspect of it, wholly alogical or irrational. And God must meet man

73. *Ibid.,* p. 300.   75. *Ibid.,* p. 46.
74. *Ibid.,* pp. 67, 69.

in this world. To do so he must, with man, enter into the completely alogical or non-rational. He must enter into the wholly contingent. And he does not thus enter into the wholly contingent unless it is his nature, his being to do so. God is inherently coexistent as well as existent.

On Barth's view there would be direct revelation only if there were no contingency anywhere. And that would be true, on his basis only, if all reality were one block of rational being. But God is not such a block or principle of rationality. He is no Platonic idea. God is the act of revelation. His being is this revelation. To have or be this being in revelation he must enter upon and pass through pure contingency. Any position that does not think of God's being as being that passes into and through contingency is, on Barth's view, docetic. Only if one *actualizes* the incarnation and thereby removes the restrictions of the Chalcedon creed can one think of God as really, because wholly, present with man. For God to be wholly present with man is to be present with him in his dependence on *pure* contingency.

Thus all revelation must be *wholly* hidden. God must in Christ on Calvary be wholly forsaken of God.

Thus Barth's stress in his latest works on the reality of God's presence with man in history is, if possible, still more inimical to the idea of direct revelation than his earlier stress on God's transcendence above man. Barth is, if possible, still more nominalist in his later work than he was in his earlier work.

But this fact is what it is because his nominalism has come to greater self-consciousness under the influence of the modern form of dialecticism. In the freedom-nature motive of Kant and his followers, the basic dialecticism of apostate thought comes to more consistent expression than could be given it in the form-matter motive of ancient thought. Only when man asserts his autonomy as self-consciously as does Kant does he operate with the idea of pure contingency. Man cannot maintain his autonomy unless he can posit himself as the only, because ultimate, source of order in himself and in the world. If man met any order over against himself, then he would have to make an adjustment to this order.

According to Kant then, man is surrounded by raw stuff. And this raw stuff is wholly pliable in the sense that it has no order in it. On the other hand, the very rawness of the stuff confronting the free man acts as a limitation on him. This limitation appears deep within man himself. Man has no self-awareness except in terms of his relation to the content of his being that comes from raw stuff. There is what may be called the formal and the material principle in his personality. Man is a combination of both. Man's self-awareness, says Kant, is nothing unless it be taken as expressed through both his formal and material principle. Self-consciousness and time-consciousness or world-consciousness are identical. But the world is nothing for man except in terms of the non-rational intuitions of space and time. That is to say, the world of man is, according to Kant, built up of two factors, one wholly rational and the other wholly irrational. Kant made the two principles of his thought, that of pure rationality and that of pure irrationality, correlative to one another in order to escape both the empirical and the rationalist thought of his days. And for him the human self was the unifying act of the principle of pure rationality and the principle of pure irrationality.

But herewith he had built abstract rationality and abstract irrationality into the center of his thinking. On his view, man himself participates in abstract rationality. In consequence, he loses his individual self-consciousness to the pull of this abstract rationality unless there be a counteracting force. But since he does not believe in man's creation by God, the only force that could keep him from being lost in abstract rationality is the force of pure irrationality. And this force is itself universalizing in its work. Unless there is some counteracting force, the idea of pure contingency or irrationality absorbs man's self-awareness into an ocean of chance and therefore into complete silence. If therefore man is to have self-awareness, it can only be if he is loyal to two mutually opposed but equally universalizing forces. It is thus that man loses himself when he will not find his unity in terms of the God who through Christ and his spoken word tells him what and therefore who he is.

Barth has not anywhere opposed this basically anti-Christian view of man. As he did not oppose the medieval synthesis of Christianity with apostate philosophy by means of the Christ of Scripture, so he does not challenge modern synthesis of Christianity with an equally apostate philosophy. He leaves the root error of both undisturbed. In fact, he builds his theology upon it.

Barth does not reject Kant's view of man as being untrue to the Scriptures. He does not reject Kant's idea of pure contingency as a constitutive factor in the constitution of the world of nature and of man himself. He is therefore only consistent with himself when he does not reject Kant's view of God as being expressed in terms of a limiting concept. In his dualistic view of knowledge, Kant asserted that man can know nothing of God. That is to say, man can know nothing of such a God as has any actual being. Plato's God was a God who had or was also being. Spinoza had a God who had content. But of such a God man can have no knowledge, says Kant. In fact, if man is to have knowledge of himself and of the world, then such a God must be cleared away. No true unification of the alogical and the logical aspects of human experience can be brought about, Kant argues, unless we do justice to both as equally ultimate. As equally ultimate, the logical and the alogical factors of experience must be brought into correlative relation with one another. Therefore, matter must have no form in it and form must have no matter in it prior to their meeting in man. And the meeting is inherently a meeting of act, for, if there were no act, then form would remain static by itself, and matter would remain irrational by itself.

Still further, the act must proceed from an Actor, a subject who acts. Not that such an act is first intelligible to itself, and then acts for the sake of the unification of pure matter and pure form. Quite the contrary, the acting subject only becomes aware of itself as the unifying agency between pure form and pure matter when it actually unifies them and itself.

And now we return to God. God has become superfluous, and worse than superfluous, as a God that has actual being apart from the unifying act of free man. On the other hand, God is not at all superfluous as an ideal principle of rationality. We cannot reach God by means of concepts *(Begriffe)*. But we need God as an ideal *(Idee)*. Science and philosophy need God as an ideal of complete comprehension in knowledge. From the point of view of science, the universe must be at the same time wholly knowable and wholly unknowable. If there is to be growth in science, there must be genuine newness. And there is genuine newness only if there is absolute contingency. So there is stability only if the whole of reality be wholly known or wholly accessible to principles of human knowledge.

And here God serves a useful and even indispensable purpose. As a limit or ideal, as a heuristic or service notion, God as pure rationality is that in terms of which alone man can continue his unifying activity.

Moreover, what holds for science holds for philosophy, and therefore for the philosophy of religion. The God that is needed for philosophy and for religion must certainly have no being. If he had being, then he would be static and could not be known. The true God of philosophy and of religion must therefore gather his being as he is brought into relation with pure contingency. Apart from this relation, God must be *pure* form. There could be no true unification of form and matter unless form is pure form and matter is *pure* matter.

In this respect, the God of modern critical philosophy resembles the God of Aristotle. The God of Aristotle is one, a unity, specifically, that is, so long as he is a principle or universal only. The God of Aristotle explodes into plurality as soon as he (or it) is given any being. In similar fashion, the God of modern dialectical thought, when truly transcendent, that is, when truly out of contact with content, is nothing but form.

It is such a universal form as correlative to pure contingency that modern philosophy as well as modern science wants as an ideal. Only by means of such a pure form as correlative to pure matter can the free, autonomous man maintain his freedom. Only by means of them does he have control of the situation.

It is this kind of man with this kind of God that Kant employs for the purpose of interpreting reality. But with his deep sense of morality he could not avoid repersonalizing this abstract principle of rationality. He was, after all, interested in the primacy of the practical reason. He therefore made provision for the subordination of the world of nature to the world of the "creator" and "redeemer." Thus, he reintroduced the notions of providence and even of redemption.

But his God and redeemer, insofar as he is transcendent above the world, is real only as supported by the postulational activity of free man. When this God manifests himself in history and thus seeks contact with man, he is at once involved in the problematics of man. As the projection of man, this God too is drawn apart by the two opposing forces of abstract rationality and equally abstract particularity. If he were not thus torn apart, he would not be really in contact with man.

Herewith we return to Barth. His principle of the freedom of God, it has been noted, stands for the same notion of pure contingency that is found in modern dialectical or critical philosophy. God is free for man in Christ and God's grace is free for man because God identifies himself in Jesus with pure contingency.

But Christ is the electing God, and God is inherently and universally gracious to man so far as he is pure form.

If there were any being in God prior to his revelation in Christ, then there would be no true universality of grace. From Barth's point of view, Calvin's doctrine of election illustrates this point all too well.

Again, if there is to be unity in the various attributes of God and grace is to be made to stand above holiness and righteousness, then there must be no being in God prior to his revelation.

Barth is quite specific on the point that the idea of God as prior to his revelation is both indispensable as a limiting concept and destructive as a constitutive concept.

God then, when he has being, has this being, for Barth, only in identity with his act of revelation.

But when we say with *his* act of revelation, we have already attributed being to him as a principle. And therewith we have anew expressed the idea that, in coming to man, God is subject to the problematics of man.

In his unwillingness really to cut himself loose from the apostate principle of modern critical and dialectical philosophy, Barth could at best produce a new synthesis theology.

This new synthesis theology is more deeply interwoven with the general dialectical interpretation of man by apostate thought than the medieval synthesis was.

Barth's criticisms of Schleiermacher and his followers could therefore never go to the bottom of the question. Barth no less than the consciousness-theologians assumed that man must seek to understand himself first in terms of himself and only afterwards in terms of God.

Chapter XII

Recent Dialecticism

In the two previous chapters, we were concerned with medieval and with modern dialecticism respectively. We turn now to a discussion of modern dialecticism as it has found expression in recent, that is, in post-Kantian, times. The term existentialism may be employed to indicate the general nature of recent dialecticism. The theology of Barth can best be understood if it is seen in relation to these three forms of dialecticism.

First and foremost among existentialist thinkers is Søren Kierkegaard. It is well known that in his commentary on *Romans* Barth spoke with favor of the idea of the qualitative difference between God and man as this was set forth in Kierkegaard's philosophy. It is also well known that in his later theology Barth seeks to cut himself loose from every form of existential thinking, from every form of philosophical speculation. Our interest now is to discover whether Barth has really turned from speculation to revelation in his later work. To do this we need first to look into the nature of recent dialecticism.

1. Kroner on Dialecticism

There is nothing essentially new in recent dialecticism. It is a carrying forth of the idea of the primacy of the practical reason as this was set forth by Kant. There is in recent dialecticism, if possible, a still greater stress on the contrast between the world of the phenomena and the world of the noumena than was found in Kant. And there is, secondly, a greater stress on the need of an ethical idea of

God as the one who must overcome this dualism by somehow unifying the two separated worlds. In other words, philosophy becomes
more and more critical and seemingly less speculative. By becoming
more critical, philosophy becomes more and more disposed to allow
for the possibility of revelation. In becoming more critical and less
speculative, philosophy is more ready to allow that revelation must
come *from above*. The deeper the gulf that is said to exist between
the world of sense (phenomena) and the world of thought (noumena), the more does their final union become a matter to be accomplished by God rather than by man. Thus, a truly critical
philosophy is said to be able to do better justice to Christianity than
any earlier type of philosophy ever could.

The argument offered for such a contention is stated in masterly
fashion by Richard Kroner. We turn to a brief analysis of his
position.

In his earlier days, Kroner was, he tells us, much influenced by
both Kant and Hegel. "With Kant I believed that philosophy approaches the incomprehensible without ever penetrating it, but
with Hegel I held that a thing-in-itself cannot express this self-
limitation of thought but that the dialectical method must vindicate
and verify this comprehension of the incomprehensible."[1]

Kroner says, faith and theology have a greater place in his thought
today than they did formerly. "Today I deviate from both Kant and
Hegel and, indeed, from all forms of philosophical idealism in my
conviction that the limit of philosophy is determined and also illuminated by faith and theology. I no longer consider religion to be a
state in the self-realization of mind or a link in the creative process
of culture."[2]

According to Kroner, the chasm between the divine and the
human minds is far deeper than was realized by either Kant or
Hegel. "It would be vain to try to deduce the duality of world and
self from any phenomenon belonging to the world or belonging to
the self. From the beginning of self-conscious experience this polarity
has made itself felt. It is an *Urphänomen*, a primordial and primary
'datum.' It is the most radical opposition we can think of. Ours is a
world of oppositions anyway. We confront them in whatever realm
of experience or thought we may move. But the opposition between

---

1. Richard Kroner, *Culture and Faith*, The University of Chicago Press,
1937, p. ix.
2. *Idem.*

the world and the self that experiences the world and itself is the most fundamental and the most astounding of all oppositions."[3]

"If" therefore "there is a realm beyond the possibilities of human thought, we simply recognize its existence by our renunciation, while it would be foolish and illusory to aim at the conquest of that realm with insufficient and inadequate weapons."[4]

But to recognize the existence of this realm beyond human thought is not enough. It is from that realm that the initiation for reunion between the two realms must come. To be sure, in order that the initiation for union may truly come from God rather than from man, we must again go beyond Kant. Kant is still too speculative. He wants, after all, to effect the union between the pure and the practical reason by means of speculative reason itself. "Consequently he conceives of the unity between morality and nature as if the question of the *cause* of nature were to be answered. He thus applies the category of causality, which has its appropriate place in scientific knowledge and in the realm of empirical objects, for the purpose of unifying theoretical and practical reason in such a way that the cause of nature insures a harmony between happiness and morality."[5]

Of course, Kant wants to make only a "practical use" of the word *cause*. He does not think of either the free act of man or the work of God as causes in the phenomenal sense of the term.[6] "But can this restriction rehabilitate a concept annihilated by critical speculation? I think that reason, whether practical or theoretical, as long as it remains reason alone, unsupported by religious intuition and imagination, is not entitled, and not able, to postulate the existence of a cause of nature, not even when this cause is conceived of as the moral author of the world in which we, as moral beings, live. It is obvious that not pure practical reason alone, but the *biblical image of the Creator* led Kant to propose that reason postulates the existence of God as the Author of the world. Kant, I would suggest, is right in defending a certain correspondence of this biblical image with pure practical reason, but he is not right in asserting that reason alone can postulate and justify this image as a rational idea or as a concept which needs no imagination to be engendered. Whereas Kant in the *Critique of Pure Reason* does not fully appreciate the

3. *Ibid.*, p. 3.   4. *Ibid.*, p. 6.
5. Kroner, *The Primacy of Faith,* The Macmillan Company, 1943, p. 55.
6. *Ibid.*, p. 59.

ability of reason to obtain positive results, in the *Critique of Practical Reason* he overrates the productive power of this same faculty."[7]

It is therefore of utmost importance, argues Kroner, to go beyond Kant by giving up every form of speculation. The Christian message makes every form of "unifying and totalitarian thought impossible. This the philosopher should learn from Karl Barth, even if he rejects his dogmatics for other reasons."[8]

"Kant approaches a right appreciation of the non-philosophical, non-speculative nature of religion, but he ruins his doctrine eventually by his conception of rational faith."[9]

At this point, Kroner stresses the place of imagination in religious knowledge. If every vestige of speculation is to be cleared out of our thinking with respect to God and his relation to the world, then it is imperative that we see the proper place of imagination in our religion. Says Kroner: "It is quite true, that in and by faith man's intellect and will are more deeply united than in any other region of his mind. But this unification is accomplished as little by practical as by theoretical reason. It is accomplished not by reason at all, but by imagination. Thus prophetic inspiration and divine revelation can be understood in their specific purport, whereas in the Kantian interpretation they lose their meaning and appear as obstacles of pure, rational faith. While Kant recognized clearly enough the superrational meaning of the *beautiful* and of creations in the realm of *art*, he did not succeed in rating the superrational in the realm of *religion* at its true value. He overcame rationalistic prejudices in analyzing the peculiar contribution of the man of *genius*, but he yielded to them in the case of the *prophet*. This is the deficiency of his philosophy seen by so many critics in the nineteenth and twentieth centuries; but none of these critics tried to supplement what is missing, and to supply philosophy with an appropriate theory of religious imagination and inspiration."[10]

It is by imagination that the antinomies found in human experience are overcome. Basic to all the antinomies of logic is the antinomy of self-contradiction. "Self-contradiction is possible only because I am a self and wish to be in agreement with myself, since my very self is at stake when I disagree with myself. The logical antinomies reflect this inner situation, this metaphysical experience.

7. *Idem.*
8. *Culture and Faith,* p. 7.
9. *Primacy of Faith,* p. 60.
10. *Idem.*

By formulating them, I clarify my perplexity and anxiety and thus begin to understand myself."[11]

There is no possible cure for the internal self-contradiction found in man by means of speculation. Man is "both real and ideal; his reality is the state of unrest and imperfection, his ideal is the completion of his selfhood by the eradication of his self-contradiction."[12] The idea of an infinite mind, a mind in which all contradiction is overcome, "transcends all categories and, indeed, all possibilities of human thought, as it also transcends the entire structure of human experience."[13]

Faith alone shows the way. It is by the religious use of the imagination alone that man can accept the revelation of God that comes to him. And this revelation must always come to man in the form of symbols.[14]

It is in this way that Kroner would follow out the process of thinking initiated by Kant. He would make reason even more self-conscious with respect to its limitations in order thus to make room for faith.

2. Kroner on Luther and Kant

But what does Kroner mean by faith? It is, of course, the act by which man believes. But what is the object of this faith? Has Kroner really made room for faith in God and in Christ in the historic Christian sense of the term? It is certainly his intention to do so. "Protestantism rediscovered the paradoxical character of the Christian creed, and opposed it to the orthodox character of the scholastic system. The fact was emphasized anew, that the Gospel is called a stumbling block and foolishness. Instead of the rational reconciliation between revelation and speculation effected by Thomism, Protestantism restated the impossibility of reconciling reason with the nature of God's mystery. In Kant's *Transcendental Dialectic* this new (and old) religious outlook is reflected. Unavoidable antinomies, natural paralogisms, fatal illusions bar the way to the throne of the Highest for human understanding. Reason must capitulate to faith. Christian dialectic, as it appears in the parables of Jesus or in

---

11. *Culture and Faith,* p. 63.   13. *Ibid.,* p. 64.
12. *Ibid.,* p. 67.
14. Cf. Kroner *The Religious Function of the Imagination,* Yale University Press, 1941, and *How Do We Know God?*, Harpers, 1943.

utterances of Paul, has not only the same implication as Kant's dialectic, but is also akin to it in spirit. Both point to the divine mystery which cannot be revealed without contradiction, and which therefore transcends the rational sphere."[15]

It is therefore the nature of this "Christian dialectic" that must be analyzed. Does it really avoid speculation? Does it really make room for revelation? Is the God of this Christian dialectic the God of the Bible? Is the Christ of this Christian dialectic the Christ of Luther or Calvin?

The answer to these questions must be in the negative. That this is the case can be seen at once if note is taken of what Kroner says with respect to the question of mystery. Barth is quite right, Kroner says, in asserting that there is no unifying and totalitarian thought for man.[16] Mystery, argues Kroner, is an element that surrounds every form of human experience. It is an "inherent and indispensable element of both experience and faith."[17] Mystery is inherent even in the efforts of science. Faith is therefore "latent in experience" even if "experience does not produce faith."[18] It is natural for experience to expect that "all reports about the highest" should be veiled. It is natural too to expect that revelation "does not remove this veil." It is natural that revelation should speak of the inaccessibility, the transcendence and the majesty of God. The Bible uses the indirect form of speech when it mentions God. "Its language becomes imaginative. Symbolic and parabolic expressions, metaphors and figurative style suggest what cannot be said in plain, literal fashion. Mysticism pervades the whole Scripture. There is an insuperable barrier between man and God. Man is not able to understand fully the purpose and action of the Creator. And His unfathomable character extends to His creation. We do not fully understand the work of His hands and His spirit; they are and remain for all time wondrous. Even man himself, if we look at him as a creature of God, assumes this marvellous character. We cannot fully understand ourselves, we are included in the universal mystery of all being. This is the impression wrought by the Bible, and it agrees with man's deepest feeling. The enduring influence and appeal of this book rests upon the agreement between the thing written and the reader."[19]

15. *Primacy of Faith*, pp. 31-32.
16. *Culture and Faith*, p. 7.
17. *Ibid.*, p. 28.
18. *Ibid.*, p. 29.
19. *Primacy of Faith*, p. 2.

Thus "Luther's doctrine that faith, and faith alone, can constitute man's relationship to God has found an adequate philosophic ally and its expression in Kant's *Critique*. While medieval Catholicism had brought about a system in which nature and grace, world and God, reason and revelation, were integral parts, supplementing each other, so that the whole was in perfect equilibrium in spite of the gap between the parts, Protestantism stressed the fact of the gap. While the Catholic system reconciled the oppositions by means of a hierarchy which mediated between the lowest and the highest spheres in accordance with the neoplatonic type of philosophy, Protestantism emphasized the mission of God's word and of Christ as the only mediator between God and man, and thus generated the Kantian type of philosophy."[20]

But surely Kroner's effort to bring Kant's approach to faith in alignment with that of Luther covers up a basic contrast. To an extent, Kroner seems to be aware of this fact. He expresses this awareness when he says: "Of course, Luther and Kant do not mean the same thing when they speak of faith. Luther means belief in the word of God as revealed in Scripture, especially in the Gospel; Kant means rational faith. But despite this difference, which must be examined carefully, there is common ground for both Luther and Kant to stand on. Both mean by faith a relation of man to God, not founded on objective facts but rather on our conscience; both mean a practical relation, i.e., a relation which concerns primarily man's will in its moral aspect; both mean, therefore, something that affects a person as a person and not something that would satisfy the human intellect or reason in general."[21]

It is precisely the claim that there is common ground on which Luther and Kant stand together that must be challenged. There is such common ground for Kroner only because Luther is first reinterpreted in terms of Kant.

Kroner himself recognizes the fact that Luther "means belief in the word of God as revealed in Scripture." For Kant, as for Kroner, faith springs from human experience as self-interpretative. For Luther, God speaks directly and in final form in history. And man, with all his endowments, must be subject to this revelation. For Kroner, there can be no such final revelation of God in history.

For Kroner, philosophy does, indeed, in distinction from science,

20. *Ibid.*, p. 31.   21. *Ibid.*, p. 47.

deal with "the question of the ultimate meaning of life."[22] But any account of the total meaning of experience is bound to beg the question. "The philosopher cannot step out of his system; whatever he may adduce as testimony to his basic principles is already informed by them. The principles are axioms, and without axioms he can prove nothing."[23] Every philosophical system must expect its own collapse. And what is true of philosophy is equally true of revelation as expressed to man. There can be no direct revelation in history for mystery is ultimate. God "is His mystery."[24]

It is no marvel that on such a view the approach of reason and the approach of faith can readily be harmonized. They are harmonized by the idea of an ultimate mystery that envelops man. And this idea is a purely negative one. The God of Kroner has no determinate content. He is "wholly other" than man. Science, philosophy and theology all need this same God. They need him, or it, as a goal. But if he were more than a goal, if he were to be present to man with any claims of his own, he would be quickly superseded.

On the surface, the recent form of dialecticism might appear to be more sympathetic to historic Christianity than was ancient dialecticism or even the Kantian freedom-nature motive. In denying man's ability to know God by reason, and in affirming the need for faith, recent dialecticism seems to draw near to the Protestant position. In reality, recent dialecticism is, if possible, more destructive of the central Protestant contention than were ancient and Kantian dialecticism. Kantian dialecticism was both more irrationalist and more rationalist than was medieval dialecticism. Similarly, recent dialecticism is, if possible, both more irrationalist and more rationalist than was Kantian dialecticism. Medieval dialecticism is therefore destructive of the Protestant principle. Kantian dialecticism is more destructive of the Protestant principle. Recent dialecticism is still more destructive of the Protestant principle.

The central contention of Protestantism is that God has revealed himself directly and clearly in history. God is, to be sure, not fully comprehensible to man. But even to say that much, and to have it carry any significance, presupposes that God is really and clearly revealed to man. It is because this God identifies himself in terms of himself to man that man can, in terms of God, identify himself as man.

22. *Culture and Faith*, p. 2.
23. *Ibid.*, p. 1.
24. *Primacy of Faith*, p. 1.

Kroner is quite right in saying that identity is "the sole guardian of truth."[25] But he assumes that man can first say *I* to himself and then turn to God. In the most basic opposition to this position, the central Protestant contention is that God must identify himself to man as man's creator and redeemer if man is to identify himself intelligently at all.

In saying this, we are not ignoring the fact, that according to Kroner, "the time has come for the philosopher to go back via the primacy of the ego to the primacy of God—the Living God, who rules the world, indifferent to the changing views of the philosophers."[26] The point is, that so long as the God of whom mention is thus made is nothing more than the goal of complete comprehension of itself which the autonomous human ego posits, then this God is not the God of Calvin, of Luther or of Paul. For Kroner "the reality of the Kingdom of God is imaginative, not factual."[27] Man can therefore "never be sure that God will eventually accept him, that he will pass in the final judgment, that his repentance is strong and sincere enough, that his faith and hope will persevere to the end. Man hovers between heaven and hell."[28]

On Kroner's view, heaven and hell, as well as God himself, are no more than limiting concepts. And thus what he speaks of as the "superiority of biblical imagination"[29] leads only to illusion. On Kroner's view man must, after all, interpret himself in terms of himself. Man has no revelation of God except such as he has projected himself.

In spite of the fact then that Kroner wants to make room for revelation, the revelation for which his philosophy makes room is not the Christian revelation. The position of Kroner is basically one of speculation, not of revelation. It is the sort of speculation that is hostile to and seeks to suppress the true idea of revelation by absorbing it into itself. It is the means by which modern men seek once again to neutralize the claims of God and his Christ upon them.

This leads in conclusion to a remark that must be made on Kroner's use of the word *ethical*. Kroner explains his usage fully. Kant's position, he says, is that of ethical voluntarism.[30] By saying this, he wants to indicate that it is not speculative or metaphysical.

25. *Culture and Faith*, p. 64.
26. *Ibid.*, p. 84.
27. *Ibid.*, p. 250.
28. *Ibid.*, p. 254.
29. *Ibid.*, p. 261.
30. Kant's *Weltanschauung*, Engl. tr., Chicago, 1956.

It is not that Kant wants to replace an intellectualistic metaphysics with a voluntaristic one.[31] He wants no metaphysic at all. He "who, on the other hand, declares that the will is supreme has to conclude that the nature of things is incomprehensible."[32] It is from the "activity of the will" in its "moral capacity" that man must take his start. Thus ethics replaces metaphysics.[33] Moral action "harbors a value of its own."[34] In moral action we escape the relativities of the world of sense. "In morality . . . the unconditional is at stake."[35] Within our will "a light is kindled which illumines another world, the world of absolute values . . ."[36] "For Kant moral obligation is something ultimate and absolute; it signifies the limit and also the summit of all human consciousness."[37]

It is this "ethical voluntarism" of Kant that Kroner incorporates into his "Christian dialecticism." He does this particularly with his idea of ultimate mystery. There simply cannot be any final revelation of God to man. If there were, he argues, we should fall back on an intellectualist metaphysic. "In order to understand the deep roots of Kant's moral Weltanschauung, we must bear in mind the words of Goethe: '*Es irrt der Mensch, solang er strebt.*' One could render this in the spirit of Kant as: 'Man strives only as long as he errs.' If man ceases to err, he ceases to strive; he who pretends to absolute truth would surely relax in the unending moral struggle."[38]

Here we are confronted again with an outspoken denial of God's ability to identify himself directly in history to man as the one who controls all things. This denial of God's ability to identify himself to man is the counterpart of the bold assertion that in man's own moral act, as independent of God, man does meet the ultimate. For Kant it is the "essence of the moral to be ultimate."[39]

It thus appears that Kroner's "ethical voluntarism" is a speculative metaphysic after all. The basic assumption of this ethical voluntarism is man's ability to say *I* to himself. But this *I* cannot say *I* to itself unless reality be wholly and ultimately mysterious. This *I* must use its intellect in order to prove to itself as will that there can be no God who speaks to man in a final revelation. In other words, this *I*, as moral act, must make a universal negative judgment

31. *Ibid.*, p. 7.
32. *Idem.*
33. *Ibid.*, p. 10.
34. *Ibid.*, p. 19.
35. *Ibid.*, p. 20.

36. *Ibid.*, p. 22.
37. *Ibid.*, p. 23.
38. *Ibid.*, pp. 24-25.
39. *Ibid.*, p. 26.

about the nature of ultimate reality in order to maintain its independence.

It is thus that the modern freedom motif has to find itself by means of a pure negation of all the relations in terms of which it could have meaning. "The moral consciousness alone should determine our Weltanschauung."[40] And yet Kant "insists that morality makes the world incomprehensible."[41]

Kroner continues to expound the philosophy of Kant by calling it ethical dualism. That is to say, the ethical freedom of man cannot be otherwise obtained than by setting it over against what is thought of as the necessity of nature.[42]

From the point of view of historic Protestantism this contrast between necessity and freedom is evidence anew that Kant's view is after all a speculative metaphysics. The assumption underneath this distinction is that, since man cannot exhaustively understand the relation of human freedom to the laws of the universe, the two must stand therefore in basic contrast to one another. This is only to carry out the idea of the ethical voluntarism already mentioned. In the latter case, man is said to know nothing of God on the ground that he cannot comprehensively know God. In the former case, this basic idea is carried through with respect to man and his relation to the created universe. "The moral freedom of man is thus not merely a freedom from nature, but also a freedom from external supernatural powers. No one before Kant had ever exalted man so much; no one had ever accorded him such a degree of metaphysical independence and self-dependence."[43]

The ethical voluntarism and the ethical dualism presuppose, Kroner says, an ethical subjectivism. "If the moral will is the center of the human self—if this self centers in morality—and if morality is the center of Weltanschauung, then this Weltanschauung must be subjective, for the human self is human just to the extent to which it is the self of a willing and thinking subject differing fundamentally from all objects that can be willed or thought. Even the moral faith which ensues from the basic moral aspect of life and the world is subjective."[44]

The implications of this point are far-reaching. In it the idea of the primacy of the practical reason shows itself in its full significance. Much is made ofttimes of Kant's epistemological subjectiv-

40. *Ibid.*, p. 29.
41. *Idem.*
42. *Ibid.*, pp. 30ff.

43. *Ibid.*, p. 36.
44. *Ibid.*, p. 61.

ism. Kant held that the theoretical reason "regulates the realm of natural existence, in so far as this realm is regular at all."[45] This "is the core of Kant's famous thesis that the intellect prescribes its laws to nature, and this in turn is the gist of his transcendental idealism or phenomenalism. This phenomenalism is the outcome of his ethical subjectivism."[46]

And now it appears that this phenomenalism is itself the outcome of Kant's ethical subjectivism. "Nature depends in the last analysis, not on the theoretical subject by virtue of its subjective forms or categories of the understanding, but primarily on the moral subject as being in the center of Kant's Weltanschauung. Epistemological subjectivism is a consequence of the ethical and not the reverse."[47] It is thus that the sovereignty of reason over nature is the result of ethical subjectivism.[48]

The purely speculative and anti-Christian character of the whole of Kant's position appears here in its true character. Man is made the ultimate source of all law. The order of paradise has been reversed. It is not God but man who now is taken to be ultimate and self-sufficient. The very idea of the incomprehensibility of God is made to serve the autonomy of man. The idea of ultimate mystery is employed as a means of keeping God indeterminate and therefore subject to man. And nature must be made subject to the moral act of man lest some law of God might be mediated to man through it and man should again lose his "freedom." "Nature can be known only subjectively, for if it could be known absolutely freedom could likewise be known absolutely. But then morality would be destroyed, for morality cannot survive inclusion in an absolute system."[49]

Kroner says quite strikingly that the "real opposite of subjectivism is therefore not objectivism but absolutism."[50] Historic Protestantism is very far indeed from claiming that man himself possesses or understands any absolute system. But it does claim that God is absolute and that he makes himself known as such everywhere to man. Even man's own self-consciousness is meaningless except it be taken to be operative against the background of God as his creator and redeemer. It is God who everywhere speaks to man. In Kant's ethical subjectivism, we have the practical substitution of man for God.

45. *Ibid.*, p. 66.
46. *Idem.*
47. *Idem.*

48. *Ibid.*, p. 67.
49. *Ibid.*, p. 74.
50. *Idem.*

This substitution is in the first place a wholly irrational one. It is an assumption pure and simple. But this substitution is at the same time a wholly rationalist one. It is taken for granted that man can logically determine what cannot be true about ultimate reality. It is said that morality cannot exist in an absolutist system. But to say this is to make the reach of man's theoretical reason, after all, the source of what is possible or impossible. Kant's position is, in the last analysis, precisely as rationalist as is that of Parmenides. Only that can be which I as a man can logically think can be. Kant's position seems at first blush to be more modest than that of rationalism, properly speaking. Does he not limit reason and say that we cannot know God? The answer is that by reason he, in effect, determines that the God of historic Christianity cannot exist. The God he makes room for is a God necessary to the man who wants no law above him and no Christ of God speaking to him, a God whom man can employ as his assistant.

The final designation Kroner gives to Kant's philosophy is that of ethical phenomenalism. "Nature takes on a phenomenal aspect for the sake of morality, and this means that its limitations are postulated by freedom."[51]

And here Kant's God comes into the picture. He must help the moral man to maintain and finally actually to realize his supremacy over nature. What Kroner here calls ethical phenomenalism may also be called monism. "Kant is a monistic thinker in so far as his philosophy leads to a faith in an ultimate unity of these separate realms, a unity in which nature is subordinated to moral ends. Such a unity is postulated by moral reason."[52]

How can the moral reason think of its idea of the good as finally being triumphant over its idea of evil? It needs the help of a God for that. It needs a God of absolute power. But then it must be a God who will reward the good. This God will not need to determine who is good and who is evil. That has already been done by the moral consciousness of man. But, even to do this service, this God must be more than something ultimately mysterious. The ultimately mysterious must be personalized. And in the process of personalization he must be ethicized. But this will not be difficult. Personality is itself inherently ethical personality. In short, the God of Kant's moral consciousness is this consciousness idealized, and it is this consciousness itself fully realized in terms of its own ideals. And

51. *Ibid.*, p. 95.   52. *Ibid.*, p. 30.

herewith we have the idea of subjectivism in the sense of solipsism and illusionism.

Kroner's own Christian dialecticism is, as earlier noted, an extension of Kant's moralism into the field of religion. By the use of the religious imagination, Kroner wants to go beyond Kant. But there is no repudiation of Kant's basic approach of ethical subjectivism. There is, to be sure, refinement of Kant's approach. But, in the process of this refinement, the God and the Christ of historic Protestantism are reduced to the requirements of a supposedly autonomous moral and religious human personality.

It may be noted here that Herman Bavinck also speaks of the Protestant position as setting forth an ethical view of the relation of God to man. Bavinck argues that in Romanism the conceptions of sin and grace have, to a large extent, been reduced to metaphysical notions. Bavinck holds that there can be no truly ethical relation between sin and grace unless man and his environment be, from the outset, placed in the relationship of total dependence upon God. Man's freedom is to be found in loving obedience to God as he speaks to man directly and clearly in general and especially in redemptive revelation. But now, in the case of Kant and in the case of the recent dialecticism, the idea of the ethical is itself secularized by the purely speculative assumption of human ultimacy and autonomy.

3. Søren Kierkegaard

With this analysis of recent dialecticism in general, we now turn briefly to Søren Kierkegaard. We deal primarily with his *Philosophical Fragments*[53] and with his *Concluding Unscientific Postscript*.[54]

In these works, the features of recent existentialism come to their first major expression. And the place assigned to Jesus Christ in this philosophy is for us of basic importance.

The *Fragments* sets the problem before us sharply. "Is an historical point of departure possible for an eternal consciousness; how can such a point of departure have any other than a mere historical interest; is it possible to base an eternal happiness upon historical knowledge?"[55]

53. Engl. tr., Fifth Printing, Princeton, 1952.
54. Engl. tr., Second Printing, Princeton, 1944.
55. *Op. cit.*, title page.

Kierkegaard's interest in this question is an existential one. He expounds this point in the *Postscript*.[56] This *Postscript* is a sequel to the *Fragments*. This sequel is "devoted to the task of investing the problem in historical costume."[57]

It is thus that the project of thought proposed becomes at once a question of every man's relation to Christ. Is that Christ to be found in history? Do I go to the Bible in order to discover him? How do I become a Christian and thus attain eternal happiness?

Kierkegaard does not ask first of all what Christianity is. He asks, how may I become a Christian? Christianity is for him a matter of personal involvement. It is not a matter of objective truth by itself; it is a matter of my appropriation and living of the truth. It is so easy to be a Christian when Christianity is the commonly accepted thing. But I must become a Christian inwardly. It must be a matter of life and death for me. It is so easy to become a Christian if the Christ I believe in fits into the pattern of general human knowledge. But the true Christ does not fit into any pattern of human knowledge; he transcends all human knowledge. Therefore he is a scandal to men. I must therefore believe in him though I do not know him. And I must be ready to be scandalized for doing so.

This approach of Kierkegaard at once draws forth our sympathy. Certainly Christianity must be *existential* to us. The very word existential has come to stand for deep personal trust in Christ. And there has always been such a thing as dead orthodoxy. All of us tend to be guilty of it. We tend to think that we are Christians when we possess a set of intellectually stated truths about Christ. The call to sincerity, to personal trust in Christ, is therefore to be taken to heart by all those who today, as well as in Kierkegaard's time, profess the name of Christ.

Immediately related to this point, there is a second. It is Kierkegaard's vigorous opposition to the idea of truth as an intellectual system. Christianity is not a philosophical system.

When Kierkegaard speaks of system, he constantly refers to Hegel and his followers. Hegel brought movement into logic. That is, Hegel attempted to explain even the course of history by means of a comprehensive system of logical relations. But how can finite man, whose very essence is that of becoming and change, presume to

56. We shall use the abbreviations *Fragments* and *Postscript* instead of the full titles.

57. *Postscript*, p. 14.

discover a system of truth? How can he ever attain to the identity of being and thought? God has, but man cannot have, an existential system. Anyone with a grain of true humility, argues Kierkegaard, will admit that God is far above man. How can human reason know that which is absolutely other than itself?[58] In Christ the eternal becomes temporal. But such a thing is logically impossible. We must therefore believe that which cannot happen according to logic.

With this second point we come into doubtful territory. It is true that man cannot and must not seek to attain to a system of knowledge in the way Hegel did. As earlier noted, any non-Christian system of philosophy is immanentistic. They are all controlled by the idea of abstract form and equally abstract matter. And the modern freedom-nature scheme is but an expression in modern form of the general form-matter scheme. The modern dialecticism of Kant and of Hegel is no less destructive of the true relation of God to man than was ancient dialecticism.

But what disturbs the Christian reader is that Kierkegaard's rejection of system refers not only to the sort of thing that Hegel believed but also to the sort of thing that Luther and Calvin believed. For Kierkegaard, any form of direct revelation of God in history is said to be impossible. Kierkegaard appears upon the scene as the great defender of the uniqueness of the event of the incarnation. He refuses with indignation to have the Christ-event reduced to an instance of a law. There must be no manner of philosophical mediation that destroys the once-for-all character of the Christ. And therewith he seeks to establish also the uniqueness of faith as over against speculation. All this sounds well enough. However, in order to establish the uniqueness of Christ and of the relation of man's faith in Christ, Kierkegaard finds it necessary to wipe out all of history as the medium of direct revelation and response between God and man. If the incarnation were to be thought of as directly identical with any fact in history, then, he argues, the purveyors of system would once more be in control of it. We cannot have a true existential relation to any fact of history as such. We cannot base our hopes for eternity on a fact of history as such. For in history there is at most an approximation to truth. Therefore, even if we had an absolutely perfect account of all that took place with respect to Jesus of Nazareth, this would not help us at all. "If all the angels

58. *Fragments*, p. 37.

in heaven were to put their heads together, they could still bring to pass only an approximation, because an approximation is the only certainty attainable for historical knowledge—but also an inadequate basis for an eternal happiness."[59]

If then we are to find the true Christ, and truly to believe in him, we must become contemporaneous with him. We must get rid of the ages that have intervened between us and the Christ. "If the thing of being or becoming a Christian is to have its decisive qualitative reality, it is necessary above all to get rid of the whole delusion of after-history, so that he who in the year 1846 becomes a Christian becomes that by being contemporaneous with the coming of Christianity into the world, in the same sense as those who were contemporaneous before the eighteen hundred years."[60]

But to get rid of the centuries intervening between the Christ and us does not mean to get closer to him historically. Those who lived with Jesus in Palestine were closer to him than are we, in the ordinary historical sense. They were contemporaneous with him in the calendar sense of the term. But they were not contemporaneous with him in the true or spiritual sense of the term. It is therefore of the greatest importance, argues Kierkegaard, that a difference be made between "the historical element in Christianity" and history in the ordinary sense of the term. "The fact that God came into existence in human form under the Emperor Augustus: that is the historical element in Christianity, the historical in a paradoxical composition. It is with this paradox that everyone, in whatever country he may be living, must become contemporary, if he is to become a believing Christian."[61] On the other hand, those who were contemporaries of Jesus in the ordinary historical sense of the term were not for that reason truly contemporaneous with him at all. "But though a contemporary learner readily becomes an historical eye-witness, the difficulty is that the knowledge of some historical circumstance, or indeed a knowledge of all the circumstances with the reliability of an eye-witness, does not make such an eye-witness a disciple; which is apparent from the fact that this knowledge has merely historical significance for him."[62]

What does Kierkegaard intend to signify with this distinction

59. *Postscript*, p. 31.
60. Kierkegaard, *On Authority and Revelation*, Princeton University Press, 1955, p. 58.
61. *Ibid.*, pp. 58-59.   62. *Fragments*, pp. 47-48.

between true and indifferent contemporaneity? Does he mean only that there were many in the days of Jesus' sojourn on earth, as well as in later times, who did not believe in him? If that were all he meant, the followers of Luther and Calvin would of course readily agree. Without regeneration and faith, there is no true acceptance of the Christ. There were in Jesus' day, as there are now, those who, when confronted with the Christ, did not accept him and did not trust in him for the remission of their sins.

But Kierkegaard obviously means something wholly different from this. What he wants his readers to hold is that nobody was or is directly confronted by Christ in history. Kierkegaard teaches what Barth has stressed throughout his whole career, namely, that, though revelation is historical, we must never say that history is revelational.

Here we have reached the same issue that was discussed when it was noted that Kroner thinks of Kant as working on the foundation laid by Luther. We saw that in reality Kant's ethical dualism and his ethical monism were in their tendency wholly opposed to the theology of the Reformers. Kierkegaard is merely carrying on in the spirit of Kant. His final reason for rejecting system and all that is bad, comes from his conviction that there is no God who can give a final revelation of himself to man in history. In other words, he seeks to attain uniqueness for his Christ in terms of the idea of pure contingency. And this idea of pure contingency of necessity has for its correlative the formal ideal of pure rationality.

Thus his position is basically no less speculative than is that of Hegel. Both are irrationalist in that they allow for the idea of pure contingency. Both are rationalist in that they use the laws of human logic in order by them to exclude the possibility of the truth of historic Christianity. The difference between them is merely one of degree. The philosophy of Kierkegaard is a form of Kant's ethical dualism and ethical monism. And his theology is adapted to his philosophy. His philosophy is, to be sure, "critical" rather than "speculative." It is *open to* Christianity. But it is only open to a certain kind of Christianity, the Christianity of the indeterminate God and of the unknowable Christ.

It is not possible to support this judgment fully in a few pages. Nor is this necessary. He who runs may read that Kierkegaard's negation of "system" and "knowledge" is directed against the possibility of the direct confrontation between God and man in history.

a. Kierkegaard's Ethical Dualism

It is well known that, over against every form of "objective" truth, Kierkegaard maintains the qualitative difference between God and man. Does Kierkegaard mean by this that God is the creator and man is the creature in the biblical sense of the term? Not at all, for he does not believe in direct communication between God and man. Direct communication would, he thinks, involve the idea of system and therefore a quantitative view of the relation of God to man.

To understand the nature of a qualitative difference between God and man we must, argues Kierkegaard, begin with the notion of man as free over against all objective revelation. With Kant, Kierkegaard thinks of man first of all as ethically free. The realm of nature is the realm of necessity, but the realm of human action is the realm of freedom. It is from this point that Kierkegaard would begin all his thinking. Let us follow his argument briefly.

In the *Fragments*, Kierkegaard sets for himself a "project of thought." He asks, "How far does Truth admit of being learned?" He wants to prepare for a Christian rather than the Socratic answer to this question.

The Socratic answer to this question is based upon the idea that he who learns as well as he who teaches are together already in possession of the truth. On such a basis, the "temporal point of departure is nothing; for as soon as I discover that I have known the Truth from eternity without being aware of it, the same instant this moment of occasion is hidden in the eternal, and so incorporated with it that I cannot even find it so to speak, even if I sought it; because in my eternal consciousness there is neither here nor there, but only an *ubique et nusquam*."[63] But if we do want the moment or instant in time to have "decisive significance" then we must think of a situation in which the eternal "which hitherto did not exist, came into being in this moment."[64] If the moment of learning is to have significance, then "the seeker must be destitute of the Truth up to the very moment of his learning it; he cannot even have possessed it in the form of ignorance, for in that case the moment becomes merely occasional. What is more, he cannot even be described as a seeker; for such is the expression we must give to the difficulty if we do not wish to explain it Socratically. He must therefore be characterized as beyond the pale of the Truth, not approaching it

63. *Fragments*, p. 8.　　　　　　64. *Idem.*

like a proselyte, but departing from it; or as being in Error. He is then in a state of Error."[65]

Going still further than this, Kierkegaard says that, if the moment is to have unforgettable meaning, then the learner must not only be in error but he must be hostile to the truth. And herewith we reach the true notion of the priority of God in relation to man. "The Teacher is then God himself, who in acting as an occasion prompts the learner to recall that he is in Error, and that by reason of his own guilt. But this state, the being in Error by reason of one's own guilt, what shall we call it? Let us call it *Sin*."[66] "What now shall we call such a Teacher, one who restores the lost condition and gives the learner the Truth? Let us call him *Saviour*, for he saves the learner from his bondage and from himself; let us call him *Redeemer*, for he redeems the learner from the captivity into which he had plunged himself, and no captivity is so terrible and so impossible to break, as that in which the individual keeps himself. And still we have not said all that is necessary; for by his self-imposed bondage the learner has brought upon himself a burden of guilt, and when the Teacher gives him the condition and the Truth he constitutes himself an *Atonement*, taking away the wrath impending upon that of which the learner has made himself guilty."[67]

Such a one who is a teacher as he "constitutes himself an *Atonement*" is thereby unforgettable. "And now the moment. Such a moment has a peculiar character. It is brief and temporal indeed, like every moment; it is transient as all moments are; it is past, like every moment in the next moment. And yet it is decisive, and filled with the eternal. Such a moment ought to have a distinctive name; let us call it the *Fullness of Time*."[68] When man thus learns from his teacher he undergoes conversion.[69] In fact, he undergoes a new birth.[70] The breach is made. Such a man cannot return.[71]

In this brief review, we have, in effect, a statement of Kierkegaard's whole conception of the relation of the believer to Christ. The believer becomes contemporaneous with Christ in the fulness of time. In that fulness of time in Christ, the eternal enters into time. And through faith the believer ignores the centuries and enters into the present with Christ.

"But is the hypothesis here expounded thinkable?"[72] To discover

65. *Ibid.*, p. 9.
66. *Ibid.*, p. 10.
67. *Ibid.*, p. 12.
68. *Ibid.*, p. 13.
69. *Idem.*
70. *Idem.*
71. *Ibid.*, p. 14.
72. *Idem.*

the answer to this question let us engage in "an essay of the imagination."[73] Why should God wish to make his appearance? The answer is that "the Moment makes its appearance when an eternal resolve comes into relation with an incommensurable occasion. Unless this is realized we shall be thrown back on Socrates, and shall then have neither God as Teacher, nor an Eternal Purpose, nor the Moment."[74]

It is God's eternal love of the learner that causes him to make his appearance. God wants to bring the learner "to equality with himself. If this equality cannot be established, God's love becomes unhappy and his teaching meaningless, since they cannot understand one another."[75] By his eternal love, God gives to the learner new being. The learner undergoes a change from "non-being to being."[76] The union between God and man cannot be attained by an elevation. It must be "attempted by a descent. Let the learner be x. In this x we must include the lowliest . . ."[77] "In order that the union may be brought about, God must therefore become the equal of such an one, and so he will appear in the likeness of the humblest. But the humblest is one who must serve others, and God will therefore appear in the form of a *servant*."[78]

This servant form "was no mere outer garment."[79] God "desires in love to be the equal of the humblest."[80] How can we believe such a thing? We "stand here before the *Miracle*."[81] Such an event therefore as God's condescending love to man is not thinkable.

The coming of God in time is unthinkable because I cannot prove the existence of God. "For if God does not exist it would of course be impossible to prove it; and if he does exist it would be folly to attempt it."[82] I must always "reason from existence," not "toward existence."[83]

What Kierkegaard means here is not exhausted in the idea that he would reject such proofs for the existence of God as "natural theology" has concocted. He means that there is no revelation of God in the facts of the universe. He rejects, in other words, not merely the "theistic proofs" of Aquinas, but the revelation of God in the universe on which Calvin laid such great stress. The "order of things" is not, for Kierkegaard, a revelation of God.[84] Kierkegaard

---

73. *Ibid.*, p. 17.
74. *Ibid.*, p. 18.
75. *Ibid.*, p. 21.
76. *Ibid.*, p. 24.
77. *Idem.*
78. *Idem.*

79. *Ibid.*, pp. 24-25.
80. *Ibid.*, p. 27.
81. *Ibid.*, p. 28.
82. *Ibid.*, p. 31.
83. *Idem.*
84. *Ibid.*, p. 33.

does here what, as earlier noted, Barth constantly does, namely, fail to distinguish between the revelation of God and the conclusions which sinful man draws from the facts of the universe with respect to the existence of God.

If the main point of Kierkegaard's argument is to be appreciated, then this distinction must be understood. On the surface it might appear that Kierkegaard means what a man like Abraham Kuyper means when he says that God's existence cannot be proved. Does it not seem that both Kierkegaard and Kuyper want to presuppose rather than prove the existence of God?

Kuyper, following Calvin and Paul, treasures what Kierkegaard violently rejects, namely, the idea of direct communication of God to man. Kuyper, with Calvin, holds to the objective clarity of God's revelation to man in nature and in man's constitution. When Kuyper says that God's existence cannot be proved, he thinks of man as the sinner who seeks to suppress the revelation of God within and about him. He thinks of man as having been, from the beginning of history, confronted directly with the revelation of God. He thinks of Adam and Eve in paradise as listening to the voice of God. He thinks of supernatural word-revelation as added to the voice of nature in order to place man in fulness of covenantal relationship with himself. In other words, Kuyper, following Calvin and Paul, thinks of man as being able to say I to himself only as he sees himself in the fulness of the covenantal relationships in which his Creator has placed him.

In contrast with this, Kierkegaard takes man out of all these relationships. He does not think of man as ethically alienated from God through the act of Adam in paradise. When he himself thinks of the "ethical" as primary in relation to the realm of nature, he thinks rather of man as autonomous and as therefore free in the Kantian sense of the term. When he therefore says that, instead of proving the existence of God, we must take the "leap" of faith, then this leap is the free and sovereign act of the would-be autonomous man.

That this is actually the case is established from the fact that the God in whom man believes through this leap is not the God of Christianity at all. The God that constitutes the object of faith as the leap is the Unknown.[85] According to Kierkegaard, if God were directly revealed, he would be knowable. And, if he were knowable,

85. *Ibid.*, p. 35.

then he could not be an object of faith. To be the object of faith he must be the "absolutely different."[86] Of the absolutely different there can be "no mark by which it could be distinguished."[87]

It is thus that the ethical dualism of Kant is perfected. God is first excluded from the realm of nature, and therefore also from man's own consciousness as revelatory of God's presence and claims. In other words, human knowledge is first interpreted as something that takes place when man imposes his own organizing principles of thought upon pure contingent material. And since man thinks in terms of concepts and general principles, it is assumed that nature operates according to these concepts. But it is also recognized that the human concepts cannot exhaustively order contingent reality. So that which is not ordered is thought of as an irrational or non-rationalizable and ultimately mysterious something. This realm of the irrational or unknown is then made the object of faith. It is in this field that man is said to be free. This human freedom is said to be operative in the realm that lies beyond the natural. Freedom is set over against the natural. And with it the intellect of man as the source of nature is set over against the will of man as operating in the irrational realm. This realm is said to be the realm of pure possibility. It is in this realm that the free man must seek to realize himself. The difficulty is that in thus seeking to realize himself in the realm of freedom man, on this view, cannot escape the mediation of nature. And so far as man must realize his possibilities in the realm of freedom through the medium of nature his freedom is compromised. Every time the free man communicates his ideals to his fellow free men, this communication is stifled because of the static produced by the human body and by nature in general. When the individual speaks it is, alas, no longer the individual that speaks. It is this dilemma in which modern thought finds itself. And it is this dilemma that mars the picture drawn for us by Kierkegaard.

It should be noted further that the dilemma involved in the relation of ethical freedom and natural law finds its counterpart in the relation of human freedom to God. The God of Kierkegaard must be unknown and unknowable. If he were known or knowable, then man would not be free. The ethical freedom which forms the starting-point of Kierkegaard's philosophy is a freedom that requires pure possibility for its environment. It requires this pure possibility in order to develop itself according to its own purpose.

86. *Idem.*   87. *Idem.*

Thus the idea of faith as a leap, in contrast with faith in God and the world as knowable in any sense, requires the idea of God as a purely limiting notion projected as a postulate by the man who considers himself autonomous.

With these facts in mind, it is clear that, when Kierkegaard says that God's existence cannot be proved, he does not mean that the God of the Scriptures must be presupposed. He means rather that God must not have any intelligible content at all. Kierkegaard is in full agreement with Hegel and other modern philosophers that proof is possible for man in the field of science without any reference to God at all. Therefore, when he says that God cannot be proved to be existing, what he means is that there is an irrational penumbra surrounding the island of rationality which man has carved for himself out of the realm of ultimate contingency.

The idea of paradox as developed by Kierkegaard can be seen for what it is in this light. When God becomes man, says Kierkegaard, the eternal becomes temporal. Thus the "news of the day" is the "beginning of eternity."[88] Here we have the paradox. "But that God himself gives this condition has been shown above to be a consequence of the *Moment,* and it has also been shown that the Moment is the Paradox, and that without it we are unable to advance, but return to Socrates."[89] People are scandalized by this paradox. What they want is system. They want to be able to reduce time and change to logical relations. Even those who lived at the same time with the coming of the eternal into time were not really contemporary with him. At least they faced the same difficulty as we of a later date do. They too had to learn that nothing could be known about the presence of God among men. They had to learn not to depend upon direct communication. They had to learn that there is no direct revelation of God in any historical fact.[90]

The distinction that Barth later made between *Geschichte* and *Historie* is virtually made here. What Barth calls *Historie,* Kierkegaard here calls "the historical in the more concrete sense." The historical in this sense is a matter of indifference.[91] With respect to this ordinary history, there may, without harm, be any amount of ignorance. We may think of this ordinary historical as "historically annihilating the historical." This does not take away the *Moment* as the true historical element. The Moment may still remain as our

88. *Ibid.,* p. 46.   90. *Ibid.,* p. 47.
89. *Ibid.,* pp. 46-47.   91. *Ibid.,* p. 48.

point of departure for the eternal. The paradox may still be there.[92] "As long as the eternal and the historical are external to one another, the historical is merely an occasion."[93] "But the Paradox unites the contradictories, and is the historical made eternal, and the eternal made historical."[94]

It is thus seen, says Kierkegaard, that faith is not knowledge. And it will also be apparent to the reader that, in thus setting faith over against knowledge, the incarnation has no more intelligible content than does God. The idea of the eternal merely stands for the idea of pure possibility which the free man needs as the area into which he may develop himself. And if this eternal, assuming that it had any content, did come into the world of space and time, it would at once lose its identity in it and could be known by no man as being eternal. The uniqueness of any revelation coming from God would be lost as soon as it made its appearance among men.

Moreover, it appears the *Miracle*, of which we heard Kierkegaard speak in connection with the coming of God, is nothing more than the idea that the irrational penumbra surrounding the world of science somehow penetrates this world for good.

b. KIERKEGAARD'S ETHICAL MONISM

The dualism of Kierkegaard therefore leads directly into an ethical monism.

According to Kant's third *Critique*, the moral realm is said to be somehow victorious over the natural realm. This is in spite of the fact that there is no knowledge relation of any sort between these two realms. We saw also that Kroner wants to supplement the ethical dualism of Kant with an ethical monism which allows for God to be somehow apparent in symbolic fashion in the world. The idea of God's direct revelation, and the idea of direct communication, have been rejected by means of a virtually universal negative proposition asserting the impossibility of the existence of such a God. God is reduced to a contentless form. But then this form is given new reality by means of a process of repersonalization. The idea of absolute power that was taken away from the God of Christianity is then ascribed to this projection by the independent moral and religious consciousness of man. And this newly created God is

92. *Idem.*   94. *Idem.*
93. *Ibid.,* p. 49.

said to come with universal love down to all men in order to help them all to realize their true selves in spite of their own sins against themselves.

Kierkegaard first makes an absolute distinction between knowledge and faith. Even the contemporary disciples can know nothing of Jesus. There is for Kierkegaard no direct identification of any manifestation of God in history. But, then, how is any man to become aware of his presence at all? "But God did not assume the form of a servant to make a mockery of men; hence it cannot be his intention to pass through the world in such manner that no single human being becomes aware of his presence. He will therefore doubtless give some sort of sign, though every understanding resting upon an accommodation is essentially without value for one who does not receive the condition; for which reason he yields to the necessity only unwillingly."[95] How is it possible that the learner shall identify the paradox? So far as God is eternal, is he not wholly different from man? And if this wholly different enters into the temporal, does he not become wholly identical with man? How then is there any recognition even of the fact of the paradox? Kierkegaard solves this question by saying: "But how does the learner come to realize an understanding with this Paradox? We do not ask that he understand the Paradox, but only that this is the Paradox. How this takes place we have already shown. It comes to pass when the Reason and the Paradox encounter one another happily in the Moment; when the Reason sets itself aside and the Paradox bestows itself. The third entity in which this union is realized (for it is not realized in the Reason, since it is set aside; nor in the Paradox, which bestows itself—hence it is realized *in* something) is that happy passion to which we will now assign a name, though it is not the name that so much matters. We shall call this passion: *Faith.* This then must be the condition of which we have spoken, which the Paradox contributes."[96]

Thus there is a happy union between a philosophy of existentialism and the idea of revelation as the Christian religion teaches it. It is, as was the case with Kroner, the idea that existentialism is a critical philosophy. It is therefore supposedly open for anything new. But then the only new thing that this critical philosophy will receive is the idea of a God and an incarnation that springs from the

95. *Ibid.*, pp. 44-45.   96. *Ibid.*, p. 47.

realm of the purely indeterminate and the purely unknown and therefore the purely meaningless. And herewith we have, to all intents and purposes, the complete secularization of Christianity by means of existential dialecticism.

The natural man will not think of this as a scandal. Man can quite readily admit that he does not know all things. If only he is allowed himself to be the ultimate arbiter of right and wrong, and is allowed to hope that his idea of right will ultimately prevail, he is ready to reduce and incorporate the ideas of God and of Christ into this, his system. Kierkegaard wants an "absolute fact" which is also an "historical fact."[97] "The absolute fact is an historical fact, and as such it is the object of faith."[98] "A simple historical fact is not absolute, and has no power to force an absolute decision. But neither may the historical aspect of our fact be eliminated, for then we have only an eternal fact."[99] "Only through placing God in particular relationship with the individual did our project go beyond Socrates."[100]

There is no reason at all why anyone should be scandalized by such an absolute fact. It is just the idea that the free man, who fears the unknown, makes himself believe that a God of all-encompassing love and power is somehow there and that he somehow will make things come out right. The God-man must require faith and must refuse direct communication.[101] But why should there be any possibility of offence in such a requirement? There is no more occasion for offence to the natural man here than there is in Kant's idea that man is free to hypostatize his moral ideas so long as he realizes that he is doing so.

That we are dealing in all this with an ethical dualism that turns into an ethical monism, in the sense in which we have seen Kroner develop it, is obvious from what Kierkegaard says about man. "Man is spirit. But what is spirit? Spirit is the self. But what is the self? The self is a relation which relates itself to its own self, or it is that in the relation [which accounts for it] that the relation relates itself to its own self; the self is not the relation but [consists in the fact] that the relation relates itself to its own self. Man is a synthesis of the infinite and the finite, of the temporal and the eternal, of freedom

97. *Ibid.*, p. 84.
98. *Idem.*
99. *Idem.*
100. *Ibid.*, p. 85.
101. Kierkegaard, *Training in Christianity*, Oxford University Press, London, 1941, p. 142.

and necessity, in short it is a synthesis. A synthesis is a relation between two factors. So regarded, man is not yet a self."[102]
There are two main elements to be noted in this description of the
self. There is, first, the relation of freedom to necessity. With Kant
freedom is set negatively over against the necessity of nature. Yet
the free man must express himself through nature. Therefore as free
he stands in dialectical relationship with nature. "The self is freedom. But freedom is the dialectical element in the terms possibility
and necessity."[103]

Secondly, man is a "synthesis of the infinite and the finite, of the
temporal and the eternal."[104] "The forms of despair must be dis-
coverable abstractly by reflecting upon the factors which compose
the self as a synthesis. The self is composed of infinity and finiteness.
But the synthesis is a relationship, and it is a relationship which,
though it is derived, relates itself to itself, which means freedom."[105]

As a synthesis between time and eternity, the self does not actually
exist at any specific time. "The self is the conscious synthesis of
infinitude and finitude which relates itself to itself, whose task is to
become itself, a task which can be performed only by means of a
relationship to God. But to become oneself is to become concrete.
But to become concrete means neither to become finite nor infinite,
for that which is to become concrete is a synthesis. Accordingly, the
development consists in moving away from oneself infinitely by the
process of infinitizing oneself, and in returning to oneself infinitely
by the process of finitizing. If, on the contrary, the self does not
become itself, it is in despair, whether it knows it or not. However,
a self, every instant it exists, is in process of becoming, for the self
κατὰ δύναμιν does not actually exist, it is only that which it is
to become. In so far as the self does not become itself, it is not its
own self; but not to be one's own self is despair."[106]

The central point in this is that the self is a self only in the process
of actualization. And this process is an infinite one. Man is therefore never fully a self. In the incarnation, nothing happens that does
not happen within the self. True, at first sight, there does seem to be
a difference between incarnation and self-development. God wants
to place man on an equality with himself. And we are told that this

102. Kierkegaard, *The Sickness Unto Death*, Princeton University Press,
1941, p. 17.
103. *Ibid.*, p. 43.   105. *Ibid.*, p. 43.
104. *Ibid.*, p. 17.   106. *Ibid.*, p. 44.

cannot be done by elevation but must be done by an act of condescension. On the other hand, the despair of man seems to come from the fact that he is seeking to elevate himself from temporality to eternality. So the incarnation may seemingly be of help to man by reaching down and helping him. But it should be noted that, in any case, what is happening both in the incarnation and in the self-development of man is the process of the infinitizing of man. And, the help that man gets from the incarnation for this purpose, he must find within himself. He cannot learn about it through history. He can only tell himself that what happened in Palestine with respect to Jesus of Nazareth is for him a symbol of help which he, somehow, thinks he gets from somewhere above.

Sin is therefore, according to Kierkegaard, sin against the self. Self-consciousness is inherently involved in despair[107] and in dread.[108] This is what should be meant by the idea of original sin. We should not look to history in order to learn about original sin.[109] Adam stands for the idea that every man is both himself and the race. Sin is basically as original in all men as in Adam. Every man in his original sin and dread must seek to realize himself. Man is a "synthesis of soul and body." He is also a "synthesis of the temporal and the eternal."[110]

Kierkegaard thinks that he has pretty well solved the idea of the synthesis of soul and body by means of a third term which is spirit. But where is the third term that will bring about unity between temporality and eternity? "Where is the third term? And if there be no third term, there is really no synthesis; for a synthesis of that which is a contradiction cannot be completed as a synthesis without a third term, for the recognition that the synthesis is a contradiction is precisely the assertion that it is not a synthesis."[111]

The incarnation must serve as the third term, as the Moment, to help man realize his own eternality. Such a third term cannot be found in the process of time as such. The problem is to escape temporality. "So time is infinite succession. The life which is in time and is merely that of time has no present."[112]

On the other hand, the incarnation cannot be an atom of pure

---

107. *The Sickness Unto Death.*
108. Kierkegaard, *The Concept of Dread*, Princeton University Press, 1957.
109. *Ibid.*, Chapter I.   111. *Idem.*
110. *Ibid.*, p. 76.   112. *Ibid.*, p. 77.

eternity. In that case it would be wholly beyond man. It must be "the first reflection of eternity in time."[113]

The Greeks could not understand this. They had no eye for the *Moment* or the Instant as the appearance of eternity in time. When they reflected upon the relation of time to eternity, they always brought time to a stop. So neither time nor eternity had justice done to them.[114] It was in Christianity that the eternal came into the temporal and therewith the Moment or Instant received significance. In this way, unity was brought into the human self. "The synthesis of the eternal and the temporal is not a second synthesis but is the expression for the first synthesis in consequence of which man is a synthesis of soul and body sustained by spirit. No sooner is the spirit posited than the instant is there."[115]

And so the future is opened up for man as the realm of pure possibility into which he can now develop himself. On the Greek basis, the idea of eternity turned into the idea of the dead past. "In general, by seeing how the past, the future, the eternal are defined, one can see how the instant has been defined. If there is no instant, then the eternal appears to be behind, like the past."[116] But on the Christian basis the eternal, instead of killing time, opens up its true possibilities in terms of the future. "The concept around which everything turns in Christianity, the concept which makes all things new, is the fullness of time, is the instant as eternity, and yet this eternity is at once the future and the past. If one does not give heed to this, one cannot save any concept from heretical and treasonable admixtures which destroy the concept. One does not get the past as a thing for itself but in simple continuity with the future—and with that the concepts of conversion, atonement, redemption, are resolved in the significance of world-history, and resolved in the individual historical development. One does not get the future as a thing for itself but in simple continuity with the present—and with that the concepts of resurrection and judgment come to naught."[117]

With this we may, says Kierkegaard, return to Adam. "Let us now picture to ourselves Adam, and then remember that every subsequent individual begins exactly the same way, only within the quantitative difference which is the consequence of the fact of

113. *Ibid.*, p. 79.   116. *Ibid.*, p. 80.
114. *Idem.*   117. *Ibid.*, p. 81.
115. *Idem.*

generation and of the historical situation. For Adam then, just as much as for every subsequent individual, there is the instant."[118]

The relation of sin and grace is, accordingly, not something that takes place directly in history. Sin is not something that comes into the world as the transgression of the known will of God by man, either at the beginning, or at any subsequent point in history. Sin is rather something that inheres in the consciousness of man as a synthesis between freedom and necessity and between temporality and eternality. Accordingly, grace is not something that comes into history at a later point of time than sin. The removal of sin is, therefore, not something that takes place in the events of history, namely, the death and resurrection of Jesus Christ in Palestine. Grace is rather something that takes place in every man as, in his development toward self-consciousness, he allows his spirit to synthesize his soul and body, and as he allows the ideal of the Moment to synthesize the temporal and the eternal. "The synthesis of the soulish and the bodily is to be posited by spirit, but the spirit is the eternal, and therefore this is accomplished only when the spirit posits at the same time along with this the second synthesis of the eternal and the temporal. So long as the eternal is not posited, the instant *is* not, or is only as a *discrimen*. Therefore, seeing that in the state of innocence the spirit is characterized merely as a dreaming spirit, the eternal manifests itself as the future, for this, as I have said, is the first expression of the eternal, is its incognito. Just as in the foregoing chapter the spirit when it was about to be posited in the synthesis or rather was about to posit the synthesis, as the spirit's (freedom's) possibility in the individual, expressed itself as dread, so here in turn the future, the possibility of the eternal (i.e., of freedom) in the individual is dread."[119]

Thus the incarnation of historic Christianity is reduced to an ideal which the autonomous ethical self-consciousness of man sets for itself. "Only in the ethical is there immortality and an eternal life. . . ."[120] Each individual "apprehends the ethical essentially only in himself, because the ethical is his complicity with God. While the ethical is, in a certain sense, infinitely abstract, it is in another sense infinitely concrete, and there is indeed nothing more concrete, because it is subject to a dialectic that is individual to each human being precisely as this particular human being."[121]

118. *Idem.*
119. *Idem.*
120. *Postscript*, p. 137.
121. *Ibid.*, p. 138.

In this way "becoming subjective is the task proposed to every human being. . . ."[122] And thus "everything is beautifully arranged."[123]

Of course, "the way of the ethical becomes a very long one."[124] In fact, it is an infinite way. The ethical leads to the religious. God is "the infinite itself."[125]

In him the ideal of total attainment of true subjectivity stands always and forever before each man. Death is one step in the process of becoming truly subjective.[126] "In the same degree that I become subjective, the uncertainty of death comes more and more to interpenetrate my subjectivity dialectically. It thus becomes more and more important for me to think it in connection with every factor and phase of my life; for since the uncertainty is there in every moment, it can be overcome only by overcoming it in every moment."[127] I must ever seek the "ethical expression for the significance of death, and a religious expression for the victory over death; one needs a solving word which explains its mystery, and a binding word by which the living individual defends himself against the ever recurrent conception; for surely we dare scarcely recommend mere thoughtlessness and forgetfulness as wisdom."[128] Thus the question or immortality is a question of inwardness. "Objectively the question cannot be answered, because objectively it cannot be put, since immortality precisely is the potentiation and highest development of the developed subjectivity. Only by really willing to become subjective can the question properly emerge, therefore how could it be answered objectively?"[129] "In passion the existing subject is rendered infinite in the eternity of the imaginative representation, and yet he is at the same time most definitely himself."[130]

Thus the "absolute difference that distinguishes man from God"[131] is gradually overcome by means of the process through which the individual, by the help of his ideal of the incarnation, becomes increasingly eternal and therewith increasingly subjective. None of this can be accomplished if we should think of Christianity as expressed objectively and directly in history. "Suppose, on the other hand, that subjectivity is the truth, and that subjectivity is an

122. *Ibid.*, p. 141.
123. *Ibid.*, p. 142.
124. *Ibid.*, p. 144.
125. *Ibid.*, p. 145.
126. *Ibid.*, p. 149.

127. *Idem.*
128. *Ibid.*, p. 151.
129. *Ibid.*, p. 154.
130. *Ibid.*, p. 176.
131. *Ibid.*, p. 195.

existing subjectivity, then, if I may so express myself, Christianity fits perfectly into the picture. Subjectivity culminates in passion, Christianity is the paradox, paradox and passion are a mutual fit, and the paradox is altogether suited to one whose situation is, to be in the extremity of existence."[132]

Kierkegaard tells us that the philosophy which he expressed in the *Fragments* and discussed more fully in the *Postscript* "takes its point of departure in the pagan consciousness, in order to seek out experimentally an interpretation of existence which might truly be said to go *further* than paganism."[133]

Taking his point of departure in the consciousness of man independently of the revelation of God through Christ directly revealed in Scripture, Kierkegaard has found his result in a complete secularization of Christianity.

In Kierkegaard's recent dialecticism, carrying forth the apostate approach to the interpretation of life, he has once more reduced the meanings of Christian terminology till there is nothing in them but immanentism. Why should the Kantian form of immanentistic dialecticism be any more open for the reception of Christianity than the ancient form-and-matter scheme? And why should the recent form of dialecticism, such as we have heard about from Kroner and such as we have briefly analyzed from the thought of Kierkegaard, be any more open to the reception of Christianity than was Kant's philosophy? The critical philosophies of Kant and of recent dialecticism are indeed open for the idea of the religious. They make room for God. But always they make room for the kind of God who opens up the future for man as a realm of pure possibility. And always the end result is a monism in which man is absorbed into the God which man himself has projected as his ideal. Thus modern man is still going around in the circles of his own consciousness writ large. The God of this religious consciousness, as qualitatively different from man, remains man's hypostatized and personalized ideal. Like a rocket that needs first to be thrown up into the sky in order then to come with light from above, this God of recent dialecticism is an eject of man's own consciousness. The riddle now is how Barth could think that by attaching himself to the thinking of Kierkegaard he could combine modern thought and the Christianity of the Bible. Zuidema is quite right when he says that, with his

132. *Ibid.*, p. 206.   133. *Ibid.*, p. 323.

mythological view of the incarnation, Kierkegaard teaches the eternal becoming of God. "God in history then signifies that God directs himself to man as the sin-forgiving one. In this case God does not want to confront man otherwise than as the God who forgives sins in Christ, as the God of all *grace*."[134]

4. Barth and Existentialism

We turn now to Barth. In chapter ten, it appeared that Barth challenged medieval dialecticism in terms of modern dialecticism. This modern dialecticism is both more irrationalist and more rationalist than was medieval dialecticism. Accordingly, Barth's theology goes *beyond* Romanism in that it is both more nominalistic and more realistic than Romanism. In the present chapter, it appears that Barth's theology is again both more irrationalist and more rationalist even than existentialist philosophy. The pendulum of Barth's thinking seeks constantly, first to go beyond that of others in terms of deeper negations, and then in terms of wider and more formal affirmations. This point may now be made more specific with respect to Existentialism.

Barth himself admits that his early thought was influenced by Kierkegaard's idea of the absolute qualitative difference between God and man. In taking note of this, evangelical Christians rejoiced in this fact. They thought of it as merely a renewed emphasis on the transcendence of God. They did not realize that the transcendence concept of Barth was based upon the idea of the purely indeterminate God. The idea of transcendence in Barth's early theology was that of pure negation.

Moreover, as was pointed out in the previous chapter, this idea of pure negation was but the correlative of the idea of universal immanence. This immanence is not that of direct pantheism. According to Barth's view, God is not reduced to man but man is virtually absorbed by God.

All this comes to striking expression in Barth's idea of *Urgeschichte*. In the idea of *Urgeschichte*, Barth seeks to accomplish the contemporaneousness of the believer with Christ. Here his thinking resembles that of Kierkegaard in striking fashion.

134. *Denkers van deze Tyd, I, Tweede Druk*, Franeker, no date, p. 46. Cf. Engl. tr., *Kierkegaard*, Philadelphia 1960, pp. 37-38.

Kierkegaard introduced his notion of the absolute paradox for the purpose of opposing all system, every form of direct revelation of God to man. In this, he was merely working out Kant's ethical dualism. Man is free when he is thought of as *act* in the ethical realm. And this ethical realm is set negatively over against the realm of knowledge, the realm of science and necessity.

But Kierkegaard's ultimate purpose was not negative. As Kant was interested ultimately in the primacy of the practical reason, so Kierkegaard was interested ultimately in a positive relationship between man and God. So in both cases ethical dualism leads to ethical monism. Faith becomes one with revelation. It is thus that the absolute paradox of Kierkegaard accomplishes precisely the same thing that Hegel's principle of mediation accomplished, namely, the commingling of eternity and time.

It was Kierkegaard's starting-point that made such an issue inevitable. When he said that truth is subjective, he did not intend this in the individualist and solipsist sense of the word. On the contrary, he intended to overcome subjectivism in the bad sense by speaking of God as the true and ultimate Subject. Even so, this God as absolute Subject was only a projection of man as the autonomous subject.

Barth's idea of *Urgeschichte*, it must be noted, is basically like Kierkegaard's notion of the absolute paradox.

Barth wants to overcome every form of consciousness-theology. Not only in *Romans*, but in his *Christian Dogmatics* (1927), he seeks for a transcendent God.

The consciousness-theologians, Barth argues, fall easy prey to the criticism of Ludwig Feuerbach. But why should we fear Feuerbach? And why should we squirm to escape his clutches?

Why not frankly admit that all theology as human speech is nothing but anthropology? Theology is a matter of knowledge. And the field of knowledge is the field of historical relativism and psychological subjectivism. "Every way to the knowledge or conceivability of God is in any case so dark, known to so few, that he who speaks of God thereby maintains a position which, regarded from the point of view of the world, is nothing more than a fantastic if beautiful dream. He who dares to speak of God must, in the last analysis, dare to do so with God alone. . ."[135] As for the Bible, we should have the "dialectical courage" calmly to join human fallibil-

---

135. Barth, *Die Lehre vom Worte Gottes*, Vol. I of *Die Christliche Dogmatik im Entwurf*, München, 1927, hereafter referred to as *Dogmatics*, pp. 55f.

ity of words with divine infallibility of content.[136] God's revelation does indeed take place not behind but in the words of Scripture. But the identification of revelation with Scripture is never direct. It is always indirect.[137] No document of history can offer anything more than a witness to primal history.

The "witnesses to the resurrection" still deal with the promise only.[138] As far as ordinary history is concerned, the facts of the gospel story from the virgin birth to the ascension are enshrouded in such mystery as to admit of various interpretations.[139] A true faith will not build its house upon the quicksands of ordinary history.[140]

In all this opposition to the idea of revelation as directly identical with history, Barth is doing, in effect, what Kierkegaard did when he argued that truth is in the Subject.

Barth tells us that a true approach to theology must be existential.[141] But a true existential approach is not possible on the basis of the idea of direct revelation. On the basis of objective or direct revelation, man is not really involved in the question of his relation to God. "Where the question is really that pertaining to man, there the subjective is the objective."[142]

Man must meet God, then, not through direct revelation in history, but man must meet God by becoming contemporaneous with God in *Urgeschichte*.

In the idea of *Urgeschichte*, God is seen to be God as the one who is Lord even of his own divinity. "God alone, the whole God, God himself," becomes man. God's whole subjectivity must triumph in man's objectivity.[143] And the man in whom God reveals himself must be truly man. Only thus there can be, as there must be, a complete incognito of God.[144] Only thus is the relation between God and man "strictly dialectical."[145] "Revelation is *Urgeschichte*."[146] Ordinary history points to *Urgeschichte*, and primal history is the meaning of ordinary history.

The realm of *Urgeschichte* is free from ordinary historical continuity; its unity is that of contemporaneity.[147] *Urgeschichte* "is history but it works directly on men of nearest and farthest times."[148]

As God, the whole God, God Himself, becomes man, man must,

136. *Ibid.*, p. 346.
137. *Ibid.*, p. 344.
138. *Ibid.*, p. 247.
139. *Idem.*
140. *Ibid.*, p. 327.
141. *Ibid.*, p. 48.
142. *Idem.*

143. *Ibid.*, p. 220.
144. *Ibid.*, p. 222.
145. *Ibid.*, p. 223.
146. *Ibid.*, p. 230.
147. *Ibid.*, p. 239.
148. *Idem.*

in response, become a new subject. As revelation on God's part is "no revelation" with respect to ordinary history, so man as the old subject cannot receive true revelation.[149] Therefore man must know himself as non-existing before he can hear the Word of God.[150] But to know himself as non-existent, he must already exist as a new man. As God, to reveal himself to man, had to become wholly man, so now man, to receive the revelation of God, must participate in the divine Subject. Thus, as the new subject, man knows God in and through God.[151] Here in the act of revelation, and in the act of faith as response, in God, to that revelation, does the truly dialectical or existential relation between God and man take place. The experience of grace cannot be identified psychologically any more than the incarnation can be identified historically.[152] True confrontation between God and man takes place in the Moment, in act.[153] When man responds in faith and obedience to God, this is in principle "not a different nor a smaller but essentially the same miracle of God that takes place in the virgin birth. . . ."[154] In faith and obedience man himself enters into the continuity of *Urgeschichte*.[155]

In all this, it appears again and again that, as Barth follows in the footsteps of Kierkegaard, both in the negations of direct revelation and in his affirmations with respect to *Urgeschichte*, he also refers to Franz Overbeck's idea of *Urgeschichte* with approval.[156]

In his *Romans* and in his *Christian Dogmatics*, Barth holds up the incarnation as the ideal of interaction between God and man. It is, in his case, as much as in that of Kierkegaard's, the human subject that projects the ideal of the absolute subject, in order by means of it to open up to the autonomous consciousness of man a field of endless advance. The grace that comes to man from the incarnate God is the grace of Kierkegaard's *Individual*. This grace is "sovereign," in that the God who gives it is indeterminate in character, and it is triumphant because it is universally operative in man. The primary relation of all men is to the Christ rather than to Adam. That is to say, men's ideal selves, their selves in their Christ, are their real selves.

It thus appears that the consciousness-theology of Schleiermacher and his followers has been "overcome" by a higher consciousness-

149. *Ibid.*, p. 287.
150. *Idem.*
151. *Ibid.*, p. 289.
152. *Ibid.*, pp. 292-293.

153. *Ibid.*, p. 295.
154. *Ibid.*, p. 319.
155. *Ibid.*, p. 320.
156. *Ibid.*, pp. 110, 230.

theology, by the notion of the Christ as the ideal *Subject* in which all human subjects participate.

It thus appears also that Feuerbach's charge to the effect that consciousness-theology is nothing more than a would-be all-inclusive anthropology has not been met. There is no way of meeting the charge of illusionism except if one really begins with God as identified directly by Christ through Scripture. Barth, no less than Kierkegaard and no less than Kant, takes the human consciousness out of the concrete relationships in which it alone can know itself. Thus set *free*, the human consciousness is condemned to operate in a vacuum. If it gets out of the vacuum, it is reduced to fate. Thus the dilemma facing all basically immanentistic thinking still faces Barth. This dilemma, earlier referred to, is that the individual, on Barth's basis, is wholly isolated. It cannot communicate. If it did, as by accident, communicate then this communication would always take place at the cost of the individual's uniqueness.

In Barth's latest theology, the approach is basically the same as that of his earlier theology. In the *Church Dogmatics*, everything centers around the idea of the *Christ-Event*. In this Christ-Event, God is wholly revealed and at the same time wholly hidden. God is so free as to include coexistence with man into his very self existence. God is what he is in the act of his revelation. On the other hand, man through faith participates in the act of God's revelation. Thus the eternal and the temporal are again intermingled as they were intermingled in Barth's earlier theology.

It has been contended that in his later theology Barth has done better justice to the idea of revelation as really entering into history than he formerly did. This contention has not been substantiated by evidence. Barth has not forsaken his principle that revelation is historical but that history is never revelational. True, as over against Rudolf Bultmann, Barth contends that when the apostles witnessed to the resurrection of Christ they were witnessing to an incontrovertible fact.[157] The resurrection, he says, is an event in time and space.[158] Even so, Barth does not at any time identify the resurrection with ordinary history. The "incontrovertible fact" of which he speaks takes place in *Praehistorie*.[159] Usually he simply speaks of *Geschichte*. The resurrection is never identified with *Historie*, with ordinary history. "The resurrection happens without our being able

157. Barth, *Kirchliche Dogmatik*, IV:1, p. 375.
158. *Ibid.*, p. 371.   159. *Idem.*

to ascribe an 'historical' character to it."[160] When we deal with the resurrection, we deal not with something that took place in the past.[161] The resurrection takes place in the present. Christ "not only went the way from Jordan to Golgotha, but He still goes it."[162]

The fact then that Barth now uses the term *Geschichte,* or occasionally *Praehistorie* instead of *Urgeschichte,* does not mean that he has turned upon his earlier total rejection of direct revelation. He still maintains the wholly hidden character of revelation.

In fact, if there is any change in Barth on this point, it is to the effect that he stresses this wholly hidden nature of revelation more than ever. There was no other way open to him of escaping Feuerbach. His rejection of the existential method in his later theology is but an expression of an ever deeper negation of every form of direct revelation.

When Barth said *Nein* to Brunner in 1929, he did so because he wanted to base his whole theology on the foundation of election. Brunner had, he argued, in an evil moment sought for negotiated peace with the consciousness-theologians.[163] We may not even use the idea of the image of God in man as a positive point of contact for the gospel. The idea of similitude expressed in the concept of the image must always be taken as correlative to the idea of dissimilitude. It is only if we begin with the idea of election in which the impossible takes place that we can answer the consciousness-theologians.

When therefore Barth begins his writing of the *Church Dogmatics,* he wipes the slate clean once more. He follows, he says, the method followed by Anselm. The existence of God must be taken for granted, not proved. This is true because God's being is free. He knows no necessity. He needs not his own being. He is free to turn wholly into the opposite of himself. Therein precisely does God's freedom exist, in that he can become the opposite of himself and take into participation in his very aseity that which is opposite to himself. It is this sort of God who meets us in Christ.[164] "For the Son of God, who in Jesus Christ became flesh, is as the eternal mode of divine being himself nothing more nor less than the principle of all the world immanence of God and thus the principle of what we have called the secondary absoluteness of God."[165]

160. *Ibid.,* p. 331.
161. *Ibid.,* p. 345.
162. *Idem.*

163. Cf. *Fate and Idea in Theology,* 1929.
164. *Church Dogmatics,* II:1, p. 354.
165. *Ibid.,* p. 356.

It is by the idea of this free God meeting us as the principle of world immanence that Barth wants to free himself from all compromise with consciousness-theology. It is the idea of God as the God of pure negation that forms the transcendence motif in Barth's latest theology. It is the God who is wholly expressed in his revelation, the God who is the act of reconciliation of all men, who is said to be present to us as an incontrovertible fact. The contention that Barth has done better justice to the idea of history as genuinely revelational of the presence of fact is therefore contrary to the evidence.

But it has also been argued that Barth has, in his later writings, done better justice to the distinction between creation and sin than he formerly did. But for this too no evidence has been adduced. Barth could do no justice to the distinction between creation and sin at all unless he first accepted the idea of creation and the fall in the historical sense of the term. But he has not done so. On the contrary, if any point in Barth's doctrine of man is prominent, it is the rejection of the idea of Adam as having any direct historical function to perform; human nature itself is said to be inherently human nature in Christ. True still to the Kantian idea of ethical dualism, Barth maintains that no true decision could be made by man unless it be in Christ as *Geschichte*. It is for this reason that no significant decision can be made, on his view, that is against Christ. Even the decisions against Christ must be made within Christ. Sin is an ontological impossibility. Man is man as fellow-man with Jesus.[166] Jesus is the only real man; other men are men by virtue of their participation in his true manhood. It is of the essence of man to be "fellow elect with the man Jesus."[167]

Thus the whole relation between God and man is in Barth's latest theology still that of the act of reconciliation of all men in the *Christ-Event*. God is free to become the creature and "in the strictest and most perfect sense to take the creature into unity with himself into his divine being."[168] "Thus time is made into the form and expression of God's eternal being."[169] Ethical dualism is still operative in Barth's latest thinking, and it is still turning into ethical monism.

Barth's treatment of the Chalcedon creed is perhaps the most

166. *Ibid.*, III:2, p. 161.   168. *Ibid.*, II:1, p. 354.
167. *Ibid,.* p. 175.   169. *Ibid.*, p. 695.

striking proof of the fact that Barth has, in no true sense, outgrown existentialism.

Orthodox theology, Barth says, has misused the Chalcedon formula. Thinking in statical categories, it has been unable to do justice to either the freedom of God or to the faith of man.

Barth therefore actualizes the incarnation. The incarnation is an event. He says that this "transposition of the static statements of older dogmatics into dynamic is undoubtedly an innovation which, although it does not really jettison or ignore any of the relatively more important elements in the older conception, may well arouse suspicion because of the radical alteration in form."[170]

The possibility of such an actualization must be answered from the point of view of Christ as *Geschichte*. We must not ask whether the concept of *Geschichte* is logically possible. "How can a being be interpreted as an act, or an act as a being? How can God, or man, or both in their unity in Jesus Christ, be understood as history? How can humiliation also and at the same time be exaltation? How can it be said of a history which took place once that it takes place to-day, and that, having taken place once and taking place to-day, it will take place again? How much easier it seems at a first glance to speak of the given fact of this person and His structure, and then of His work, or, to use the language of more modern theology, of His 'significance for all succeeding ages, or His influence and effects'! How can the birth and life and death of Jesus Christ be an event to-day and to-morrow? Are these thoughts and statements that can really be carried through? But again, if there is a genuine necessity, even suspicions as to the possibility cannot be regarded as finally decisive. Difficulty or no difficulty, we must attempt to think and state the matter along these lines."[171]

The incarnation must, therefore, be interpreted in terms of the *prima veritas* that in the Christ-event there is involved the whole essence of God and the whole essence of man. Let us note something of what this implies for Barth.

1. In the first place, Barth wants to do away with the idea that the states of humiliation and exaltation of Christ follow one another in time. Revelation can never be a predicate of history. The suffering and death of Christ are not to be identified as in themselves steps in the humiliation of Christ. Nor is the resurrection, or any fact

170. *Ibid.*, IV:2, p. 119; Engl. tr. p. 108.
171. *Ibid.*, p. 120; Engl. tr. p. 108.

following upon it, as such to be identified as a step in his exaltation. Christ's work cannot be divided into different stages or periods of His existence. Christ's humiliation and exaltation take place together in the present.

2. In addition to rejecting the idea of the two stages of Christ's life and work as following one another, Barth also rejects the idea of two natures as separate from one another.

The two natures must be interpreted in terms of the one act that takes place within both.

It is thus that, by the actualization of the incarnation, Barth provides the basis for grace as both sovereign and universal. On the older view, the immutability of the divine nature kept it from becoming really human, and the immutability of human nature kept it from participation in God. But God, whose essence is the act of saving grace for man, and man, whose essence is to be fellow-elect, are what they are in the Christ-Event. Thus grace is both sovereign and universal.[172]

This actualization of the incarnation on the part of Barth cannot fairly be taken to be indicative of a return to the historic Christian view. Barth has never expressed his negation of a direct revelation of God in history more emphatically than he does in the idea of the actualization of the Chalcedon creed. And Barth has never expressed the idea that manhood is essentially manhood in Christ more emphatically than he does in this same idea of the actualization of the Chalcedon creed.[173]

Our general conclusion then must be that, in all the stages of the development of his thinking, Barth has followed without basic alteration the type of dialecticism that we found in Existentialism and, back of it, in Kant. And this type of dialecticism is not basically different from the form-matter scheme of ancient dialecticism. Barth's effort to get beyond Romanism by means of a modern dialecticism cannot be accounted successful. And his attempt to go beyond modern existentialist dialecticism by means of his Christ-Event cannot be accounted successful either. With Berkouwer we would hold that he who sets his feet on the way of subjectivism cannot suddenly stop himself from sliding into illusionism.

172. *Ibid.*, IV:2, p. 38.
173. For a fuller discussion of this point see *The Westminster Theological Journal*, May, 1960, pp. 147ff.

Section Four

The New Consciousness-Theology

Chapter XIII

Hans urs Von Balthasar

In the previous section we found that Barth's theology, together with Roman Catholicism and New Protestantism, is basically informed by dialectical principles that spring from the assumption of human autonomy. The basic divide, we found, is between historic Protestantism on one side, and every form of dialectical theology on the other side. The difference between Barth's theology and that of Romanism and of New Protestantism are differences that operate upon a common dialectical presupposition, and this presupposition is the diametrical opposite of that of Luther and Calvin. Man as interpreted in terms of Aristotle's philosophy and man as interpreted in terms of Kant's philosophy do not differ too greatly from one another. And a theology that compromises either with Aristotelian or Kantian anthropology can never be a theology of the Word. A theology of the Word worthy of its name requires of man that, as a creature and as a sinner, he submit his every thought captive to the obedience of Christ as he speaks by his Spirit in the Scriptures. Barth's essentially Kantian view of man keeps him from being a theologian of the Word as surely as any Roman Catholic theologian's view of man keeps him from being a theologian of the Word. And any theology that assumes human autonomy has no real Christ to offer unto men. Any theology that assumes human autonomy condemns human predication to the necessity of operation in a vacuum.

In the present and final section, the truth of this contention is further established. In the light of recent theological discussion, the great divide between the biblical and the dialectical forms of theology has come to stand out more clearly than ever. Outstanding

319

Roman Catholic theologians see clearly that in Barth they have found a friend as over against Luther and Calvin. They see clearly that the activist principle of Barth is basically similar to their own dynamic principle. They see full well that they and Barth have a common cause to defend against the Reformers.

On his part, Barth has expressed a large measure of agreement with their point of view. By the same token, he has reconsidered his earlier opposition to New Protestantism. He now finds that his earlier criticism of Schleiermacher and his followers was one-sided and too negative.

In short, recent discussion seems to have led Barth to a recognition of the fact that his theology differs at most gradationally from Romanism and from New Protestantism. The development of his own anthropology has apparently strengthened him in this conviction. Thus, we must not say that belief in God excludes humanity. We must rather say that "His deity encloses humanity in itself."[1] After all, however true it is that God must speak from above, it is also true that there must be a man to whom God speaks. The Romanists and the New Protestantists were right in so far as they merely contended for this truth. And were not Romanism and New Protestantism also interested in giving a Christological interpretation to man?

It is thus that Romanism, New Protestantism and Barth's theology are drawing ever closer together. The followers of Luther and Calvin now stand out more clearly than ever in their isolation. It now appears more clearly than ever that the cleavage between them and Barth is as great as, if not greater than, the cleavage between them and Romanism and New Protestantism. The followers of Luther and Calvin now stand alone in their contention for the reality of the revelation of God's grace in history in Christ. The Christ of the various forms of dialectical theology cannot be found. He is composed of a cross between an abstract form of unity which, when it comes into touch with diversity is lost in it, and an abstract principle of diversity which, when it comes into contact with abstract unity, is lost in it. Thus the conclusion of the matter must be that, with the loss of any discernible Christ, man himself is lost. There is no triumph of grace for the Christian minister to preach. He can offer nothing to men that are lost in the cauldron of utter meaninglessness.

1. Karl Barth, *The Humanity of God,* Richmond, 1960, p. 50.

To indicate the inevitability of this conclusion, chapters XIII and XIV of this section are devoted to Roman Catholic thinkers as they make their estimate of Barth's theology, and chapter XV is devoted to Barth's own re-evaluation of New Protestantism, and the last chapter is devoted to the general conclusion of the argument of the book as a whole. It indicates that Barth's theology may properly be designated as humanism.

The present chapter considers the work of Hans Urs von Balthasar. Von Balthasar finds that, in the theology of Barth, Protestantism has, for the first time, found its fully consistent expression.[1a] How has Barth attained to this high position? Has he simply gone back to the Reformers and restated their theology? Not at all. He has, to be sure, gone back to them. But he has also radicalized their position and therefore has gone beyond them.

In a sense, Barth has relativized the theology of the Reformers. Barth has a broader view of the church and its theology than the Reformers had. He sought therefore to be true to their principles by means of making an approach to a more Catholic point of view.[2]

It is therefore imperative, argues Von Balthasar, for a Roman Catholic to understand the basic principles of Barth's theology. Barth has been, throughout his writings, true to his own principles.[3]

We can best see these principles at work in Barth when he discusses subjects that find their center in creation, in the incarnation and in reconciliation. When he deals with these subjects his central Christological view comes clearly to the fore. In dealing with these subjects, Barth is creative and original. This is less true when he discusses subjects that center about the idea of the church, the sacraments and the Christian life.[4] Our main concern will therefore be with the first group of doctrines.[5]

It is interesting, says Von Balthasar, that in his exposition of the first group of subjects, the one with which we shall be primarily concerned, Barth approaches Roman Catholicism, while in his exposition of the second group of subjects a further departure from the Church may be discerned.[6]

What did Barth mean when he said that in the Roman Catholic idea of the analogy of being (*analogia entis*) we can discern the

1a. Hans Urs von Balthasar, *Karl Barth—Darstellung Und Deutung Seiner Theologie*, Verlag Jakob Hegner in Köhn, MCMLI, p. 32.
2. *Ibid.*, p. 33.
3. *Ibid.*, p. 34.   5. *Ibid.*, p. 53.
4. *Ibid.*, p. 52.   6. *Idem.*

spirit of the Antichrist?[7] To answer this question it is imperative to realize that for Barth the principle of theology is the content of revelation. This content of revelation must be thought of as an act of the sovereign God. There can, therefore, be no direct revelation of God to man. Revelation must always be revelation in hiddenness. Revelation must always be indirect.[8] From Barth's point of view, the Roman Catholic notion of the analogy of being constitutes an attack on this indirect character of revelation.

All the various heresies of Roman Catholicism may, according to Barth, be traced back to this failure to fathom the indirect character of revelation. When we hear of "faith *and* works," of "nature *and* grace," of "reason *and* revelation," we expect to hear "scripture *and* tradition." This Roman Catholic *and* is a symptom of the idea of the analogy of being. For this fatal *and* always indicates that man is supposed, in part at least, to be able to possess and control the revelation of God.[9] On the basis of the Catholic principle of the analogy of being, the grace of God is reduced to a relation of reciprocity between God and man. The Roman Catholic notion of man's cooperation with the grace of God, Barth asserts, assumes that man has some claim on the grace of God.[10] The Roman Catholic notion of the Church as something directly ascertainable in history, as something "given," involves a reduction of grace into a physical event.[11] It is therefore impossible to do justice to the idea of the "triumph of the grace of God" on the principle of the analogy of being.[12]

At this point Von Balthasar assures Barth that the Roman Catholic *and* is not so fatal to the idea of grace as it might seem. Roman Catholicism does not believe in direct revelation any more than does Barth. The discussion between Barth and himself must start from the common presupposition that revelation is revelation in hiddenness.[13]

It is this common presupposition between Barth and the Roman Catholic position, we believe, that determines the nature of the argument between them. It also accounts for the fact that the differ-

7. *Ibid.,* p. 56.
8. *Idem.*
9. *Ibid.,* p. 58.
10. *Idem.*
11. *Ibid.,* p. 60.
12. *Ibid.,* p. 61.
13. *Ibid.,* p. 56. "Die Gegebenheitsweise des sich offenbarenden Gottes ist jedenfalls—dies ist wiederum gemeinsame Voraussetzung—ein Offenbarsein in Verhüllung, ein Gegebensein des wesenhaft nie im Sinne rein-weltlicher Gegenständlichkeit Gegebenen."

ence between the two positions cannot be so great as it might at first seem to be. If Roman Catholicism as well as Barth believes in the hiddenness of revelation, then it too, as well as Barth, Von Balthasar continues, can maintain the free and sovereign nature of the grace of God. For then the absoluteness which Roman Catholicism claims for itself is not a directly given something. For the claim to absoluteness is made as the answer of obedience to Christ. And the certainty that the church claims for the truth of its teachings depends altogether on its task and its mission. For every member of the church, including the infallible Pope, to be in the church means to be the recipient of the promise of salvation, not a guarantee of it. It is therefore quite out of place to speak of an "attack on God" in connection with Roman Catholicism.[14]

On the other hand, since Barth as well as the church has to speak of revelation in hiddenness, he also must, in some sense, deal with a givenness. Granted that the difference between the two positions must primarily be sought in the difference between their formal principles, it remains true that any formal principle must express itself in content. A final understanding between the two positions cannot, therefore, be attained unless the formal principles be considered in relation to the content in which these principles find expression. Only in the forward and backward movement of the theological *a priori* and *a posteriori* can progress be made in mutual understanding.[15]

When, therefore, Barth develops his notion of the analogy of faith in order to place it over against the analogy of being, he may quite properly warn Roman Catholicism against any direct identification of something given in the world with the revelation of God in Christ. But, on Barth's own view, revelation must also and quite

14. *Ibid.*, p. 62. Die «Absolutheit», die die katholische Kirche für sich in Anspruch nehmen muss, erweist sich darin als Gehorsam, dass sie die Souveränität der göttlichen Freiheit der Gnade in nichts antastet und einschränkt. Nie hat die Kirche den Raum ihrer Sichtbarkeit mit dem Raum der Erwählten und Gerechtfertigten gleichgesetzt. Und die Sicherheit, die sie besitzt, hängt ganz an ihrem Auftrag und ihrer Sendung. Für jedes Glied der Kirche, auch für den unfehlbaren Papst, ist das Sein in der Kirche Verheissung des Heils, nicht «Garantie». Von einen katholischen «Griff nach Gott» weiss der Katholik nichts.

15. *Ibid.*, p. 57. Nur in einem beweglichen Hin und Her zwischen theologischem «Apriorismus» und «Aposteriorismus» wird sich die Diskussion wirklich *vorwärts* bewegen.

properly take the form of things in this world.[16] The difference between the two positions can in consequence be at most one of degree. It is true that, to counteract the theology of the Reformation,
the Council of Trent laid great stress upon the necessity of works
and of the institution of the church. But this does not in the least
militate against its maintenance of the triumph of the grace of God
in Christ which the Church as well as Barth is anxious to maintain.

At this point, it is well to pause and to indicate, at least in general
terms, the far-reaching significance of this general description of
Barth's principle of theology as made by Von Balthasar. If we apply
the criterion of Bavinck or of Berkouwer, we shall have to say that
here two forms of subjectivism are to be compared with one another. God's once for all and direct revelation in history through
Christ as set forth in Scripture is not even mentioned by Von Balthasar as a matter of difference between the Roman Catholic and
the Protestant views of theology. Herewith we are on subjective
ground. The difference between Barth and von Balthasar is the
difference between two forms of subjectivism. Such a difference is,
in the nature of the case, no more than gradational.

Being subjective, both the theology of Barth and that of Von
Balthasar are also dialectical. All non-biblical thinking assumes the
ultimacy of the self-consciousness of man. With this assumption of
human ultimacy or autonomy goes a principle of continuity and a
principle of discontinuity that together overarch the difference between God and man. Ancient dialecticism, as it found its expression
in Plato and in Aristotle, had an abstract idea of being, of truth and
goodness that was supposed to be the means of unifying all the
multiplicity of differences found in human experience. In this Idea,
all was light and there was no darkness at all. But over against this
impersonal and abstract Idea of unity or continuity, there was an
equally ultimate and abstract idea of plurality or discontinuity. The
latter was called non-being or pure potentiality. In reality it was
Chance.

As he sought for truth, the Greek thinker had therefore to seek to
combine his abstract principle of continuity and his equally abstract
principle of discontinuity. But, suppose he would be successful in
subsuming every diversity of experience under his principle of
unity: in that case he would not be aware of his success, because

16. *Ibid.*, p. 61.

he himself, together with all the multiplicity of facts about him, would have been lost in his principle of unity. His principle of continuity would have swallowed up both the knower and all that he knew. On the other hand, suppose that the Greek thinker succeeded in bringing down his principle of continuity from the realm of the wholly other into contact with the world of time; then what would happen? In that case the principle of continuity would have lost itself in multiplicity and therewith would have lost all unifying power. In the first instance, Chance would have been wholly rationalized, and, in the second instance, rationality itself would have been wholly immersed in Chance.

In order to avoid both extremes, the seeker for truth therefore tried to effect a compromise. He made the idea of complete or absolute rationality correlative to the principle of complete irrationality. It is this compromise that constitutes the essence of dialecticism. According to the principle of pure rationality or continuity, the whole of reality must be thought of as wholly lit up to the mind of man. But, according to the principle of discontinuity or irrationality, reality must also be thought of as being purely contingent and wholly dark, even to the mind of God. The two ideas, that of pure rationality and that of pure irrationality, must be kept in balance with one another. The form-matter scheme of the Greeks expressed this principle of dialecticism. And this form-matter scheme was adopted into the philosophy and natural theology of Roman Catholic thought.

It is not necessary now to restate the modern form of this form-matter scheme as it derives largely from the philosophy of Immanuel Kant. Dooyeweerd speaks of it as the freedom-necessity scheme. According to this scheme, there is again a principle of continuity according to which reality is altogether light, and a principle of discontinuity, according to which reality is altogether contingent and therefore dark. In order to avoid the obvious contradiction involved in saying that reality is both wholly light and wholly dark, it is said that darkness and light are correlative aspects of one another and together constitute reality. It is from this background that, as earlier indicated, Barth derives his notion that God is wholly revealed when revealed at all and yet when thus wholly revealed is still wholly hidden.

What we are to witness now, in the analysis of Barth's theology by Von Balthasar, is the evaluation of modern dialecticism by an adherent of medieval or ancient dialecticism. Both parties, Von Balthasar tells us at the outset, agree that revelation is revelation in hiddenness and that this agreement excludes the idea of any form of direct revelation in history.

Of course, lip service will be paid to the Bible, but it will not be presented as the once for all and finished interpretation of the once for all and finished work of redemption of Christ in history. So far as God speaks through Christ and through the Bible in history, this revelation must be thought as still wholly hidden there. And this wholly hidden character of revelation must be taken as correlative to the notion that God is wholly revealed in history.

It is thus that one synthesis theology is to judge another synthesis theology, one form of subjectivism to judge another form of subjectivism, and one form of dialecticism to judge another form of dialecticism. This is what we are to see as we follow the argument of Von Balthasar. The argument will center on the question as to which of the two theologies has the more truly Christological and more truly biblical approach. But the answer to that question will be given in terms of the question as to which theology better than the other attains to the dialectical ideal of first keeping in balance the notion of a Christ in whom God is both wholly revealed and wholly hidden and then of tipping this balance in favor of the triumph of grace in Christ.

1. *The Period of Dialecticism*

After his general analysis of the problem facing him, Von Balthasar then proceeds to trace the development of the thinking of Barth. He speaks of this development as going from dialecticism to analogy.[17]

The reader will observe the fact that Von Balthasar limits the use of the word dialecticism to the earlier works of Barth, while in the preceding paragraphs we have used the term dialecticism to describe the whole of Barth's work. Our broad usage of the term dialecticism is not made in the interest of impressing Barth's later writings into the schematism of his earlier writings. This broad usage, taken from Dooyeweerd, is made exclusively in the interest of gettting at the root of the difference between an essentially Christian and an essentially non-Christian form of thought.

17. *Ibid.*, p. 71.

(a) The First *Römerbrief*

In the first edition of Barth's exposition of Paul's letter to the Romans, he seeks to set forth the good news of the gospel. The divine economy of redemption is developed, but it is developed, says Von Balthasar, in a schematism that is not primarily borrowed from Scripture, or even from Luther or Calvin, but from philosophical sources. Von Balthasar mentions the influence of Plato, of Hegelianism of the right, and of religious socialism.[18] He points out that, due to his essentially Platonic approach, Barth is unable to have a proper appreciation of nature. If he had only had the true idea of analogy from the start, he would not have identified nature with evil.[19] On the other hand, he would not have had nature absorbed in God. As it is, in his essentially pantheistic view, Barth presents an idea of grace as that which is inherent in man.[20]

Barth has christianized his Platonism with the help of Origen. His Hegelianism could not add much that was new to this Origenist Platonism but only underscores the dynamic notion of *apokatastasis* as world movement.[21] And here appears the notion of *Urgeschichte*. In terms of Hegel's Phenomenology, Barth develops the notion of the subjection of the finite spirit to the absolute Spirit which is the Holy Spirit.[22]

Still further, this Hegelianized Platonism is touched up with the brush of religious socialism. Individuality must be absorbed in universality. The whole aristocracy of the spirit, from Moses to John the Baptist, and from Plato to religious socialism, teaches this same truth.[23] With what vehemence do the motives of philosophical mysticism, of the radical historicity of the world, and of an unrestrained universalism, find expression in it.[24]

(b) The Second *Römerbrief*

Who does not know that Søren Kierkegaard's notion of the absolute qualitative difference between God and man was a guiding principle for Barth when he rewrote his commentary on *Romans*? And who does not know that the Reformers appear in this work in

18. *Idem.*
19. *Ibid.*, p. 73.
20. *Idem.*
21. *Idem.*

22. *Ibid.*, p. 74.
23. *Idem.*
24. *Idem.*

the light of the fire that he kindled from such men as Overbeck, Nietzsche and Dostoevsky, as well as Kierkegaard?[25] In this second edition of *Romans*, the dialectical principle appears as pure eschatology.[26] In it man's self-sublation is complete.[27] Man is not what he is and is what he is not. Nature is sin and religion is the attack on God.[28]

Underneath this absolute qualitative difference between God and man lies a principle of identity that derives from Plato's idea of remembrance.[29] The idea of redemption in Christ is the idea of the return to unity. Christ takes the place of Adam. There is no fall in Adam that is not automatically sublated through redemption in Christ.[30] "Only against the background of an original, presupposed identity does the entire dialectic of *Romans* appear to be possible."[31] The tremendous stress on the qualitative difference between God and man does not in the least qualify this principle of identity. On the contrary, this qualitative difference finds its expression only in relation to this very principle. It is through this principle as the principle of the immediacy of origin that nature appears to be identical with grace. And the idea of the identity of nature and grace virtually involves the identity of nature and sin.[32] Thus we are led from *Baius* to *Jansenius*.[33] There must be a radical subsumption of the human subject into the new subject, which is the new man Christ Jesus.[34]

What shall we say of this new form of dialecticism? We can only say that it is hyper-Christian and therefore un-Christian.[35] Barth absolutizes his method and makes it a "standpoint." Therewith he commits what he himself considers the greatest of all sin, namely, of turning toward the creature *(conversio ad creaturam)*.[36] Barth's approach is demonic in that it stretches all the mysteries of the Godhead on the rack of his method. Herein lies his Hegelianism.

25. *Ibid.*, p. 75.
26. *Idem.*
27. *Ibid.*, p. 76.
28. *Idem.*
29. *Ibid.*, p. 77.

30. *Ibid.*, p. 77. «Kein Fallen von Gott in Adam, kein Todesurteil, das nicht seinen Ursprung hätte an dem Punkt, wo dem Menschen, in Christus mit Gott versöhnt, das Leben [immer schon] zugesprochen ist» [143].

31. *Ibid.*, pp. 77-78.

32. *Ibid.*, p. 78. Der Zusammenfall der Begriffe Natur und Gnade führt notwendig zum Zusammenfall der Begriffe Natur und Sünde.

33. *Idem.*
34. *Idem.*
35. *Ibid.*, p. 79.
36. *Ibid.*, p. 98.

Accordingly, that which constitutes the heart of Christianity, namely, the incarnation, is made impossible.[37] Since, on Barth's view, the divine only touches the world as a tangent touches a circle, there can be no true life of Christ revealed in history. It is only in his death that the life of Christ has meaning.[38]

(c) THE TASK OF DIALECTICISM

But perhaps Barth only intended to use his method of dialecticism as a means by which to give new and fresh expression to the gospel. Perhaps he used philosophy as a servant of revelation after all.[39] Was Barth perchance merely using the method of dialecticism or paradox because of the inherently abstract nature of all human knowledge? Was he impressed by the fact that the object of human knowledge can never be fully caught by means of human concepts? Perhaps the fact that the object of revelation is in reality the free and self-determining subject called God made him use the dialectical method.[40]

According to Barth, says Von Balthasar, God does indeed reveal himself to man in the forms of human speech, in terms of precepts and concepts.[41] Man can therefore believe and understand his revelation. But, inasmuch as it is *God* who appears to man in a human form or scheme, the understanding of this form or scheme is not as such the understanding of God. God appears in human word but at the same time hides himself in it.[42] If God were not hidden in his revelation, he would not be God.[43] And at this point precisely dialecticism as a theological method takes its point of departure. Dialectic must act as a perpetual warning against man's tendency to think that he possesses truth as something given. To be sure, God's revelation of himself in human form is not itself a contradiction. It is rather the possibility of this revelation from which the *Sic et Non* of dialectics starts and in which it finds its criterion.[44]

---

37. *Ibid.*, p. 79.
38. *Idem.* «Eben darum muss der Sinn des Lebens Jesu ein Sterben sein, weil die ganze diesseits des Todes liegende menschliche Möglichkeit als solche die Möglichkeit der Sünde ist». «Der Sinn, das Letzte, der Tod in diesem Tod ist Gott» [186]!

39. *Ibid.*, p. 80.
40. *Ibid.*, pp. 80-82.
41. *Ibid.*, p. 83.

42. *Idem.*
43. *Ibid.*, p. 84.
44. *Ibid.*, p. 85.

Properly used, the dialectical method defends the openness of theology toward the revelation of God.[45] Dialecticism, properly conceived, wants to be only a *pointer* toward God.[46]

If therefore we are to speak properly of Christ as well as of sin and grace, we must do so in terms of dialecticism. Unwilling to do this, Schleiermacher reduced the antithesis between sin and grace in advance to something relative.[47] When God reveals himself in Christ, he always does so as the incomparable one.[48] And as the principle of dialecticism must protect the aseity of God, so it must also protect the divinity of his Word. God's speech is always in the form of a *concretissimum*. Behind all the objectivity of the revelation of God is his subjectivity.[49] In revelation it is God's holiness that comes into the medium of total sinfulness as a hot iron comes into cold water. The sinfulness of man comes to light in the act of the revelation of God to him.[50]

Holding to this view of dialecticism, Barth said that he had no standpoint but only a mathematical point.[51] We might conclude from this that it would be unfair to him to say that he has subjected the mysteries of God to a standpoint of clarity supposedly found in his method.

But even after taking careful note of this, says Von Balthasar, we must still maintain that Barth's theology is not open to revelation at this stage, for Barth yielded to the temptation of seeing in the impossibility of the speaking of God the equivalent of a permanent position.[52] How can pure emptiness be an actual pointer to God? Why can such emptiness not indicate pure nothingness as well as God?[53]

But perhaps we find such pure emptiness in Barth's dialectical starting-point because we do not see that his Kierkegaardian or static dialecticisms must be supplemented with his Hegelian or dynamic dialecticism. Perhaps the idea of the self-movement of truth should be added to the idea of the impossibility of revelation as something directly given.

Von Balthasar answers that the real defect of dialecticism as an exclusive and final method comes to its clearest expression when the

45. *Idem.*
46. *Idem.*
47. *Ibid.*, p. 86.
48. *Ibid.*, p. 87.
49. *Idem.*

50. *Ibid.*, p. 89.
51. *Ibid.*, p. 91.
52. *Idem.*
53. *Idem.*

two aspects, the static and the dynamic, are combined, for then it appears that there is a principle of identity underneath the method which swallows up the difference between God and man.[54] Thus the second edition of *Romans* itself illustrates that which Barth has most violently castigated. It is a product of religious genius. The distance between God and man has disappeared in it.[55] It is only when Barth turns away from the idea of dialecticism to that of analogy that he can really give us what he wanted to give us, a theology that is more than a theology in philosophical garb.[56]

2. Turning Toward Analogy

(a) THE CHRISTIAN DOGMATICS

It is clearly possible to see the development in Barth's theology away from dialecticism and toward analogy in the period of 1922 to 1932. Among the many writings of this period, it is well to pay special attention to the *Christian Dogmatics* of 1927. In it he is concerned with the concrete word of God as it has become man in Jesus Christ.[57] In speaking of this concrete word of God, Barth is trying to get away from every form of philosophy.[58] He is also concerned in this volume to set off his theology from every form of consciousness-theology.[59] And as he is opposed to the consciousness-theology of Schleiermacher, so he is also opposed to every form of natural theology.[60]

Barth constantly militates against the idealism of Schleiermacher, for behind this idealism he finds Roman Catholicism.[61] Religion as a "human apriori" is the archenemy of Revelation.[62] In religion we

54. *Ibid.*, pp. 91-92. Wo Dialektik sich als das Absolute versteht, werden lauter [statische oder dynamische] Identifikationen vorgenommen: zunächst Gottes [in seiner reinen aktualen Aseität] mit seiner Offenbarung. Dann des Geschöpfs mit dem reinen Gegensatz zu Gott und somit mit dem Nichts. Schliesslich, da das Geschöpf in der Offenbarung von Gott eingeholt und durch die dynamische Bewegung [die eine absolute, weil göttliche ist] zu Gott zurückgebracht wird, die Gleichsetzung des Geschöpfs mit Gott selbst, zumindest in seinem Ursprung und Ziel. Diese Gleichsetzungen sind es denn auch, die wir in den beiden Fassungen des «Römerbriefs» feststellen konnten.

55. *Ibid.*, p. 92.
56. *Ibid.*, p. 91.
57. *Ibid.*, p. 94.
58. *Idem.*

59. *Ibid.*, p. 95.
60. *Idem.*
61. *Ibid.*, p. 97.
62. *Idem.*

have the idea of unquestioned givenness and possession of the revelation of God.[63]

Even so, we hear in this work a new emphasis. While in *Romans*
religion was always pure negation, in the *Christian Dogmatics* it
may be redeemed by the grace of God.[64] There is, however, even
throughout this work, the same mistrust of every form of continuity
that was found in *Romans*. Accordingly, Barth cannot do justice to
the incarnation of the Son of God, to the idea that God really became *man* and that he really *became* man.[65] All possible stress is
still laid on the act character of revelation. In consequence, the
theology of the *Christian Dogmatics* is that of an inner circle of the
speaking God into which that which pertains to the creature is
absorbed.[66] The creature is still seen as being inherently identical
with contradiction. Barth still has no eye for the creature as something which stands over against God but is, as such, willed by him.[67]

(b) Ways of Change

The breaking through of the fatal monistic dialecticism may be
noted in three areas.

(1) Culture and Philosophy

In 1926 Barth wrote *The Church and Culture*, wherein Barth
speaks of that in creation which has not been wholly destroyed by
sin.[68] Man is man even when a sinner, and, as such, God speaks to
him in Christ. Man is able to participate in the promises of God.[69]

If only Barth had been mindful of this in his own theology when
he had his controversy with Brunner all would have been well. Then
that controversy might have been avoided. And then too his attitude
toward Roman Catholicism would have been expressed differently
and with greater nuance.[70] As it is, Barth's tendency toward the
recognition of a proper place for the human is, once again, suppressed by his schematism of actualistic monism.[71]

63. *Ibid.*, p. 98.
64. *Idem.*
65. *Ibid.*, p. 99.
66. *Idem.*
67. *Idem.*

68. *Ibid.*, p. 104.
69. *Ibid.*, p. 105.
70. *Idem.*
71. *Idem.*

In 1929 Barth's *Fate and Idea in Theology* appeared.[72] In this work Barth again discusses the question of the relation of philosophy to theology.[73] One cannot say that philosophy is necessarily sinful.[74] As long as one realizes that philosophy is simply an aspect of worldly reality, then the whole enterprise is unavoidable.[75] Theology must of necessity use the concepts and schematism of thought developed by philosophy.[76] But the theologian must be careful not to identify the living word of God with any philosophical concept.[77] With this the Roman Catholic can agree.[78] Yet, even so, the monistic motif of *Romans* again takes control. Philosophy is, in the last analysis, said to have no legitimate independence at all.[79]

(2) Ethics

A second road by which Barth made advance from dialecticism to analogy is found in his various writings on ethics in the period under discussion.

In 1922 Barth wrote *The Problem of Ethics in the Present.*[80] This piece of writing is still controlled by the philosophical categories of *Romans.*[81] All created reality is seen in the light of sin. Everything must be condemned.

In 1927 *Keeping the Commandments* appeared. Here things have changed. In this publication one no longer looks from the impossibility of existence toward the possibility created by grace. On the contrary, in the light of grace the impossibility of existence appears.[82] The same position is taken in another publication entitled *Justification and Sanctification.*[83]

In 1933 *The First Commandment as Theological Axiom* was published. In it we see a more Christological approach to ethics.[84] In his first discussion of ethics, Barth speaks of the absolute condemnation of all existence. In the second stage of his thought, he seeks to mitigate this purely dualistic approach. In this stage, he wants concrete obedience to the concrete command of God. The third stage finds

72. *Ibid.*, p. 103.
73. *Ibid.*, p. 106.
74. *Ibid.*, p. 107.
75. *Ibid.*, p. 106.
76. *Ibid.*, p. 107.
77. *Idem.*
78. *Idem.*

79. *Ibid.*, p. 108.
80. *Ibid.*, p. 109.
81. *Idem.*
82. *Ibid.*, p. 110.
83. *Ibid.*, p. 111.
84. *Ibid.*, pp. 109, 112.

expression in the publication now under discussion, for in it the Christological principle makes its appearance.[85]

(3) The Church

A third way in which Barth's thought changed from dialecticism to analogy is found in his discussion of the church. During his Münster period (1925-1930), Barth wrote three treatises dealing in different ways with the concept of the church. And in each of the three he sets off his view over against what he considers to be the Catholic position.

First there is *Church and Theology*. Then there is *The Concept of the Church*, and finally there is *Roman Catholicism as a Question to Protestantism*. These writings all indicate that Barth has not yet self-consciously laid the foundation for his own theology.[86] These writings are still controlled by the principles of *Romans* and its idea of dynamic actualism.[87] In *Romans* the church is said to be the great negation of revelation.[88] Atheism is said to be the real essence of the church, but, in spite of this and even because of this, the church is necessary. There is no salvation outside the church.[89] When Barth discusses the idea of the church in relation to Roman Catholicism, he takes all the attributes of the church as Roman Catholicism sees them and radicalizes them. This radicalization takes place in terms of his dynamic actualism.[90] No room is left for any actual center of action outside of God himself.[91] In relation to God, passivity is the only proper attitude.

Even so, in these various writings Barth is seeking to overcome the hopeless dualism that marks his early dialectical approach. But he cannot overcome his dualism so long as he does not allow the Christology of Chalcedon to have the upperhand in his thought.[92]

By thus carefully tracing the development of Barth's thought in the period of 1922 to 1932, Von Balthasar enables us to see how it was with great difficulty that Barth attained to the substitution of the principle of the analogy of faith for that of dialecticism. At the

---

85. *Ibid.*, p. 112.
86. *Ibid.*, p. 113.
87. *Idem.*

88. *Idem.*
89. *Idem.*
90. *Idem.*

91. *Ibid.*, p. 114. Die Kategorientafel des Aktualismus, mit seiner ständigen, unaufhaltsamen Reduktion aller Aktivität auf den Actus purus, Gott, hat für ein echtes Aktzentrum ausserhalb Gottes keinen Raum.

92. *Ibid.*, p. 115.

same time, Von Balthasar shows us what it was that drove Barth to this substitution. Barth was driven to the conclusion that the actualistic monism of *Romans* could not express the true nature of the grace of God. This actualistic monism virtually absorbed man into God. All the activity of this monism was within the divine circle.

3. Analogia Fidei

We come now to Von Balthasar's description of the idea of the analogy of faith as this is found in the *Kirchliche Dogmatik*. Even in this work, says Von Balthasar, the idea of analogy of faith grows only gradually. It is not found in its full-blown form till we reach the volumes that deal with creation (1945), Incarnation (1948) and providence (1950). In the first volume there is a negative preparation for it in that the existentialist-anthropological approach of the *Christian Dogmatics* is rejected. In its place Barth uses the purely theological approach. In this first volume, the idea of analogy is mentioned, but it is not yet based on the Christological motif on which it later rests.

When in the first volume of the *Church Dogmatics* Barth deals with the analogy of faith, he sets off his idea of it over against the idea of the analogy of being. He does so by saying that the latter deals with the category of being, while his own idea of analogy rests on the idea of Act. God is pure act. We must, indeed, speak of a similarity of man to God.[93] But this similarity of man to God is created in man through restoration from above.[94]

In the third volume, Barth again speaks of the necessity of having an idea of analogy. We cannot speak of God as wholly other than ourselves, and we cannot speak of God as simply similar to ourselves. The idea of analogy must give expression to an idea that lies in between these two extremes.[95] In everything in which God is similar to man, he is *also* different from man. Man's concepts of God are in themselves relative and finite. If we are to know God through them, God must restore us to relationship with himself. God uses our truth for the expression of his own truth.[96] "His truth is not our truth. But

93. *Ibid.*, p. 117.   95. *Idem.*
94. *Ibid.*, p. 118.   96. *Idem.*

our truth is his truth."[97] God speaks originally and authentically, and we speak derivatively and unauthentically.[98] Even so in the midst of our error we must, as human beings, live by God's truth. God's authentic speaking takes place in our unauthentic speech. Our words are not ours but his property. God accomplishes a restitution in us.

When Von Balthasar gives his analysis of Barth's view of analogy at this point, he speaks of it as being "highly Platonic speech," for authentic speech about God is found only there where human speech is made the property of God. Even so, Barth finds it necessary to refer to the idea of creation in order to justify the idea that God takes possession of human speech.[99] Moreover, Barth speaks of the analogy of attribution and makes God primary in the whole analogical relation. This shows that he wants grace to be the ontological and the epistemological foundation of analogy.[100]

In the same volume Barth finally reaches the notion of created being as true being, as the product of God's positive creation. Here Barth takes the idea of nature seriously. Creation is no longer identified with sin. Sin presupposes freedom. Therefore, when sin comes into the picture, the result is not the reduction of all to chaos.

Here then we have a reality that is distinct from God and which is not evil. This reality stands over against God, but this fact merely points to distinction not to opposition.[101] God permits his creature to have relative independence.[102] God is not only transcendent above, but also immanent in, his creature. Precisely because God is above he is also present in it.

As time goes on, Barth continues to praise the goodness of creation. In his work on Providence, he reaches the point where he says that, as the creature has been given relative independence by God, so it cannot be reabsorbed by God.[103] Thus even revelation is said to presuppose a world in which God can reveal himself.[104] The reality of the creature finds its highest expression in the fact that it stands over against God as highly active.[105] Thus we may speak of a secondary subject in connection with man who receives the

97. *Idem.*
98. *Ibid.*, p. 119.
99. *Ibid.*, p. 119.
100. *Ibid.*, p. 120.
101. *Ibid.*, pp. 120-121.

102. *Ibid.*, p. 121.
103. *Ibid.*, p. 122.
104. *Idem.*
105. *Ibid.*, p. 123.

revelation of God.[106] And thus we have reached theological analogy.[107]

4. Full-Blown Analogy

(a) ITS CHRISTOLOGICAL FOUNDATION

From time to time Von Balthasar has intimated that we must not look for Barth's full-blown statement of analogy till we have seen him place it on his Christological foundation. As we proceed in our reading of the *Church Dogmatics*, it cannot escape our notice that the idea of the Word of God is being replaced by the idea of Jesus Christ as God and man.[108] Since in Christ God becomes man, creation has from the beginning a relation to him. Herewith we have a new perspective. Christ is the Redeemer. Therefore all creation is good in advance and is justified in advance. It is a foregone conclusion that God should have man for his partner.[109]

Christ is now the measure of all things.[110] When the implications of the idea of the incarnation are carried out, then there is no longer any final opposition to God. Any presentation of opposition to God is then found within the suffering son of man. This presupposes that this opposition is overcome in him. In the obedience of the Son, all opposition of the creature to God is already overcome.

Through his Christology, Barth is able, Von Balthasar asserts, to give a place to the idea of *nature* next to that of *actuality*.[111] This nature of Christ grounds and justifies all human nature.[112] Man is what he is because he participates in advance *(zum vornherein)* in the history of victory that has appeared in Christ.[113] Since human nature is founded in Christ, it is impossible that this nature should stand in final opposition to grace.[114]

Here we reach a point of great importance. Henceforth Barth points out that sin has affected all the relations of human existence

106. *Idem.*   108. *Ibid.,* p. 124.
107. *Idem.*
109. *Idem.* Die Perspektiven haben sich umgekehrt: weil er in der Zeit als Erlöser Mensch wird, darum ist alle Schöpfung von vornherein gut, von vornherein gerechtfertigt, darum ist es von vornherein recht, dass Gott den Menschen zum Partner hat.
110. *Idem.*   113. *Idem.*
111. *Ibid.,* p. 126.   114. *Idem.*
112. *Idem.*

but has not changed its structure.[115] Christ has founded human nature. This makes it to be something constant.[116]

Protestant theologians have often suppressed this constant element in human nature in order to magnify the depth of the contrast between sin and grace. We must not follow that path, says Barth. Even if, with the idea of human nature as a continuum unaffected by sin and redemption, we seem to come close to the Roman Catholic and the humanist position, we must nevertheless hold on to it.[117]

It is clear that, by this review of Barth's theology, Von Balthasar is leading us closer and closer to a final comparison between the Roman Catholic and the Barthian view of analogy. The two positions seem to have come very close to one another. But before confronting the two positions with one another in final form, another and final step in Barth's development must be noted. Barth himself senses that there seems to be a difficulty in his position. He has set forth Christ as the Archetype of human nature. But Christ is God. And so it is impossible to deduce from the incarnation as such the notion of human nature. As human nature must be interpreted in terms of Christ's incarnation, this incarnation must, in turn, presuppose human nature. Christ has become one of us. Thus human nature must at least be presupposed as a possibility. Unless we have the idea of a general presupposition of the possibility of the Incarnation in the idea of the *humanum*, then either Christ is the only man or he is no real man.[118] We need therefore a ground-form of humanity that may serve as the presupposition for the possibility of the work of Christ in saving men.[119]

(b) CREATION AND COVENANT

How then are we to harmonize the idea of the priority of grace in Christ and the idea of the *humanum* as a ground-form of hu-

115. *Idem.*

116. *Idem.* Von Christus her muss also offen und nicht verschämt von einer «notwendigen and *konstanten* Bestimmung» des menschlichen Wesens gesprochen werden [6, 84], und es ist die Aufgabe der theologischen Anthropologie, dieses Unangreifbare, dieses Kontinuum . . . sichtbar zu machen [6, 246].

117. *Ibid.*, p. 128. "Humanität also als eine in sich gute, in der Sünde unzerstörte, wenn auch gänzlich missbrauchte, in der Gnade bestätigte, wenn auch gänzlich überstrahlte Möglichkeit: das ist die Natura Humana. So ist es nur folgerichtig, wenn nun auch das Wort «Naturrecht» fällt, das von keinem Ort her relativiert werden kann [6, 581]."

118. *Ibid.*, p. 129.   119. *Ibid.*, p. 130.

manity? Barth finds the unity between the two in the idea that creation is the external ground of the covenant and that the covenant is the internal ground of creation.[120] This formula, he argues, maintains the priority of grace. It preserves the newness of the work of salvation through Christ. Grace is the mystery, the hidden sense of nature.[121] At the same time, the new act of salvation does not sublate nature. How could it since God is its creator? Through grace creation obtains perspective depth.[122]

Thus we reach the point where we can, without fear of losing the priority of grace, assert that there is analogy between nature and grace. Grace is truly a new work. It is not merely the crown of creation, though it is also that. Yet it is nature that experiences grace.[123] Thus revelation, new as it is, is not absolutely new.[124] It is in this manner that we are to see the proper relation between creation and redemption. We may look at nature as the symbol of grace.[125] We have then a sacramental universe.[126]

(c) Partner of God

In thinking of creation as the external ground of the covenant, and of the covenant as the inner ground of creation, we have the true notion of the image of God in man. It means that man is inherently open for God. Man is not that hopelessly self-immanent being that Barth formerly thought he was. The very definition of man is *to be with God*.[127] Godlessness is an ontological impossibility. Together with the Son of God, man is the object of God's electing grace.[128] If Christ is really elected by and loved of God, then man, every man, is as man elected along with Christ.[129] In this sense man is a free subject.[130] As such he has a transcendent destination, a destination determined by the history *(Geschichtlichkeit)* and factuality of the incarnation.[131]

120. *Ibid.,* p. 131.
121. *Idem.*
122. *Ibid.,* p. 132.
123. *Ibid.,* p. 133.
124. *Ibid.,* p. 134.

125. *Ibid.,* p. 135. "Dieses Verhältnis lässt formal die ganze Schöpfung wie einen grossen Symbolismus der Gnade erscheinen."
126. *Idem.* "Die Schöpfung ist «selber schon ein einziges Bundeszeichen, ein wahres Sakrament» [5, 262-263], ein «Zeichen und Zeugnis des Geschehens, das auf sie folgen wird» [5, 264]."
127. *Ibid.,* p. 138.
128. *Idem.*
129. *Idem.*
130. *Ibid.,* p. 132.
131. *Ibid.,* p. 139.

At this point Von Balthasar asks the question whether in this description of man as inherently the partner of God Barth has been true to his idea of analogy. Has he not fallen back into the monism of *Romans?* Is he not simply deducing the idea of creation from that of grace? Is not Barth bringing in man's relation to Christ in every word that he says about creation?[132] Or is this the case because Barth is, at all costs, seeking to avoid both extremes, namely, that of defining man in terms of grace alone and that of defining him without any relation to grace. Surely Barth's principle of analogy requires him to avoid falling into extremes. Only if he avoids extremes will he, according to his own view, avoid speculation.[133]

But there is another and deeper reason, says Von Balthasar, why in his attempt to do justice both to creation and to grace Barth tends constantly to overstress the latter. This deeper reason is his basic commitment to an Augustinian concept of human freedom.[134] Barth always defines human freedom in terms of the true freedom that springs from redemption.[135] When Barth discusses the problem of the providence of God, he naturally returns to the question as to what is meant by the activity and freedom of the creature. Barth speaks of man's cooperation *(Mitwerken)* with God.[136] He says that in the field of nature there is real mediation *(Vermittlung)*. Not so in the field of grace.[137] There God works alone. Yet the two fields or realms are related. And nature is subordinated to grace. So the real working of man in the realm of nature may also be spoken of as cooperation with God.[138]

Barth therefore speaks of *concursus*. And with respect to it he makes qualifications that are self-evidently acceptable to Roman Catholics too: (1) He says that human cooperation must not be thought of as being mechanical, (2) The whole relationship between God and man must always be purely personal, (3) We must not begin with a concept of highest cause under which God and man may be subsumed, (4) We must not slip into philosophy but argue on the foundation of revelation alone and (5) The whole doctrine of cooperation must therefore be explained in terms of the first article of the Christian faith. It is only in terms of this first article that all the questions pertaining to the relation of man's freedom to God receive their meaning.[139]

132. *Idem.*
133. *Ibid.*, p. 140.
134. *Idem.*
135. *Ibid.*, p. 143.

136. *Idem.*
137. *Ibid.*, p. 144.
138. *Idem.*
139. *Ibid.*, pp. 144-145.

In beginning with the sovereignty of God, the question of the possibility of human freedom in relation to it is not so much as asked. Barth takes his point of departure from it as a simple and self-evident truth.[140] It is thus that in his volume on Providence Barth has made a great advance toward his final idea of *analogia fidei*. This advance consists in his allowance of the idea of secondary causes in the realm of nature.[141] In his creatureliness and in his being a self, man is a second cause.[142]

At this point, Von Balthasar argues, Barth approaches the Roman Catholic doctrine of the relation of nature to grace. It is to the effect that nature, to be truly nature, needs inherently to be complemented by grace.[143] Secondary causality, however real it is in itself, must yet be founded in the destiny of man that is set by God.[144] It is the goal of man as placed before man by God through his grace that is the source of Barth's idea of freedom. It is also that of the Roman Catholic idea of cooperation.[145]

Von Balthasar does not mean to suggest that there is complete identity between the Roman Catholic and the Barthian view of human freedom and of second causes. He thinks that Barth stresses too much his notion of the priority of grace over nature. But the all important point is that according to Von Balthasar there is no basic difference between the Barthian and the Roman Catholic views of the relation of nature to grace.

(d) Faith and Knowledge

The question of the relation of faith and knowledge is a particularly important aspect of the general problem of nature and grace.[146] Barth's book on Anselm is the first work that interests us on this matter.

If man is the partner of God and as such has his reality from the fact that he is the brother of Jesus Christ, then his knowledge of God has its authenticity in the act of faith. Faith is the organ of

140. *Ibid.*, p. 145. 142. *Idem.*
141. *Ibid.*, p. 146.
143. *Ibid.*, pp. 146-147. "Und nun wird die Unstimmigkeit offenkundig: wenn es wahr ist, dass das Geschöpf in seinem Geschöpfsein und Selbstsein causa secunda ist, wenn es anderseits wahr ist, dass die Freiheit vom Raum der Gnade her zu interpretieren ist, dann ist der Schluss unabweisbar, dass— entgegen der protestantischen Lehre—die Kausalität des Geschöpfs gerade im Raum der Gnade ihre Eigentümlichkeit und höchste Entfaltung gewinnt."
144. *Ibid.*, p. 146. 146. *Ibid.*, p. 148.
145. *Idem.*

absolute truth, of *veritas increata,* as the organ of absolute truth is none other than faith. This is the case because the Absolute can be known by the Absolute only. And this is so because man finds his foundation in the Word of God.[147]

It is pointless, says Von Balthasar, to call this position sceptical, inasmuch as it is based upon the certainty of the Word of God in faith. It is meaningless to call this position irrational, inasmuch as it is based upon the idea of the revelation of the Logos inherent in every rational being. Finally, it is pointless to speak of this position as noetic Ontologism, inasmuch as it makes its appeal, not to a hidden vision of God, but to the recognition of the revelation of God in faith. On the other hand, we must not call Barth's position Fideism, at least not in the sense that it was used during the nineteenth century in the acts of the Vatican Council. Bautain thought in terms of Kant's philosophy. He talked of nature that had powers in itself. But Barth's basic thinking is theological.[148]

What then constitutes faith for Barth? It is not a magical capacity of a given nature. It comes from above, from the Word of God. This does not mean that it is added to nature as something foreign. On the contrary, it leads man to his own act. Through faith man's destiny toward salvation is restored in Christ.[149]

As such, faith is not a subordination of man's intellect and will to a law that comes from without, nor is it a conviction attained by the independent activity of man's judgment with respect to the objective truth of that which he believes.[150] Faith enlightens the human mind and will from within. Faith requires no sacrifice of the intellect; rather it sets the intellect free. Faith stands above all such antitheses as above and within. It is not partly the work of God and partly the work of man. "Faith is wholly the work of God and wholly the work of man, complete imprisonment and complete liberation."[151] Faith does not spring from human nature but completes it according to the purpose of the Creator.[152] It is therefore participation in the action of God.[153] Grounded in the Word of God, it is at the same time wholly the act of man.[154] God reveals and hides himself in earthly things. And faith looks through earthly things toward God.[155]

147. *Ibid.,* p. 149.
148. *Ibid.,* p. 151.
149. *Ibid.,* p. 152.
150. *Idem.*
151. *Idem.*
152. *Idem.*
153. *Ibid.,* p. 153.
154. *Idem.*
155. *Idem.*

The Christological foundation of this view of the relation of faith and reason lies in the fact that Jesus Christ is both the ontological and the epistemological foundation of creation. Man is real because he is related to God through the grace that comes to him in Christ. So also this real or true man has true knowledge because it has its foundation in Christ.[156]

Barth therefore believes in a *Veritas increata,* but only when it is properly and immediately founded on the grace of God in Christ. According to Barth, Roman Catholicism fails to give human knowledge this proper foundation. Barth does believe that God reveals himself in nature, but this revelation must never become a quality of nature.[157]

According to Barth, it was Anselm who gave human knowledge its proper Christological foundation. He maintained the primacy of faith. At the same time, he showed that the unbelief of the "fool" consists in the fact that he does not believe in his own faith.[158] God has created man as able to receive the revelation of God. It is true that, when Brunner spoke about such a thing, Barth said *Nein* to him. But in his *Church Dogmatics* Barth has materially altered his view. In it he is more sympathetic toward the position of Brunner.

Of course this does not mean that Barth wants to return to the idea of natural theology. The Christological foundation of all human knowledge must, argues Barth, be at all costs maintained. But this point itself requires that man be inherently one who can receive revelation.[159] Man cannot help but perceive God.

It may now be clear, says Von Balthasar, how Barth can seemingly both deny and affirm man's ability to perceive God.[160] Barth denies man's ability to start from his own self-consciousness in order to work up to God. Barth affirms man's ability to know God in that, beginning with the revelation of God he sees himself for what he is, dependent upon God. A truly theological anthropology thinks of faith as man's unavoidable perception of God.[161]

156. *Ibid.,* p. 154.   158. *Ibid.,* p. 158.
157. *Ibid.,* p. 155.
159. *Ibid.,* p. 166. "Wir können formulieren: der Mensch ist dazu geschaffen und als Geschöpf von Natur dazu ausgerüstet, Gott in allen Dingen zu begegnen und zu finden und darum auch finden zu *können.*"
160. *Ibid.,* p. 168.
161. *Idem.* "Der Glaube aber fällt überein mit dem echten Vernehmen, das heisst mit dem Urakt der Vernunft."

(e) Sin

From the preceding, it now becomes clear why Barth no longer thinks of sin as simple contradiction but as an "impossible possibility."[162] In the *Römerbrief*, the relation of revelation and faith was simply expressed by the principle of identity. On this basis sin had to be thought of as non-being. To avoid this conclusion, Barth insisted that redemption is the ultimate or original reality which overtakes and envelops contradiction. The idea of dialecticism was involved in this view of the relation of sin and salvation. The identity of the subject as sinner and the same subject as justified was that of a mathematical point.[163] Even so, the transition from sinner to saint did not wholly destroy the subject that was changed.[164]

At a later stage, Barth stresses the fact that the subject that is changed by redemption is still the same subject that it was before redemption.[165] This subject is moreover now constantly seen in the light of Christ. In Christ the contrast between God and man is overcome. In Christ there is no contradiction but only obedience. By his incarnation, the chaos in the world is already sublated. Through Christ there is peace between God and man.[166] It is thus that man's opposition to God has become an impossible possibility.[167] It is *impossible* in Christ who has made it impossible *(aufgelöst hat)*. It is still *possible* in man who, though he is in fact a brother in Christ, nevertheless says *no* to this fact.[168] When man resists the salvation that is his in Christ, then he acts in contradiction with his own nature. Thus there is an essential relation *(seinshafter Beziehung)* which cannot be broken by sin.

In his book on Anselm, Barth discussed the difference between the ontical and the noetical *ratio* in the creature. According to Barth, both of these rest in the uncreated *ratio veritatis* which, in turn, is identical with the *ratio summae naturae*, i.e., the divine Word, consubstantial with the Father. The divine Word is the measure of both that which is ontical and that which is noetic in the creature.[169]

By what right then, asks Von Balthasar, does Barth set the ontic *ratio* above the noetic *ratio*?[170] Man's actual knowledge, i.e., the

162. *Ibid.*, p. 169.
163. *Idem.*
164. *Idem.*
165. *Ibid.*, p. 170.
166. *Idem.*

167. *Idem.*
168. *Idem.*
169. *Ibid.*, p. 171.
170. *Ibid.*, p. 172.

noetic *ratio,* is said to depend upon man's moment by moment decisions, while in his ontic *ratio* truth is present to him constantly. The ontic *ratio* is that which has not been because it could not be destroyed by sin. Therefore the noetic *ratio* must first be measured by the ontic *ratio* as its immediate standard in order that afterward, and only through the ontic *ratio,* it may be measured by the divine Word.

But why, asks Von Balthasar, cannot the knowledge structure of man, i.e., the noetic *ratio,* be said to be a reflection of the original subject which is God, as the ontic *ratio* is said to be a reflection of the original object which is God? And why, therefore, should sin have any more effect on the one than on the other? The *act* of knowledge involves, to be sure, decision, but it rests on a structure of knowledge *(Erkenntnis-Natur)* which, however corrupt the act may be, remains intact.[171] It must always be remembered that spontaneity is an aspect of the nature of knowledge and cannot be destroyed by sin.[172]

There is therefore no reason why Barth should not, on his own view, recognize the apriori character of the spontaneity of human thought. He has, to be sure, asserted that God can be known by himself only.[173] But did he not himself explain that this fact does not exclude a partnership between God and man?[174] A spontaneity of faith as well as of unbelief can be maintained only if nature and all its powers be, from the outset, interpreted Christologically. Disobedience on the part of the creature is, from the outset, disobedience against Christ.

(f) *Analogia Entis*

It appears then that a properly conceived concept of *analogia entis* is quite in accord with Barth's own idea of the *analogia fidei.* If properly conceived the idea of *analogia entis* is one in which the entire concept of nature is seen to be inherently in need of complementation through grace. We then have an *analogia entis* within the *analogia fidei.*[175] Man is then seen to be created not *as* in but *unto* covenant relationship.[176] In the idea of *potentia oboedientialis,* the concept of *analogia entis* is seen to be a function of the *analogia*

171. *Ibid.,* p. 173.
172. *Idem.*
173. *Ibid.,* p. 174.
174. *Idem.*
175. *Ibid.,* p. 179.
176. *Ibid.,* p. 180.

fidei.[177] In viewing the matter thus, we perceive that God enables the creature to do what in itself it could not do, namely, to outreach itself and thus to attain to its intended meaning.[178]

5. *Praedestinatio Gemina*

It is now time to recall, says Von Balthasar, that from the beginning Barth was zealous for the triumph of the grace of God. If at first he spoke of the absoluteness of God as though it were a consuming fire, it soon appeared that the wrath and judgment of God must be regarded as forms of his grace. This idea of the triumph of the grace of God finds its climactic expression in his doctrine of election.[179] All the ways and works of God have their source in grace.[180] There is no created nature that does not derive its final meaning from grace.[181] The election of grace is accordingly inherently universal in nature. To be sure, election is always double election; it involves rejection as well as acceptance. But the rejection is subordinate to the acceptance. The gospel is wholly and exclusively good tidings.[182] In creation we find the realization of cosmos and, in a secondary and accompanying fashion, the exclusion of chaos.[183] In all their godlessness and perversity, the reprobate cannot bring upon themselves the wrath of God inasmuch as Christ has borne this for them.[184] And in all their opposition to one another the elect and the reprobate are brethren in Christ.[185] The church is for Barth an inherently dynamic notion.[186]

It is true, says Von Balthasar, that Barth rejects the idea of *Apokatastasis.*[187] But he rejects this notion because it is based upon a view of nature that is not, from the outset, Christological.[188] Even so, says Von Balthasar, the idea of the all-inclusiveness of salvation is built into the very foundation of Barth's theology.[189] Man's origin and destiny is in Christ. For this reason sin is an impossible possibility. When man sins, he sins against his own nature. It is this

177. *Ibid.*, p. 181.
178. *Idem.*
181. *Ibid.*, p. 187. "Es gibt keine geschaffene Natur, die nicht aus der Gnade ihr Dasein, ihr Wesen und ihren Bestand hätte, und die in ihrem Dasein, Wesen und Bestand anders als wieder durch die Gnade erkannt werden könnte."
182. *Ibid.*, p. 188.
183. *Ibid.*, p. 190.
184. *Ibid.*, p. 193.
185. *Ibid.*, p. 194.

179. *Ibid.*, p. 186.
180. *Idem.*
186. *Ibid.*, p. 197.
187. *Ibid.*, p. 199.
188. *Idem.*
189. *Ibid.*, p. 200.

inherently universal nature of the triumph of grace that constitutes the great passion of Barth's theology.[190]

6. Die Denkform

All that has been said so far may now be concentrated in the idea that Barth's major concept is that of *Act*. Barth seeks to start all his thinking from the point of the highest reality. To say this is, in effect, the same as to say that Barth interprets all things Christologically. For Christ is wholly and exclusively the history of the divine salvation of all and every man.[191] Here we have what may be called "intensive universality."[192]

Every man must be seen in the light of this Christ.[193] In all this we have, says Von Balthasar, the basic thought-form of Barth's theology, and the approach of Scholasticism is not basically different from this. For it too act precedes potentiality. Only Scholasticism has not applied this principle to the relation of nature to history.[194]

7. Die Herkunft

The source of Barth's type of thinking, says Von Balthasar, must obviously be found in German idealism, and, from Schleiermacher's

190. *Idem.* Nur darum kann ja der Mensch existieren, weil er von der Gnade Christi herkommt und auf sie hingeht, nur darum bleibt seine Natur auch in der Sünde konstant und nicht endgültig verdorben, weil sie durch die Gnade Christi vor dem totalen Abfall bewahrt wird, ja nur darum kann er letztlich überhaupt sündigen, weil er seine Erlösung, nur darum ungläubig sein, weil er seinen Glauben nicht wahrhaben will. Darum ist ja Sünde nicht einfach eine Möglichkeit, sondern eine «unmögliche Möglichkeit». Um diesen Preis hat Barth seine lückenlose Systematik der oeconomia saluti durchzuführen vermocht. Das gibt ihr ihre unerreichte Geschlossenheit, ihre Siegesgewissheit, ihre trumphale Allüre.

191. *Ibid.,* p. 208. "«Er ist ganz und gar und ausschliesslich die Geschichte der göttlichen Rettung für alle und jeden Menschen. Der Mensch—dieser Mensch—existiert also, indem diese Geschichte geschieht. Er ist selbst diese Geschichte» [6, 81]."

192. *Ibid.,* p. 210.

193. *Ibid.,* p. 209. Der Mensch ist Hörer des Wortes, oder er ist nichts [4, 832]; er ist Geschichte, oder er ist nichts [6, 188, 297], er steht im Ereignis der göttlichen Offenbarung [6, 418f.), oder er stünde sonst im Nichts. Aber wiederum sind diese Aussagen keine solchen, die die «Natur» des Menschen als solche beschreiben, sondern jenes freie, gnadenhafte Geschehen Gottes, das die ganze Sphäre der Natur allererst begründet: «Von ihm her *ist* sein Wesen und seine Existenz . . .

194. *Ibid.,* p. 203.

scheme of thinking, Barth has never been able to set himself free.[195] Of course, he adds, this says nothing as to the theological value of his views.[196] After all, a philosophical scheme is only a form that may be filled with any content. And the content of Barth's theology is not identical with that of German idealism.[197] Barth wants to be a theologian, nothing else.[198] Granted he learned to think out his theology, when young, in idealistic categories, still he was aware of what he was doing. After all, why should revelation be limited in its expression to one thought-form?[199]

8. Idealism and Revelation

Shall we then still speak of a system of theology in connection with Barth?[200] Is there an inner necessity in the development of his thought (innern Systemzwang)?[201] The answer to this question may best be found by looking again at his view of predestination, for this leads us at once to the basically existential character of Barth's theology, namely, his category of Act.[202] In terms of Act, God's victory of grace is accomplished, but for this very reason man can speak of this grace in broken language only.[203]

(a) THE WORD AND FAITH

Even so, as was noted, Barth turned from the pure Actualism of the Römerbrief toward the idea of analogy.[204] This turning toward analogy does not imply a change in the basic act-character of his view of revelation. The "factual necessity" of the primacy of revelation is still maintained. But the idealistic construction of the circle of his thought was henceforth broken.[205] We now have the idea of the free confrontation of God and man.

(b) DIALECTICISM AND JUDGMENT

German idealism was a method of thought in which by means of the idea of contradiction and its dynamic resolution, the essence of

195. Ibid., p. 201.
196. Ibid., p. 211.
197. Ibid., p. 215.
198. Ibid., p. 228.
199. Ibid., p. 229.
200. Ibid., p. 229.
201. Ibid., p. 230.
202. Ibid., p. 231.
203. Ibid., p. 233.
204. Ibid., p. 236.
205. Idem.

reality was said to be nature and spirit.[206] Using this method in the *Römerbrief*, Barth resolved every genuine relation between God and the creature, and attained to a Pantheism of a pure actualistic and eschatological hue.[207] In turning away from this dialecticism toward analogy, i.e., toward the recognition of the idea that the divine and the human can be united in Christ, Barth broke both with the static (Kierkegaard) and the dynamic (Schelling, Hegel) forms of dialecticism as an exclusive method in theology. When, after this, Barth uses the dialectical method it is no longer philosophical but purely theological. When, after this, Barth sees, for example, contrasts of light and darkness in the universe, the contrasts are not dialectical. They do not, as such, indicate opposition to God. Creation is no longer identified with sin.[208] Creation as such is said to be good. It is only the "infamous trick" of evil *(des Nichtigen)* that brings opposition to God.[209] God's judgment no longer rests on creation as such but on the evil that is operative in it.[210]

A new problem appears herewith, and it is strictly theological. In this change toward analogy, the act-character of revelation is, if possible, more basic than ever. Everything now depends on the *no* and *yes* of God. There is no systematic relation between them that is traceable by man.[211] One cannot say that the lie (which is the essence of *das Nichtige)* has a place in the system of truth. And herewith the non-existent character of evil is given all the greater emphasis.[212]

It is on this basis that Barth can go so far as to say that in the incarnation God makes himself the object of his own wrath.[213] Thus evil derives its "reality" inasfar as it is the correlate of the divine *no*, and this means that evil is an "unreality" so far as it is only an accompanying function of the divine *yes*.[214] And demons are in the same position as *"das Nichtige."* They are only inauthentic.[215] One cannot say that God has created them, for he hates nothing that he has created. Neither can one say that God sustains them; their

206. *Ibid.*, p. 238.
207. *Idem.*
208. *Idem.*
209. *Ibid.*, pp. 238-239.
210. *Ibid.*, p. 239.
211. *Ibid.*, p. 240.
212. *Idem.* "Das Nichtige ist, von Gottes Standort aus, das absolut Nicht-seinsollende und, weil Gott allmächtig ist, Nichtseiende, und wenn der Mensch es gegen das Urteil Gottes dennoch als seiend setzt, dann setzt er das Nicht-seiende als seiend, das Unmögliche als möglich. Sünde ist «unmögliche Möglichkeit»."
213. *Ibid.*, p. 241.
214. *Ibid.*, p. 242.
215. *Ibid.*, p. 243.

reality consists in their being an expression of rejection, and as such move toward the eternal fire and disappearance.[216]

(c) THE CONCRETE AND HISTORY

It remains to note that according to Von Balthasar, Barth's theology has gone beyond idealism in his view of Christ as the *concretissimum* in which God is for the world as the world is for God. Barth now deals with concrete reality.[217] In the historicity of Christ *(die Geschichtlichkeit Christi)* we have the measure of all things else.[218] Christ, in his work, is the ground of the reality of creation *(Realgrund der Schöpfung)*. So he is also the ground of human obligation.[219] Only as we begin from Christ can we understand human freedom.[220]

In conclusion, then, it must be said that Barth used the transcendental categories of idealistic philosophy as a means for the expression of his Christological theology. These categories were his servants. Even so, says Von Balthasar, it must also be maintained that Barth has not altogether escaped a tendency toward systematization.[221] His tendency toward systematization is discovered in the fact that, though he admits a place to the *humanum,* he frequently deduces its place from the idea of the priority of Christ.[222] It is here that the Roman Catholic senses Barth's Protestantism.[223] True, Barth denies that he seeks to deduce the meaning of nature from Christ. Yet, he frequently speaks of Christ as the true man as if remaining humanity were only an *Epiphänomen Christi.*[224]

This is a serious point. For if it is true that Christ is the prius of nature, then he is also the prius of sin. Then his cross is not conditioned by sin but by his eternally planned self-revelation. On this basis, a final condemnation of sinners is possible.[225]

9. The Thought-Form of Roman Catholic Theology

What then must be the final evaluation of Barth's theology by a Roman Catholic theologian? The criterion to be employed as we answer this question is the Roman Catholic thought-form. But this

216. *Idem.*
217. *Ibid.,* p. 244.
218. *Ibid.,* p. 245.
219. *Ibid.,* p. 246.
220. *Ibid.,* p. 247.

221. *Ibid.,* p. 253.
222. *Ibid.,* p. 254.
223. *Idem.*
224. *Ibid.,* p. 255.
225. *Ibid.,* pp. 255-256.

is not to be identified with the idea of *analogia entis*. The church as such has no metaphysics; it wants merely to proclaim the grace of God in Christ.[226]

Of course Roman Catholic theologians use, as Barth uses, philosophical categories. And they too must be careful not to allow their theology to degenerate into a process of Egress and Regress after the pattern of Origen. Barth's doctrine of predestination is controlled by such a scheme.[227] This same scheme has, in the past, had a detrimental influence on Roman Catholic theology.[228] But the basic thought-form of Roman Catholic thought is not this Egress-Regress scheme. The basic thought-form of Patristic thought and even of that of St. Thomas is that the idea of the *analogia entis* is subordinate to the idea of the *analogia fidei*. Roman Catholics used Greek categories of thought only for the purpose of establishing the proper order between these two.[229] Accordingly, the only fruitful question to be discussed between Barth and Roman Catholic thought is their relative faithfulness to Christ as the *Concretissimum*.[230]

10. The Nature Concept of Roman Catholic Theology

If Barth thinks that the Roman Catholic view of nature makes it unfaithful to the primacy of the *analogia fidei*, this is based on a mistake. Roman Catholic theologians think of the idea of pure nature as a limiting concept.[231] As such, it does not pretend to be intelligible without the supernatural order, the order of grace. According to them, the very idea of nature is interpreted in terms of the primacy of grace. Only through grace can man participate in the divine nature.[232] And this is the divinely ordained goal of man.[233] Barth's radical Christocentric vision is therefore quite possible for Roman Catholic theology.[234] Roman Catholic thought does want to maintain a distinction between the order of nature and that of grace.[235] But even Przywara, the great defender of the idea of *analogia entis*, held to the primacy of the *analogia fidei*.[236] Surely Christ is the ground of creation.[237]

In recent Roman Catholic thought there is a great desire to center

226. *Ibid.*, p. 266.
227. *Ibid.*, p. 271.
228. *Ibid.*, p. 272.
229. *Ibid.*, p. 273.
230. *Ibid.*, p. 278.
231. *Ibid.*, p. 294.

232. *Ibid.*, p. 297.
233. *Ibid.*, p. 298.
234. *Ibid.*, p. 320.
235. *Ibid.*, p. 334.
236. *Ibid.*, p. 338.
237. *Ibid.*, pp. 336-344.

the entire meaning of history in Christ.[238] The same is true of all leading Protestant theologians.[239] Both groups of thinkers are seeking to overcome the historicism of the nineteenth and the existentialism of the twentieth centuries.[240] As the true *scientia de singularibus,* theology must make the incarnate Logos the norm and consummation of all genuine *Logoi* in nature and history.[241]

It must even be said, argues Von Balthasar, that Roman Catholic thought is more genuinely Christocentric than is that of Barth. As already noted, due to his Protestant background Barth tended to narrow down his Christology. It was unfortunate that the Reformers wanted to build their theology on a philosophical principle, namely, that of nominalism.[242] Barth's narrowing down of his Christological principle, as noted, springs from this source. It is well to insist on the primacy of the order of grace. But the first act of the human mind cannot be grace or there would be no grace.[243] It is in the very interest of maintaining the true primacy of grace that Roman Catholic theology insists on a relative independence of nature.[244] If we are not to reduce grace itself to an aspect of a philosophical system, then the human factor must be respected as well as the divine.[245] Only if this is done is there room for the idea of genuine appropriation and cooperation.[246]

The very idea of man's supernatural goal, of his participation in the being of God, can be best maintained on this Roman Catholic view. Barth first made the idea of Act and Decision central in his thought. This led him to a Theopanismus, a dialectical sublation of the creature, into God. But true grace does not signify the destruction of man. It signifies rather his participation in deity. To attain this goal, the Act in terms of which the whole relation of God to man must be interpreted is the act of the incarnation. For only in the incarnation is there genuine unity without identity between God and man. Roman Catholic thought simply draws out the full significance of this fact. There is real and genuine change of being in man

---

238. *Ibid.,* p. 344.
239. *Ibid.,* p. 345.
240. *Idem.*
241. *Ibid.,* p. 346. "Die Person Jesu Christi in ihrer geschichtlichen Einmaligkeit und ewigen Herrlichkeit ist selbst die Kategorie, welche Sein, Tun und Lehre des Christlichen bestimmt . . ."
242. *Ibid.,* p. 345; *cf.* also 278.
243. *Ibid.,* p. 372.
244. *Idem.*
245. *Idem.*
246. *Idem.*

even while he is in this world. This indicates that the full implication of the idea of act is that of being.[247]

Barth has recently himself rejected his earlier overdrawn eschatologism.[248] He now no longer thinks merely in terms of *Urgeschichte*. He wants Christ to come into our history.[249] This really involves the idea of the participation of man in the divine nature even in this life. Even Reformers did not entirely neglect this teaching.[250] We need a real participation in the merits of Christ, and this not only in the passive but also in the active sense of the term.[251] The grace of God is participation in the inner life of God. As such it is a gift of God. This gift is neither purely forensic nor purely eschatological. It is real, internal and present.[252] To be properly thought of, this participation must be thought of as the act of God by which the being of man is changed.[253]

In his conclusion, Von Balthasar takes note of a general rapprochement as between several leading Roman Catholic theologians and Barth. The remaining differences between them, he says, are really not more basic than differences between Protestant or between Roman Catholic theologians.[254] Of course, says Von Balthasar, we have not discussed the complex of questions centering around the ideas of the church and the sacraments.[255] But so far as the basic problems of nature and grace are concerned, there is no basic difference. Why does Barth continue to reason as though there were a fundamental difference between him and Roman Catholic theology on this point? When Barth interprets his *analogia fidei* Christologically, then it includes the idea of *analogia entis*. Similarly, when Roman Catholic theologians properly interpret their idea of *analogia entis*, then they subordinate it to the idea of the *analogia fidei*.[256] Both seek for a truly Christocentric theology, and therein the two forms of theology can be harmonized.[257]

11. *Evaluation of Von Balthasar's Argument*

Von Balthasar has given a thorough and fair oversight of the development of Barth's theology. Barth is not to be judged any

247. *Ibid.*, p. 374.
248. *Ibid.*, p. 375.
249. *Ibid.*, p. 377.
250. *Ibid.*, p. 381.
251. *Ibid.*, p. 382.
252. *Ibid.*, p. 386.
253. *Idem.*
254. *Ibid.*, p. 389.
255. *Idem.*
256. *Ibid.*, p. 390.
257. *Idem.*

longer by the principle of dialecticism that he espoused in his earlier work. On the other hand, Barth has been remarkably true to himself throughout his work. Barth's substitution of the idea of the analogy of faith for the idea of dialecticism does not indicate a radical change in the method of his thought. There has, indeed, been a change. One must take due note of it. Even so, the change from dialecticism to analogy is a change that takes place within the general overarching activist notion of revelation. According to this notion of revelation, God is wholly revealed and wholly hidden in his revelation. Von Balthasar is not mistaken when he appeals to this basic principle as the criterion by which he must measure the relationship of Barth's theology to that of the Roman Catholic church. Barth has not changed his basic view of revelation. And the all important point is that Von Balthasar as a Roman Catholic theologian expresses basic agreement with this principle. This fact has significance of the most basic sort in opposite directions.

In the first place, it calls attention to the fact that Barth and Von Balthasar together stand utterly opposed to the principle of the Reformation. Von Balthasar calls Barth the theologian in whom the principle of the Reformation has come to its most consistent expression. But he also says that in a certain sense Barth has both relativized and radicalized the Reformers' principle of revelation. He has done this by means of his idea that revelation expresses the whole of God's being and that the whole of God's being is wholly hidden in this his complete revelation. This radicalizing of the Reformation principle amounts to a radical rejection of that principle.

In the second place, Von Balthasar finds the basic unity between his own theology and that of Barth in this *radical* Protestantism of Barth. Von Balthasar makes no effort to show how his Roman Catholic theology can be harmonized in principle with the Protestant theology of Barth in terms of a common submission to the Bible as the direct and finished revelation of God. On the contrary, their discussion is to be carried forth on the common presupposition that such a thing must not be done. When the methodology of the Reformers is mentioned at all, it is assumed, if it is not stated, that they are wrong. This appears pointedly in the fact that so far as Barth's earlier view, that is, his dialectical method, is said to be mistaken, this is said to be due to the fact that at that time he had not yet fully outgrown the speculative notion of the Reformers to the effect that God works *alone* in salvation.

When Barth turned away from the speculation of the Reformers toward a more truly Christological approach, Von Balthasar argues, then he, at the same time, did better justice to the reality of man as a creature in distinction from man as sinful. As a consequence, he then no longer thought of the circle of the saving work of God as taking place exclusively within the divine being. He then realized that God is identical with his incarnation in Christ, and therewith man was accorded the proper place in the scheme of salvation. Therewith too the priority or primacy of grace over nature has really been preserved. According to Von Balthasar, then, Barth has been able to preserve the primacy of grace only because he departed from the views of the Reformers and developed his own idea of the Christ-Event.

It was this primacy of grace that Roman Catholic theology has always been concerned to maintain. Long before the day of the Reformation, Von Balthasar contends, the Church taught its members that man has a supernatural goal and that it is only by grace that this supernatural goal can be attained. For the Church the independence of nature is therefore always subject to this primacy of the supernatural grace of God. Without presupposing this supernatural grace, man cannot even be maintained as man. The very notion of *liberum arbitrium* must serve the primacy of the grace of God in Christ.

If the Reformers had been concerned to maintain the sovereignty of the grace of God, says Von Balthasar, then they might better have remained within the church. Seeking to defend such sovereignty by means of a speculative nominalism in the way that Luther did in reality constitutes an attack on this sovereignty. Not only is it the sovereignty of grace that is best maintained in the Church, but the same is true for its unity and universality. For if man's nature is inherently in need of supernatural grace for its true fulfillment, then grace is inherently universal.

The Roman Catholic theologian is, accordingly, in agreement with Barth's basic Christological approach and with his idea of the primacy of the analogy of faith. On the fundamental questions of creation, of incarnation and of salvation, the differences between Barth's Protestantism and his, i.e., Von Balthasar's, own Roman Catholicism are not such as to warrant separate church existence.[258]

With this judgment of Von Balthasar it is impossible to disagree.

258. *Ibid.*, p. 393.

When Berkouwer writes a book on *Conflict with Rome*, he speaks frequently of the dynamical categories of Roman Catholic thought. The church is said to be the continuation of the incarnation.[259] Roman Catholic theologians do not hesitate to speak of the identity between the church and Christ.[260] In every conceivable direction, this notion of the identity of the church with Christ is worked out.[261] Of course, the identity spoken of is not absolute. There is difference within this identity.[262]

The basic objection of the Reformation to Roman Catholic thinking springs from the fact that on the basis of its idea of identity, the place of Christ as the head of the church has been compromised.[263] Roman Catholic theology will not give its thought captive to the obedience of Christ as he speaks in his word.[264] The Church refused to test the question of heresy by the exegesis of Scripture alone (Chapter 2). It was because the Reformers did measure the church by the Word that the Council of Trent condemned their theology of grace. The Church's course of action was guided by the twilight of its identity principle.[265]

Because of its identity principle, the Church took for granted that man did not become spiritually impotent through the fall in Adam. Its view of man may, in consequence, be spoken of as anthropological optimism.[266] This optimism is not to be identified with humanism.[267] Yet the church rejected the idea of the radical ethical depravity of man as taught in Scripture.[268] The punishment that man was to receive for sin is described in negative terms.[269]

The conclusion must be that, though the Roman Catholic church speaks and speaks emphatically[270] of sovereign grace, this fact must be seen in the light of the frame of reference of its theology as a whole.[271] So also when Calvin and the Reformed Confessions speak of some light of nature and some remnants of the image of God remaining in man even after his fall into sin, this too must be seen in the light of their theology as a whole.[272] Only by regarding the teachings on sin and grace in each case in the framework of which

---

259. Berkouwer, *Conflict met Rome*, Eng. tr. (Pres. Ref. Pub. Co.), p. 31.
260. *Ibid.*, p. 30.
261. *Ibid.*, p. 31.   267. *Idem.*
262. *Ibid.*, p. 33.   268. *Ibid.*, p. 126.
263. *Ibid.*, p. 38.   269. *Ibid.*, p. 127.
264. *Ibid.*, p. 46.   270. *Ibid.*, p. 130.
265. *Ibid.*, p. 88.   271. *Ibid.*, p. 132.
266. *Ibid.*, p. 125.   272. *Ibid.*, p. 133.

they form a part can we see them for what they are. And, thus regarded, it appears that there is a deep religious-ethical difference between Romanism and the Reformation. It is a difference "of the first order."[273]

On the basis of its principle of identity, Roman Catholic thought thinks of the church as a prolongation of the incarnation. This gives to its view of the incarnation a "universal cosmological structure."[274] Thus Roman Catholic theologians employ the idea of "progressive incarnation." Mascall, e.g., says that "we may indeed see the effects of the incarnation in a gradual supernaturalisation of the whole created order."[275]

It is, we conclude, not difficult to see why Von Balthasar, using such a dynamical principle welcomes the development of Protestant theology by means of the activist categories employed by Barth. These activist categories of Barth's theology are not basically different from the dynamic categories of Von Balthasar. The Christ constructed in terms of Barth's activism is not appreciably different from the Christ constructed in terms of Von Balthasar's dynamism. Barth too speaks of the identity of the being of the church with that of Christ. But, as in the case of Romanism the identity of Christ with his church is dynamic, so, in the case of Barth, this identity is that of pure act. And, as it is the dynamics of Rome that accounts for its opposition to the finished character of God's revelation in Christ and in Scripture as conceived of by the Reformers, so it is the idea of revelation as pure act that accounts for Barth's opposition to the Reformers' view of Christ and of Scripture.

273. *Ibid.*, p. 134.   275. *Ibid.*, p. 281.
274. *Ibid.*, p. 275.

Chapter XIV

Hans Küng

A second Roman Catholic theologian to be discussed is Hans Küng. As the title of his work indicates, Küng deals with Barth's teaching on justification. He, as well as Von Balthasar, is interested in asking whether the theology of Barth represents a Protestant approach to the Roman Catholic position.

Barth's basic objection to the Roman Catholic doctrine of justification, says Küng, is not valid. Roman Catholic theology is as much interested in the gracious sovereignty of God as is Barth. And this sovereignty can come to expression in the Roman Catholic doctrines of election, creation and redemption as well as in Barth's theology. In fact, this sovereignty is for Roman Catholic thought the absolute measure of all other problems.[1] Roman Catholic teaching is in agreement with Barth when he seeks to stress the theocentric aspect of grace.[2]

Moreover, both the Barthian and the Roman Catholic doctrines of justification must be studied in the light of the total theology of which they are a part. When thus considered, it appears all the more clearly that the Catholic and the Barthian doctrines of justification are not essentially different from one another.

It is of interest to note that Küng's book contains an accompanying letter by Barth. In this letter Barth says that Küng has represented his views fairly. He adds that, if Küng's views on justification are truly those of his church, then his own views are also in basic agreement with those of the church.[3]

1. Hans Küng, *Rechtfertigung—Die Lehre Karl Barths Und Eine Katholische Besinnung*, Paderborn, p. 272.
2. *Ibid.*, p. 201.   3. *Ibid.*, p. 12.

With these few remarks as our background, we now turn to a brief analysis of the argument of Küng's work.

Küng's work is divided into two parts. In the first part he sets forth Barth's view and in the second part he sets forth the Roman Catholic view of justification. After that, he makes his comparison between the two views.

1. Barth's View of Justification

The first part is divided into two sections. The first of these sections deals with the framework of Barth's theology. The second deals with the doctrine of justification in the light of this framework.

It is getting monotonous, says Küng, to hear people speak of Barth's theology as being dialectical. Surely Von Balthasar has shown clearly that Barth has gone on from dialecticism to analogy.[4] Von Balthasar seems also to have convinced Barth of the fact that the idea of the *analogia entis* does not adequately express the central point of Roman Catholic theology. At least since the appearance of Von Balthasar's book in 1951, Barth no longer used the idea of the analogy of being as the epitome of Roman Catholic thought. Even so, we must examine whether Barth's objection to Roman Catholic thought is still basically what it was before the appearance of Von Balthasar's book.

The first two parts of volume four of the *Church Dogmatics* appeared in 1953 and 1955 respectively.[5] In these books Barth deals specifically with the doctrine of reconciliation. In them the question of justification is discussed from every possible point of view.[6] We shall therefore be chiefly concerned with these volumes.

Barth is, above all else, concerned with thinking *from above*. For him this means thinking from the point of view of the supremacy of God. In the whole of his doctrine of reconciliation, Barth speaks in terms of Christ. This implies negatively that the "Christian triad of covenant, sin and reconciliation must not be understood in Hegelian fashion."[7] Von Balthasar has spoken well of Barth's use of idealist thought forms.[8] The use of these thought-forms does not as such make Barth a heretic. Moreover, Barth passed through a genuine development. As Augustine carried with him the effects of his early Neoplatonism and Manicheanism all his life, so, no doubt, Barth

4. *Ibid.*, p. 18.
5. *Ibid.*, p. 17.
6. *Ibid.*, p. 18.

7. *Ibid.*, p. 41.
8. *Ibid.*, p. 21.

will carry with him all his life the effects of his idealistic style of
thought and of his anti-humanistic existentialism.[9]

Thinking "from above" signifies for Barth positively to start from
Christ as the electing God and the elected man. To start thus
Christologically is, at the same time, to start theologically. For we
know God only in Christ. When we speak of the attributes of God,
we do not, according to Barth, speak of anything but the grace of
God to man in Christ. For each of the attributes of God is identical
with the whole of the essence of God. Each attribute is a form of
love in which God is free or a form of freedom in which God loves.[10]
What God is in himself he is, therefore, also *for us* in his electing
grace.[11]

Following upon his doctrine of God comes Barth's discussion of
his works. First comes his doctrine of creation. In its deepest meaning, the doctrine of creation is the doctrine of reconciliation. The
work of creation is not as such to be identified with reconciliation.
But reconciliation and consummation presuppose creation and therefore begin with it.[12] As a result, the doctrine of justification is to be
regarded in this broad context of God's electing grace in Christ
toward man effected through creation, reconciliation and consummation.

What Küng presents, by way of fuller elucidation of this context
in which Barth sets his view of justification, may now be given under
the following heads.

a. THE ETERNAL GROUND OF JUSTIFICATION

As noted, for Barth the justification of sinners is based upon
God's electing grace in Christ.[13] From all eternity God determines
himself for sinful man and sinful man for himself. It is in this
eternal self-determination that God is God. He is God as the one
who does his work of creation, reconciliation and consummation. It
is as such too that he is the justifying God.[14]

Inasmuch then as in his electing grace God determines himself
for sinners and sinners for himself, there are two questions that
must at once be faced. In the first place, does not God's election or
predetermination of his creature destroy the genuine self-existence

9. *Ibid.*, p. 271.   12. *Idem.*
10. *Ibid.*, p. 127.   13. *Ibid.*, p. 29.
11. *Ibid.*, p. 27.   14. *Idem.*

of this creature? Barth contends that it does not. On the contrary, it is within the original electing act of God that the independence and full reality of the creature is founded.[15] In the second place, we must note that election is election of *sinful* creatures. Does not then their election in Christ virtually deny the reality of their sin? Barth answers that predestination is not a particular act of God. It is the act that precedes and includes creation, reconciliation and consummation. Jesus Christ is the elected man. Other men are elected in the one man Jesus of Nazareth. Every man participates in Christ's election. Every man participates in Christ's creatureliness, which as such is already the gift of grace. Every man participates in his adoption, which is grace in pre-eminent fashion.[16]

Election is, for Barth, inherently double election *(praedestinatio gemina)*. If there is election, there is also reprobation. But the reprobation falls upon Christ. Reprobation is not meant for man. God takes reprobation upon himself in his Son.[17] The sinless one takes sin upon himself and therewith its punishment, condemnation, death and hell. Christ suffers for all. Christ is the only one rejected of the Father, in order that in him we all might be the elect of the Father. For it is the positive side of predestination that constitutes its reality and meaning.[18] The *no* of reprobation is subordinate to the *yes* of election.[19] Even when a man claims to stand where Christ alone can stand for all, he can only affirm what he attempts to deny. "The one truth is and remains: the election of *all* rejected men in Christ Jesus, who as the reprobate is the elect: election to God's kingdom, to salvation and to eternal life. On this, man's justification is founded."[20] The justification of sinners in time is possible and real because God has from eternity chosen condemnation in his Son for himself and forgiveness for sinners.[21]

b. The Covenant as Presupposition of Justification

In describing Barth's view of justification more specifically, Küng goes on to deal with the question of the covenant. For Barth its all-

---

15. *Ibid.*, p. 32.
16. *Ibid.*, p. 30.
17. *Idem.*
18. *Ibid.*, p. 31. Gott wählt für sich Verdammnis, Tod und Hölle, um für den Menschen zu wählen das Überströmen seiner Herrlichkeit, die Seligkeit und das ewige Leben.
19. *Idem.*
20. *Idem.*
21. *Idem.*

enveloping character is the important point. Without the idea of the covenant, justification, and with it the whole of reconciliation, might appear to be of only relative importance. It might appear as pertaining not to all but to some men only.

Undoubtedly, justification is a reaction to human sin as something that comes between (Zwischenfall), but this fact does not make justification an arbitrary thing. It is anything but that, for the eternal will of God's covenant is established through justification in reconciliation.[22]

It follows that, even in creation, man is placed within God's grace. The grace of the covenant envelops in advance (von vornherein) the grace of creation.[23] Founded in creation, God's covenant of grace with man has a universal character.[24] God creates in Jesus Christ. Herein lies both the realization and the justification of the creature.[25] Man was created good; he was justified through God's creation. Man broke the covenant. But God justifies him in spite of (trotzdem) sin. He maintains his eternal covenant.[26]

c. JUSTIFICATION IN RECONCILIATION

Justification and, in general, reconciliation must be seen as the fulfilling of the covenant. Justification is the fulfillment of the broken covenant.[27] Reconciliation includes justification.[28] But if we are to see the proper relation of justification to reconciliation, then we must first exclude all abstract modes of thought. We must not set Christology over against Soteriology and Ecclesiology. We must not set the person of Christ over against his work, or his natures over against his states. We must not develop an independent doctrine of

---

22. Ibid., p. 33. Der ewige, in der Zeit aufgerichtete Gottesbund macht die Rechtfertigung zu einem unbedingten, ewig gültigen und allgemein verbindlichen Geschehen. Zweifellos ist die Rechtfertigung eine Reaktion auf des Menschen Sünde, ein Dennoch und Trotzdem auf diesen Zwischenfall. Aber die Rechtfertigung in der Versöhnung ist «alles andere als das blinde Paradox eines Willküraktes göttlicher Allmacht «(IV/1, 11), sie ist vielmehr» die von Gott selbst vollzogene Behauptung, Durchsetzung seines Bundes mit dem Menschen» (IV/1, 35), die göttliche Geltendmachung seines ewigen und ursprünglichen Bundeswillens.

23. Ibid., p. 35.   26. Ibid., p. 37.
24. Ibid., p. 36.   27. Idem.
25. Idem.   28. Ibid., p. 38.

sin over against reconciliation. Finally, we must not speak of a fore-ordination of individual Christian men from the congregation.[29]

Stated otherwise, Barth wants a concrete doctrine of reconciliation. Küng gives a schematic survey of Barth's doctrine of reconciliation.[30]

In this scheme, Christ Jesus forms the center and standard. He is the key to the whole doctrine of reconciliation. From him we turn to the question of sin, then to the objective accomplishment of reconciliation, and after that to its subjective appropriation by the church and by individual believers. Thus Christology, the doctrine of sin, the doctrine of soteriology and the work of the Holy Spirit are four horizontal layers that together constitute the work of reconciliation. But of these Christology forms the center.[31] Corresponding to these horizontal layers, there are three perpendicular perspectives. These too proceed from Christology. Christ is (a) true God, (b) true man and (c) true God-man.

Looking at these three perspectives we note: (a) Jesus Christ is true God; he is the Lord as servant. He is the High Priest (*munus sacerdotale*), (b) Jesus Christ is true man; he is the servant as Lord (*munus regale*) and (c) Jesus Christ is God-man; he is the surety and witness of our reconciliation (*munus propheticum*).[32]

According to the Barthian scheme, justification must be viewed under the light of the first perspective. Justification is founded on the fact that Christ is true God, that he reveals his divinity in his humiliation and his Lordship in being a servant and thus reconciles man to himself.[33]

By setting the doctrine of justification in this framework of reconciliation, and then regarding reconciliation as the consummation of the covenant of grace with Christ as its center, Barth seeks to escape "Hegelianism."[34] And with his own view of justification set in its proper framework, Barth thinks he is able to evaluate the Roman Catholic view of it properly.[35]

We shall not follow Küng as he works out in detail Barth's view of justification in the light of the framework presented in the second section of part one of Barth's work. Reference will be made to this

29. *Ibid.*, p. 39.
30. *Ibid.*, p. 40.
31. *Ibid.*, p. 39.
32. *Ibid.*, pp. 39-40.
33. *Ibid.*, p. 40.
34. *Ibid.*, p. 41.
35. *Ibid.*, p. 43.

section as we now turn to the second main part of Küng's work, which has for its title: An Attempt at a Catholic Answer.

2. A Catholic Answer

The one question that Barth is constantly interested in asking us as Roman Catholic theologians, says Küng, is whether our doctrine of justification does justice to the sovereign act of the grace of God.[36] Barth sees in Roman Catholicism a threat to the sovereign grace of God. For that reason, his attack on Roman Catholic theology is sharp, even emotional, and he raises many questions. What about the Roman Catholic doctrine of sin? According to Catholic doctrine, sin leaves man wounded, but does it touch him in the depth of his being? And what of the Roman Catholic doctrine of grace? Is God taken seriously here? Is not Catholicism more interested in man than in God? Again, what about the Roman Catholic doctrine of justification? Does it not speak of man *becoming* righteous rather than of the declaratory act of the judging and justifying God? Furthermore, what about the Roman Catholic doctrine of the justified? Does not the Catholic seem to forget that he is a sinner still? Moreover, what about the Roman Catholic doctrine of faith? Does not man in it really justify himself, inasmuch as he cooperates with justification? Finally, does Roman Catholic thought take Jesus Christ seriously? Does Christ play a role in the Roman Catholic doctrine of creation? Is sin regarded in the light of the work of Christ or in the light of a God apart from Christ? In short, is not Roman Catholic thought after all an attempt to control God, and therefore an attack on grace?[37]

Küng's answer to Barth's central question and its subordinates is set forth in two sections. The first of these sections deals with the framework of Roman Catholic theology, and the second with the question of justification in the light of this framework. Our concern will be chiefly with the former. This will best enable us to follow the basic point of comparison between the Barthian and the Catholic doctrine of justification that Küng is out to make. This will also prepare us best for our own evaluation of this comparison in the light of Reformation theology.

36. *Ibid.*, pp. 97-98.   37. *Ibid.*, pp. 99-100.

a. FOUNDATIONS

To a large extent, Küng's answer to Barth's questions are given indirectly. They are given by a positive setting forth of Roman Catholic teaching. The reader may then draw his own conclusions. The first point considered is that of the authority of the church. Küng is out to show, as was Von Balthasar before him, that the Catholic system of thought is an open system. If Barth had only realized this fact when he so mercilessly criticized the doctrine of grace as set forth by the Council of Trent! The decrees of the infallible church are not frozen formulas. They are living pointers for deeper research into the infinite riches of the revelation of God in Christ.[38]

The history of dogma, says Küng, proves this point.[39] Dogmatic definitions do strike the truth infallibly, yet they cannot exhaustively express the truth. They may therefore always be explained and developed. In performing the task of explaining and developing truth, the church is not bound to one form of philosophy. The implicit truth content always exceeds any formulation given. The church seeks constantly to set forth the truth in terms of more inclusive perspectives. It is thus that the embodiment of the truth as the realization of the incarnation (*Auswirkung der Menschwerdung*) is accomplished in the church through the working of the Holy Spirit.[39a]

Of course this development of doctrine involved in the past the setting aside of heresies as they appeared from time to time. The particular formulations of doctrine will always be made with a particular heresy in view. This is apparent in the Tridentine decree on justification.[40] This decree did not say everything that is to be said on justification. It said only what at that time needed to be said in the light of the heresies of the Reformation on this subject.

In making reply to these heresies, the church did employ a certain anthropocentrism in its formulation of the doctrine of justification. But this was not done in the interest of the primacy of man. It was done in the interest of truly saving the primacy of God in his act of grace. How can that primacy be maintained if there is no real man that is to be saved? The Council of Trent emphasized that

38. *Ibid.*, p. 106.
39. *Ibid.*, p. 107.

39a. *Ibid.*, p. 108.
40. *Ibid.*, p. 111.

aspect which the Reformers in their false zeal overlooked. Barth has not fully realized this circumstance.

In setting forth Roman Catholic doctrine, Barth not only appealed to official decrees of the church but also to manuals of theology.[41] But it must ever be realized that in the strictest sense the Scripture is for Roman Catholic thought alone the Word of God.[42] The Scripture is without error and valid for all times and places.[43] It is as such the primary norm for theologians. Of course, in using this norm the theologians are subject to the interpretation of Scripture given by the church. For only in the church can the Scriptures be read properly. Scripture and church go together.[44]

There is also the matter of tradition as a source of revelation. But, as is apparent from the pronouncements of Trent, it is only divine tradition, such as was revealed by Jesus Christ or by the Holy Spirit, that is to be taken as a source of revelation.[45]

Still further, tradition is expressed in the symbols of the faith and in the decrees of popes, councils and bishops.[46] But these are subject to Scripture as the final norm.[47] Such formulations are, indeed, to be regarded as the end of a development, but then they must also at the same time be regarded as the beginning of new development.[48]

As theologians, we construct our system of theology subject to the Scriptures and to tradition as itself subject to Scripture.[49] The idea of papal authority is not inconsistent with, but is rather an expression of, the idea that all proof of doctrine must be of the Spirit and of power. Did not Barth himself allow that the idea of a pope is not inconsistent with the gospel?[50]

b. The Christocentric Foundation of Justification

Having established the fact that the Roman Catholic theologian has an open system of theology, Küng proceeds to show that in it Christ truly has the primacy. Of course, a Christocentric position must not be set over against a theocentric position. For Christ has his origin in the eternity of God.[51] In Jesus Christ the fulness of the Godhead appears bodily.[52]

41. *Ibid.*, p. 114.
42. *Ibid.*, p. 116.
43. *Ibid.*, p. 117.
44. *Ibid.*, p. 118.
45. *Ibid.*, p. 121.
46. *Idem.*
47. *Idem.*
48. *Ibid.*, p. 122.
49. *Ibid.*, p. 124.
50. *Ibid.*, p. 127.
51. *Ibid.*, p. 130.
52. *Ibid.*, p. 128.

Throughout its history, the Church has held to the primacy of Christ.[53] And, in the present day, there is a whole spate of Christ-books. It is in terms of Christology, and in terms of the doctrine of creation and of sin as dependent on Christology, that the answer is being given today, as it was yesterday, to the nature of justification.[54]

Our justification must be brought into relationship with our election in Christ from all eternity.[55] From all eternity, God has in his Son thought of the salvation of all men.[56] From the beginning, the whole of world-history is determined by God's plan of salvation. Thus through God's special grace this world-history becomes history of salvation (Heilsgeschichte) and even church history.[57]

(1) Creation as Salvation History

What happens in time has been determined by God from eternity. All temporal eventuation happens in fulfillment of the eternal plan of salvation in Jesus Christ.[58] This implies that creation took place in Jesus Christ.[59] The whole of creation bears the form of Christ (christusformig) and as such has a hidden trinitarian structure.[60] Everything comes into being and exists in Jesus Christ.[61] John the apostle warns us that without him not anything was made that was made.[62] Of course, creation has its own existence, but its ground of being is factually in Jesus Christ.[63]

To say all this is not to deny the fact of gradation. Material creation is not conscious of existing in Christ. The sinner who rebels against his being in Christ exists in Christ in a different manner from the righteous man. The damned are in Christ in a different manner than the blessed. But the idea of gradation must never reduce the fact that all things are in Christ.[64]

(2) Sin and Death in the Plan of Salvation

God's eternal plan is against sin.[65] Sin is a falling away from the covenant and therefore from God.[66] But through Jesus Christ as the redeemer, the sinner continues to exist and continues to exist as

53. Idem.
54. Ibid., p. 129.
55. Ibid., p. 134.
56. Ibid., p. 137.
57. Idem.
58. Ibid., p. 138.
59. Ibid., p. 139.

60. Ibid., p. 140.
61. Ibid., p. 146.
62. Idem.
63. Ibid., p. 147.
64. Ibid., p. 149.
65. Ibid., p. 150.
66. Ibid., p. 156.

man. Christ frustrates the destruction of himself which man under-
takes through his sin. Thus creation in Jesus Christ is not as such to
be identified with redemption. Creation is the presupposition of redemption,[67] and as such is the hidden beginning of redemption.[68]
Scripture frequently speaks of creation in Christ. It now appears
that all creation is imbedded in a redemptive context.[69] Even the
damned sinner has his existence in Christ, for where else could he
have it if he were not to fall back into non-being.[70]

The doctrine of justification must now be regarded in the light of
what has been said about creation and sin, for now we know what
the sinner is. We now understand the final power and the ultimate
powerlessness of sin, and therefore we know now the starting-point
of the justifying event.[71] As *aversio a Deo* and as *conversio ad
creaturas*, sin strives toward the fulness of death, toward the disappearance of the creature. Here we discover the final radicality and
power of sin. But when the Council of Trent confessed this radicality
of sin, it did not hesitate to pronounce its anathema on those who
held that since the fall of Adam the free will of man was extin-
guished.[72] In this pronouncement, the Council had no desire to
minimize the fact of sin. It was only concerned to assert that, in becoming sinful, man has not lost his manhood.[73] The *terminus a quo*
of justification is this sinner who owes his very manhood to Christ.
As such this sinner has no capacity for self-justification.

The mistake of the Reformers was not that they took sin too radically, but, rather, that they did not take it radically enough. They
took the condition of the sinner as that of being entirely without
grace. They overlooked the fact that even the being of the sinful
creature is in Christ. If such were not the case, then the sinner
would simply have been wiped away from the face of the earth. If
the Reformers had seen the truly radical nature of sin, then they
would have, together with Trent, attributed such freedom to man
as would enable him to allow himself to be turned about through
the mercy of Jesus Christ and to work out his salvation alone
through the power of Christ.[74]

In order to point up the fact that the Roman Catholic doctrine
of sin is alone truly radical, Küng asks three questions: (1) Is the

67. *Ibid.*, p. 163.
68. *Idem.*
69. *Ibid.*, p. 166.
70. *Ibid.*, p. 168.

71. *Ibid.*, p. 175.
72. *Idem.*
73. *Ibid.*, p. 175-176.
74. *Ibid.*, p. 179.

sinner free or not free? (2) What are we to say of the being of the sinner? and (3) what are we to say of his acts?[75]

Starting from the primacy of Christ, he avers, we speak first of freedom as the freedom of the children of God.[76] Of course the church also confesses to believe in man's freedom of choice. The great themes of Scripture, such as covenant, guilt, punishment and conversion, would be meaningless without it. Freedom of choice forms the anthropological substratum of Christian freedom. Without this substratum, Christian freedom would lose its meaning.[77]

If the idea of freedom of choice is thus, from the beginning, subordinated to freedom in Christ, then the whole question of determinism is seen to be irrelevant. When through sin man's will is enslaved, we are not speaking of determinism at all.[78] We can thus also see that man's freedom, lost through sin, is given back to him through Christ.[79]

It now appears that only the will of the justified man can really be called *liberum arbitrium*. His will is not against grace. It is rather the fruit of grace.[80] Roman Catholic teaching on man's freedom does not abolish but rather establishes the primacy of grace.

The same point must be made with respect to the sinner's being. The whole man sins, but even as such he retains his manhood in Christ.

Finally, the same point must be made with respect to the deeds of sinful men. No act of the sinner is good in terms of his autonomy. Only from Christ comes his strength to do penance, to convert himself and thus do what is "good."[81] But this "good" is not meritorious *sensu stricto*. Only through justification is man enabled by God to do good deeds in the full sense of the word.[82]

With the primacy of grace in Christ thus established, Roman Catholic theology cannot fairly be charged with showing any resemblance to humanism.[83] By the same token, the basic similarity between the Barthian and the Roman Catholic approach to theology is also established.[84]

---

75. *Idem.*
76. *Ibid.*, p. 181.
77. *Ibid.*, p. 182.
78. *Ibid.*, p. 184.
79. *Idem.*

80. *Idem.*
81. *Ibid.*, p. 186.
82. *Ibid.*, p. 187.
83. *Ibid.*, p. 189.

84. *Ibid.*, p. 193. Unser vorläufiges Ergebnis in diesen ersten Kapiteln ist also: Was die Grundlagen der Rechtfertigungslehre angeht, steht Barth, aufs Ganze gesehen, mit uns Katholiken auf dem gleichen Boden.

The fact that Barth and the Roman Catholic theologian build on the same foundation does not imply that their houses will look alike. There will be differences between Barthian and Roman Catholic theology. But such differences cannot be serious. Roman Catholic theology is happy to see Barth stress the theocentric aspect of grace. And Barth on his part has not neglected the anthropological aspect of grace. Barth realizes that it is *man* who receives grace and that man's being is changed through grace *(dass der Mensch seinshaft verändert wird)*.[85] Thus both are concerned to maintain the unity of grace.[86]

Again, Roman Catholic thought is as eager as is Barth to do justice to the forensic aspect of justification.[87] So Cardinal Newman says: "Here I am to consider it, not as it is in fact, but as it is in idea: as an imputation of righteousness, or an accounting righteous; and I shall offer remarks in behalf of three positions, which arise out of what has been said; first, that justification is, in the proper meaning of the word, a *declaration* of righteousness; secondly, that it is *distinct* from renewal; thirdly, that it is the *antecedent* or *efficient cause* of renewal" (p. 66).[88]

Of course the forensic aspect of justification must not be separated from the idea of inner renewal.[89] Paul's teaching on justification combines the juridical and the mystical aspects of the believer's relationship to Christ.[90] The central event that happens to the believer in Christ is both justification and sanctification.[91] This event is a pronouncement which makes righteous *(Gerechtsprechung, die gerecht macht)*.[92]

Küng again calls attention to the fact, as he sees it, that the Reformers required the Council of Trent to bind itself to a certain particular form of anthropology. He also refers to Luther's "nominalism." But he adds that the Council rejected any form of overstress on the extrinsic aspect of justification.[93] Trent had a view of justification which included imputation. But for this very reason Trent refused to identify justification with imputation.[94]

As for Barth's views and his own, as a Roman Catholic, Küng finds no basic difference between them.[95] Barth understands by

85. *Ibid.*, p. 201.
86. *Ibid.*, p. 198.
87. *Ibid.*, p. 208.
88. *Ibid.*, p. 210.
89. *Idem.*
90. *Ibid.*, p. 211.

91. *Ibid.*, p. 212.
92. *Ibid.*, p. 213.
93. *Ibid.*, pp. 214-215.
94. *Ibid.*, p. 216.
95. *Ibid.*, p. 213.

justification primarily God's pronouncement on man in relation to the death and resurrection of Jesus Christ.[96] Trent understands by justification primarily the inner change in man. But these are, in reality, not to be regarded otherwise than as aspects of one another. If Barth had kept this fact in mind, he would not have contrasted his own view of justification with that of Trent in the way he did.[97] The Tridentine conception of justification is open, and therefore complementary. Why then should Barth think of this view as basically different from his own?

Man is not merely called righteous; he *is* righteous. He is not righteous in a merely external but in a truly inward sense. Man is not partly but wholly righteous. He is a new man not merely in a negative but in a positive sense. All this is indisputable common ground between Barth and Catholic thought.[98]

Finally, it is only to be expected, from all that has been said, that Roman Catholic thought follows Paul in ever bringing justification into relation with faith rather than with love.[99] The Roman Catholic believed in the idea of *fides sola* and in *fiducia sola*.[100] Man is justified through faith alone.[101] This faith is a living faith. It binds the believer to the person of Christ. Roman Catholicism does not believe in justification by faith *and* works.[102] It believes that he who believes and is baptized will be saved.[103] Thus again, on this all-important point, there appears to be basic agreement between the Barthian and the Roman Catholic teaching on justification.[104] Both hold that in the crucifixion and resurrection of Jesus Christ justification has taken place for all men. Both believe that justifying faith is the recognition and realization of the once-for-all pronouncement of justification by God.[105]

In this justifying faith we have what Roman Catholic theologians have called *gratia increata* or *inhabitatio Spiritus Sancti*.[106] Barth himself has done full justice to this idea. He allows that in faith a new and special reality makes its appearance. This new reality is the Christian subject. He allows that the justified is different in reality from the sinner.[107] In analogy with Trent, Barth distinguishes

96. *Ibid.*, p. 228.
97. *Idem.*
98. *Ibid.*, p. 231.
99. *Ibid.*, p. 246.
100. *Ibid.*, p. 248.
101. *Ibid.*, p. 249.

102. *Ibid.*, p. 250.
103. *Ibid.*, p. 251.
104. *Ibid.*, p. 252.
105. *Idem.*
106. *Ibid.*, p. 255.
107. *Idem.*

between that element of faith which comes from below, from man, and that which comes from above, from God.[108]

Why then should Barth charge the Tridentine doctrine of cooperation with being synergistic? Everything comes from God, man's cooperation no less than anything else. In its teaching on justification and faith, Trent was only concerned to declare that to say that all comes from God should not be interpreted to mean that God alone works.[109]

It is on this basis, namely, that even man's power to cooperate with God comes from God, that Trent based its view of sanctification in relation to justification. What possible objection could Barth, from his point of view, have to such a view?[110] The Roman Catholic will agree that justification is a gracious declaratory act of God that follows upon the death and resurrection of Jesus Christ. The Roman Catholic will agree that this act of judgment happening once for all is for all men without exception. Surely sanctification is implied in justification so conceived.[111]

In the comparison between the Barthian and the Roman Catholic doctrine of justification instituted by Küng the one main problem has been that of the relationship of God and man in the history of salvation.[112] Barth asks Roman Catholic thought whether it has given due prominence to the fact that justification is due to the sovereign grace of *God* in Christ.[113] Roman Catholicism asks Barth whether he takes seriously the fact that justification is always justification of *man*.[114] What is the net result of the comparison made? Not every doctrine has been discussed. But so far as the basic doctrines of creation, sin and grace are concerned, there is in them no ground for Barth's separation from the old church.[115]

3. Küng on the Reformation

The reader has no doubt observed that in making his comparison between the Roman Catholic and the Barthian doctrine of justification, Küng was compelled, at every major point, to introduce a polemical note against the teachings of the Reformers. His opposition centers chiefly on the following points:

108. *Idem.*
109. *Ibid.*, p. 258.
110. *Ibid.*, p. 262.
111. *Idem.*

112. *Ibid.*, p. 267.
113. *Ibid.*, p. 268.
114. *Ibid.*, p. 269.
115. *Idem.*

(a) The Reformers Are Said to Think Dialectically

The Reformers held to a "dialectical" position with respect to the doctrinal background of justification. But Barth, starting concretely from Christ[116] and through his actualization of the incarnation[117] has broken with this dialecticism.

This point is also made by Von Balthasar.[118] Von Balthasar says that "historical Protestantism" is based on thinking in terms of the philosophical contrast between realism and nominalism. Historical nominalism may have meant to refer to Christ, but, because it thought in terms of philosophy as such, it could not think of him concretely. The saddest result of this philosophical approach was— Luther. But Barth has, in contradistinction from Luther, really thought Christologically and concretely.[119]

According to both Küng and Von Balthasar then Barth has, as over against the Reformers, left false speculation far behind and has, like Romanism, become truly Christological. This means that he, as well as Roman Catholicism, is said to have an open system. And this is, basically, the reason why Barth and Roman Catholicism are said to be in basic agreement on the question of sin and salvation.

(b) The Reformers Are Said to Have a Speculative View of Sin

Due to this lack of a Christological approach the Reformers had a defective view of sin. They did not realize that, without Christ, the sinner would not exist.[120] But Barth, together with Roman Catholicism, having a truly concrete Christology, also has a truly radical view of sin. Both of them realize that a true doctrine of sin must take its start from the idea of man's true freedom in Christ.[121] Only in the light of this true *libertas* does sin appear to be exceedingly sinful. For only thus does it appear that all sin is what it is because it involves the rebellion of the whole man against the grace of God in Christ. Both Barth and Roman Catholicism have lifted the whole question of sin out of the level of predestinationalist speculation. And thus Barth is able to escape the determinism involved in the position of the Reformers.[122]

116. *Ibid.*, p. 41.
117. *Ibid.*, p. 39.
118. Von Balthasar, *op. cit.*; p. 278.
119. *Idem.*

120. *Ibid.*, p. 179.
121. *Ibid.*, p. 181.
122. *Ibid.*, p. 58.

(c) THE REFORMERS ARE SAID TO HAVE AN EXTERNALISTIC VIEW OF JUSTIFICATION

The Reformers had too externalistic a view of justification.[123] Barth, together with Trent, in opposition to the Reformers, confesses that justification involves an inward change of being as well as a pronouncement of righteousness.

4. Berkouwer on Trent

According to Küng's judgment, both Barth and the Roman Catholic Church have open systems of theology. This allows them, Küng thinks, to do full justice to the biblical idea of the primacy of the sovereign grace of God to all men in Christ. The Reformers, having no such open system, cannot be truly biblical and therefore cannot be truly Christological.

Those who live in the camp of "historic Protestantism" may well agree that the Barthian and the Roman Catholic systems are alike because they are "open." But this is true because they are closed to God's revelation through Christ in Scripture. Historic Protestants cannot agree that Barth and Romanism are more biblical and more truly Christological than were the Reformers. It is precisely because the Reformers submitted their thinking to Scripture that they were compelled to oppose the Roman Catholic concept of justification and the "open" approach to theology as this finds expression in the categories of Romanism.

In the previous chapter, it was shown that, according to Berkouwer, Roman Catholic thought works with dynamical categories. This fact results in the idea that the church is the continuation of the incarnation. We are fortunate in that Berkouwer has also written a book on justification. In it he points out that because of its dynamical categories the Roman Catholic doctrine of justification is not truly biblical and therefore not acceptable to those who hold the Protestant position. The whole of his criticism is centrally expressed by saying that Rome wants to preserve the ethical character of justification over against what it considers mere extrinsic imputation. In doing this Romanism interprets the concept of justification

123. *Ibid.*, p. 231.

in such ethical-dynamic categories that the character of grace in it is obscured.[124]

Over against the procedure of Roman Catholic thought stands that of the Reformation. Roman Catholic theologians were bound in their exegesis by traditionalism and confessionalism.[125] With the coming of the Reformation, God was really allowed to speak to men through Christ in the Scripture. The light of the gospel of God's grace broke through to men once again in the time of the Reformation. The full salvation that is in Christ shone upon them anew.[126] Only by submission to Scripture without reserve could men visualize and enjoy the priority of divine grace and love.

The Reformation did not teach a one-sided stress on the juridical relation of God to man. All that concerned the Reformers was that men should realize that salvation is by grace alone without the works of the law. With their idea of *sola fide* the Reformers were concerned to praise the justice and mercy of God. It was with the simplicity of the gospel that they busied themselves. It was the gospel that Paul preached "which, in its integrity, was brought to life again by the Reformation."[127] "Thus, in the forensic idea of justification the *sola fide-sola gratia* finds its purest incarnation."[128] The Council of Trent emphatically rejected "the imputation of Christ's righteousness and therewith *sola fide*."[129]

Of course, in its way Trent also wanted to give recognition to God's grace. ". . . justification is described as translation of man from the situation in which he is born, as child of Adam, into the status of grace, as child of God (Trent, VI, 4). This fundamental translation is then elucidated in its various relationships. Grace, standing at the beginning, precedes human merit and puts the sinner in a position to prepare his own justification through free acquiescence to and cooperation with this grace (Trent, VI, 5)."[130]

According to Trent, we should hold that "through infused righteousness the sinner is justified to the root of his being, really and effectively, so that he is not only counted as just, but in reality *is* just. Justification occurs when the Holy Spirit is poured into the heart, and abides there."[131]

---

124. Berkouwer, *Geloof en Rechtvaardiging*, Kampen, 1949; Engl. tr., *Faith and Justification*, Grand Rapids: 1954, p. 98.

125. *Ibid.*, p. 65.   129. *Ibid.*, p. 94.
126. *Ibid.*, p. 72.   130. *Idem.*
127. *Idem.*   131. *Ibid.*, p. 95.
128. *Ibid.*, p. 91.

But, if we think that Trent really holds to justification by faith, we are soon disillusioned. Trent warns "against the idle delusion that one is made an heir of Christ *sola fide,* through mere faith" (Trent, VI, 11). Again, after pronouncement of the decrees, the canons reject the Reformed confession: "If any say that the sinner is justified through faith alone, in the sense that nothing else is necessary that cooperates to obtain the grace of justification and that it is not necessary for the sinner to prepare himself by means of his own will, *anathema sit* (Trent, VI, 9)."[132] Compare also Trent, VI, Canon 12.

Summing up the matter, Berkouwer says: "The conflict over justification is focused as sharply here as is possible within Christian confessions. Trent threw at the Reformation not merely a rejection of antinomianism, but a confession in which infused grace and love are subsumed within justification. This is what Trent maintained in opposition to the Reformation, and it must be granted that they made the contrast lucid enough. For it was against this very depreciation of God's 'favor' that the reformers bolted. They did not merely formulate justification as 'only the favor of God.' This might make it appear that something else might be posited alongside of this favor. Their position was not an opposition to love and good works, but the defense of the forensic and declarative character of justification, and of the righteousness of Christ *extra nos.* For this they drew sovereign grace around the problem of the human situation, and conceived man as encircled by grace. In this Lutheran and Calvinistic theologians were one. They saw and understood the debates that went on at the Council of Trent about twofold righteousness and clearly grasped why Rome was not prepared to make a concession. They perceived that Trent's respect for faith as the beginning, foundation, and root of salvation could not hold back a radical condemnation of the Reformation, for they knew that when the chips were down, Rome would hold *infused* righteousness to be *the* justification."[133]

The following important facts now emerge. Berkouwer and Küng agree that there is a basic disagreement between the Reformation and the Tridentine concept not only of justification but of grace in general. And both of these men trace the reason for this difference back to an all-important difference in methodology. Berkouwer

132. *Ibid.,* pp. 95-96.   133. *Ibid.,* pp. 96-97.

speaks of Roman Catholicism as working with dynamic categories. Küng speaks of Roman Catholicism as having an open system. For all practical purposes, these are the same. According to Berkouwer, Roman Catholicism is unable to maintain the true primacy of grace because it thinks of Christ and his Word in Scripture in terms of its dynamical categories. According to Küng, the Reformers were unable to maintain the true primacy of grace because they did *not* think in terms of an open system.

Thus Berkouwer and Küng agree that there is a radical difference between the concept of Christology and therefore of sin and grace as held to by the Reformers and as held to by the Roman Catholic Church. But they are in radical disagreement as to the question where the true primacy of grace is maintained. Berkouwer holds that it can only be maintained if the method of the Reformers is followed. He therefore thinks it imperative that even today those who think like the Reformers must engage in a "conflict with Rome." Küng holds that the primacy of grace can be maintained only if the dialectical method of the Reformers be rejected and the open system of Trent accepted.

We have not lost sight of Barth in discussing Berkouwer's analysis of Trent in relation to that of Küng. The entire discussion was introduced exclusively for the purpose of understanding Barth in relation to Reformation theology. We assume that Berkouwer and Küng are essentially correct in holding that the Christology of the Reformers and that of Trent are mutually exclusive of one another. And we assume that Berkouwer and Küng are right also in thinking of this difference as one that springs from a fundamental difference in methodology. Moreover, we assume that Berkouwer rather than Küng is right on the question where a true Christology and true primacy of grace may be found. It may be found with the Reformers and not with Trent.

Still further, it seems clear that Küng has established his point when he makes comparison between the Roman Catholic and the Barthian view of Christology and of grace. There is no more than a gradational difference between them. And this is true because the dynamic categories of Roman Catholicism are not basically different from the activist categories of Barth.

The dynamic categories of Romanism spring from a synthesis between Christian and Greek thought. The activist categories of Barthian theology spring from a synthesis between Christian and modern existentialist thought. Modern existentialist thought and Greek thought are alike based upon the assumption of the self-sufficiency of man's theoretical reason. They are two forms of the dialectical principle of human thought become apostate through the fall of man.

According to Küng, Barth was able to maintain the primacy of grace in Christ just because he had escaped Reformation method-ology. Moreover, according to Küng, the act concept, in terms of which Barth maintains his idea of the primacy of grace, does allow for the reality of the creature and for the reality of an inward change in the creature toward participation in the being of God.

To be sure, argues Küng, in his earlier theology Barth was too much under the influence of philosophy. This fact accounts for the dialectical method employed in this early theology. In that early theology he was unable to maintain the primacy of grace just be-cause he could not do justice to man as the creature to be saved. Therefore also he could not do justice to grace as being a real change of being in a real man.

But with his turning away from dialecticism derived from the Re-formation, and his advance toward the idea of the analogy of faith, Barth has attained to the truly biblical idea of the primacy of grace and therefore to the reality of the existence of man, and of his par-ticipation in God through grace.

There are, says Küng, certain evidences that Barth has, even in his latest writings, not wholly outgrown the evils of his earlier dia-lectical method. Notably, there is the tendency in Barth toward *apokatastasis*. There is, in addition, a tendency to depreciate the in-dependence of man. Again, in his view of sin there is still the tend-ency toward dialectical neutralization and justification. In his view of redemption, there is still the tendency toward a neglect of its ontic-creaturely aspect. There is still the tendency to sublate the difference in being between the righteous and the sinner, between believers and unbelievers. There is still the tendency toward the reduction of justification to a flowing movement without real deci-sions. There is still the tendency to underestimate the idea of growth in grace and to ignore the possibility of falling from grace.

But to point to these dangerous tendencies is not, says Küng, to deny that Barth's basic views are not essentially different from those of the "old church."[134]

134. *Op. cit.*, p. 271.

It remains now to point out that if Küng is basically right in his analysis of Barth's theology, then those who follow the Reformers are as much duty bound to engage in a conflict with Barth as they are to engage in a conflict with Rome.

Barth's idea of act is not less, perhaps more, destructive of the Reformation concept of God's revelation of grace in Christ than are the dynamical categories of Rome.

5. *Back to Dialecticism*

We have heard Küng say that it is becoming monotonous to speak of Barth's theology as being dialectical. Is it not obvious that Barth has gone on from dialecticism to analogy?

In reply, it may be said that, of course, Barth must be judged by his latest works. But regarded from the point of view of historic Protestantism, Barth's latest procedure is still dialectical. In saying this, it must be added at once that the term dialecticism is then used in a wider sense than that given it by Küng. It is also at the same time used in a different sense.

The usage of the term dialecticism in this wider and different sense has been explained in earlier chapters, particularly in section three of this work. By dialecticism we mean the methodology employed by all non-Christian thought.

When conceived in this sense, dialecticism makes its start from the self-consciousness of man as autonomous. Dialectical thinking is therefore thinking *von unten*. In the second place, dialectic thinking has a non-rational principle of individuation. For it the facts of the universe, consisting of man and his cosmic environment, exist by chance. They do not exist because they are created and controlled by God. Therefore, it may be said that for dialecticism existence is as such independent of rationality. But in the third place, it should be noted that it is quite impossible to think of such facts. Therefore, if facts are not from the beginning regarded as being what they are because of God's decision with respect to them, then they are what they are, in effect, because of what man by the categories of his thought, acting independently of God, orders them to be. This means that dialecticism has a rationalist principle of unification or continuity.

Dialectical thinking may accordingly be called apostate thinking. It is the thinking of man who through sin has broken the covenant that God had made with him. And, through the fall of the first man

Adam, all men—he being their representative with God—became covenant breakers. Through dialectical thinking apostate man seeks to suppress the truth about himself and his proper relation of subordination to God.

It has been noted earlier that Dooyeweerd describes apostate or dialectical thinking as employing the form-matter scheme of thought. The principle of unity is expressed by the idea of pure form and the principle of discontinuity is expressed by the idea of pure matter. The Greek form-matter scheme was largely influential in the construction of Roman Catholic thinking, notably in that of Thomas Aquinas. What Berkouwer speaks of as the dynamic categories of Roman Catholic thought springs largely from the Greek form-matter scheme. The modern form of dialectical or apostate thinking is expressed in the idea of the freedom-nature scheme. But the freedom-nature scheme itself may be included in the form-matter scheme as a general expression of all apostate thought. The modern freedom-nature scheme sprang in its large outlines from Kant's philosophy as the Greek form-matter scheme came to its climactic expression in Aristotle. But both in Aristotle and in Kant it is would-be autonomous man who is the ultimate source of predication. In both Aristotle and Kant too this would-be autonomous man employs a purely irrational scheme of individuation and a purely abstract impersonal principle of unity.

Why then should not Küng and Barth agree in all essential matters? Why should Küng, who interprets Scripture in terms of the typical synthesis-theology of the medieval period, not agree essentially with Barth, who interprets Scripture in terms of a synthesis-theology born in modern times?

Barth has been violently critical of Romanist theology. But, significantly enough, this criticism was made on the basis of something that Romanism does not actually teach. Barth's criticism of Rome was made on the assumption that Romanist thinking not only allows for but demands the idea of direct and identifiable revelation of God in history. But both Von Balthasar and Küng have pointed out that Romanist theology does not believe in any finished revelation of God, either in Christ or in Scripture. Von Balthasar says that Roman Catholicism is as anxious as is Barth to maintain that the revelation of God is always wholly hidden. And Küng says that the Roman Catholic system is an open system. Both assure us that the absolutist claims of the church at no point contravene the idea of process as found in the open system of the church. Berkouwer's criticism of the Tridentine doctrine of justification and its idea of the church as the continuation of the incarnation only corroborates the analyses given by both Von Balthasar and Küng.

Again, when Küng finds dangerous tendencies in Barth, he speaks of things which Barth does not really believe. Küng thinks that Barth has retained a measure of dialectical thinking and that this fact might lead him to the idea of *apokatastasis*. But what is dialectical thinking in the mind of Küng? It is the type of thinking in which all things are determined in advance. It is the type of thinking used by Barth in his earlier work when for him the human subject had no existence at all except it were participant in and eventually identical with the divine. Such a position would lead naturally to the idea that all men must be saved. Men simply could not exist unless they were in God, and as such saved by God.

But Küng does not really need to fear that Barth will hold to *apokatastasis*. We are saying this not primarily because Barth has verbally rejected the idea. We are saying this primarily because one of the basic principles of Barth's thinking, to which he has been true throughout his career, is the idea of pure contingency. It is this aspect of his thought that was so prevalent in his early thought that Berkouwer spoke of it as proving that Barth was more nominalist even than Occam. And, though in his later theology Barth has stressed the universalist idea to the effect that all men are inherently in Christ, he has never lost sight of his principle of discontinuity. He has used it to date in order by means of it to maintain the idea of the sovereignty of God's grace. For Barth grace is inherently sovereign as well as universal, so there is no danger that Barth will teach *apokatastasis*. It is true that his principle of continuity would by itself lead directly toward identification of man with God, but then this principle of continuity is always employed in Barth's thinking in correlativity with his principle of discontinuity. So long as Barth maintains that God is both *wholly* revealed and *wholly* hidden, just so long will his tendency toward *apokatastasis* be counteracted by his tendency toward thinking of the disappearance of both God and man into the realm of chance. Barth's realism is always counterbalanced by his nominalism.

Küng need not then be fearful lest Barth has retained any of his earlier dialecticism in his later thought because of the fact that his earlier dialecticism sprang from the "dialecticism" of the Reformers. Küng is apparently unable to distinguish between the dialecticism as entertained by Barth in his early writings and the position of the Reformers. Barth's early dialecticism, Küng rightly asserts, involved the virtual absorption of the human subject into the divine. Küng thinks that the same must be said for Reformation theology. It was Trent, he argues, that had to defend the genuineness of the existence and the free existence of the human subject over against the determinism of the Reformers. But it is by virtue of their view of creation as taken from Scripture that the human subject can never be absorbed by the divine.

The very inability on the part of Küng to distinguish between the position of Barth's early theology and the position of the Reformers is evidence of the fact that his thinking is bound by his dialectical categories and that for this reason he cannot understand what the Reformers were saying. The Reformers believed in the actual creation of men by God. They believed therefore in the direct confrontation of man by God both in the cosmos and in the penetralia of the human consciousness. And they believed that God spoke to man directly through Adam, the first man, as the representative of all other men, in paradise at the beginning of history. They believed that the sin of man is what it is, namely, guilt and pollution, because man broke the known will of God. The Reformers did not pretend that they could logically understand how a creature wholly dependent on God could, for that very reason, have the power of genuine and permanently significant choice. They did not seek to explain the relation between God and man by means of a dialectical scheme. Their presupposition was that their logical thinking had to be subordinated to the revelation of God as directly given by Christ to his church in the Scriptures.

So far then from being dialectical, the theology of the Reformers is the only position that is not dialectical. It is the only position that does not seek for human freedom in the idea of autonomy. It is therefore also the only position that is not given over to the hopeless tasks confronting dialectical thinking. Its Christ is not the victim of a death struggle between a principle of continuity that would destroy the possibility of his appearance in history and a principle of discontinuity that would swallow him up in the bottomless and shoreless ocean of Chance should he appear.

6. The Dilemma of Dialecticism

Thus the situation of dialecticism is inescapably a dilemma. At an earlier point, Bavinck was quoted to the effect that the ethical relation between God and man as taught in Scripture was rediscovered by the Reformers. Roman Catholic thought had reduced this ethical relation, in large measure, to one of ontology. Conceived of as existing in *puris naturalibus,* man is from the outset of his existence said to be in need of supernatural grace. It is his lack of being that constitutes the reason for this need. Man is so near non-being that only by grace can he be lifted to that scale of being for which God intends him. When sin enters into the picture, man needs more grace but not radically different grace than he already needed as a creature. Through sin man was working himself in the direction of non-being. So a larger measure of grace was required to keep man from his tendency toward self-destruction and to lead him onward toward his supernatural goal.

Working with this approach, Küng says that, if it were not for the presence of Christ to man, he would have fallen into non-existence through sin. Does not the Roman Catholic then maintain the primacy of grace and therewith the proper ethical relation between God and man as well as does Barth, asks Küng?

The answer must be that he does. And then Plato may be said to outdo both in maintaining the primacy of grace. For Plato the ethical is wholly identical with ontology. For Plato the ideal world is the only real or fully real world. To the extent that man has any reality at all, it must be by way of participation in the Ideal world and finally in the idea of the good. And man is evil to the extent that his being is separate from God.

Küng and Barth both build grace into the very being of man. When Barth says that the original relation of every man is to Christ rather than to Adam, he is, in effect, doing what Küng does when he insists that all men, even in their sin, have their being in Christ. Neither Küng nor Barth has any room for Adam, the first man, as being confronted at the beginning of history with the known will of God and deliberately disobeying it. Accordingly, the work of the substitutionary atonement of Christ does not for them take place at one point in history, and there completely. Atonement is virtually identified with the incarnation, and the incarnation, as the inner ground of creation, begins with creation and continues through Christ in the church till this day, and will continue forever. That is to say, in this view creation is turned into emanation.

Küng is, of course, quite right when he points out that in his earlier theology Barth worked out the consequence of this ontologism by saying that the whole transaction of creation and salvation is within God. Man participates in this transaction only to the extent that he is absorbed in deity. And Küng fears that Barth may still be carrying with him some of this tendency toward monism and therefore toward *apokatastasis*. In this too we do not think he is mistaken. Barth has no other means by which to maintain the primacy of grace than by building grace into the very being of man. And, as noted earlier, this is also the only means available for Küng when he seeks, if possible, to outdo Barth in his maintenance of the primacy of grace.

But now comes the other side of the story. A little earlier we asserted that Küng need not fear that Barth will really go onward toward *apokatastasis*. Does he not always have available to him his principle of discontinuity? In fact, does not his monistic principle of continuity depend for its very operation upon his atomistic principle of discontinuity? And is not the same thing true of Küng's own theology?

In both cases there is the monistic or realistic tendency which would lead to the absorption of the human subject into the divine. For both Barth and Küng the goal of man is participation in the being of God. In both cases too this participation is an active something. It cannot exist unless it moves forward and that means onward toward absorption into deity. The primacy of *Christ* depends for both upon this tendency toward absorption of man in deity. For both Barth and Küng the triumph of grace depends upon this realistic or monistic aspect of their thought. All men are *in advance* already in Christ. The triumph of grace in Christ is *objective* because essentially eternal. The objectivity of that triumph lies in this very eternity. The *analogia fidei* idea of both Barth and Küng reckons on this objectivity for all their criticism of the supposed subjectivism of historic Protestantism. Their own procedure, they hold, is true thinking, thinking *von oben* and not *von unten*.

However, when their realistic principle of continuity would lead them directly into the idea of the absorption of the human subject into the very aseity of God, then there is available to them their nominalistic principle of discontinuity or individuation. If the formal principle of human personality depends for both Barth and Küng on the idea of virtual pre-existence of Christ and of all men in Christ as God, then the material principle of human personality may be said to be for both of them the idea of pure chance. Neither Barth nor Küng depend for the origination and continued existence of human personality upon the biblical idea of creation and providence. When they refer to creation and providence, these are virtually absorbed into Christology. And this is only consistent. To maintain the true triumph of grace and, therefore, its true universality or objectivity, they *need* a purely irrational principle of individuation. Since the idea of universality is for both of them a pure form, this pure form needs for its correlative pure matter. And neither pure form nor pure matter can ever function without standing in relation of correlativity to one another. Their God is *wholly* hidden and at the same time *wholly* revealed. Barth and Küng can never reproach one another for holding heresy. When Küng points out the dangers of *apokatastasis* in Barth, then Barth can answer, "Your system too has the same danger." And he can add, "But neither of us need really fear this danger, for our common form of universality is meaningless without its correlative in pure matter." So the "open situation in preaching" always obtains, and the freedom of man is supposedly preserved.

And here the dilemma of the dialectical procedure of both Barth and Küng appears clearly. This dilemma is well expressed in the words of Goethe, *Spricht die Seele so spricht ach schon die Seele nicht mehr.* In the activist-dynamic system of both Barth and Küng, men are made to swing back and forth between a pure form in which their individual being would be saved by being absorbed, and a pure matter into which their individuality would be saved by being lost in Stygian darkness. To be lost would be no worse than to be saved. In fact, it would be the same thing, inasmuch as both principles must function in man at the same time.

The basic objection to this whole ontologist approach to Christianity, as Berkouwer has pointed out, is that in it there is no transition from wrath to grace in history. The incarnation, the death and resurrection of Christ are all caught up into history at a common juncture point of a timeless and abstract form and a timeless realm of non-being or chance. On this basis the primacy of Christ consists in nothing more than in his being somewhat nearer to pure form than are other men. But this primacy would involve at once his being also more deeply imbedded in pure matter than are other men. If in Barth's system Christ is the only elect man, he is such because he is at the same time the only reprobate man. In him God as pure form has been more deeply hidden than he could be in other men. Christ's priority over other men must be in terms of his greater formality, and this greater formality itself requires deeper immersion in non-being. The idea of God as being identical with Christ in his incarnation, and of the incarnation as being identical with reconciliation, is built upon the idea that all reality is one act. And this one act must be inherently an act of salvation of all men. At the same time, it must be an act in which sin is essentially one with non-being, and this non-being is correlative to being. So, on the one hand, all men have from all eternity been saved in Christ, and, on the other hand, no one can be saved to all eternity in him. This is thinking *von unten*, not *von oben*.[135] The grace of God in Christ as proclaimed by the apostles, and as brought to light anew in the Reformation, is lost so far as Barth and Küng act upon their own principle. To say this is, of course, not to deny that, as Berkouwer has stressed, the Bible has had a great influence on Barth. The same may be said for Küng. But in so far as a true theology of grace finds expression in their theology, we must say, however reluctantly, that this is in spite of their basic principles.

135. We are not concerned to ask to what extent the officials of the Roman Catholic Church agree or disagree with the analysis of Barth's thought by such men as Von Balthasar and Küng.

Chapter XV

The New Protestantism

Barth's ever-present aim is to point out that true Christian thinking is thinking *from above*. For many years his criticism of Roman Catholicism has been that it was too largely characterized by thinking *from below*. And this has also been his criticism of New Protestantism. Von Balthasar says that Barth takes his position between these two.[1]

Perhaps it may be said that Barth takes his position above Roman Catholicism and New Protestantism, for it is from the point of view of a radical Christology that he judges them both. Moreover, Barth also wants at the same time to carry on and carry forward the Reformation motif in theology. Barth wants to retain his standing as a Protestant. But, to do so, he finds that he cannot simply return to the Reformers. He must purify and radicalize the theology of the Reformers.[2] And this purification and radicalization must also be done in the light of his Christology. This purification and radicalization requires that God be thought of as wholly revealed to man and as wholly hidden in this revelation.

Here then we seem to have the picture as a whole. Barth is *against* Roman Catholicism. He is *against* New Protestantism. He is *for* the Reformers, provided he be allowed to purify and radicalize their theology in terms of his Christological principle.

But now something strange has happened. Von Balthasar and especially Küng have convinced Barth that he and Roman Catholics can be friends, providing Barth will renounce his friendship

1. Von Balthasar, *op. cit.;* p. 39.   2. *Ibid.*, p. 32.

with the Reformers. Do not Barth and Roman Catholicism both have open systems? And do not both subject their anthropology to their Christology? As to the Reformers, they had an anthropology that will not be subject to the primacy of Christ. Theirs was dialecticism of a speculative nature. In their dialecticism neither the sovereignty nor the universality of grace could be maintained. According to Küng, the theology of the Reformers cannot be purified or radicalized so as to make it do justice, as do Barth and the Church, to the primacy of grace. The anthropology of Rome need not, and that of the Reformation cannot, be radicalized in terms of a proper Christology.

Barth has not, of course, openly expressed his readiness to disavow friendship with the Reformers, but his frank agreement with the argument of Küng virtually commits him to a rejection of the theology of the Reformers. Moreover, and this is even more basic, Barth's whole argument for the primacy of a Christ in terms of whom God is wholly revealed and wholly hidden is, as before noted, destructive of the basic principles of the Reformation theology.

But, in the present chapter, our attention is to be turned to the question of New Protestantism. More particularly, the question must be asked as to what extent Barth's criticism of New Protestantism continues to be of a basically negative sort. If he can now allow that Romanist anthropology can be properly subordinated to Christology, why should not the same thing be true of New Protestant anthropology?

When Emil Brunner and Barth developed a difference between themselves, it was on the question of the relation of the gospel to the general cultural consciousness of man. How sadly, says Barth, has Brunner slipped back into ascribing to man a power over the Word of God. How dare he speak of Christianity as being in some sense a consummation of creation? The reparation of which the New Testament speaks is in no sense a development or consummation. It is only and exclusively a miracle. As such, it has nothing to do with any formal or material principle that precedes it. What has been repaired becomes wholly new in Christ. As Brunner walks upon his road of nature *and* grace, it becomes increasingly difficult, said Barth, to distinguish his position from that of Rome or of New Protestantism.

The theologian, Barth says, must take the first commandment to be his theological axiom. His principle is the reverse of that of philosophy. The first commandment is *written*. It comes from without. It is in no sense the product of human reason.[3]

It was thus that Barth wrote his farewell to Brunner, and at the same time to Gogarten, whose anthropology had interested Brunner. He would make no compromise of any sort with the consciousness-theologians. But, more recently, Barth has developed an anthropology that satisfies such men as Küng, the Roman Catholic theologian. Has Barth come to realize that one can go *too far* with stressing the *wholly other* character of God? If God can be known by God only, must not man, to know God, become divine? The consciousness theologians, says Barth, had no true view of sin as the uncrossable gulf that separates man from God. But is it better to have men sin *in* God? Can salvation precede sin and creation altogether? Does insistence on the primacy of grace mean that there is nothing but grace?

In his own anthropology, Barth answers such questions by stressing the *humanity* of God. God *is* his act of revelation in the incarnation. God *is* his act of reconciling the world unto himself in Christ. Therefore there is a world that is to be saved. There is a creation that must serve as the external ground of the covenant as well as a covenant that serves as the inner ground of creation. It is man, not God, that believes. Man sins *against* God and not merely *in* Christ.

The question now arises whether Barth has in his later theology realized that even the anthropology of New Protestantism can be radicalized so as to make it acceptable to him. If the *analogia entis* of Rome can be properly related to Christology, why is not the same thing true of the autonomous consciousness that forms the starting-point of New Protestantism? Perhaps Barth can make friends with the consciousness theologians as well as with Von Balthasar and Küng. But will not these consciousness-theologians too insist that, if he wants to be friends with them, then he must renounce the theology of the Reformers?

Barth's more recent attitude toward New Protestantism can perhaps best be discovered if we follow him in his analysis of some of its leaders. In his work *Die Protestantische Theologie im 19. Jahrhundert*, Barth gives a connected account of the development of New Protestantism. From this work it is possible to discover his recent estimate of the value of this theology in relation to his own.

3. *Zwischen den Zeiten*, 1933, pp. 297ff.

In particular, we can discover in this work whether and to what extent the anthropology of New Protestantism can, in Barth's estimate, be properly Christologized.

1. The Philosophers

(a) LESSING'S BIG DITCH

Barth knows very well, of course, that the anthropology of New Protestantism is grounded in the philosophy of the great idealist philosophers. Accordingly, he traces with considerable care the development of this philosophy so far as it has bearing on modern Protestant theology.

By way of background, Barth sketches the development of the absolutist attitude of eighteenth century man. Eighteenth century man knew that God is mighty and that man is *also* mighty, that God is wise and that man is *also* wise, that God is benevolent and that man is *also* benevolent. Man is ultimately of the same substance as God and is what God is but in an infinitely less perfect form than God.[4] Eighteenth century man "assumed it to be self-evident that in taking himself to account, and himself answering the account, and then acting in obedience to it he was also showing the existence of God, justifying and guaranteeing anew his relationship with God and thereby affirming that his own existence was possible."[5]

Complete autarchy was the ideal of the eighteenth century man. Not that he left God out of his thought, but his God had to serve the purpose of establishing his own autonomy. Here we have full-blown humanism.[6] It is Gottfried Wilhelm Leibniz who best typifies this autonomous man.[7] His "utterly self-sufficient monad is an emanation, an image, a mirror of God himself and is therefore nowhere limited by things outside it, but only in its own being; which has no windows, and changes only by its inner principle, its own most peculiar striving; which is always the best it is possible for it to be, and which can therefore transform itself by the tendency of its own most peculiar nature; but it cannot be destroyed, cannot perish, and is immortal like God himself who created it?"[8] In Leibniz then we

---

4. English translation: *Protestant Thought: From Rousseau to Ritschl*, p. 52.
5. *Ibid.*, p. 54.
6. *Idem.*

7. *Ibid.*, p. 55.
8. *Ibid.*, p. 56.

have a theodicy "which decisively refers man to himself."[9] Is there no room for grace in such a philosophy? O yes, there is.[10] There is room for God, but only for a particular kind of God. The God of Leibniz has the task of guaranteeing the concordance between the truths of reason and the truths of fact by means of a pre-established harmony.[11]

In Rousseau and in Lessing, we have two men who, though typical of the eighteenth century attitude, yet are also strangers to it.[12] We omit the former and turn to the latter. Our interest is to see how far, in the eyes of Barth, Lessing has gone beyond the idea of autarchy of the eighteenth century man. Has he made more room for grace than Leibniz did? This much at least must be said, namely, that he has, together with Rousseau, discovered a second dimension, the dimension of "existence as such, as distinct from what man can know and desire."[13] With Rousseau he had a knowledge of something beyond morals and science. "He spoke of the heart and of feelings less often and with less emphasis than Rousseau, but he, too, did refer to them, especially at decisive points."[14] Lessing appeals to "that inner place of existence" as the "source of the whole." It was in this inner place of existence that, together with Rousseau, Lessing found his freedom. And while Rousseau used this freedom as a haven to which he could withdraw from the realm of the outer world, Lessing used this freedom as the point from which he made his contact with the outer world.[15] His freedom was a "freedom to act."[16] In both of these men we have therefore a "deeper rationalism, a rationalism deepened in the direction of an independent and permanently independent awareness of one's own existence."[17]

Lessing's preoccupation with drama was an expression of this deeper rationalism, and in his dramas his theme was not simply man but man in action. His contemporaries noticed that here was something new. Lessing's influence on Protestant theology takes off from this point.[18] Did holding to his deeper rationalism imply for Lessing a sympathy for positive religion? In his most mature dramatic work, *Nathan the Wise* (1779), Lessing gives expression to his view of the relation between natural and positive religion.[19] In his work, *The*

9. *Ibid.*, p. 57.
10. *Idem.*
11. *Idem.*
12. *Ibid.*, p. 119.
13. *Idem.*
14. *Idem.*

15. *Ibid.*, p. 120.
16. *Idem.*
17. *Idem.*
18. *Ibid.*, p. 121.
19. *Ibid.*, p. 122.

Education of the Human Race (1780), he dealt again with the same problem.[20]

In both of these works the influence of Reimarus is apparent.[21] Lessing found it his duty to " 'test with his own eyes,' *quid liquidum sit in causa Christianorum.*"[22] In Lessing's view "The religion of Christ is the religion which Christ himself knew and practised as a man; . . . ."[23] Christians who think that Christ was more than a man are mistaken.[24]

Man's duty, says Lessing, is to practice "natural religion." But " 'From the religion of nature a positive religion had to be constructed, just as a positive law had been made out of the natural one.' This positive religion acquired its sanction by the respect accorded to its founder, who alleged that the conventional element in this religion came just as certainly from God, only indirectly through himself, as its essentials came directly through the reasoning powers in each one of us.' "[25] Thus all positive and revealed religions are for Lessing equally true and equally false, "equally true to the extent that an agreement concerning non-essentials was everywhere necessary, and equally false as far as every such convention signified a weakening and suppression of the essentials. 'The best positive or revealed religion is the one containing the fewest conventional additions to natural religion and least limits the good effects of natural religion.' "[26]

But all this is only one line of Lessing's thought.[27] Lessing can also quite abruptly dismiss all theologians both in theology and in philosophy.[28] Then he makes his appeal to the "great misjudged man, Luther."[29] However, he does not want those who are committed to positive religion to appeal to history for its defense. For, according to his best known statement: "Accidental historical truths can never become proofs for necessary truths of reason."[30] "Historical truth as such, the truth which is in need of such investigation and is not yet part of my own experience, cannot be the legitimate and fully-authorized messenger of the truth of revelation, i.e., the truth which necessarily imposes itself upon my reason, which is ultimately certain."[31] "No historical truth, even when it is supplied with the best

20. *Idem.*
21. *Ibid.,* p. 123.
22. *Idem.*
23. *Ibid.,* p. 125.
24. *Idem.*
25. *Ibid.,* p. 126.

26. *Ibid.,* p. 127.
27. *Ibid.,* p. 128.
28. *Ibid.,* p. 129.
29. *Idem.*
30. *Ibid.,* p. 137.
31. *Ibid.,* p. 138.

evidence, can be demonstrated."[32] "But if," says Lessing, " 'no historical truth can be demonstrated, then neither can it in turn be used
to demonstrate anything'."[33] There is a "nasty big ditch" between
the accidental truths of history and the necessary truths of reason.[34]

In saying this, Lessing is not, however, speaking as a rationalist
pur sang. Lessing "is aware of one proof of Christianity, i.e., a
growth of a knowledge of God through Christ, through present-day
man's encounter with the Christian tradition. But this proof must
be 'the proof of the spirit and the power' as the title of the famous
writing of 1777 runs, from which comes the famous sentence just
quoted."[35] The proof of the spirit and the power appeals to feeling,
experience and the heart.[36] "It is not as historical truth but through
experience, that the historical element in Christianity assumes the
power of proof for Christianity itself, and that, by way of historical
truth, necessary truths of reason are proved. The way of Lessing's
victor is the direct way from historical truth to the *heart* of present-
day man."[37]

Appealing from Luther's writings to the spirit of Luther, from the
letter of the Bible to the spirit of the Bible, thence to religion, to St.
John's testimony:—Little children, love one another—we finally
reach the religion of Christ himself.[38] This religion of Christ himself,
as noted earlier, every man can have in common with him.[39]

In the famous fable of the three rings of *Nathan the Wise*, we are
again taught that the truth of Christianity must be brought as a
proof of the spirit and the power.[40] In this case the problem is not
that of "Christian history itself studied for its own sake."[41] The
problem is rather that of the history of Christianity and of other
religions in relation to the universal history of religion.[42] "Is Christianity, when ranked with the other religions, really the true religion,
or, as was to be said later, the absolute religion? And how should
the justification for his claim show itself, if and in so far as it is
justified? That is the theological question which is discussed in
Nathan."[43] "The fable of the three rings is as follows: In an ancient
family it is the custom for the father to give his favourite son a ring
for his inheritance, a ring possessing the miraculous power of mak-

32. *Ibid.*, p. 135.
33. *Idem*.
34. *Ibid.*, p. 136.
35. *Ibid.*, p. 137.
36. *Ibid.*, p. 138.
37. *Idem*.

38. *Idem*.
39. *Ibid.*, p. 125.
40. *Ibid.*, p. 140.
41. *Idem*.
42. *Idem*.
43. *Idem*.

ing whoever owns it beloved in the sight of God and man. One father, in this family, has three sons whom he loves equally. In order to hurt none of them he has two perfect imitations of the true ring made, which even he cannot detect and gives each of the three sons his blessing, and one of the rings, and dies. What happens then is obvious, of course. Each of the three sons considers that the other two are deceivers."[44]

When the three sons hasten to the magistrate, that officer might take the position that all three of the rings are counterfeit. This would signify that all positive religions are false. But the judge "opts—without knowing it, only sensing it, although the author knows—for the true view in opposition to the false one: the true ring was in fact *not* lost. . . And that is precisely why no proclamation of a universal religion comes about in Nathan."[45]

The reader may ask at this point whether Lessing has now been able somehow to cross his "big nasty ditch." The answer is, obviously, that he has not. Lessing has a purely rationalist principle of unity and a purely irrationalist principle of plurality. Accordingly, he can never make intelligible how learning by experience is possible. If Lessing's positive religions are really positive, then they are wholly out of contact with one another and with truth. Again, if Lessing's natural religion is really natural, then it cannot allow that even in a thousand thousand years from now one positive religion could prove itself any better than any other, let alone being the only one that is true. If the individual speaks then, alas, it is no longer the individual that speaks.

But how will Barth seek to cross the ditch? Will he follow the way of the Reformers and of Paul? Will he, with them, take the position that the big ditch is of man's own making? And will he take the position that this fact itself can be known by sinful man only if God in Christ through Scripture reveals it to him from above? Or will Barth dig the ditch still deeper and confront God himself with it so that God too must seek for some makeshift compromise as he tries to cross it? Will Barth construct his advance beyond Leibniz and Lessing without questioning their dialectical assumptions, based as these are upon the idea of human autonomy? Will he repress the biblical idea that God in Christ realizes his plan for the created universe and develop instead an inner teleology within a Universe that includes God and man? The advice of the judge in the parable

44. *Idem.*   45. *Ibid.*, p. 143.

"consisted in the pointing out of the self-proving miraculous power of the genuine ring."[46] But on Lessing's view, miracle has power only so long as it is out of touch with nature. When miracle makes contact with nature, it is itself reduced to nature. Will the Christ of Barth be in any better position with respect to man the creature and his sin than was the judge in relation to the "genuine ring"?

Barth complains that "it is precisely the Protestant doctrine of Scripture that Lessing is trying to juggle away" by means "of the *regula fidei*, in favour of the spirit and the inner truth and the 'ever-continuing miracle of religion itself,' in favour of the whole 'edifice' of the Christian Church. In short, he seeks to achieve this end in unison with Roman Catholicism and the whole of Protestant modernism (and as one of the first quite obvious heralds of the programme of Protestant modernism) in favour of history itself as distinct from and as against the Lord of history, who is indelibly denoted precisely by the Protestant doctrine of the Scriptures."[47]

Summing up his verdict on Lessing, Barth says: "With Lessing there is no such thing as a Lord of history within history."[48] Is the final verdict on Barth's theology perhaps to be expressed in these same words which he employs with respect to Lessing? The judge in the parable simply chose irrationally for the idea that the genuine ring was not lost. It was to manifest its salutary miraculous power later, much later, in experience. But, as noted earlier, the final verdict might as well have been the one first given to the brothers, namely, that they were all three deceived deceivers. So also Barth judges that the truth is *not* lost. It will show itself at last in his Christ as victor. But until Barth will, with the Reformers, really maintain that the truth of God is present to man plainly through Christ in the Scriptures, his choice has no better foundation than that of the judge in Lessing's parable. Barth's principle of revelation, according to which God is both wholly revealed and wholly hidden, is as much an unsuccessful compromise as is the "deeper rationalism" of Lessing.

(b) Kant Offers Peace Terms to Theology

In Kant the eighteenth century "understood and affirmed itself in its own limitations."[49] Kant's position is called Criticism.[50] By means

---

46. *Ibid.*, p. 145.
47. *Ibid.*, pp. 146-147.
48. *Ibid.*, p. 147.

49. *Ibid.*, p. 150.
50. *Ibid.*, p. 153.

of his Criticism Kant sought to give enlightenment to the Enlightenment.[51] He demands "an almost unconditional faith in reason. But the only kind of reason he considers worthy of his trust is the reason which has first of all come to be reasonable as regards itself."[52] "The Enlightenment before Kant was the absolute and boundless self-affirmation of reason, which, as such an affirmation, was ultimately bound to be uncertain of itself. Even if we wish to characterize Kant's intellectual quality and that of the time after him as part of the Enlightenment—as in a certain sense we not only can but must —it is now at all events a relative and bounded self-affirmation of reason, critical and now for the first time sure of itself, to the extent that it possesses these qualities. That is what is new in Kant."[53] Reason in Kant is sure of itself because it has finally understood the nature of its own capacity.[54] In Kant reason has reached maturity.[55] "From now on theology would no longer be able to formulate its tenets, no matter on what foundation it might base them, without having acquired a clear conception of the method of reason, which it also uses in the construction of its tenets."[56] To be sure, of itself and at the same time reason knows its limits. Reason must realize that concepts without intuition are empty.[57] Concepts by themselves cannot be made to yield any knowledge of what exists.[58] "When assertions or denials about what exists are made by means of forming concepts which lack any actual or at least possible intuition, the illusion of genuine theoretical knowledge and not the reality is achieved. For there is wanting any basis in transcendental apperception and thus any test of pure rationality. This illusion will very soon produce difficulties in its train by developing antinomies, necessary self-contradictions in which at once such a desire for ideal knowledge of a merely conceptual kind will be entangled. Examples are the contradiction between the assumption of a First Cause and that of a *regressus in infinitum;* or that between the assumption of human free-will and the assumption that there is no such thing. So far as the objects of intuition and the Understanding, of empirical knowledge, are concerned, God, Freedom and Immortality are not objects of our knowledge. That means: they are not objects of our

51. *Ibid.,* p. 154.
52. *Ibid.,* p. 155.
53. *Ibid.,* p. 156.
54. *Idem.*

55. *Ibid.,* p. 157.
56. *Idem.*
57. *Ibid.,* p. 158.
58. *Idem.*

theoretical knowledge."[59] "All theoretical proofs and disproofs of God's existence, for example, fail equally, since the propositions, 'God exists' and 'God does not exist,' can express in their theoretical meaning only the illusion of knowledge and not knowledge. For they apply the Category of being, positively and negatively, to an object which lacks intuition. God is a limiting concept, a regulative idea, a pure thing of thought. We imagine that when we assert or deny God's existence we have said something about God. In fact to speak of existence or non-existence is *per se* not to speak of God."[60] But reason is practical as well as theoretical. "Surely the union of intuition and concept, whence empirical knowledge derives its reality, is in fact action, practice, having its basis in transcendental apperception. It is in this act as such that man is laid hold of not only by the being of things, i.e., by nature in its reality in time and space, but beyond this and above all by the thing that must be, hidden from us as a 'thing in itself' which is, as a thing, undiscoverable; by the world of freedom which limits time and space and resolves them in itself."[61] "Abstract man, the man who is held to be a creature of theoretical reason, is not the real man. I am not a real man, a real creature of reason, simply by virtue of this capacity I have for perceiving things in time and space, but this capacity for perceiving things in time and space is itself based upon the true and essential reasoning capacity, namely that by which I perceive necessity and law, in such a way that law and necessity are imposed upon me as a person who acts. God, freedom and immortality—these ideas which in their regulative use are indispensable also in empirical knowledge—cannot be perceived *in abstracto*, i.e., by contemplation in isolation, but they can be perceived *in concreto*, i.e., in actual fact."[62]

(1) Pure and Practical Reason Harmonize

Kant was not slow to indicate the importance of his view of reason as having two aspects, one pure and one practical. He dictated his own terms for peace with theology.[63]

Theology must remember that it too *"makes use* of reason in the establishment of its propositions."[64] And Kant reserves the right as

59. *Ibid.*, pp. 158-159.
60. *Ibid.*, p. 159.
61. *Ibid.*, pp. 159-160.

62. *Ibid.*, p. 160.
63. *Ibid.*, p. 162.
64. *Ibid.*, p. 163.

a philosopher to assess religion as a "phenomenon of reason."[65] Philosophy must critically examine theology's interpretations. And philosophy must seek for its own sake " 'to form some coherent idea of those things in the Bible . . . which can also be perceived by reason alone'."[66] It must, says Kant, " 'seek that meaning in the Scripture which is in harmony with the holiest of reason's teachings'."[67] Philosophy is interested in Christianity as a positive religion in order by it, as an illustration, to demonstrate the universal truth of religion.[68] Thus, on the one hand, religion is not a matter for theology alone. It must also be studied within the limits of *reason* alone. On the other hand, "within the limits of reason alone, and secondly that within the limits of reason alone *religion* too is to be contemplated."[69] By reason alone Kant means reason not illuminated by revelation.

Barth reminds us here that by *ratio* Kant does not refer to "the isolated theoretical, intellectual human capacity but to that human capacity which is, decisively even, determined by practice."[70] As such it refers to the idea of God as "an influence upon the human will for the fulfilment of every human duty."[71] In religion morality appears "in its majesty." Says Kant: "Morality inevitably leads to religion, and in so doing extends itself into the idea of a moral legislator possessed of power and existing outside man."[72] Revelation is not necessary to this extension of morality. Morality is spontaneous with man and religion, as an extension of morality, is also. In fact, external revelation would be meaningless for religion as well as for morality. " 'For if God really spoke to man, he would never be able to know that it was in fact God who was speaking to him'."[73] If we were as men to receive any revelation from God and should recognize it for what it was, then we should "have some prior knowledge of what revelation is, and of what God is."[74]

"If then there is no empirical criterion, and therefore no empirical knowledge either, of true revelation of the true God, this criterion can only ever be perceived by its 'correspondence with that which reason declares to be proper for God,' and it should now be clear where in fact we must look—judging always from the standpoint of

65. *Idem.*
66. *Idem.*
67. *Ibid.*, pp. 163-164.
68. *Ibid.*, p. 164.
69. *Idem.*

70. *Ibid.*, p. 165.
71. *Idem.*
72. *Ibid.*, p. 166.
73. *Ibid.*, pp. 166-167.
74. *Ibid.*, p. 167.

the religion of reason—for the true, original revelation, if we might speak of such a thing."[75]

Kant's attitude toward positive or statutory, revealed religion is as follows. He says it is "based upon facts." "It is a 'historical faith.' It has need, in so far as it has its basis in books, of the control of historical science. In consequence 'its validity is always only of a particular kind'—it is valid, that is to say, only for those who have been reached by the history upon which it rests. Its knowledge is not necessary and uniform, but accidental and diverse; it is not *per se* the one, pure religious faith which should distinguish the one true Church. Such a historical faith is, however, as such not a living, not a salutary faith, and is therefore not necessary either. It is 'dead in itself.' The idea that 'it is our duty and essential to salvation, is superstition.' "[76]

(2) Kant Makes Room for Christ

To say this does not mean that he thinks of revelation as "completely unnecessary and superfluous."[77] Due to a weakness in human nature, man needs positive religion. Dogma may be used "to set the religion of reason publicly in motion."[78] Ideally, positive religion is one with the religion of reason. In ideal circumstances men could convince themselves by their own inner resources of the truth of the true religion. ". . . In this case the religion is objectively a natural one, although subjectively it is a revealed religion, for which reason also it is the former name which truly befits it'."[79] "This supposition that the revealed and the natural religion might be one and the same, is, in Kant's opinion, true of Christianity. And thus the Christian preaching has also at any rate the task of presenting the biblical teaching of the faith in the form in which we can develop it from within ourselves by means of reason."[80]

When Kant proceeds to read the Bible, he finds that "the incarnate Son of God is interpreted as 'the idea set before us for our emulation' of moral perfection, an idea which as such cannot be any created thing, but only God's only begotten son. We cannot conceive of the 'ideal of the humanity in whom God is well-pleased' other than as it is contained 'in the idea of a man who is prepared not only

75. *Idem.*
76. *Ibid.*, p. 168.
77. *Ibid.*, p. 169.

78. *Idem.*
79. *Idem.*
80. *Ibid.*, pp. 169-170.

himself, to exercise every human duty . . . but also, although . . .
tempted, to take upon himself every suffering, even a shameful
death for the best good of the world and for the sake, even, of his
enemies'."[81] Immediately involved in this Christology is the idea of
vicarious atonement as the work of Christ. "The *work* of the Son of
God, however, in so far as it exceeds his teaching—his vicarious
suffering above all—is, according to one passage in Kant, to be interpreted as meaning that from a moral point of view *intelligible*
man is in God's eyes different from empirical man; that as the latter's
vicar he carries empirical man's guilt incurred by sin, meets the
demands of the highest justice through suffering and death and is
therefore his Saviour, so that empirical man, in so far as he is yet
identical with intelligible man, can hope to appear before his Judge
as one vindicated by him."[82] As empirical men, we therefore must
have a righteousness which is not our own.[83] If we are to be men
who are well-pleasing in the sight of God, then it is God who must
forgive us.[84] But how could men possibly understand the meaning
of the words, "thy sins are forgiven thee?" An experience of the forgiveness of sins would be a "super-sensory experience, because it is
impossible."[85] Kant saw that "the notion of a historical faith that
justifies, i.e., one achieving this unfathomable improvement of mankind fundamentally, just as much as the notion of vicarious atonement as the object of this faith 'ultimately leads to the conception of
an absolute divine decree: God "hath mercy on whom he will have
mercy, and whom he will he hardeneth,"' which, as Kant at one
point says, 'represents, if taken literally, the *salto mortale* of reason,'
whereas elsewhere he says: 'It must at all events refer to a wisdom
the rule for which is utterly and completely hidden from us'."[86]

Therefore Kant's conclusion is that "Grace, miracle, the mysteries
of the call to faith, of atonement and of election, and the possibility
of means of grace, are '*Parerga* of religion within the limits of reason
alone' as the methodically very illuminating expression runs; 'they
do not belong within it, but are yet adjacent to it. Reason, in the
knowledge of its incapacity to satisfy its moral requirements, extends itself to extravagant ideas, which could supply this need,
without, however, appropriating them as its own extended possession. Reason does not dispute the possibility or reality of the objects

81. *Ibid.*, p. 172.
82. *Ibid.*, p. 173.
83. *Ibid.*, p. 183.
84. *Ibid.*, p. 184.
85. *Ibid.*, p. 185.
86. *Idem.*

of these ideas; it is just that it cannot include them in its maxims for thought and action'."[87]

Of the main tenets then of Kant's system, as well as those of Lessing, it must be said, "These roads must all lead to Rome!"[88] Yet there are deviations in Kant's thought which point to something better. These may well lead us to ask whether Kant does, after all, understand what justification is in the sense in which the Reformers spoke of it.[89] But we must beware against the desire to reinterpret Kant "as if what he said and meant were at bottom the same as what Luther and Calvin said and meant."[90]

Even so, it is important to take note of the deviations; "the deviations which occur precisely at the most significant point: are '*parerga* of religion' which, according to Kant's own explanation, *abut* upon the 'religion within the limits of reason alone.' And in this, incidentally, we are certainly at liberty to take this 'abutting' as implying not only adjacency but a clash."[91]

In his main tenets, Kant makes man the measure of God. Such is Barth's conclusion to this point. But in his notion of the church, Barth argues, Kant seems to allow some room for the idea of a statutory religion.[92] Secondly, in his idea of radical evil Kant seems to hold to that which is against reason.[93] In the third place, beyond the idea of atonement by means of one's own deeds, Kant seems to allow for something beyond, namely, grace. Kant allows for mysteries of religion which at least *abut* upon the religion of reason.[94]

Our general conclusion then must be "that the dictation of peace terms with which Kant, commandingly enough, advanced upon theology, does at least contain a certain gap."[95] Aware of this *gap* or inconsistency, the theologians of the nineteenth century go *beyond Kant*. Barth speaks of three movements in theology that sought to build on Kant and also to go beyond him.

The first of these movements or tendencies is found in the "so-called rationalistic theologians." Wegscheider is the first and chief representative of this tendency. And later, "as a result of the great Kant-revival of the second half of the nineteenth century" there is "A. Ritschl, and particularly distinct among his pupils W. Herr-

87. Idem.
88. Ibid., p. 187.
89. Ibid., p. 183.
90. Ibid., p. 187.
91. Ibid., pp. 187-188.

92. Ibid., p. 189.
93. Idem.
94. Idem.
95. Idem.

mann."[96] This group tried as best as possible to carry out and develop Kant's program.

The second of these movements is represented by Schleiermacher and later by Troeltsch. These men sought to subject Kant's thinking to an "immanent critique." They sought to "broaden and enrich" Kant's concept of reason. They said "that there is yet another capacity *a priori* which is part of the necessities of human reason, apart from the theoretical and practical ones: the capacity of feeling, as Schleiermacher put it, or that of 'presentiment' as de Wette preferred to express it, linking up with the philosophers Jacobi and Fries."[97]

These two possibilities of building on Kant "have it in common that theology desires in principle to keep to the Kantian terms for peace, and to enter into negotiations, merely, with their dictator, whether it be upon the conditions he has laid down for their execution, or upon the actual terms for peace themselves. It is in pursuing these two lines of development that nineteenth-century theology is destined to be the direct continuation of the theology of the Enlightenment."[98]

(3) Kant Makes Room for the Preacher

Barth obviously does not want to work for the development of either of these possibilities. But there is a third one which, he says, we must explore further. This third possibility "becomes visible on the borders of the Kantian philosophy of religion."[99] Hegel and some of his pupils, particularly Marheineke and I. A. Dorner, visualized this possibility. Even so "right up to our own time it could not get the better of the actual trend of the time."[100]

Kant sought to establish a border between philosophy and theology, but he could not help, even as a philosopher, taking a half step over this border. Standing on the border, he said some things that might have led theology into thinking of this third possibility in addition to the former two. What then is this possibility? It will be recalled that, with his notion of the Church as a starting-point, Kant "pondered the possibility of the Bible having a position and significance, which, even if it were not 'divinely statutory' would

96. *Ibid.*, p. 190.   99. *Ibid.*, p. 191.
97. *Idem.*   100. *Idem.*
98. *Idem.*

yet be extraordinary and qualified, and he went on from this to ponder also the possibility of a theology which would be *different* from the philosophical theology he himself was propounding. He explicitly calls this other theology, which limits philosophical theology, 'biblical theology,' and it is his wish that the affairs of this biblical theology should not 'be allowed to mingle' with those of philosophy."[101]

Moreover, the minister of a Church is to preach and teach in accord with the symbols of his church. Only if he should find the content of this symbol to be "flatly in contradiction of the 'inner religion,' as he must understand it as a philosopher" would he be obliged to abandon his office. And even then the scholar in him "can always explain that it is not completely impossible for 'truth to lie hidden' in the things he has to represent in the Church as one holding office."[102]

And, with this, we have what Kant called the "material possibility of a biblical theology."[103] Thus Kant guards against the reproach that his critical teaching presumes to dispute revelation. This is not his intention.[104] Says Kant, "Even at that point where philosophical theology seems to accept principles in opposition to those of biblical theology, e.g., in respect of the teaching concerning miracles, it confesses and proves that it does not assert them as objective principles, but only as subjective ones; they must, that is, be understood as maxims, *when* we merely wish to make use of our own (human) reason in judging of theological matters; and in so doing we do not dispute the miracles themselves, but merely leave them without restraint to the biblical theologian, in so far as he wishes to judge solely as a biblical theologian and scorns any alliance with philosophy."[105]

(4) Kant Cannot Cross Lessing's Big Ditch

What conclusion may we draw from this association of philosophy and theology in Kant's thinking? Perhaps the old gentleman smiled again when he made his assignment to theology. There was a one-sidedness in his view. It is therefore "only to be regretted that there was apparently no one among Kant's theological contemporaries

101. *Ibid.*, p. 192.
102. *Ibid.*, p. 193.
103. *Idem.*

104. *Idem.*
105. *Idem.*

who had the insight, the courage and the humour expressly to draw the great man's attention, in all respect, to the mutual quality of this relationship."[106] As for ourselves, Barth concludes, "we cannot see why his determination of theology's place should not be right simply because the place he indicates for the theologian is in fact such that in it the theologian—seen from the point of view of a philosophy attentive to the concerns of 'mere reason'—must right at the outset feel himself threatened and also probably an object of ridicule. It is only necessary to take quite seriously what Kant said half in mockery, in order to hear something very significant, even though we reserve in every respect our right to object to his formulations. Or is it not the case that the philosopher of pure reason has said something very significant to the theologian in telling him in all succinctness that *'The biblical theologian proves that God exists by means of the fact that he has spoken in the Bible'?*"[107]

The reader may perhaps be surprised by this conclusion of Barth's. Barth did warn us against thinking that Kant said and meant the same thing that Luther and Calvin said and meant. Barth has also shown us that in Kant's view positive religion would ideally be the same as natural religion. Are we then to say that one who holds such a view of the religion of reason as did Kant might also hold to the religion of the Reformers? Barth seems to hesitate on this point. At one point he says that at least it is not impossible that he might. At another place he affirms without hesitation: "And I further dare to say that Kant understood what grace was, in the sense of the Church of the Reformation."[108]

To the extent that Barth gives any justification for thinking this, he relies on Kant's view of the primacy of the practical reason. We have heard Barth speak of three possibilities that opened up to men as they sought to build their theology on Kant's philosophy. There was, first, the way of the more rationalist theologians who sought to cling as closely as possible to Kant. There was, second, the possibility of those who submitted Kant's thinking to an immanentist critique. But there was also, finally, the possibility of saying that Kant had developed only one side of the religious problem, namely, the side which deals with the human function in it. If this possibility is followed out, then we may indicate that the human function needs to be related to the divine whence it springs: "It might be possible to

106. *Ibid.,* p. 195.
107. *Ibid.,* p. 196.

108. *Ibid.,* p. 223.

object that with the problem conceived as 'religion within the limits of reason alone' only the one side of the problem, namely religion as a human function, is seen, and not the other side, the significant point to which this function is related and whence it springs, the dealings, namely, of a God who is not identical with the quintessence of human reason, with the 'God in ourselves'—thus restricting the validity of the enquiry in a manner which must also of necessity adversely affect the presentation of the first side, the interpretation of this human function."[109]

And why should there then not be a place for a theology in which the primacy of grace is maintained alongside of Kant's philosophy? Barth obviously pins his hopes for such a theology on the fact that even in Kant's philosophy of religion it is the primacy of the practical reason that obtains.[110] Barth knows well enough that, from the point of view of Kant's basic notion of philosophy, there cannot possibly be any knowledge of anything super-sensible and therefore no knowledge of God. He knows that on this basis "The God who is within us is the interpreter."[111] On this basis, the Trinity has to be "held together by the idea of love."[112] On this basis, the incarnate Son of God is an ideal that "does not require any historical realization."[113] "To the religion of reason the Son of God is not a man, but 'the abstraction of humanity.' "[114] Barth knows that on Kant's philosophy the atonement consists of man's clinging to the archetype of humanity and in remaining true to his example in faithful imitation.[115]

But, after all this is said, it must be remembered that Kant has limited reason. Therefore, though by his view of reason as theoretical Kant is the greatest exponent of the idea of the enlightenment, he yet by his idea of the primacy of the reason as practical takes a "quite strikingly systematic interest in the notion of the Church."[116] And "it is here for the first time that something becomes visible of the borders of the conception of the problem peculiar to him. The reign of the good principle of humanity demands and makes necessary—as he puts in at this point—the setting-up and spreading of a 'society in accordance with the laws of virtue and for the purpose of the same.' This demand, however, presupposes a higher moral

109. *Ibid.*, p. 191.
110. *Ibid.*, p. 279.
111. *Ibid.*, p. 171.
112. *Idem.*

113. *Ibid.*, p. 172.
114. *Idem.*
115. *Ibid.*, p. 173.
116. *Idem.*

being beyond the insufficiency of the individuals, upon which this demand is made a supreme law-giver and universal searcher of hearts, a moral world-ruler. It would be 'against all reason to say that the kingdom of God should be instituted by men . . . God himself must be the originator of his kingdom.' 'The creation of a moral people of God is therefore a work the execution of which cannot be expected of men, but only of God himself.' "[117]

The reader may here wish to recall Kroner's analysis of Kant's thinking, as earlier summarized in this work. Kroner spoke first of Kant's ethical dualism. Barth's analysis of Kant starts from the same point. According to Kant, says Barth, conceptual knowledge, the knowledge of science, is limited to sensuous experience. The rationalists and the empiricists were quite wrong in thinking that man could reach out beyond sensuous experience and attain to knowledge of God conceptually. To solve the problem of uniting the facts of existence to the principles of rationality, Kant found it necessary to say that these principles are *a priori* forms of the human mind. As forms these principles need the purely non-rational stuff of sensuous experience for their filling. By combining this purely abstract form of rationality and the equally abstract principle of pure contingency, Kant sought to save science. He sought by means of this combination to attain to the universality and objectivity of scientific knowledge.

Obviously this universality is, on this basis, located in the knowing subject. And this subject is certainly not God. For by definition there is no theoretical knowledge of God at all. The ultimate reference point for all knowledge is therefore placed in man. If then there is any relation of necessity in nature and any relation of order in history, these relations spring ultimately not from God but from man. Therefore, if God is to be revealed to man in nature or in history, he must be *wholly* revealed in it and *wholly* penetrable by the theoretical reason. And thus positive or statutory religion must become identical with natural religion. The incarnation must become the abstraction of ideal humanity.

However, on this view man himself too would be swallowed up by nature as nature in turn would be swallowed up by man. In other words, the only way by which man can retain his freedom or assert his autonomy, an autonomy in terms of which the whole of nature

117. *Idem.*

and history has to be constructed, is by means of pure negation. As autonomous and free, man must be as little known by his own conceptual reason as is his God, for if man were known to himself by means of this theoretical reason then he would no longer be he. He would then be reduced to nature. It is for this reason that Kroner's phrase, "ethical dualism," expresses so accurately Kant's conception of the negative relation of nature to the human self.

In the previous chapter, we spoke of the problematics of dialecticism. It is in Kant's thinking that this problematics is clearly seen to have its taproot in the assumption of the autonomy of the human self. In dealing with Lessing's parable, we saw that the judge simply *assumed* that the genuine ring was not lost. Kant also assumes this. He did not ask *whether* knowledge was possible; he simply sought for the presuppositions that make the fact of knowledge intelligible. No one could, in the last analysis, do anything less. The Reformers, following Paul, also did so. But the all important point is in which direction does one look for the presupposition of the fact of knowledge? The Reformers looked for it in the direction of the triune God as revealed through Christ in Scripture, while Kant looked for it in the direction of man. The Reformers looked for it in Christ as the one in whom the eternal Word was made flesh; Kant looked for it in the abstraction of humanity. The Reformers looked for it in the Scripture as the Word of Christ. Kant looked for it in the autonomous reason of man. The Reformers interpreted human self-awareness in terms of the speech of God available to them through Christ in the Scriptures. Kant sought for human self-awareness in terms of abstract form and abstract matter as correlative to one another. The Reformers knew that there was no gulf between God and man inasmuch as God has made man in his image. Kant had a great gulf between man and God because he made God in the image of man. The Reformers had no "nasty big ditch" between man and his environment because God is the source and director of nature and history as well as of man. Kant could only enlarge the "nasty big ditch" of Lessing between man and nature because for him the matter of human experience is purely contingent and the unity brought into this matter was abstract form. The Reformers could account for the rise and continuance of human self-awareness, because they placed it in the concrete situation of the revelation of God as surrounding them and being present within them from the beginning of history. Kant could not account for either the rise or the continuance of human self-awareness, because for him it has to take its beginning and take its permanent stance in a vacuum. The Reformers recognized mystery between themselves and God. Kant surrounded both man and God with mystery. The thinking of the Reformers may therefore be said to be thinking from above, and the thinking of Kant may be said to be thinking from below.

(5) Barth Still Stands Before Lessing's Big Ditch

Will Barth side with the Reformers as over against Kant? Will he challenge the basic presupposition of Kant? No, he will not. He will seek to go *beyond* Kant. He will seek to go beyond Kant further, *much further* beyond Kant than any other theologian has done since Kant. But with them he will still *start* with Kant in assuming that human self-awareness can initiate itself and after that continue its functioning in a vacuum. And so his God and his Christ will also function in a vacuum.

Barth recognizes the validity of Kant's method as he builds up the world of human experience in terms of abstract form and purely contingent matter as these are based upon the assumption of human autonomy. But he pins his hopes on the fact that Kant himself seeks to limit the autonomous interpretative activity of man to science and philosophy. He seems to take comfort from the fact that even Kant himself, in distinction from Lessing, had a quite systematic interest in the church. And are not the office-bearers of the church, even according to Kant, allowed quite simply to prove "that God exists by means of the fact that he has spoken in the Bible"?[118] The office-bearer of the church, even according to Kant, is allowed to speak of the Church, the Bible, historical revelation and grace.[119]

One wonders, however, why Barth did not see that, on Kant's basis, theology could never preach and teach in the name of God as really speaking to man. Even the illustration employed by Barth of the possible tension between the man who is an office-bearer in the church and at the same time a scholar, should have made this point clear to him. The preacher must simply preach according to the symbol of his church, says Kant. He need not concern himself about the truth of what he preaches in terms of the claims of scholarship, except in an extreme case. Says Kant: "A preacher would be bound

118. *Ibid.*, p. 196.   119. *Ibid.*, p. 195.

to abandon his office for this reason, only if he should find something flatly in contradiction of the 'inner religion,' as he must understand it as a philosopher, in the teachings of his Church, but not if these teachings do not happen to correspond exactly with his historical-philosophical convictions. Even if such a conflict between the office-holder and the scholar in him should take place, the scholar can always explain that it is not completely impossible for 'truth to lie hidden' in the things he has to represent in the Church as one holding office."[120]

Two remarks are in order at this point. In the first place, it is impossible to indicate the border line between that which the scholar in the preacher should find flatly contradictory and that which he should find merely not to "correspond exactly with his historical-philosophical convictions."[121] If the scholar in the preacher holds his convictions with any intelligence, then he does so precisely because with Kant he knows that percepts without concepts are blind. If he were a scholar worthy of the name, then he would, with Kant, demand that the supernatural lose its supernatural character by being brought into contact with the natural. The scholar in the preacher would demand that all the positive teachings of the preacher should be reduced to that which is fully manipulable by the conceptual processes of the philosopher. And, in demanding this, the scholar in the preacher would have no occasion ever to face the question as to whether there was anything flatly contradictory between the content of preaching and the truth discovered by philosophy. Nothing of the preacher's sermon could even *appear* to be contradictory, because, by the time it had appeared at all to the scholar, it would already have lost its supernatural character. The scholar in the preacher would therefore always silence the preacher unless he were first put to silence by the preacher. But then the preacher would have to be a scholar in terms of his preaching. He would have to interpret the possibility of philosophy as well as of science in terms of the revelation of God that comes from above.

On Kant's basis, however, this way is not open. He must forever stand on the border between a philosophy which must claim to say everything even in the field of theology and a theology which cannot claim to say anything to philosophy without in the very act of its speech losing itself in philosophy. Not willing to face this dilemma,

120. *Ibid.*, p. 193.   121. *Idem.*

Kant says that the scholar in the preacher need not object to anything except in the extreme case of open contradiction, and the preacher "can always explain that it is not completely impossible for 'truth to lie hidden' in the things he has to represent in the Church as one holding office."[122]

Barth has virtually taken over this position from Kant. He does not question the rightful claims of Kant's scholar, that is, of his philosophy. Yet this claim amounts to the demand that any revelation that is to be accepted by man must be wholly penetrable by the conceptual operations of man as the final reference point in predication. Barth simply seeks to satisfy this claim by saying that God must be wholly revealed if revealed at all. For him the being of God is therefore wholly expressed in his revelation. So far as the Reformers hold to God as being not wholly identified and expressed in his revelation, Barth purifies their theology. He purifies the theology of the Reformers in the interest of meeting the demands of autonomous reason. It does not seem to occur to him that then, together with the preacher of Kant, he can only say that it is "not completely impossible" for truth to lie hidden in the Bible and the creeds that are based upon the Bible. In other words, he must fall back on pure mysticism. To meet the demands of the philosopher, Barth is willing to live by such a concession of mere possibility. On such a basis he cannot discover a God or a Christ who speaks from above. Barth is willing to have God's revelation wholly hidden even when God is wholly revealed. Nothing intelligible can ever be said by God to man on Barth's basis. Barth's basic concept of a revelation as wholly revealing and wholly hiding God to man is based upon the assumption of the autonomy of man. From the point of view of Reformation theology, the final position as well as the earlier position of Barth must therefore be said to be dialectical. In it, as well as in all other dialecticism, there is the rationalistic demand that all reality, to be accepted by man, must be penetrable by his conceptual or logical powers. But Kant's dialecticism, and that of the modern theologians and philosophers following him, allows more readily than did ancient and medieval dialecticism for the fact that man cannot equate reality with the reach of his logic. Kant limited science to make room for faith. But this limitation of reason does not make room for faith in any Christian sense of the term. It simply makes

122. *Idem.*

room for faith in the irrational. Such a faith is itself irrational. It makes room for the idea of an abyss of unrelatedness surrounding the floating island of rationality that men call science and philosophy.

Barth says that certain post-Kantian theologians are on their way to Rome. But why should he think that his own way does not lead to Rome? Is there any basic difference between his way and that of those who closely follow Kant or those who subject Kant's position to an immanent criticism? The answer must be that there is only a difference of degree between Barth's own theology and that of the men whom he describes as on the road to Rome. Their system as well as his allows room for the irrational. Barth's system differs from theirs in allowing *more* room for the irrational. But then, just because of this fact, his system is more insistent on the purely formal nature of its principle of unification. His system is therefore both more irrationalist and more rationalist than that of his predecessors. It is by being thus both more irrationalist and more rationalist that Barth seeks to outreach Romanism and the theology of Emil Brunner. It is thus too that he seeks to outreach Schleiermacher and all his followers. But as time goes on, it appears ever more clearly that the difference between his view and that of Rome is not basic. It also appears that his quarrel with Modern Protestantism is not basic. The speech of Romanism and that of Modern Protestantism is *from below*. So too is the speech of Barth's theology, and as such it shows itself to be meaningless. Kant's philosophy has made it clear that on the basis of all apostate thought the human consciousness, in seeking to escape from God, *cannot even find itself*. It has to construct itself in terms of an abstract freedom that stands over against a necessitarian nature. This is Kant's ethical dualism. Then, when this dualism must be overcome, it can be overcome by no other means than by a God who speaks "from above." But this God who is supposed to be able to speak from above turns out to be a projection of the human consciousness in its vaunted independence. Unless one begins by the interpretation of both man and his environment in this world in terms of the God of Scripture, illusionism is the only result. Kant's primacy of the practical reason over his theoretical reason is the clearest modern expression of this illusionism. For the God of this practical reason is a mere projection into the unknown on the part of the supposedly independent theoretical reason of man. This God is nothing more than an absolutely abstract form made correlative to absolutely abstract or pure matter.

Yet it is on such a God that Barth suspends his idea both of the sovereignty and the universality of grace in Christ. The very reason for his identification of God with his revelation in Christ and of Christ with his work of salvation of all men is the rationalistic one that any God, to be acceptable, must have no sort of existence that is not accessible to man. A pure form serves this Barthian universalistic purpose perfectly. But then this pure form must itself be seen to be wholly correlative to pure contingency. The pure form must be wholly hidden in pure matter as pure matter must be wholly revealed in pure form. It is by thus assuming that his God is wholly revealed and wholly hidden to him that man can make sure that he has no God who has any existence prior to himself and who can make any demands on him. Thus Barth's theology is a more consistent form of consciousness-theology than has been seen in history thus far.

(c) Hegel Cannot Cross Lessing's Big Ditch

After Barth is through with his discussion of Kant, he takes up Herder and Novalis. But we must hasten on to see what he has to say on Hegel. Even here we must be brief.

"Hegel's philosophy," says Barth, "is the philosophy of *self-confidence.*"[123] And Hegel's "brand of self-confidence" is "confidence in mind which for its own part is one with God and the same with God."[124] And to say this is the same thing as to say that it is confidence in "universal human *reason.*"[125] Barth says that, in saying this, we are saying that Hegel is taking up the inheritance of the Enlightenment.

Hegel is also supposed to have overcome "the dualism of the eternal truth of reason and the accidental truths of history."[126] And he is said to have accomplished this "within his concept of reason, and not by referring to some intuitive and emotional Beyond, which could not be apprehended, but only experienced."[127] "Hegel believed in the possibility, legitimacy and sovereignty of pure thought."[128] "And Hegel of course also affirmed Kant's transcendentalism."[129] But Kant's critique of knowledge had not been thorough enough. Kant's distinctions between the knowledge of ideas

123. *Ibid.*, p. 275.
124. *Idem.*
125. *Ibid.*, p. 276.
126. *Idem.*

127. *Idem.*
128. *Ibid.*, p. 277.
129. *Idem.*

and empirical knowledge on the one hand and theoretical and practical knowledge on the other hand must be thought of as preliminary stages of mere reflection. "All knowledge comprehending and surpassing these distinctions, is knowledge of God."[130] Fichte with his teaching of the ego understood Kant better than Kant understood himself. But we should allow neither of them to detain us. "The distinction between knowledge and the thing in itself, between ego and non-ego is a provisional matter. Upon this point Hegel proceeds with Herder and Romanticism."[131] Hegel is the Enlightenment philosopher with a "completely protected rear."[132] Hegel was able to include Lessing's discovery of historical experience, Kant's teaching of radical evil and the primacy of practical reason, Herder's protest against pure rationalism and the Romantic discovery of the immediacy of the individual in his all-inclusive concept of reason.[133] Thus God is no longer "an offence or foolishness" to man's understanding. The true reason of man is at the same time the reason of God.[134]

It is quite in accord with this concept of reason when Hegel asserts that for him method is everything. His views on history and of religion as well as his views on all other subjects depend on his method. "The only centre is the *method* which is to be applied and proves true in every discipline and in every field of life and learning."[135] But it is not so much the triadic movement of thesis, antithesis and renewed thesis that interests Hegel. It is the fact that through this triadic movement he attains to the invention of a "universal method altogether" that is of importance to him.[136] His method, he thinks, will reach not only "the problems of natural reality" but also the "incomparably harder concreteness of history."[137] By it Hegel can reach, as he thinks, the "most primitive paths of the human psyche" just as well as "the decisions of the Lord himself."[138]

Thus Hegel produced a philosophy in which theology seemed to be better taken care of than theology could take care of itself.[139] Hegel seems to be able to make keys to fit every lock.[140]

It is no wonder then that Barth feels that he must finally say

130. *Idem.*
131. *Ibid.*, p. 278.
132. *Idem.*
133. *Ibid.*, pp. 278-279.
134. *Ibid.*, p. 279.
135. *Ibid.*, p. 290.

136. *Idem.*
137. *Idem.*
138. *Idem.*
139. *Ibid.*, p. 293.
140. *Ibid.*, p. 291.

"No" to Hegel.[141] But, as was the case with Kant, Barth's *No* is not the *No* that any follower of the Reformers would give. Barth's entire criticism of Hegel, as was the case with his criticism of Kant, is to the effect that his principle of unity is *too* rationalistic and therefore *too* deterministic. Barth hopes to cure this rationalism and determinism by a liberal dose of irrationalism and contingency. Barth hopes to safeguard the "dialectic of grace" by means of his notion of the freedom of God.[142] And this freedom, as the reader knows, involves the idea that God can turn wholly into the opposite of himself.[143] God knows no necessity; he needs not his own being.

But this conception of the freedom of God is either purely factual, pre-conceptual, supra-conceptual and contra-conceptual and therewith purely meaningless or, if it is to have meaning, then it must be wholly expressed in a system of logic such as a Hegel or a Kant might construct. Barth is not willing to place the whole notion of the historic factual and the humanly conceptual upon the foundation of the self-contained God who has spoken to man through Christ in the Scripture. And for this reason he has no other means with which to say *No* to Hegel than of the Wholly Other which, if it is to be known, becomes of necessity the wholly identical with man.

Barth's attitude toward Hegel is the same as that which he has toward Kant. Both hold to a method of philosophy which is calculated to eat up and consume every teaching of Christianity. Both Hegel and Kant use a method which by their own word is universal in its significance and all-determinative of the nature of reality as a whole. Barth is unwilling to face the fact that this is actually the case. Consequently, the "dialectic of grace" that he seeks to vindicate over against Kant and Hegel is one that lives by the mercy of what is virtually an identity philosophy.

Barth does not feel comfortable when Hegel speaks of the devil "in tones of unfeigned admiration."[144] He disapproves of the fact that "in his paraphrase of the relation of man to God he did not call a halt before the concept of sin."[145] In consequence Hegel had no place for reconciliation as something that is new. Hegel sought sin "in the finite nature of man as such."[146] All in all, in Hegel's philosophy God can never speak to man. "Hegel's living God . . . is actually the living man."[147] For Hegel God is "utterly manifest."[148]

141. *Ibid.*, p. 281.
142. *Ibid.*, p. 304.
143. II:1, p. 352.
144. *Op. cit.*, pp. 286, 290.

145. *Ibid.*, p. 302.
146. *Idem.*
147. *Ibid.*, p. 303.
148. *Ibid.*, p. 304.

But all that Barth can offer in relation to this entire situation is to say that God is wholly hidden *even as* he is wholly revealed. He fails to see that this cure is as bad as the disease. There is in Barth's analysis of Hegel no release from the entanglement of an apostate dialecticism in which the pendulum swings backward and forward from pure abstract identity to pure meaningless contingency. Hegel is as little able to cross Lessing's Nasty Big Ditch as is Kant.

2. *The Theologians*

(a) SCHLEIERMACHER AND HIS ELLIPSE THEOLOGY

We come now to the "father of modern theology," Friedrich Schleiermacher. And in coming to him we have come to the heart of consciousness-theology. As earlier noted, it is especially in Barth's *Christian Dogmatics* (1927), that he sets his own theology, the theology of the Word, sharply over against the theology of Schleiermacher and his followers.

Consciousness-theologians, Barth said in that earlier work, start from the human consciousness as a given something. Then they ask whether there is another pole that is anything more than an illusion. They think from below and ask whether revelation from above is possible. They do not realize that he who dares to speak of God at all "must, in the last analysis, dare to do so with God alone. . . ."[149]

No one has the right on any ground to speak of God.[150] When we preach, says Barth, we ought to speak of God not because on an intellectual or an experiential basis we *can*, but because of the fact that, though *we cannot*, yet we must. Ludwig Feuerback is entirely justified in maintaining the impossibility of speaking otherwise than of ourselves. All theology as speech is only anthropology. Even so, we must maintain that God speaks through this anthropology.[151]

It is evident that at this early time Barth was seeking to cure consciousness-theology, although not in terms of the Reformation principle of the direct revelation of God through Christ in the Bible. On the contrary, it was by the idea of the wholly hidden character of revelation that Barth sought to overcome the weakness of consciousness-theology. He wanted a God who really speaks from above instead of from below. But in seeking to find such a God, he charges

149. *Op. cit.*, pp. 55ff.   151. *Ibid.*, p. 61.
150. *Ibid.*, p. 59.

consciousness-theologians with holding to a theology of possession. Over against this theology of possession, he argues that the preacher, in speaking of God, must wait for the *actus purus* of the Person of God.[152] A little later Barth argued that if we are not with Brunner to walk the road of nature *and* grace but rather to maintain the true primacy of grace alone, then we must not speak of the consciousness of man as having even so much as the power to receive the Word of God. What then is the proper relationship between philosophy and theology? They walk, to be sure, on the same road, but they walk in opposite directions. There can, says Barth, be no contact, except a negative one between them. Philosophy seeks, rightly, for a comprehensive system. Theology does no such thing. If theology seeks for a unity between the two worlds of truth and of reality, this unity can only be a matter of faith. Such unity must be thought of as existing only in God. Only thus can we escape the danger of holding to an already present, instead of an ever coming God. There is no polarity relationship of any sort between God and man. Between theology and philosophy there lies the fact of sin. And this constitutes an uncrossable gulf.

It is only by God's predestination and election that the impossible takes place. The doctrine of election, argues Barth in effect, is the answer to the consciousness-theologians. For the idea of election is the opposite of system of any sort.[153] And this idea of election in Christ is expressed in the *Church Dogmatics* in the idea of the freedom of God.

But in recent years, as noted in an earlier chapter, Barth has himself developed an anthropology. He found it impossible to do without it. Without an anthropology theology would remain up in the air. There must be, to be sure, a *primacy* of faith but this primacy must not destroy the human subject that believes. How then does Barth now feel about the anthropology of New Protestantism? Does he still feel that it swallows up theology? So far as Schleiermacher, the father of New Protestantism is concerned, the following points must be made. Barth recognizes that in Kant's philosophy autarchic reason claims a dictator's right even over the domain of theology. Theologians can (a) simply submit to the claims of the dictator and do the best they can, or (b) theologians can subject Kant's principles to an immanentistic critique. Schleiermacher fits into this second

---

152. *Ibid.*, p. 64.   153. *Zwischen den Zeiten*, 1929, pp. 309ff.

class. In pursuing either of these lines nineteenth century theology became a direct continuation of the theology of the Enlightenment.[154]

How then does Schleiermacher express the immanentistic criticism that he thinks is required with respect to the philosophy of Kant? He does this by saying that there "is yet another capacity *a priori* which is part of the necessities of human reason, apart from the theoretical and practical ones." This capacity *a priori*, says Schleiermacher, *is feeling*.

Barth feels, however, that this kind of criticism of Kant is not adequate. We have seen how he himself appeals to a third possibility for theology in relation to Kant. The all-important question now is how this third possibility that Barth sees for theology in relation to Kant's philosophy differs from the second, the one followed by Schleiermacher. It is the third one that Barth himself develops and it is the second which, together with the first, he says, continues the Enlightenment and also leads to Rome.

In dealing with Schleiermacher, says Barth, we must at all times think of the fact that he too is "within the sphere of the Church."[155] Schleiermacher attacked the problem of theology where it must be attacked "with a basic consideration."[156] He was deeply in earnest "to safeguard the specifically theological quality of theology."[157] He saw "the danger of a theology which is essentially apologetic in its approach—its impending metamorphosis into a philosophy; and if there was one thing he fought almost desperately against as an academic theologian, it was this danger. He saw also what the offence was wherewith he had to present philosophy, or at least the philosophy of his own time, if he wanted to be a theologian, and he did in fact dare to offend it in this way. It is the problem of Christology which is here at stake."[158]

But was Schleiermacher really able to present the claims of Jesus of Nazareth to the philosophy of his own day? Was there not that in his own philosophy that kept him from doing so effectively?[159] Barth's answer is plain: "Jesus of Nazareth fits desperately badly into this theology of the historical 'composite life' of humanity, a 'composite life' which is really after all fundamentally self-sufficient;

154. *Ibid.*, p. 190.
155. *From Rousseau to Ritschl*, etc., p. 310.
156. *Ibid.*, p. 312.
157. *Idem.*
158. *Idem.*
159. *Ibid.*, p. 313.

in Schleiermacher's sermons, too, Jesus only plays the striking *role* he does because, one is tempted to think, he is simply there. He obviously gives Schleiermacher, the professor and preacher, a great deal of trouble! But nevertheless he is in fact there. And the professor and preacher goes to this trouble, swims ceaselessly against his own current, and wishes under all circumstances, and be it at the cost of certain artifices and sophistries, to be a Christocentric theologian. Whether he really is, who can say? Perhaps in fleeing from one kind of philosophic speculation he became all the more deeply embroiled in another. Perhaps after all he avoided the offence of a real Christology."[160] After all, Schleiermacher wants to speak about Christ "in terms of the premises achieved by the philosophy and history and natural science of his day, and on no account in any others."[161]

Schleiermacher did not, of course, wish to identify theology with philosophy. He "did not give theology or the principles of Christianity a speculative basis."[162] He did not wish simply to derive these principles from human knowledge.[163] "He too is a philosopher of identity, approximating to Schelling's doctrine of the point of identity as the point at which the ideal and the real are seen to be as one, and approximating also to Hegel's philosophy of the mind as the synthesis of logic and natural philosophy."[164] But as a theologian he derived his principles independently of philosophy. The assertions of faith must, according to Schleiermacher, be presented in terms of themselves.[165] They must be "represented as a correct statement of Christian self-awareness."[166]

Here then, says Barth, we have reached the central point of Schleiermacher's theology. The great formal principle of Schleiermacher is also his material principle; it is that of Christian pious self-awareness contemplating and describing itself.[167]

By thus concentrating on pious self-awareness, Schleiermacher did not forget that theology must speak of God as well as of man. It is true that "in the very places where the theology of the Reformation had said 'the Gospel' or 'the Word of God' or 'Christ' Schleiermacher, three hundred years after the Reformation, now says, religion or piety."[168] But it must be remembered that, as every

160. *Idem.*
161. *Ibid.*, p. 316.
162. *Ibid.*, p. 328.
163. *Idem.*
164. *Ibid.*, p. 329.

165. *Idem.*
166. *Idem.*
167. *Ibid.*, p. 338.
168. *Ibid.*, p. 339.

theology must speak of God, so every theology must also speak of man. By birth and upbringing the Reformers were led to begin with God and Schleiermacher was led to begin with man. Yet, both the Reformers and Schleiermacher spoke of both God and man.[169] Schleiermacher too acknowledges two basic motifs and thus "enters into the course of Trinitarian theological thinking together with the Reformers."[170]

What interests Schleiermacher is "the question of man's action in regard to God."[171] And "we must not condemn him for this out of hand . . . A genuine, proper theology could be built up from such a starting-point."[172] "Theology could remain true to its own theme while it went with the times and thus completed this reversal. What Schleiermacher constructed by means of his theology of awareness by planting himself in the centre which for the Reformers had been a subsidiary centre, *could* be the pure theology of the Holy Spirit; the teaching of man brought face to face with God by God, of man granted grace by grace."[173] There is no doubt, says Barth, that Schleiermacher wanted his theology to be like theocentric Reformed theology.[174] He is "very much aware of a second centre beside his original one, and seeks to grant it its full validity."[175]

The only question is whether in stressing the divinity of the Holy Spirit, "which is his actual centre or rather is apparently meant by what he presents as his actual centre," he can still do justice to the "divinity of the *Logos.*"[176] As a "theology of the Word," the theology of the Reformers "is at once a theology of the Holy Spirit to such a degree that it can largely be understood as a theology of faith too, and it is this very fact which proves that it is the divine Word that forms its true centre. Will Schleiermacher's theology also pass this test, thus proving that for all the great reversal which is its starting-point, as compared with Reformed theology, its proceedings are theologically unexceptionable?"[177]

The answer is not clear. His second motif, the divinity of the Logos, does not fit in well with his first motif, the *divinity* of the Spirit. Are we then certain that we can even identify his *divinity* of the Spirit with the "divinity of the *Holy* Spirit"?[178]

169. *Idem.*
170. *Idem.*
171. *Ibid.*, p. 340.
172. *Idem.*
173. *Ibid.*, p. 341.

174. *Idem.*
175. *Idem.*
176. *Idem.*
177. *Idem.*
178. *Ibid.*, p. 343.

Why was it so difficult for Schleiermacher to do justice to his second motif? The answer is that he wanted to understand "revelation not strictly as revelation but in such a way that it might also be comprehensible as a mode of human cognition."[179] Accordingly, the object of faith became for him the correlate of human experience.[180] "When Schleiermacher speaks of Christ and Christians and their mutual relationship, what he primarily has in mind is neither the one nor the other, but one single concept embracing both, namely the 'composite life,' humanity, the history of 'human nature.' In this history it is a question of the 'redemption' of human nature. This redemption, however, is at the same time its fulfillment. It is a question of the furtherance of its 'higher life,' of its gradual ascent from the sensory to the spiritual state, from a dim to a powerful consciousness of God. To this extent it is a question of its approach to the way in which man was originally determined, which was thrown into question by sin. Piety is the condition of being involved in this approach."[181] "According to Schleiermacher Christ is the Revealer and Redeemer in so far as he effects the higher life."[182] To be sure, he did not want a speculative Christology. Even so, "he was bound" by the premise of his religion "to renounce the idea of the Deity of Christ or, to put it differently, to understand the Deity of Christ as the incomparable climax and decisive stimulator within the composite life of humanity. And it was not possible to arrive at an unequivocal opposition of Christ and Christians from this angle either. The antithesis between the two is seen through even before it is elaborated, and cannot be a final one. The first thing, and therefore the final thing too is the unity between the two, and the point at which this unity can be perceived is not by any means Christ, but the Christian, the view of Christ being in principle a view back towards him."[183]

"The two foci of the ellipse" that tie the relation of Christ to the Christian "draw relentlessly closer to one another, and how is the dissolution and disappearance of the objective moment in the subjective to be prevented? *The Word is not so assured here in its independence in respect to faith as should be the case if this theology of faith were a true theology of the Holy Spirit.* In a proper theology of the Holy Spirit there could be no question of dissolving the Word. Here, quite seriously, there is a question of such a dissolution. The

---

179. *Ibid.,* pp. 343-344.
180. *Ibid.,* p. 344.
181. *Ibid.,* p. 345.

182. *Ibid.,* p. 347.
183. *Ibid.,* pp. 349-350.

only thing which prevents it is Schleiermacher's good will in not allowing things to develop so far. This good will must once again be formally acknowledged, but that in no way alters the fact that we feel ourselves here in all seriousness threatened by this dissolution."[184]

Schleiermacher did not wish, of course, to destroy Reformation theology. He wanted to continue it in a way that suited his time. Even so, we have to maintain that in his theology there is an obscurity in the question of the relation of God to man. And within this obscurity "every identifiable sign points to the fact that here man has alone remained master of the field to the extent that he alone is the subject, and Christ has become his predicate."[185]

(b) FEUERBACH'S SMILE

The final sentence of this chapter of Barth's on Schleiermacher will remind the reader of Feuerbach. Feuerbach criticized consciousness-theology, stating that for it the Word of God is nothing but the divinity of the word. Feuerbach wanted to celebrate the divinity of the attribute rather than the attributes of divinity. In short, Feuerbach said that consciousness-theology was nothing but self-sufficient anthropology in disguise.[186] And Barth said that Feuerbach was right. Now, in his more recent estimate of Schleiermacher's theology, Barth once more asserts that in it Christ has become the predicate of man as the subject.

After discussing Schleiermacher Barth turns once again to Feuerbach. Will he still find that Feuerbach is right in relation to Schleiermacher?

Feuerbach, says Barth, was an outsider. He was a philosopher but "engaged in nothing but theology."[187] As such "he sought to take Schleiermacher and Hegel seriously, completely seriously, at the point where they concurred in asserting the non-objective quality of God."[188] In his eyes even Kant, Fichte and Hegel are supernaturalists in that they seek for divine Being in reason, separately from man.[189]

Of course, Feuerbach does not deny either God or theology. "In

184. *Ibid.*, pp. 352-353.   185. *Ibid.*, p. 354.
186. *Cf.* article on Ludwig Feuerbach in *Die Theologie und die Kirche,* München, 1929, pp. 212ff.
187. *Ibid.*, p. 355.   189. *Idem.*
188. *Idem.*

denying the existence of an abstract divine Being, divorced from nature and man, he is merely affirming God's nature as man's true nature."[190] His feeling is positive. "He, too, is singing his *Magnificat*."[191]

This theology of Feuerbach represents a question to the theology of his time, and perhaps not only of his time.[192] The theology of the time was constantly seeking to show that the relationship of God to man could "also be understood as a necessary predicate of man."[193] And Feuerbach asks the theologians whether in thus formulating the question they are not primarily interested in the apotheosis of man.[194]

"Was he in fact completely in the wrong?"[195] Was not Schleiermacher's "Christology and doctrine of atonement, seemingly projected back from the personal experience of the human subject?"[196] And how about the might which Hegel and his disciples "bestow upon the human mind in its dialectic self-movement?"[197] Feuerbach's question is always in point and becomes acute "whenever incautious use is made in theology of mystical ideas, of the union of God and man; in fact, whenever these ideas are used other than in an eschatologically ensured connexion."[198]

Unfortunately, the theologians of the time of Feuerbach were unable to answer him. Feuerbach's own conception of man is an illusion. He identifies the individual with the species. He had no eye for the true man as an individual and for the wickedness of this individual or for the fact that he must surely die. "But the theology of the time was not so fully aware of the individual, or of wickedness or death, that it could instruct Feuerbach upon these points. Its own hypotheses about the relationship with God were themselves too little affected by them. In this way they were similar to Feuerbach's, and upon this common ground his rivals could not defeat him. That was why the theology of his time found it ultimately possible to preserve itself in face of him, as it had preserved itself in face of D. F. Strauss, without summoning an energetic cry of 'God preserve us!' "[199] When Feuerbach smiles his condescending smile, we must laugh in his face.

190. *Ibid.*, p. 356.
191. *Idem.*
192. *Ibid.*, pp. 357-358.
193. *Ibid.*, p. 358.
194. *Idem.*
195. *Idem.*
196. *Idem.*
197. *Idem.*
198. *Ibid.*, p. 358-359.
199. *Ibid.*, p. 361.

(c) Strauss and His Projected Christ

It is well to consider what Barth has to say about D. F. Strauss along with his remarks on Feuerbach. Together they again present the problem of Lessing's big ditch and pose the question as to whether Schleiermacher or the idealist philosophers and theologians could cross it. Strauss' work on the *Life of Jesus* was an achievement that paralleled that of Feuerbach's "concerning the problem of religion."[200] Perhaps we shall find that in Strauss "a secret ailment of the whole of modern theology is focused and represented in a special way."[201] His achievement lies, of course, chiefly in the historical sphere.[202] In his second *Life of Jesus* (1862) Strauss set forth the religious consciousness as it really was according to the synoptic gospels.[203] At this time Strauss was able to think "with understanding mildness" of Jesus' messianic claims. But of what help is Jesus as history really presents him to us? "Our historical information concerning him is incomplete and uncertain. It is out of the question that faith and salvation can depend on things only the smallest part of which are not in doubt. And, in any case, it is a matter of principle that there should be no such dependence. 'Just as certainly as the destiny of man is a universal one and accessible to all, so the conditions upon which it is to be achieved . . . must be accorded to every man'; the perception of the goal must 'not only be an accidental one, a historical perception coming from without, but a necessary perception of reason, which each man can find in himself.' "[204] Strauss feels that the transference of faith that saves from the figure of the historical Christ to reason is required by "the imperative result of the more recent development of mind. It is 'the continued development of the religion of Christ to a religion of humanity, towards which all the nobler endeavour of our time is directed.' "[205] Of course this is not to say that the historical Christ served no useful purpose. He was the chief among those who helped forward the realization of the human ideal.[206] Here we have an ordinary garden type of liberalism.

In his first *Life of Jesus* (1835–36) something more dramatic was presented. In this first *Life of Jesus* it was the method that caused

200. *Ibid.*, p. 363.
201. *Idem.*
202. *Ibid.*, p. 364.
203. *Ibid.*, p. 373.

204. *Idem.*
205. *Ibid.*, p. 374.
206. *Idem.*

the great offence.[207] And why did it cause such great offence? It was because of the simplicity or even naiveté of the theologians of the time. The historical element had always given these theologians a measure of trouble. But "quite naively they thought man could be conscious and possessed of religion, of the consciousness of God, the experience of transcendence, the Christian quality within himself, as something which was there and given, something which could be joyfully reckoned with. They thought man could be conscious and possessed of the historical basis for religion in the same way, no matter whether one understood it like Schleiermacher, more as a historical beginning, or, like Marheineke, more as a metaphysical origin, or lastly, like Tholuck and Menken—the 'Positives' of that time—more as the supernatural divine imparting of religion. They used history just as unquestioningly as they used psychology."[208]

Jesus was thought to be "a human personage who is in principle accessible to historical knowledge in precisely the same measure as Tiberius is accessible to it."[209] We can "in some way come to terms with his miracles, with virgin birth and resurrection, divesting them of their true miraculous character by describing them as misunderstandings, hidden secrets of nature, or as myth; or by somewhat enlarging *ad hoc* the concept of what is historical, calling historically real something one would never otherwise be prepared to call historically possible."[210] ". . . if something like the feeling of utter dependence can find a place in the picture we form of ourselves, then why cannot someone like Jesus Christ also find a place in our picture of history? It will be a Jesus reduced in stature and hammered into shape, perhaps, a Jesus who is perhaps a trifle groomed, domesticated and made practicable when compared with all the strange things which are said of him in the texts, even in the 'Life of Jesus' versions of positive theology. But it is precisely in this way that he will find a place there, even if only just so that a historically immanent connexion between him and our faith becomes possible in principle."[211]

Now "the name of D. F. Strauss stands for no more and no less than the breaking-up of this concerted body of opinion about research into the life of Jesus, the protest against its method, the declaration that its entire undertaking was impossible to execute."[212]

207. *Ibid.*, p. 375.
208. *Ibid.*, p. 375.
209. *Ibid.*, p. 378.
210. *Ibid.*, pp. 378-379.
211. *Ibid.*, p. 379.
212. *Idem.*

Against the commonly adopted view, Strauss asserted: (1) that "we cannot expect to find what we believe, as such, in history."[213] Thus Strauss challenged "the historical immanence of the connexion between Christ and faith,"[214] (2) Such being the case, we need not much concern ourselves about source-criticism. "Upon all points, so to speak, the form of the New Testament narrative is not that of a historical report, but simply that of a myth. So strong is Strauss's impression of the particular nature of these sources that he makes their disqualification as historical sources the starting-point for his method,"[215] (3) Again, such being the case, he "does not even begin to enquire after" any such thing as the "historical core" of the life of Jesus,[216] (4) Once again, such being the case, Strauss took no pains to "work out a character picture of Jesus."[217] Theologians had taken for granted that Jesus should be accessible "so that we could 'have' him, as we have other men."[218] "But Strauss's lack of concern and his silence upon this point made it seem as if Jesus were inaccessible and incomprehensible as a man, and as if we might not, therefore, be able thus to have him"[219] and (5) All this being the case, Strauss denied the possibility of ascribing a "unique and absolute quality" to this historical phenomenon.[220] Barth here quotes Strauss as follows: "If reality is ascribed to the idea of the unity of divine and human nature is this as much as to say that it must once have become real in one individual, as it was never again either before or since? This is by no means the way in which the idea realizes itself, pouring out its whole abundance upon one example and begrudging itself to all others. Rather it likes to unfold its wealth in a diversity of examples which complement each other, in the interchange of individualities one in decline, the other rising."[221]

Here we reach the point also openly avowed by Feuerbach that humanity is the absolute, the true content of Christology.[222] Jesus served the useful purpose of lifting the sense of absolute value into the universal human consciousness.[223]

This then is the substance of Strauss' view. Historical research can at best produce a Christ who, as a revealer of God, can be only relative. As such he can at most be a symbol of the "thing itself."

213. *Ibid.*, p. 380.
214. *Idem.*
215. *Ibid.*, pp. 380-381.
216. *Ibid.*, p. 381.
217. *Idem.*
218. *Ibid.*, p. 382.
219. *Idem.*
220. *Idem.*
221. *Idem.*
222. *Idem.*
223. *Idem.*

This Christ "could on no account be the Word that became flesh, executing God's judgment upon us and challenging us ourselves to make a decision."[224] "This is what D. F. Strauss asked theology, just as Feuerbach asked it, whether the Godhead man sought and thought he had found in his consciousness was anything but man's shadow as it was projected upon the plane of the idea of the Infinite."[225]

Strauss had no solution for his problem. He merely saw through the bad solution that was given in his day and "gave up any further attempt to improve upon it." Therefore the problem "pursued him to the last like a fate."[226] Even so, it must be maintained "that together with Feuerbach, Strauss is the theologian who was most significant for the situation of theology in the time after Schleiermacher's death."[227] "Proper theology begins just at the point where the difficulties disclosed by Strauss and Feuerbach are seen and then laughed at."[228]

(d) Barth's Failure to Answer Feuerbach and/or Strauss

It is now time to ask how Barth himself seeks to face and answer the question that confronts him in the Feuerbach-Strauss criticism of consciousness-theology. Barth has traced for us the development of Enlightenment philosophy in Kant. By his primacy of the practical reason, Kant tried to get beyond the Enlightenment but did not really succeed in doing so. He made room for the church indeed. He allowed the preachers in the church to preach according to their creeds indeed. But the scholar in the preacher would either have to stop his ears or else reduce the words of the preacher to symbols of self-sufficient rational truths. Hegel went beyond Kant. He had a deeper view of reason than did Kant. Hegel sought by means of this deeper reason to allow genuine room for the historical and the positive in religion. But the scholar in his preacher must also stop his ears when the latter speaks of sin and reconciliation. He too must reduce the particular to the universal whenever it meets him. He too must reduce the supernatural to the natural. Schleiermacher goes beyond Kant in a different way from that of Hegel. Schleiermacher insisted that there is another "capacity *a priori* in addition to the

224. *Ibid.*, p. 387.   227. *Ibid.*, p. 388.
225. *Idem.*   228. *Ibid.*, p. 389.
226. *Idem.*

theoretical and practical aspects of reason." Even so, he did not overcome the Enlightenment. In him too the object of faith loses itself at last in the subject. And Feuerbach and Strauss, each in his own way but with the same intent and result, simply bring out the failure of one and all of these and many other men. Feuerbach is quite right in saying that if one assumes at the start the self-sufficiency of the human consciousness that then one can only go round in circles within it. Strauss shows that one who, like Jesus, claims to have escaped this circle, saying that he, and he alone, is God and man thereby only proves that he is a fanatic. The end result is that we stand still before Lessing's nasty big ditch. Every attempt that was made since the day that Lessing looked into it so hopelessly has only resulted in making it more apparent that the ditch cannot be crossed if the initial assumption of the autonomy of man is not forsaken.

How does Barth propose to cross this ditch? Does he propose to return to the theology of the Reformers and start with the presupposition that God has really spoken from above to man? Does he forsake the assumption of the Enlightenment, of Kant, of Hegel, of Schleiermacher, of Feuerbach and of Strauss, and with Calvin set the consciousness of man, from the beginning, in the concrete relationship of God's unavoidable revelation directly present to man in history? No, he does not!

On the contrary, at the conclusion of his survey Barth simply expresses complete agreement with Strauss in saying that God cannot be present directly in history. "Something absolute as a part of world and of human history as such is a sword of lath."[229] To be sure, here as elsewhere Barth assumes that the idea of direct revelation in history and in Scripture is identical with the rationalist notion that man can then master history. He does this again and again throughout his work. Barth simply cannot think of a directly ascertainable presence of God in history that cannot be mastered by man. But this fact all the more establishes the point that his own view of the human consciousness is not different from that of the consciousness-theologians and as such is not different from that of Kant and the Enlightenment. Barth constantly asserts that it is the proper business of philosophy to seek for a comprehensive system in terms of itself. At the same time he knows that theology must somehow be related to philosophy. If it is not so related, then it has no message

229. *Ibid.*, p. 383.

to tell to the nations. How then will he make philosophy stop at a certain arbitrary point in order to leave room for faith? His own review of Kant and Hegel should be clear evidence of the fact that any theology that wishes to live in the same world with their philosophy must either keep silence or speak according to the demands of autonomous reason.

Herewith we return to the "third possibility" in relation to Kant in terms of which Barth hoped to cross Lessing's big ditch. The first two possibilities, the way of the direct followers of Kant and the way of Schleiermacher and his followers, said Barth, lead directly to Rome or to Feuerbach and to Strauss. But it was in terms of his third possibility that he would give the preacher something to preach without being silenced by the scholar. As earlier noted, this third possibility was nothing more, and could in the nature of the case be nothing more, than an attempt to seek a Christ in the realm projected by self-sufficient reason. This *wholly other* of Barth can never do the one thing it is above all else supposed to do, namely, speak from above. This wholly other cannot speak at all unless it becomes wholly identical with man and then it is no longer other in any sense. Quite rightly Barth says that in the theology of Modern Protestantism the object of faith recedes of necessity into the subject. This is equally true of his own theology. And so he cannot cross the big ditch of Lessing and he cannot smile at Feuerbach. Of the theology of the nineteenth century Barth makes this final statement: "The situation was such that in running away from Feuerbach they ran straight into the arms of Strauss. And if they managed somehow to escape Strauss they were still not free of Feuerbach. That was the deeply disturbing feature of the state of theological discussion a hundred years ago: the deeply disturbing background to the history of theology in all the ensuing decades."[230] The same thing must also be said of Barth.

Barth's system is *open* in terms of Lessing's big ditch. It is open, that is to say, because he assumes with Lessing, with Kant, with Hegel and with Schleiermacher that man's reason or intellect must of necessity make the demand that any God it is to worship must be penetrable to itself. Then when this man is faced with that which he cannot penetrate, and there is nothing that he can penetrate, then he assumes that God cannot penetrate it either. His rationalist as-

230. *Idem.*

sumption requires him to asume that he can penetrate all that God can penetrate and that God cannot penetrate anything that man cannot penetrate. Thus God and man are assumed to be identical in being as they are identical in the reach of their logical powers. In other words, the principles of an identity philosophy account for the supposed rationality of the system of thought thus constructed. God must be wholly expressed in his revelation; he must be identical with his revelation.

Strictly speaking, there should on this view be no revelation at all. Plato was quite consistent with the principles of his rationalistic motif when he said that any reality that is not eternal is not real at all in the full sense of the term. Even so, Plato had to allow some sort of reality to temporal existence; so modern philosophy has to allow some sort of reality to historical existence and with it to bare possibility.

For this reason Kant limited reason and made room for faith. But the object of this faith was and could be for Kant nothing determinate. So also in Barth's theology. His God and his Christ, so far as they are above man, are indeterminate. And as soon as his God is in his Christ present to man, he is wholly identical with man. To be sure, when this God is wholly identical with man, he is also again wholly different from man. But this is true because man is also wholly different from himself. In other words, in Kantian and post-Kantian idealism man explains himself in terms of abstract form and abstract matter. He is therefore wholly revealed to himself in terms of form and wholly hidden to himself in terms of pure matter. The same thing holds true for the Christ that comports with this sort of philosophy.

There is no reason then why the open system of Barth, largely springing as it does from the primacy of reason as found in Kant's philosophy, should not comport with the open system of Von Balthasar and Küng that largely springs from Aristotle's idea of the analogy of being. And there is no reason why the analogy of faith in the theology of Barth should not live at peace with the analogy of being in Roman Catholic theology. And Feuerbach will smile at them all and yet fail to smile about himself. But there is every reason why the theology of Barth, that of Rome, and of Modern Protestantism should unitedly oppose the theology of the Reformers.

Chapter XVI

The Higher Humanism

The burden of the argument of the three preceding chapters has been to the effect that the God of Barth's theology is like the god of modern consciousness-theology, a projection of the would-be autonomous man. Berkouwer said in his work on *Karl Barth* (1936) that Barth's idea of the sovereignty of God rests upon a nominalism more extreme than that of Occam.[1] Occam still believed in a positive revelation of God to man. Back of this revelation he placed the sovereignty of God. This sovereignty became a threat to the trustworthiness of the revelation given in Christ and through him in the Scriptures. But Barth no longer believes in any positive revelation at all. In his theology the whole of positive revelation has been absorbed by the idea of the "actualistic unapproachable reality of God."[2] Thus everything in the church and in theology is made uncertain.[3] Even when Barth speaks in very positive fashion of the certainty of faith, of experience and the church, we must always think of such statements as being conditioned by his nominalist idea of the sovereignty of God.[4] Barth's criticism of all "given and direct revelation" is even more extreme than that of Brunner. "It is in the last analysis the *dependability* of God, which is in Barth's theology the point of importance. The revelation of God is deprived of its meaning, when over against all that is 'given' we are directed toward the 'deeper reality' of the hidden God."[5] Berkouwer points out that

1. *Karl Barth*, p. 80.
2. *Ibid.*, p. 92.
3. *Idem.*
4. *Idem.*
5. *Ibid.*, p. 93.

all-destructive character of Barth's view of revelation by indicating what it does to the biblical revelation of the covenant of God with man. The covenant is the revelation of God's faithfulness with respect to his people as he leads them, draws them and preserves them continually "in the horizontal line of history." How could this idea of the covenant be given a place in the "actualistic sovereignty scheme of Barth's theology? It is precisely *this* continuity that Barth opposes passionately."[6]

Thus on this very vital point the divine actuality destroys "all continuity of the work of God in this world and the bearing reality of his covenant."[7] As a red thread this basic motif of the actuality of God runs through all of Barth's theology. "Here lies the source of Barth's view of revelation, his conceptions with respect to Scripture, with respect to the canon, with respect to the *open* canon, with respect to the facts of salvation, with respect to the trinity, Christology, pneumatology, ecclesiology and eschatology."[8]

Hans Michael Müller drew out the destructive consequences of Barth's own idea of the sovereignty of God as a condition *(Vorbehalt)* of all that Barth said in the field of theology. Barth rejects this criticism by saying that even his *method* stands under the control of his *Vorbehalt.*[9] What then are we to say of this argument between Barth and Müller? Berkouwer gives us the clue. We are to appreciate the fact that Barth wants to apply the brakes when his view is carried through to its inevitable destructive consequences. But Barth's view of the divine condition was seldom so clearly seen in its destructive significance as it was in this debate between Müller and himself.[10] Through this one theme of God as being exlex "which reappears in all its subdivisions, Barth's theology has become the opposite of a scriptural dogmatics."[11] In a scriptural dogmatics there is no such thing as a condition. In such a dogmatics every dualism in the idea of God is rejected. Only by clinging to the idea of revelation as given in Scripture can we avoid all speculation. Barth may warn against all speculation, but his idea of revelation as conditioned by the sovereignty of God leads him directly into it. Forsaking the idea of "direct" revelation, his theology is inevitably bound up with speculation.[12]

6. *Idem.*
7. *Ibid.,* p. 94.
8. *Idem.*
9. *Ibid.,* p. 96.

10. *Ibid.,* p. 97.
11. *Idem.*
12. *Idem.*

Other Reformed writers, mentioned earlier, have as with one voice expressed essentially the same sort of criticism of Barth here made by Berkouwer. Even the philosophers discussed build up their own views on the basis of the "direct" revelation of God in history. And they, as well as the theologians, know that the natural man is ethically hostile to God and therefore misinterprets this revelation of God. By his hatred of God the natural man is bound to repress the truth of revelation given him. He does not want to be confronted with the demands of the God against whom, ever since the day of Adam at the beginning of history, he is in rebellion. Even in the field of philosophy this opposition to God appears. Everywhere, in man's own constitution as well as in his environment, God speaks to man. But everywhere too man, the sinner, seeks to suppress the truth about himself and his relation to God his creator. Even when God in his grace speaks redemptively to man through Christ, and then Christ speaks redemptively to man through the Scriptures, the natural man again seeks to repress this revelation. He uses his scientific and philosophic as well as his theological systems in order to keep under the challenge of the revelation of God to him. Everywhere God meets man and everywhere asks man to answer. Man is inherently a covenantal being. He is one who cannot help but answer to God. He can give the right answer to God only through Christ's atoning blood and through the regenerating power of the Holy Spirit. Once Christ has become a curse for him on the cross, and once Christ has risen from the dead for his righteousness and he has by the Spirit's power accepted this salvation wrought for him in history, then he seeks at every point to be a covenant-keeper. He then seeks to be a covenant-keeper in the field of science and philosophy no less than in the field of theology. The great presupposition of all his efforts at interpreting himself and the world about him is the fact that he and the world are first interpreted by God in Christ as revealed in Scripture.

On this basis human self-awareness is awareness of self in relation to what God has revealed himself as being for man through Christ. On this basis God speaks to man from above and man answers to God as a scientist, as a philosopher and as a theologian. All his predication constitutes one great answer of covenant gratitude to his redeemer through whom he has been brought back to God the father.

Berkouwer quite rightly says that on the biblical approach there is no dualism in the idea of God. But this does not mean that man claims to have at any point an exhaustive understanding of things. It does not even mean that in some field, for instance, the field of science or that of philosophy, man aims at an exhaustive knowledge of reality. On the contrary, the biblical views involve the recognition of mystery everywhere. There is no fact in the universe that man understands or will understand comprehensively. But his presupposition is that, because God has created all things, therefore he also controls and directs all things. Of course the believer does not seek to prove the existence of such a God. This God must be presupposed as the basis of all proof in any field. Thus the biblical position is not like that of rationalism or like that of irrationalism. Nor is it like any combination of these two. It is based on the presupposition that man knows truly though not comprehensively because God does know all things in terms of his self-contained being and has revealed himself to man.

This is the analogy of faith based on the scriptural revelation with respect to man's creation in the image of God. But this analogy of faith is at the same time the analogy of being. The redeemed sinner knows that he is what he is, that sin is what it is and that salvation is what it is, because in the Scriptures as the Word of God his creator and redeemer has so told him. He is not afraid to say that he *knows* this. His very knowledge, that is his very conceptual activity, is subject to the revelation of God in Christ. Therefore his knowledge is always existential in character. And it is *everywhere* existential in character. There is for him no phenomenal realm in which he, as the subject of knowledge, stands above the objects of his knowledge. For the objects of his knowledge, including his very self, are themselves subject to God, the great subject of knowledge, who alone is the great *I am*.

Moreover, the redeemed sinner does not hesitate to say that he knows all this *with certainty*. His certainty is, of course, based on the authority of the revelation of God in Christ. At the same time he knows that unless he gives the answer of faith in every field he has no answer even of science or philosophy in any field. Even the knowledge that those who do not submit themselves to Christ possess in any field is finally to be accounted for by the fact that they and their environment are what God through Christ in the Bible says they are. If the universe were controlled by Chance, as the non-biblical position in the last analysis assumes it to be, and if man must think of himself as the ultimate source of all coherence that he experiences, then life has no meaning. With Paul the biblical believer may therefore say in all humility but also with all boldness: "Where *is* the wise? where *is* the scribe? where *is* the disputer of this world? hath not God made foolish the wisdom of this world? For after that in the wisdom of God the world by wisdom knew not God, it pleased God by the foolishness of preaching to save them that believe" (I Cor. 1:20-21).

Barth believes none of all this. His actualistic concept of revelation requires him to take sides with modern science, with modern philosophy and modern theology against this simple biblical view of men and things. That Barth holds to the modern view of autonomous science is well known. That he holds also to the modern idea of autonomy in philosophy is equally well known. And that his actualist view of revelation is the implicate and expression of the view of autonomy in science and in philosophy is also clear. What Berkouwer has said about Barth's actualist view of revelation is but to point out how fundamentally hostile Barth is to any approach to theology that is based upon the idea of the direct revelation of God to man in history at any point.

Neither has Barth's view of the sovereignty of God become any less actualist in more recent years. To be sure, we have heard Berkouwer and Runia speak of the Christo-monistic tendency of Barth's recent thought. But this monist tendency of Barth's more recent theology, no less than his dualistic tendency in his earlier work, also constitutes a threat to the direct revelation of God in history. Berkouwer again points out this fact with all possible clarity. He indicates that Barth has no proper respect for the mystery of God in his revelation. He complains of Barth's desire to make God's revelation perspicuous to man. Barth therefore again makes a violent attack on the gradual step-by-step revelation of God in history. Barth's present tendency toward monism, as was the case with his earlier tendency toward dualism, is expressed in his opposition to the idea of the direct work of the covenant-salvation of God through Christ in history.[13]

This monistic tendency, as much as his earlier dualistic tendency, strikes right at the heart of the principle of grace. It involves the idea of sin as overcome *in advance* by grace. Sin is said to be an

13. *De Triomph der Genade,* etc., p. 248.

ontological impossibility. There is, as Berkouwer pointedly observes, on Barth's view no transition from wrath to grace in history.[14] On Barth's basis the wrath of God is merely a form of grace *(Gestalt der Gnade).*[15] It is true that Barth seeks to attribute reality to sin. But whatever the reality of sin, it is overcome *in advance (zum vornherein)* by grace.[16] The nature of the *triumph* of grace in the theology of Barth lies precisely in this *zum vornherein.* Barth holds the supralapsarian view of election just because he thinks that in this view the idea of this triumphant nature of grace is best expressed.[17] It is in this supralapsarian view that Barth's opposition to the step-by-step nature of salvation in history comes to its most striking expression.[18] It is in this purified supralapsarian view of election that "the way to the decisive significance of the history is blocked."[19]

It appears then that Barth's theology lies between his nominalist view of election, his *Vorbehalt,* and his realist view of the triumph of grace, his *zum vornherein.* In the former we have the sovereignty of his grace and in the latter its universality. And these two, in the nature of the case, supplement one another. This is well brought out by the criticism Berkouwer makes both of the notion of *Vorbehalt* and of the notion of *zum vornherein.* The former stands for the idea of pure contingency and the latter for the idea of pure determinism. Neither can stand by itself. Each needs the other in order to attain even the appearance of meaning, and together they deny any decisive significance either to the fall of man or to his redemption. Together they deny, in effect, the decisive meaning of history altogether.

1. *Barth and Roman Catholicism*

One source of great confusion in the interpretation of Barth's theology has been the fact of his constant claim that he is carrying forth Reformation theology and, by the same token, opposing Roman Catholicism. But it is now more obvious than ever that Barth does not carry on Reformation theology. How can one whose main target of criticism throughout the years has been the identifica-

14. *Idem.*   17. *Ibid.*, p. 251.
15. *Idem.*   18. *Ibid.*, p. 253.
16. *Ibid.*, p. 244.   19. *Ibid.*, p. 252.

tion of history with revelation be said to carry on Reformation theology? How can one who with his earlier dualism and with his later monism denies that there is any transition from wrath to grace in history be said to carry on Reformation theology?

Barth's opposition to Romanism has always been in terms of his *Vorbehalt* or of his *zum vornherein*. The great error of Rome's fatal "and," its synergism, its reciprocity, its natural theology and its *analogia entis,* has always been, on Barth's view, that in it all there is hidden the serpent of direct revelation. On Barth's view, if Rome was in error, then the Reformation was in far greater error. We can therefore do nothing less than express agreement with Berkouwer on this point when he says that the opposition of Barth and the opposition of "protestant dogmatics" against Romanism, is structurally different. If Reformed dogmatics were to subscribe without qualification to Barth's criticism on Rome, it "would sign its own death-sentence."[20] The fact that Barth and the Reformers both oppose Romanism does not prove that their opposition has the same foundation. Barth opposes Romanism from the point of view of his actualistic concept of revelation.[21] Calvin opposed Rome in a different way. In his struggle with nominalism he had excluded the basic motif of Barth.[22]

When in the *Church Dogmatics* Barth continues to defend the idea of "sovereign grace" against Rome, he does so in terms of his *zum vornherein*. According to Barth, Romanism does not do justice to the primacy of grace because it does not hold that man's very manhood presupposes his salvation in Christ. If therefore Reformed theology were to agree with Barth in this his recent opposition to Rome, it would again be signing its own death warrant. For, as Berkouwer has shown, on Barth's latest view of grace, sin is an *ontological impossibility.* Barth did change the nature of his polemics against Rome in the course of the years. As he formerly stressed the notion of the *Vorbehalt,* so he now stresses the notion of the *zum vornherein*. If formerly he opposed Rome from the point of view of his actualist concept of revelation, he now opposes Rome from the point of view of his idea of the triumph of grace.

The change in the nature of Barth's polemics against Rome is therefore not a basic one. Barth is always opposing the idea of a

20. *Karl Barth,* p. 187.   22. *Ibid.,* p. 188.
21. *Idem.*

given revelation. And he has always done so from the point of view of his concept of sovereign universal grace. Formerly he stressed the idea that the concept of *analogia entis* was opposed to the *sovereignty* of grace. More recently he stresses the idea that the concept of *analogia entis* is opposed to the *universality* of grace.[23] It is therefore not as though Barth's theology has only recently come to resemble that of Roman Catholicism. As earlier noted, Barth's activist categories have from the beginning made him construct a theology that is even more hostile to Reformation principles than is the theology of Romanism.

Rome has made alliance with Greek immanentist philosophy. Therefore its theology is largely based on human autonomy. But Barth has made alliance with modern immanentist philosophy. And this modern immanentism, while ostensibly making room for faith in God and Christ, is in reality more autonomous than was ancient philosophy. The God and the Christ of modern immanentist philosophy is merely the projection of a human ideal. This human ideal is hypostatized and personalized and thus made into a God. In other words, this God is a limiting concept, not an actually existing and acting being. This God has not created the world and does not direct it. When this God became incarnate in Christ to save man from sin, he does only that which man has made him to do.

Modern idealist thinking, both in theology and philosophy, is opposed to all forms of naturalism and mechanism. Modern idealist thought opposes ordinary earthy humanism. But its own position is still man-centered. As such it is still humanistic. We may call this position the *higher humanism.*

Barth's theology has at no time outreached the principles of this higher humanism. Its very notion of the primacy of Christ as the embodiment of sovereign universal grace is a projection of would-be autonomous man. The whole argument of this work has established this fact. We shall not now recapitulate that argument. Instead we shall bring to the fore some of the high points in it. This will bring out the fact that if Barth's position is to be called Protestant, it must be so called in the way that Schleiermacher's theology is called Protestant. It is a man-centered Protestantism, not the Protestantism of Luther or Calvin.

23. *Cf.* II:1, p. 275 where Barth militates against A. Quenstedt.

2. *Barth and New Protestantism*

That Barth's theology is in line with and a development of New Protestantism is apparent from its starting-point. This starting-point may be called its principle of identity.

At this point too Barth seems on the surface to be on the side of the Reformers and opposed to the New Protestants. Suppose we set Calvin and Descartes over against one another. Both start their thinking by telling us who man is. For Descartes man is a being who can explain himself, his world and his God in terms of himself. To be sure, he too needs a god, but he makes a god in the image of man. For Calvin, man is from the outset placed in the configuration of his relation to God as his creator and to Christ as his redeemer revealed once for all in Scripture. On whose side is Barth? Ostensibly and verbally he is on Calvin's side, but actually, by virtue of the content of his theology, he is on Descartes' side.

The fact that Barth's theology as a whole and his anthropology in particular is based on Christology does not prove the contrary. For everything depends on what the nature of Christ is said to be. And what is the nature of the Christ of Barth's theology? For Barth Jesus Christ is the *Christ-Event*. Barth has actualized the incarnation. He has reinterpreted Chalcedon. The two natures of Christ are therefore related to one another in terms of God's saving of all men. Jesus Christ is the history of the salvation of all men.[24] In this history *(Geschichte)* the steps of Christ's exaltation do not follow those of his humiliation as temporal events. There is no transition from wrath to grace in history.

Thus man is what he is as fellow-man with Jesus. Man is what he is as one who has been saved in Christ. It is in this sense that the idea of creation is said to be subordinate to that of the covenant of grace. Man is to be identified for what he is in terms of this "grace-objectivism." Man is man as elected in Christ. Man is man as the one for whom the wrath of God is absorbed *in advance* by Christ. Man the sinner is what he is as the one who participates in the inter-trinitarian life of God himself.[25] God's history completes itself as world-history.[26] God is inherently coexistent as well as existent, and as such takes man up into the cycle of his history.

24. IV:1, p. 138.   26. *Idem.*
25. *Ibid.*, p. 236.

Of course man is all that he is *through Christ*. Barth spurns every form of direct identification of man with God. Even so, there are no men except as they are men by participation in Christ. This idea of man's indirect identification with God is just as destructive of the Creator-creature distinction of Scripture as the crassest forms of identity-philosophy could be. In Barth's theology the Christ-Event stands for the idea of Reality as a whole. In Greek philosophy the ideas of permanence and change stood antagonistically over against one another. Aristotle did try to overcome their opposition by the notion of *analogy of being*. In this notion pure contingency and pure changeless form were made correlative to one another. But it was not till modern times, and especially through Kant, that the aspect of contingency was given equal standing with the aspect of form. The Act-principle of post-Kantian thought seeks to express this full cor-relativity between pure form and pure chance. And Barth has built his theology on this Act-principle. Accordingly, his God becomes wholly lost to himself in the bottomless sea of pure contingency. But, of course, his man always comes out of chance with Christ, victorious over Chaos. This is the essence of his higher humanism.

Barth knows full well that the Reformers had no such views. His "radical correction" of Calvin's view of election in terms of his own purified supralapsarianism indicates this fact. Barth argues that be-cause Calvin does not take grace to be sovereign-universal grace in his own sense of the term, he does not understand grace at all.[27] Barth bewails the fact that Reformation-theology did not properly put Christology at the foundation of all its teachings about the rela-tion of God and man to one another.[28] He says this after he has told us about his actualizing of the incarnation.[29] Our fundamental start-ing-point must be the Christ-Event.[30] Starting with the *Christ-Event*, and interpreting everything in terms of it, we know that grace is the all-overarching and all-unifying attribute of God. Accordingly, there can be no such thing as a wrath of God that is not borne by God himself in Christ for all men. Not starting from the *Christ-Event* as their master-concept the Reformers, and particularly Calvin, did not understand the comfort of the gospel. They did not fathom the triumph of grace in Christ. They did not have a true standard for judging the nature of sin and even of right and wrong.[31]

27. *Cf.* Chapter IV, *Beyond the Reformers.*
28. *Church Dogmatics,* IV:1, p. 40.
29. *Ibid.,* pp. 145ff.
30. *Ibid.,* p. 193.
31. *Ibid.,* p. 404.

Only if we think along truly Christological lines, Barth argues, can we understand that God's righteousness, subject as it is to his all-encompassing grace, is identical with man's justification.[32]

The reader will now have sufficient evidence to see that Barth's view of man's participation with God in Christ allows no room at all for the Reformation view of grace. The grace of Barth's theology is the grace of a Christ who is himself nothing more than a projection of man himself.

3. Lessing's Big Ditch

It has been pointed out earlier that for Barth the *Christ-Event* is the ground of knowledge as well as of being. Christ is the solution for the problem of knowledge and of being alike. For Barth the two problems are one problem. For Barth man has both authentic existence and authentic knowledge through his participation in Christ. Only God can know God, but man can also know God because by grace and through faith he participates in Christ.

In the previous chapter, it was pointed out that Barth seeks to solve what he calls the *Lessing-Frage* by means of his Christ concept. In typical modern fashion Lessing tried to unite history and rational thought. But he could not succeed in crossing the "nasty big ditch" between the accidental truths of history and the necessary truths of reason.[33] How is it possible to say anything about the truth of Christianity?

Lessing had no answer. With his purely rationalist principle of continuity and his purely irrationalist principle of discontinuity, history cannot be thought of as the bearer of meaning. Barth quite rightly says that on Lessing's view there is no Lord of history present within history.[34] In Lessing's parable of the three rings, the judge had no good reason for not saying that all three rings are false. So also, Barth has only his purely individual preference as the foundation for choosing his *Christ-Event* as the starting-point for his thought. It is not Barth's Christ who has first chosen him; it is rather Barth who has first chosen his Christ. Only if we start with Luther and Calvin and their idea of God's speaking directly in Christ and Scripture, do we have a Christ who chooses us before we choose him.

32. *Ibid.*, p. 613.
33. Barth, *Protestant Thought*, etc., p. 136.

34. *Ibid.*, p. 147.

To say this, is not to fall back on natural theology. It is to presuppose the Reformation framework of thought. Unless we may presuppose with Luther and Calvin that the triune God, creator and redeemer, has clearly and finally revealed himself in deeds explained by words, then pure subjectivism results. Barth's idea of the actualization of the incarnation involves the notion that it is God's being to go into the realm of pure contingency, and then, out of pure contingency, he takes man up with himself into participation in his pure rationality. Of course, this is not a process that happens in time. The steps of Christ's exaltation do not follow upon those of his humiliation in time. God is in Christ both in humiliation and in exaltation. He is this in the divine presence, that is, in *Geschichte*. How is this possible? The answer is that we do not answer the problems of rationality and irrationality in terms of laws of logic or in terms of fact. On the contrary, we interpret logic and fact, as well as their relation to one another, in terms of the *Christ-Event*.

However, the *Christ-Event* of Barth is, as a matter of fact, a construct composed of Lessing's two mutually exclusive principles. Accordingly, Barth is as unable to cross Lessing's big ditch as is Lessing himself. This ditch cannot be crossed unless, in terms of Reformation principles, it is seen as an artificially constructed ditch. It is created by the natural man's assumption that human knowledge must rest on man as self-sufficient. If Barth were really a follower of Calvin, then he would, with Calvin, have regarded man as from the beginning confronted by the self-sufficient God who speaks through Christ in the Scripture. Then he would have had mystery, mystery for man the creature, but he would not have submerged God himself in the realm of chance.

4. Barth's Polemics

Unable to cross Lessing's nasty ditch, Barth is unable, as we also saw in the previous chapter, to harmonize Kant's philosopher and his preacher. He is unable to escape the sardonic grin of Feuerbach. He cannot himself escape from the "secret ailment" from which Strauss suffers.[35]

Barth does not, like Calvin, find God speaking directly to him in the facts of nature, history or Scripture. He rejects what Polman, working on Reformation principles, calls *fundamental revelation*.

35. *Ibid.*, p. 363.

The phenomena of the world about us, says Barth, are dumb.[36] God is revealed in them as wholly hidden.

To escape from and get beyond lower views of man, Barth argues, we must do so in terms of Christ, the one and only real man.[37] In terms of this real man we may first get beyond the idea of man as a rational animal. To find the real man, we may therefore use Calvin's terminology, but we must put it in the proper Christological framework.[38]

When next we look at man in terms of the ethical approach of post-Kantian idealism, we see that it is still insufficiently Christological. The ethical as well as the naturalistic view of man regards him as a closed entity.[39]

Even the existentialist view, such as that of Karl Jaspers, has not reached the Christological plateau. Jaspers does indeed speak of man as open toward the *beyond*. But the beyond into which Jaspers' man stretches out his arms is indeterminate. Why should he not meet a demon there instead of God?[40] On Jaspers' view, man has more than one real alternative to choose from.[41] On the basis of the true transcendence of Christ, man has only one true choice, the choice *for*, not *against* Christ.[42] On any but a true Christological basis, faith has no object. But on the true Christological basis, faith appears to be true faith because it has no authentic alternative. Sin and unbelief are then ontological impossibilities.

Thus, according to Barth, the natural, the ethical and the existential views of man are still based on the idea of autonomy.[43] On their basis man must, in the last analysis, still understand himself by principles that spring from himself. Real or authentic man cannot be found in any of these views.

Even Emil Brunner does not discover the authentic man. He does indeed employ the concept of act.[44] He does seek therefore to go beyond the self-enclosed man of existentialism.[45] He tells us that man must be known not by man himself but by God, that is, by the Word of God.[46] Brunner deals not merely with a border-situation but with real transcendence. And this transcendence, Brunner tells us, is

36. III:2, p. 91.
37. *Ibid.*, p. 158.
38. *Ibid.*, p. 84.
39. *Ibid.*, p. 120.
40. *Ibid.*, p. 136.
41. *Idem.*

42. *Ibid.*, p. 138.
43. *Ibid.*, p. 143.
44. *Ibid.*, p. 151.
45. *Ibid.*, p. 153.
46. *Idem.*

identical with Jesus Christ. We are with Brunner very near to the true position.[47]

Unfortunately Brunner thinks he has actually reached a resting point in his description of man.[48] And therewith the primacy of Christ is once more placed in jeopardy. On Brunner's view there appears once more the danger that faith and unbelief are equally possible alternatives. How then could the triumph of God's *Yes* as over against man's rebellion be maintained?[49] In short, Brunner has no proper appreciation of the ontological impossibility of sin as the correlative to the triumph of grace, in terms of which all men can be and *must be* saved in Christ.

It will now be noted that the criticism made by Barth on these several views of man is to the effect that they have not done justice to the primacy of grace. But naturally he understands this primacy of grace in terms of his own purified supralapsarianism. Only in terms of *this* Christ does faith have an object. Only in terms of *this* Christ is sin and unbelief seen to be an unauthentic possibility. But suppose now that Jaspers should choose to reply to Barth. What would he say? He would only need to indicate that if Barth's argument for the need of the primacy of grace is sound, then grace is no more grace. Grace would be a universal necessity. And this necessity itself would be meaningless unless it were taken as the correlative of the idea of chance. Or, otherwise stated, Jaspers could tell Barth that, in insisting on his *universality* of grace, he has lost its *sovereign* character. And he could add that the sovereignty of grace can, on Barth's view, be maintained only if it is stated in terms of pure irrationalism.

In earlier days Barth went beyond Romanism, beyond the Reformers, beyond Schleiermacher and beyond others by means of his actualistic concept of revelation. In recent times Barth seeks to go beyond Romanism, beyond the Reformers and beyond modern existentialists by means of the idea of a necessitarian universalism. Yet his nominalist notion of actualism and his realist notion of determinism are meaningless, the one without the other. And he is still seeking to go beyond others by means of grace that is sovereign as well as universal. His movement of thought again appears to be a swinging back and forth between pure irrational nominalism and

47. *Ibid.*, p. 154.   49. *Ibid.*, p. 155.
48. *Idem.*

pure rationalist realism, with emphasis on the latter. If someone opposes him as being a nominalist, then Barth can answer him as a realist. If someone opposes him as a realist, Barth can answer him as a nominalist. When in earlier days Brunner argued for the need of making contact with the cultural consciousness of man, Barth replied with his resounding *Nein*. That was pure nominalism on his part. When Brunner, more recently, contends that, on the basis of Barth's universalism, faith has no real significance, Barth answers that a theology which allows for the equal possibility of belief and unbelief is no real Christianity. This is pure realism on his part.

Moreover, each time that Barth opposes men by means of his idea of grace, he seems to be right. Of course it is true that on Jaspers' view there is no way of distinguishing the voice of Satan from that of God. But the same is true of Barth's actualist view of the sovereignty of grace. Of course, Barth was right when earlier he argued that Brunner was allowing Christianity to be re-absorbed into the cultural consciousness of apostate thought, but the same may again be said of Barth. He has no universal grace unless it be grace that is built into the very nature of man and is not given on the basis of the once-for-all finished work of Christ in history.

Mention may finally be made of Barth's running polemics against Rudolf Bultmann. Evangelical thinkers sometimes look for help from Barth to stem the tide of subjectivism represented by Bultmann's program of demythologizing the message of Scripture. Has not Barth, we are told, especially in recent times, insisted that we must have no parthenogenesis of the faith? Has not Barth, against Bultmann, maintained that the resurrection faith took its start from a real encounter on the part of the disciples with the risen Lord? Does not Barth then have a truly objective basis for the Christian Faith?

The answer is obvious. What Barth considers to be the objective basis for the faith is found in *his* Christ, and in the resurrection of *his* Christ. And *this* resurrection of *this* Christ does not follow upon his death as one event in time follows another. "Where and when is He not both humiliated and exalted, already exalted in His humiliation, and humiliated in His exaltation."[50] Or again, "We have to do with the being of the one and entire Jesus Christ whose humiliation detracts nothing and whose exaltation adds nothing."[51]

50. IV:1, p. 146; Engl. tr. p. 133   51. *Idem.*

On Barth's view, there would be no true objectivity for the gospel message if the resurrection were directly identified with a fact of history following upon the death of Christ as another fact of history, for then the revelation of God in the resurrection would no longer be divine revelation. Then revelation no longer would be *hidden* as well as revealed. Therewith all the evils of a natural theology and of a self-enclosed anthropology would have returned. If Barth's idea of the objectivity of the gospel is to be maintained, then, on his own view, that of the Reformation must be rejected. Barth answers Bultmann, as he answered Romanism and all others, in terms of his Christ-Event, and this answer is based on a purely subjective foundation. We cannot walk down this incline of subjectivism for some distance and then arbitrarily stop. Bultmann and Barth stand together in their common opposition to the gospel of grace as founded on the Christ of the Scriptures. We dare not follow Barth any more than we dare follow Bultmann.

The choice must therefore be made between Barth and the Reformers. On Barth's view there is no transition from wrath to grace in history. And on Barth's view grace is inherently a meaningless idea. For his Christ is composed of the interaction between a principle of continuity based on the idea of timeless being and a principle of discontinuity based on the idea of pure contingency. He has therefore no gospel of grace to present to men. He cannot challenge men by presenting them with the Christ of the Scriptures because his Christ is a mirage. It is the Christ of modern reconstruction. It is the Christ of the higher humanism.

The late J. Gresham Machen was confronted with the Christ of the higher humanism in his day. In 1924 he published his book, *Christianity and Liberalism*. In it he pointed out that "the great redemptive religion which has always been known as Christianity" was "battling against a totally diverse type of religious belief, which is only the more destructive of the Christian faith because it makes use of traditional Christian terminology."[52] Said Machen, "The chief modern rival of Christianity is 'liberalism.' An examination of the teachings of liberalism in comparison with those of Christianity will show that at every point the two movements are in direct opposition."[53] The two religions, argued Machen, have mutually exclusive views of Jesus the Christ: "The liberal Jesus, despite all the efforts of

52. New York, 1924, p. 2.   53. *Ibid.*, p. 53.

modern psychological reconstruction to galvanize Him into life, remains a manufactured figure of the stage."[54] The two religions, argued Machen, therefore also have mutually exclusive views of grace. Having diverse views of sin they naturally have opposite views of grace.[55] "A cardinal doctrine of modern liberalism is that the world's evil may be overcome by the world's good; no help is thought to be needed from outside the world."[56]

When Machen found himself compelled thus to speak of "liberalism" as having denied in fact, though having confessed in word, the gospel of the grace of God in Christ, he did not do so from personal animosity. He did so from a deep desire in his heart that "liberals" might return to an acceptance of the grace of God in Christ as the only way of salvation for man and his world. If then we are forced by the facts of the case to think of Barthianism, for all its speaking of "election in Christ" as being, like "liberalism," a religion of man's own devising, we too, like Machen, must do so from a sincere desire for the salvation of men through the Christ of the Scriptures. Speaking as objectively as we can, we must say that, as in Machen's time "Liberalism," while propagated in the church as though it were the gospel, was in reality a man-made religion, so Barthianism, using the language of Reformation theology, is still only a higher humanism.

54. *Ibid.*, p. 116. 56. *Ibid.*, p. 136.
55. *Ibid.*, p. 129.

Index

447

Thomism, 178, 187, 278
Thomists, 50, 51
Time, 93, 113
Trent, Council of, 356, 365, 368, 370,
371, 372, 374, 375, 376, 377, 382
Trimp, C., 164, 165, 166
Troeltsch, E., 72, 124, 402

U
Urgeschichte, 185, 297, 308, 309, 310,
312, 353

V
Vahanian, G., 54
Van Dyk, M. P., 196, 197, 198, 199,
200, 208
van Teylingen, E. G., 192, 193, 196
van Til, S., 70, 71, 72, 73, 74
Vollenhoven, D. H. Th., 173, 238

von Balthasar, H. U., 89, 319, 321,
322, 323, 324, 325, 326, 327, 329,
330, 334, 335, 336, 337, 338, 340,
341, 342, 343, 344, 345, 346, 347,
350, 352, 353, 354, 355, 357, 359,
365, 373, 380, 387, 389, 429

W
Walaeus, A., 69
Wegscheider, 401
Weltgeschichte, 20
Wendeln, M. F., 69, 70
Wobbermin, 143
Woelderink, J. G., 164, 165
Wolleb, J., 69, 83

Z
Zuidema, S. U., 179, 180, 181, 182,
183, 184, 185, 186, 187, 188, 189,
190, 191, 192, 196, 215, 263, 306